THE INCLUSIVE ECONOMY

THE INCLUSIVE ECONOMY

How to Bring Wealth to America's Poor

Michael D. Tanner

CATO INSTITUTE

First printing in paperback, 2020.

ISBN: 978-1-948647-01-4
Paperback ISBN: 978-1-948647-97-7
eISBN: 978-1-948647-02-1

Jacket design: Spencer Fuller, FaceOut Studio.
Cover imagery by Shutterstock.
Printed in the United States of America.

Library of Congress Cataloging-in-Publication Data

Tanner, Michael, 1956- author.
The inclusive economy : how to bring wealth to America's poor /
Michael D. Tanner.
page cm
Washington, D.C. : Cato Institute, 2018.
Includes bibliographical references.
ISBN 9781948647021 (ebook) | ISBN 9781948647014 (hardback)
1. Poverty—United States. 2. Public welfare—United States.
3. Equality—United States. 4. United States—Economic policy. 5. United States—Social policy.

HC110
339.4/60973 2018034548

Cato Institute
1000 Massachusetts Avenue NW
Washington, DC 20001
www.cato.org

TABLE OF CONTENTS

PREFACE

Writing this book was something of a personal journey. I have studied poverty and welfare for more than 30 years. I have written two previous books on the subject, numerous studies, and innumerable columns. But over the years, I have come to believe that the issue is not as simple as some of my previous work may have portrayed it. More specifically, because my earlier work dealt primarily with government welfare programs, it was easy to focus on the failures of those programs without delving deeply into the larger questions of poverty and its causes. To the degree that I have previously portrayed poverty issues as government welfare versus pulling yourself up by your bootstraps, I was wrong. Any successful fight of poverty must deal with deeper issues, including those of race, gender, and class in America.

That does not mean that I now favor increased redistribution or government activism—far from it. As this book will show, government has generally made matters worse, both culturally and structurally. Almost every government intervention to help the poor has had unintended consequences that have actually trapped millions of Americans in poverty. Some of these interventions were malign; others were well intentioned. But nearly all hurt far more than they helped. The best thing that government can do now, therefore, is to stop doing all the bad things it currently does.

In particular, I would like to thank three remarkable women who helped raise my consciousness on issues of poverty, race, gender, and other issues. First, blogger and activist Cathy Reisenwitz challenged me to understand how privilege can distort the way I have viewed issues and weighed priorities. Given the angry and unjustified criticism that Cathy has received for trying to show that free markets and social justice are not contradictory ideas, I think it important to acknowledge how her views have helped shape my approach to this book, and, more generally, my philosophy of a libertarian approach to poverty. She is a social justice warrior in the best sense of the word, and my work has benefited from her work.

Second, Melissa Greenwald, much more than just my closest friend, constantly cautioned me against judging people without understanding the context of their decisions. Having escaped poverty herself through hard work and determination, she nonetheless reminded me that choices always existed within the contexts of upbringing, culture, and environment. She also reminded me frequently that "absence of evidence is not evidence of absence." Sometimes research simply doesn't exist because our society doesn't value the results of that research. It remains important, therefore, to try to fill in those gaps.

And, finally and most important, my wife, Ellen Maidman-Tanner, never ceases to remind me that behind all the studies and dry statistics are the lives of real people. I've written similar words in regard to other books, but this statement has never been truer. Ellen's love, support, encouragement—and critical review—were essential to the completion of this book, as they have been for all my work. Whether I was bouncing ideas off of her or relying on her editing skills, she has been part of this research from the start. She is one of the smartest and most accomplished people I know, and that is reflected in this text. But more important was her refusal to allow me to stray from the fundamental goal of trying to improve people's lives. In many ways, her commitment to making the world a better place undergirds the heart and soul of this book. Frankly, without her, this book doesn't exist.

While I am thanking people, let me acknowledge the contributions of some other unsung heroes who contributed to the research that shows up in these pages. First and foremost, I had the extraordinary benefit of working with two of the finest researchers I have known, Charles Hughes and Robert Orr. Actually, the title of researcher does not do them or their contribution justice. Their work is reflected on virtually every page. They made this a better book, both in the writing and in substance. In particular, Robert's willingness to play devil's advocate, to constantly push back and challenge assumptions, narratives, and data, proved essential to making the final product as rigorous as possible.

In addition, Peter Van Doren not only championed this book when few others would, he was also an inexhaustible source of advice, and the sort of ruthless editor that I needed. Without his help, this book would certainly never have seen the light of day. And speaking of editors, this book was immeasurably improved through the diligent editing and suggestions of Jason Kuznicki, Cato's book editor. I have been truly lucky to have had input from scholars as diligent and knowledgeable as Peter and Jason.

This book also benefited from the input of Cato policy analyst Vanessa Brown Calder—who had much to add in both thought and substance, especially on housing policy, where she is one of the nation's leading experts—as well as our indefatigable interns, Hejin Wang, Ali Ahmed, Jacob Hyre, Colin Combs, and Brian Camilleri, who spent countless hours at libraries, scouring the internet, fact checking, and meeting all sorts of my unreasonable demands. A particular shout out to Kelly Lester, who was one of the best interns who has ever worked for me. Beyond exemplary research, she joined Robert, Vanessa, and me for some of our most productive morning discussions that helped clarify my theories of poverty.

I should also note the assistance of Jeff Miron, Cato's director of economic policy, who provided both guidance and insight. And, finally, a word of thanks to my copy editor, Christine Stinson of Publications Professionals, for turning my mangled syntax into understandable prose.

Along the way, I consulted several outside readers who provided much-needed perspective from across the ideological spectrum. Among those I am indebted to are Aaron Yelowitz of the University of Kentucky, Michael Lewis of Hunter College, and Sven Larson with the American

Institute for Economic Research. Their advice was extremely helpful and greatly improved this book, yet I don't want to imply their agreement with either my approach to the subject or my conclusions. That lies with me alone.

I believe that the vision offered in this book, and the policy proposals I put forward, can help offer millions of Americans an opportunity for a brighter, more hopeful future for them and their children. I hope you agree.

Michael Tanner
Fall 2018

INTRODUCTION

If you want men to build a ship, don't gather the wood, divide the work, and give orders. Instead, teach them to yearn for the vast and endless sea.

—*Antoine de Saint-Exupéry*[1]

This year, federal, state, and local governments will spend more than $1 trillion to fund more than 100 separate anti-poverty programs.[2] In fact, since President Lyndon Johnson declared war on poverty 52 years ago, anti-poverty programs have cost us more than $23 trillion.[3] That's a huge sum of money by any measure.

What has all this money bought us? Although far from conclusive, the evidence suggests that this spending has successfully reduced many of the deprivations of material poverty. This finding shouldn't be a big surprise. As George Mason University economist Tyler Cowen notes, under most classical economic theories, "a gift of cash always makes individuals better off."[4] Regardless of how dim a view one takes of governmental competence in general, it would be virtually impossible for the government to spend $23 trillion without benefiting at least some people in poverty.

The evidence certainly appears to bear this out. The sort of deep poverty that existed at the start of the War on Poverty in the mid 1960s is largely eliminated. By international standards, it could be reasonably claimed that poverty has been all but eliminated in this country.

Take hunger, for example. In the 1960s, as much as one-fifth of the U.S. population and more than one-third of poor people had diets that did not meet the Recommended Dietary Allowance (RDA) for key nutrients. Conditions in 266 U.S. counties were so severe that they were officially designated as "hunger areas."[5] Today, malnutrition has been significantly reduced. According to the U.S. Department of Agriculture, just 5.6 percent of U.S. households (7.0 million households) had "very low food security" in 2013, a category roughly comparable to the 1960s measurements.[6] Even among people below the poverty level, only 18.5 percent report very low food security.[7]

Housing provides another example. As recently as 1975, more than 2.8 million renter households (roughly 11 percent of renter households and 4 percent of all households) lived in what was considered "severely inadequate" housing, defined as "units with physical defects or faulty plumbing, electricity, or heating." Today, that number is down to roughly 1.2 million renter households (1 percent of all households).[8] In 1970, fully 17.5 percent of households did not have fully functioning plumbing; today, just 2 percent do not.[9]

And if you look at material goods, the case is even starker. For instance, in the 1960s nearly one-third of poor households had no telephone. Today, not only are phones nearly universal, but also roughly half of poor households own a computer. More than 98 percent have a television, and two-thirds have two or more TVs. In 1970, less than half of poor people had a car; today, two-thirds do.[10] Clearly, the material circumstances of poor families have improved significantly over the past 50 years.

Conservative critics of welfare frequently point out that the U.S. Census Bureau poverty measure has remained virtually unchanged over the past 50 years.[11] In fact, the only substantial decline since the mid 1970s occurred in the 1990s, a time of state experimentation with tightening welfare eligibility, culminating in the passage of national welfare reform (the Personal Responsibility and Work Opportunity Reconciliation Act of 1996).

The official poverty measure is misleading because it fails to consider the non-cash benefits that constitute the majority of welfare payments as well as refundable tax credits such as the earned income tax credit (EITC). For this reason, it would be better to consider alternative measures that more fully account for these benefits as well.

For example, a 2012 paper from the Brookings Institution modified the official poverty rate to account for in-kind transfers such as food stamps and the tax system (as well as correcting for what they perceive as an upward bias in the inflation adjustment). Using this measure, Bruce Meyer and James Sullivan found that only 8.3 percent of Americans were living in poverty in 2010, a year in which the official poverty rate was 15.1 percent.[12] Using their methodology to look back in time, they conclude that the poverty rate actually fell by 23.5 percentage points between 1960 and 2010.[13] A second study by Christopher Wimer and other researchers at the Columbia Population Research Center using a similar methodology estimates that the actual poverty rate, fully accounting for non-cash welfare benefits, is about 5.5 percentage points lower than the official rate.[14]

Studies have also looked at specific programs and their effects on poverty rates. For example, the Center on Budget and Policy Priorities estimated in 2014 that without the Supplemental Nutrition Assistance Program (SNAP, or food stamps) some 4.7 million more people would be poor.[15] The Census Bureau also suggests that food stamps reduce the number of people in poverty but by slightly less than half as much, roughly 2.2 million.[16] Similarly, the Census Bureau suggests that Temporary Assistance for Needy Families (TANF) reduces the number of poor Americans by 304,000 and that housing subsidies lift 1.2 million Americans out of poverty.[17] Certainly the methodology behind these figures can be questioned; but even if the numbers are off substantially, there is no doubt that these programs have a substantial effect on rates of material poverty.

The evidence that welfare spending has reduced poverty—or at least the degree to which it has reduced poverty—is not wholly unqualified. Other factors such as the passage of the Civil Rights Act, the expansion of economic opportunities to African Americans and women, increased private charity, and general economic growth all may have played a role in whatever poverty reduction occurred. Besides, studies suggest that improvements that resulted from spending in the early years after these programs began have plateaued more recently and that we are no longer seeing marginal declines in poverty commensurate with increased spending.

We should also at least consider the counterfactual. What actions would the poor have taken in the absence of welfare? We know that incentives matter, and there is a vigorous debate about the degree to which the availability of welfare creates incentives toward poverty-inducing behavior by discouraging work and encouraging nonmarital births. Some observers, such as Charles Murray, who explored these issues in his groundbreaking book *Losing Ground*, see a significant effect, while others, such as Robert Moffitt of Johns Hopkins point to a much smaller impact.[18] The evidence in this area is limited and contradictory. Poverty rates declined following Clinton-era welfare reform, and experts attribute part of that decline to the reform.[19] However, studies following Reagan-era benefit cuts found that in most cases increases in wages did not fully offset benefit reductions. My own research for the Cato Institute suggests that someone leaving welfare for an entry-level job would likely suffer an initial loss of income, although I do not address the likely long-term impact, which could well be more positive.[20] The incentives and other unintended consequences of welfare will be explored in depth later in this book.

Still, looking at the totality of available evidence, it is hard to argue that welfare spending has not been a contributing factor to the decline in the material deprivation and hardships of poverty. Surveying the available literature, Rebecca Blank of the University of Wisconsin concludes "transfer programs unambiguously make people less poor."[21]

This line of research has led many conservative critics to focus on the systemic failings of welfare and their impacts on the larger economy. For instance, the taxes or debt required to support welfare transfers may slow economic growth or limit innovation. And work disincentives reduce the labor pool, further eroding growth and international competitiveness.

These concerns about economic growth are not abstractions. Rather, the evidence is overwhelming that over time economic growth lifts more people out of poverty than any achievable amount of redistribution. In a world of scarcity, some will always be relatively poor. Good anti-poverty policy, therefore, should seek to encourage growth and reduce scarcity.

What we need is inclusive growth—economic growth to which the poor have access. By any measure, the vast majority of the population was poor 100 years ago. In fact, even the richest individuals 100 years ago would be considered poor by many of today's standards. What changed that was the enormous growth and innovation that took place since then. What remains to be done is to remove the obstacles that still remain, while preserving the institutions that promote continued economic growth.

If our economy grows robustly into the future, we can expect that 100 years from now, all Americans, including the poor, will have far more material abundance than today. Yet the converse is also true; to the degree that the welfare state undermines or otherwise encumbers the free market that helps drive economic growth, Americans will be poorer in the future than they would otherwise be. To put this in perspective, if U.S. economic growth from 1870 to 1990 had been just one percentage point lower, our country would be no richer than Mexico.[22] Thus, even if current welfare policies benefit individual poor people at a given time, they may well be problematic for the poor as a group over the longer term.

As important as such large-scale systemic considerations are, the view from those in poor communities provides an even more convincing critique of our current welfare system.

For example, visit the Washington, D.C., neighborhoods of Bellevue, Congress Heights, and Washington Highlands, just a short drive from the White House and Capitol Hill. Almost 40 percent of the households living in these communities have incomes below the poverty line, and more than half of children live in poor households. Unemployment tops 30 percent, and single mothers head one of every five families. Nearly 20 percent of residents lack a high school diploma. Roughly two-thirds of the people living in the communities receive food stamps. All of this occurs in a city with a median annual income of almost $95,000 per year.[23]

At the same time, just 45 miles to the northeast lie Baltimore's Sandtown-Winchester and Harlem Park communities. In 2015, this community saw riots in the wake of the still unsettled death of Freddie Gray while in police custody. A third of houses are boarded up and abandoned. The community lacks a supermarket or even a fast-food restaurant. Unemployment exceeds 20 percent, three times the city average, and one-third of families live below the poverty line. Two of three births are to unmarried women, and more than 60 percent of households are headed by single mothers. More than a quarter of students citywide fail to graduate, and the numbers are worse in Sandtown. Incarceration rates here are the highest of any neighborhood in Baltimore.[24]

Across the country in Fresno, California, the poverty rate nudges 30 percent and is closer to 40 percent for children. Nearly one-third of Fresno families receive public assistance. More than half of all births in the city are to unmarried women.[25] But overall statistics may disguise the reality of poverty in Fresno, which has some of the highest concentrations of poverty in the nation. Nor does the future hold promise for better, especially for the city's children. Nearly half of Fresno 11th graders fall short of grade-level proficiency in English. The high school graduation rate for African-Americans is just 72 percent, while one out of five Latino children also fails to graduate.[26]

Nor is poverty the exclusive domain of minorities or big cities. America's poorest county is Owsley, Kentucky, which is rural and 98.5 percent white. The poverty rate here reaches an astounding 40 percent, including 56 percent of children. More people in Owsley receive government assistance per capita than in any other county in America. Like poor inner cities, much of the area is a service wasteland. The county, for instance, has just one grocery store. The nearest FedEx office is 37 miles away. Male life expectancy is nearly a decade shorter than in, say, Fairfax County, Virginia, less than a half day's drive away. Drug use, particularly methamphetamine and opiates, is ubiquitous.[27]

The same story can be seen across this country from Detroit, Michigan, to the Mississippi Delta and from Monticello, New York, to Centralia, Washington. It can be found equally in inner cities, small towns, and rural counties. One needn't accept a Trumpian vision of "American carnage" to understand that millions of Americans are suffering, trapped in lives of poverty and despair.[28]

In every town and city noted here, government has spent heavily to reduce poverty. A high percentage of residents are receiving some form of government assistance. The poor may well be better off financially than they would be in the absence of government aid. Yet no one could honestly describe those communities or the people living in them as thriving or flourishing in any sense of the word.

And therein lies the real failure of our anti-poverty efforts. Our efforts have been focused on the mere alleviation of poverty, making sure that the poor have food, shelter, and the like. That may be a necessary part of an anti-poverty policy, but it is far from sufficient. A truly effective anti-poverty program should seek not just to alleviate poverty's symptoms but to eradicate the disease itself. We should seek not only to make sure that people are fed and housed, but that they are able to rise as far as their talents can take them. In a sense, we focus too much on poverty and not enough on prosperity.

Perhaps *The Economist* put it best:

> If reducing poverty just amounts to ushering Americans to a somewhat less meagre existence, it may be a worthwhile endeavor but is hardly satisfying. The objective, of course, should be a system of benefits that encourages people to work their way out of penury, and an economy that does not result in so many people needing welfare in the first place. Any praise for the efficacy of safety nets must be tempered by the realization that, for one reason or another, these folks could not make it on their own.[29]

President Johnson himself called for something more than simply fighting material poverty. The War on Poverty was created not only to "relieve the symptom of poverty, but to cure it and, above all, to prevent it."[30] Yes, he sought to meet the "basic needs" of those in poverty, but also to "replace despair with opportunity."[31] Yet in focusing on the material aspects of poverty, we have neglected the more important aspects of human flourishing. Our tax and spending policies should be better designed so as to enable all people to become fully actualized beings, capable of being all that they can be.

Such flourishing requires a level of autonomy and self-sufficiency that is, in fact, compromised by the reliance on government assistance (or charitable assistance, for that matter). Individuals cannot be said to have control over their own lives if they are perpetually dependent on another. As William Ernest Henley's poem *Invictus* so eloquently puts it:

> I am the master of my fate,
> I am the captain of my soul.

Of course, none of us is an island. We interact with others all the time, and we both survive and prosper because of that interaction. In addition, all of us will experience times when we are dependent, in childhood or old age, for instance. In times of distress, our community, private charity, or possibly even the government may need to intervene.

Yet such an intervention will always be a second-best solution. Of necessity, it reduces an individual's autonomy, self-ownership, and ability to make choices in life. There is a reason that, even in the case of individuals with mental and physical disabilities, we attempt to maximize everyone's self-sufficiency and ability to run their own lives.

Increasingly we are finding that programs once intended to be stopgap or emergency measures have become a form of long-term, even multigenerational, dependency. The poor are becoming, in effect, wards of the state. Seen in this way, the gap between poverty levels with and without benefits can be seen as a measure of failure.

The poor themselves recognize how the existing welfare system fails to address their larger needs. According to a joint American Enterprise Institute and *Los Angeles Times* poll, 71 percent of individuals living below the poverty level believe that the government lacks the knowledge to eliminate poverty, even if willing to spend whatever was necessary.[32] Moreover, the poll showed that people living below the poverty level were split evenly at 41 percent, for and against whether the welfare system actually helped people escape from poverty or encouraged the poor to stay poor. And, by a 48 to 41 percent margin, the poor believed that people who had been poor for a long time were likely to remain poor despite government assistance. Indeed, people with incomes above the poverty level were more likely to have a favorable impression of the welfare system and government's role than did the poor themselves.[33]

Cowen suggests that if the poor truly felt this way, then they ought to refuse benefits, which they are free to do, and the fact that so few of them do suggests that they see welfare as a net positive. However, that view seems to underestimate both the tendency of people to discount long-term consequences (we all do things that are bad for us in the pursuit of immediate gratification) and to prioritize immediate need over nonmaterial concerns. Maslow's hierarchy of needs puts physical needs such as food before self-actualization.

In proposing a better way to fight poverty, we should not blindly support cutting programs for the sake of cutting. Nor should we assume that what we are doing now is working just fine and that we should simply do more of it. Rather we should ask whether it is possible to ameliorate the suffering of those living in poverty at least as well as existing efforts, while also creating the conditions that would enable people to live a fulfilled and actualized life. Is it possible to achieve or even expand on the poverty reductions that we have seen, without the negative side effects accompanying such accomplishments today? Can we fight poverty in a way that is compatible with the economic growth that will reduce poverty in the future? Finally, can we fight poverty in a way that empowers poor people to control their own lives?

In part, answering those questions is hampered by the limits of the available evidence. Few questions in social science are definitively settled. We cannot go back in history, change a single policy, and observe the resulting effects. For both moral and practical reasons, we are seldom able to do the sort of double-blind or random assignment experiments commonly relied upon in the physical sciences. The few natural experiments that exist are limited in scope and inextricably linked to a specific context, meaning it is difficult to draw generalizable conclusions from the results. As a result, it is frequently impossible to definitively establish causality. At best, we can see that B is correlated with A, and then we must use our own intellect and common sense to decide whether A likely caused B, B caused A, whether a third thing caused both, or if A and B exist wholly independent of each other despite the apparent correlation.

We can also weigh the total body of academic evidence in favor of one or the other interpretation. Writing in *A Companion to the Philosophy of Science,* Peter Lipton, former head of the Department of History and Philosophy of Science at Cambridge University, calls this process "inference to the best possibility," and likens it to a situation with which we are all familiar. "When a detective infers that it was Moriarty who committed the crime, he does so because this hypothesis would best explain the fingerprints, blood stains and other forensic evidence. Sherlock Holmes to the contrary, this is not a matter of deduction. The evidence will not [prove] that Moriarty is to blame, since it always remains possible that someone else was the perpetrator. Nevertheless, Holmes is right to make his inference, since Moriarty's guilt would provide a better explanation of the evidence than would anyone else's."[34]

Take, for example, one statistic widely discussed by those who study poverty. Unmarried women who have children are five times more likely to be poor than women who do not have children until marriage. We might conclude that reducing nonmarital births would reduce poverty. Yet we cannot say this with certainty. It could also be the case that those women most likely to give birth outside marriage have other characteristics that may incline them toward poverty or that women who are more likely to be poor for a variety of unconnected reasons are more likely to have children outside marriage. We observe a correlation between poverty and nonmarital birth but cannot definitively attribute causation in a manner that is generalizable to every distinct context.

Nevertheless, we can apply experience and reason to understanding this correlation. Trying to support a child on one income is likely to be more difficult than on two incomes. A single mother is more likely to have trouble with childcare that could interrupt education or employment opportunities. Employers may be consciously or unconsciously more hesitant to hire single mothers, who may have to take time off to care for their children. An unmarried birth may not itself cause a woman to fall into poverty, but common sense suggests that it may make it more difficult to climb out of poverty. Even still, we cannot rule out the possibility that causation flows in both directions, meaning poverty and single-mother childbearing may form a vicious circle. While there is much that we don't know, we cannot be paralyzed by the difficulties in collecting and interpreting data. Acknowledging the limits of what we know—and can know—we still need to try to understand the essential causes of poverty and the best policies to enable people to escape it. In fact, the lack of definitive proof should itself inform government policy. As the Nobel Prize laureate in economic sciences Milton Friedman said, modesty is important in government, precisely because we may be wrong.

But while lack of certainty should limit the grandiosity of our plans, it does not excuse inaction.

I conclude that the provision of welfare to at least some people may (or may not) be necessary and justified but is insufficient (and sometimes counterproductive) to provide an environment that enables humans to flourish. We should judge the success of our efforts to end poverty not by how much charity we provide to the poor, but by how few people need such charity; not just by whether we have reduced the suffering of poverty, but by whether we have enabled people to flourish; and not by the alleviation of poverty, but by its eradication.

Perhaps apocryphally, Einstein is reputed to have said that the definition of insanity is doing the same thing over and over but expecting different results. But for decades we have essentially pursued the same anti-poverty strategy—creating more and more government programs and spending more and more money without visible improvement in the lives or opportunities of the poor and vulnerable.

It should be apparent, therefore, that truly improving the lives of the poor will not be achieved through more small changes to the existing social welfare system. It is not a question of spending slightly more or less money; of tinkering with the number of hours mandated under work requirements; or of rooting out fraud, waste, and abuse. We need a new debate, one that moves beyond our current approach to fighting poverty to focus on what works rather than on noble sentiments or good intentions.

I believe there is a more effective approach to fighting poverty, one based firmly on libertarian principles. It suggests that, before we discuss whether or how much redistribution is needed, we should attack the underlying barriers that can prevent poor people from prospering. As Nobel Prize laureate in economic sciences James Buchanan once put it, "A strong defense of the liberties of individuals, which can only be secured in an operating market economy, may be joined with an equally strong advocacy for the reform of basic social institutions designed to produce greater equality among individuals in their initial endowments and capacities."[35] I would go further, suggesting not that these two principles "may" be joined, but that they *must* be joined.

Specifically, we should do the following:

- *Reform the criminal justice system and curtail the War on Drugs.* The criminal justice system is discriminatory against the poor and minorities at every level. That fact would be a problem regardless of context. But in the context of poverty, it is even more of an issue. Large numbers of the poor are burdened with a criminal record that makes it far more difficult for them to find jobs. Moreover, dragging large numbers of poor and minority youth into the criminal justice system severely limits the pool of marriageable men, and a wave of fatherlessness afflicts poor communities. An effective anti-poverty policy should remove barriers to work and family formation.
- *Reform education to give more control and choice to parents and to break up the public school monopoly.* The days when it was possible to drop out of school and still find a job that enabled a person to support a family are long gone. Education is now vital to escaping poverty. At the same time, despite our spending more and more money on education, our public schools are failing many poor and minority students. The type of innovation necessary to turn this situation around is unlikely to occur under a system dominated by a government-run monopoly. Instead, our education system needs to be opened up to greater competition and choice.
- *Bring down the cost of housing.* Restrictive housing regulations primarily benefit the wealthy who own homes, while they drive up rents for the poor. Rather than chase rising housing costs with ever higher subsidies, we should focus on lowering the cost of housing, and of rents in particular.
- *Make it easier for the poor to bank, save, borrow, and invest.* Income is critical to dealing with the immediate needs of the poor, but savings are vital to long-term prosperity. Yet too many poor

people find it difficult to access the banking system. We should review banking regulations that primarily harm the poor, while easing access to nontraditional banking alternatives. At the same time, we should review welfare eligibility requirements to ensure that they do not unnecessarily discourage the poor from accumulating savings.

- *Increase economic growth and make it more inclusive.* Economic growth does more to reduce poverty over time than any government intervention. Therefore any effective approach to fighting poverty should include policies that encourage economic growth. But that growth must be inclusive. We should also make it easier for the poor to find work today by eliminating regulations that make it harder for the poor to find jobs or to start a business.

Rather than create new programs and spend more money, we should start by undoing the harmful legacy of past and current government policies. Reforming criminal justice, education, and housing policy while encouraging job creation, economic growth, and individual savings will do more to help reduce poverty than anything we are doing today. Taken as a whole, these reforms would give far more poor people the opportunity to partake in the prosperity that they seek.

I won't pretend that I have come up with the definitive answer to poverty. Readers will undoubtedly find more than enough room for argument. But in a debate too often frozen between hostile camps on left and right, I hope to offer a different perspective, one that can draw support from both sides.

The stereotype of libertarian attitudes toward the poor ranges from indifference to outright hostility. Libertarians have too often failed to focus on the aspects of their agenda that can offer the greatest benefits to the poor. But as a libertarian, I believe in the inherent dignity and equality of every human being. One cannot believe that and ignore the millions suffering in poverty today.

As we shall see, an agenda based on liberty, choice, and free markets has much to offer women, African Americans, the poor, and other individuals and groups too often marginalized in today's society.

CHAPTER ONE: A HISTORY OF THINKING ABOUT POVERTY AND POLICY

The conduct of society toward poverty continues to oscillate between two evils—the evil of insufficient care for the indigent, with the resulting appearance of ever increasing impoverishment . . . and the evil of a reckless poor-relief, with the resulting appearance of far-reaching abuses, the lessening of the spirit of independence. . . . The history of poverty is for the most part a history of these constantly observed evils and of the efforts to remove them, or at least to reduce their dimensions. No age has succeeded in solving this problem.

—*Emil Munsterberg*[1]

No doctor would attempt to treat a patient without first attempting to determine the underlying cause of the patient's condition. After all, both excess gas and a heart attack might cause chest pain, but they need to be treated in very different ways.

So too is it with poverty. How we believe society or government should react to poverty depends in large part on what we believe are the causes of poverty. But the answer to that question is one that has bedeviled scholars for centuries.

For much of human history, poverty was simply accepted as a given. "The poor you will always have with you," Jesus said.[2] Few people attempted to understand the deeper underlying reasons for poverty, other than, say, misfortune, or the "will of God."

There were, of course, efforts to help the poor, but they were mostly private—although more often public than commonly portrayed. Sometimes these efforts were undertaken out of compassionate or humanitarian impulses and sometimes as a way to pacify the masses. The Romans, for example, distributed free or reduced-price grain (c. 4th century BCE–476 CE). The Islamic Caliphate under Umar ibn al-Khattab (586–684 CE) offered a broad range of welfare benefits including old-age pensions and government-paid physicians.[3] In China, the Song Dynasty (960–1200 CE) established programs to provide for the aged and unemployed.[4]

In the western world, virtually all organized charity from the Middle Ages through the Renaissance was handled through the Roman Catholic Church or related organizations, particularly "confraternities," hospitals, and "poor tables."[5] The Church saw an obligation to help the poor as a matter of faith. Almsgiving was considered the duty of all Christians, from those high born to low. Christians were directed to feed the hungry, welcome the stranger, and perform other acts of compassion.[6] Two gospel passages in particular were used by church fathers to point in this direction: "Whenever you did one of these things to the least of my brothers, you did it to me"[7] and "give alms and, behold, all is clean for you."[8] A review of church writings shows that the terminology used in referring to such charitable acts expresses a clear belief that an exchange is taking place. In return for the believer practicing charity and giving alms, God grants heavenly treasures and the forgiveness of sins.[9]

At the same time, the Church condemned the accumulation of wealth. It saw materialism as a barrier to spirituality, which is one reason monastic orders often stressed poverty and humbleness among their virtues. In the secular realm, material possessions were accepted grudgingly as a "necessary evil resulting from the fall of man."[10] Christians were well aware of the biblical admonition that "It is easier for a camel to pass through the eye of a needle than for a rich man to enter the Kingdom of God."[11] A rich man could effectively hedge his bets through charity.

It would be a mistake, of course, to believe that such teachings were universally implemented, certainly not by the laity and not even by the Church. The Third Council of Mâcon in 585 CE actually had to admonish bishops for using guard dogs to keep paupers away from their benefices.[12]

Poverty was widespread during this period, even on a relative basis. The vast majority of people were poor or in danger of falling into poverty. Poverty, therefore, was seen as a natural condition, not the result of a moral failing on the part of the poor. Moreover, as noted previously, Christians saw almsgiving as a transaction with God, not necessarily with the specific individual being helped. Perhaps for this reason, the Church did not distinguish between the "deserving" and "undeserving" poor, a practice that we will see develop in subsequent eras, but assisted all on a universal basis. "The one who gives alms to the needy and does not spurn him on account of some sin which he committed, rightly and justly upholds mercy, since nature is to be considered in almsgiving, not the person," Rabanus Maurus Magnentius, the influential archbishop of Mainz wrote in the ninth century.[13]

A similar tradition could be found in Judaism, where helping the poor was considered a mitzvah (or commandment). As one passage from the Talmud explained, "*Tzedakah* (charity) is equal to all the other commandments combined."[14] And Islam prescribed the *zakat*, a requirement that all believers contribute 2.5 percent of their wealth and assets to charity each year. The Arabic term *zakat* means "purification," and giving the zakat was intended to purify the soul from greed. The zakat was to be used to support the poor and the needy, as well as to free slaves and debtors.[15]

Thus all three of the major Abrahamic religions called for charity without distinction as to the recipient (other than that they be part of the same community, meaning religion, as the giver). Nor was there any expectation that the recipient would do anything in return.

Gradually, however, the commitment to the universality of charity receded. Several reasons are suggested for the change, including an expanding economy that led to the rise of a trade and commercial middle class; increased crime and social unrest; and the growth of towns and the movement away from a rural, agricultural-based population. Concentrations of poverty in urban areas, for example, were far more problematic than higher poverty rates spread over a rural countryside. This period also saw the collapse of the Carolingian effort in the ninth century to create a unified Christian Europe. In the 14th century, the Black Death wiped out much of the labor supply and created a premium for wages and a need for workers. As people became more mobile and towns grew larger, more of those seeking charity were strangers, rather than friends and neighbors, creating both more opportunity for the undeserving and less trust all around.

For whatever reason, by the 10th century, we begin to see warnings about the provision of alms to those "choosing begging over work due to laziness."[16]

The change was gradual, but by the 14th century, countries all over Europe were taking steps to restrict begging and to punish "vagabondage," and those laws became increasingly strict throughout the 15th and 16th centuries.[17] The idle and the homeless were particular targets of such laws. For example, a 1530 English law permitted the elderly and disabled to beg, but established strict penalties prohibiting the "sturdy" from doing so. "A vagabond, whole and mighty in body, who should be found begging, was to be whipped . . . and the sworn to the place where he was born . . . and there put himself to labour."[18] Other laws permitted the able-bodied who were found begging to be branded with a V for "vagabond" or P for "pauper."[19]

At the same time, the provision of charity was rapidly moving from a voluntary private activity to a mandatory, public responsibility, enforced by the state. For example, a 1536 English law directs the head officers of corporate towns and the churchwardens and two others of every parish "to collect voluntary alms for the purpose of relieving the impotent poor."[20] Note that the provision of alms was to be "voluntary." In fact, the law went on to say that "Every preacher, parson, vicar, and curate, as well in their sermons, collections, bidding of the beads, as in the time of confession and making of wills, is to exhort, move, stir, and provoke people to be liberal for the relief of the impotent, and setting and keeping to work the said sturdy vagabonds."[21]

By 1563, admonition had become coercion.

> If any person of his forward, willful mind shall obstinately refuse to give weekly to the relief of the poor according to his ability, the bishop shall bind him to appear at the next sessions . . . if he will not

> be persuaded, it shall be lawful for the justices, with the churchwardens, or one of them, to tax such obstinate person, according to their good discretion, what sum the said obstinate person shall pay weekly towards the relief of the poor within the parish wherein he shall dwell; and if he refuse, the justices shall, on complaint of the churchwardens, commit the said obstinate person to [jail], until he shall pay the sum so taxed, with the arrears.[22]

Finally, in 1572, Queen Elizabeth I extended the power of bishops and churchwardens to impose taxes for the purpose of supporting the impotent poor to "every inhabitant in their divisions," and to imprison those who refused to pay.[23] Thus, within the span of fewer than 30 years, the system moved from one relying on choice and persuasion to one relying on broad-based taxation, backed by the threat of jail and other coercion.

All of this was building to one of the most consequential laws in the history of the welfare state. In 1601, the English Parliament passed "An Act for Relief of the Poor," which came to be known as the Poor Law. It was to serve as the foundation for how to care for the poor for centuries to come.

The Poor Law codified the principle that care for the poor was a public responsibility, albeit one that should be undertaken at the local level. Purely church-based charity had been in decline for some time, a process accelerated by Henry VIII's dissolution of monasteries, hospitals, lazar houses, and other institutions. In fact, one of the charges leveled against monasteries by Henry was that they provided "daily relief to very numerous and very idle Poor."[24] Even though, as noted, Elizabeth I had given bishops and churchwardens the power to impose taxes to provide for the poor, such efforts were viewed increasingly as insufficient.

The Poor Law ordered families of the blind, lame, and poor to care for them. But where that was not possible, as was most frequently the case, local officials were directed to provide assistance, paid for through taxes.[25]

Although amended or revised many times in the years that followed, the Poor Law would serve as the foundation for dealing with poverty for the next five centuries. Most significantly, the concept that there are different categories of poor who should be treated in different ways, who were more or less responsible for their plight and therefore more or less deserving of assistance, became the moral underpinning of anti-poverty policy.

The Enlightenment and the Laboring Poor

The legal foundation for dealing with poverty would remain stable following the Elizabethan Poor Law, yet it was only a few decades before the dawning of the Enlightenment saw renewed debates over the nature of poverty and the proper response to it, with many of the era's most prominent thinkers offering competing perspectives.

For the first time as well, societies appeared to show an interest not just in helping individual people who were poor but also in actually reducing or eliminating poverty. A just society was seen not simply as one with charity but one where charity was unnecessary. And accomplishing this goal required an inquiry into the causes of poverty. Whereas previously poverty was seen as a brute fact of life—something that simply was and always would be—people now began to inquire into its ultimate causes.

It was during this period that attention began to be paid to a new category of poverty, the "laboring poor."[26] These were not idle "paupers," nor were they traditional "deserving poor" such as the aged or infirm. Rather these were laborers whose wages were insufficient to provide the necessities of life. They included both rural farm laborers and domestics (many hired seasonally or even daily and earning as little as six or seven pounds—no more than $600—a year) and urban factory and mill workers. Some estimates suggest that the laboring poor comprised as much as a quarter of the British population in the 18th century.[27]

The laboring poor forced a reevaluation of attitudes toward poverty. Jean-Jacques Rousseau, for example, was one of the first to suggest that poverty had causes that lay in the structures of society, as opposed to the failures of the poor themselves. Rousseau saw several causes of poverty, but chief among them was the unequal distribution of resources. Some people were poor because others were rich, for "How is it possible to become wealthy without impoverishing someone else . . . ?"[28]

Rousseau goes far beyond practical measures to relieve poverty, maintaining that the state also has the obligation to eliminate the conditions that lead to poverty. And because he saw the unequal distribution of wealth as a cause of poverty, the "social contract" required measures that prohibit some from becoming rich.

Rousseau's attitude toward inequality sprang, in part, from his adoption of the idea of "relative" as opposed to "absolute" poverty.[29] In the "Considerations on the Government of Poland," for example, he says, "what does it matter to me, after all, to have a hundred guineas instead of ten, if the hundred do not bring me a more comfortable living?"[30] And, in the "Constitutional Project for Corsica," he notes that the inability of some Corsicans to pay their taxes has made them feel poor.[31]

John Locke, too, saw poverty as not the fault of the poor in some cases, but as a failure of governance. While drawing traditional distinctions between "the deserving poor" and the "idle, improvident, and undeserving poor," Locke believed that everyone has an "equal right" or "right in common . . . to provide for their subsistence."[32] Locke saw this right to subsistence as a necessary means to fulfill the general obligation laid upon each individual by the law of nature to preserve mankind. By extension, the right to subsistence leads to a right to the surplus of another's goods because natural law "gives every man a title to so much out of another's plenty, as will keep him from extreme want, where he has not means to subsist otherwise."[33]

Adam Smith is generally thought of as the father of free-market capitalism. However, he took an unquestionably compassionate view of poverty.

> No society can surely be flourishing and happy, of which the far greater part of the members are poor and miserable. It is but equity, besides, that they who feed, clothe, and lodge the whole body of the people, should have such a share of the produce of their own labour as to be themselves tolerably well fed, clothed, and lodged.[34]

Smith saw the answer to poverty in a growing economy, a "universal opulence which extends itself to the lowest ranks of the people."[35] Everyone, from lowest to highest, had the same capability to flourish in a free economy, and therefore efforts to combat poverty should focus less on the individual poor, whether deserving or undeserving, and more on creating the economic conditions for prosperity. After all, according to Smith, labor would receive a substantial portion of increasing national wealth, whereas a slowing economy led to increased poverty.[36] Smith presented, in essence, an 18th century version of "a rising tide lifts all boats."

Some theorists, such as Bernard Mandeville, had claimed that wages should be kept at sustenance levels because if workers were paid more than immediate necessity, they would have no incentive to keep working, choosing increased leisure over continued labor. Smith rejected this idea. It was not low wages that ensured economic growth, but the division of labor. By lowering the unit cost of manufactured goods, the division of labor made it possible for wages to rise, as the economy as a whole expanded. It was possible, therefore, to increase wages even as the economy grew as a whole. Therefore, economic growth could improve the lot of the laboring poor. That is an argument that would not be foreign to many economic conservatives today.

Despite all this intellectual ferment, the government structure for assisting people who were poor remained tied to the concepts of the Elizabethan Poor Law. Indeed, in 1834 Great Britain updated and toughened the Poor Law, with an emphasis on reducing eligibility generally and reinforcing the distinction between the deserving poor and "pauperism."

The commission drafting the new law explicitly rejected the idea that poverty was a natural result of societal structures, allowing that, if poverty was "principally the result of unavoidable distress, we must have inferred the existence of an organic disease." Instead, in a swing back to Elizabethan moralism, poverty was viewed as a result of such vices as "fraud, indolence, and improvidence."[37] The commission also rejected the idea of a right to relief as "a monstrous and anarchical doctrine."[38] Nor did the new law offer any particular assistance for the laboring poor.

The commissioners responsible for the law appeared to be distressed by the increasing frequency with which relief was given without any associated requirement for work. They noted that under the Elizabethan Poor Law, "relief [was not] to be afforded to any but the impotent, except in return for work."[39] Indeed, working was in itself felt to have value for the poor. It need not even be productive labor. As Lord Chief Justice C. A. Tenterden wrote in an 1827 case, "whatever may be the difficulty of finding *profitable* work, it is difficult to suppose the existence of a parish in which it would not be *possible* to provide some work, were it merely to dig holes and fill them again," which the commissioners cited approvingly.[40]

In contrast, the commissioners complained that many localities were "giving to those who are or profess to be without employment a daily or a weekly sum, without requiring from the applicant any labor. Sometimes relief (to an amount insufficient for a complete subsistence) is afforded, without imposing any further condition than that the applicant shall shift, as it is called, for himself, and give the parish no further trouble. In many districts the plan had become so common as to have acquired the technical name of "Relief in lieu of Labour."[41]

Gertrude Himmelfarb, an American historian, notes that the renewed emphasis on pauperism in the New Poor Law—the Poor Law Amendment Act 1834—may have had the unintended perverse effect of stigmatizing the deserving poor as well.[42] Opponents of the Poor Law revisions, such as Conservative Party Prime Minister Benjamin Disraeli declared that they announced to the world that in Great Britain "poverty is a crime."[43]

Despite such criticism and public debate, the New Poor Law remained the basis for British anti-poverty policy through the 19th century. It wasn't until a series of welfare reform laws passed by the Liberal Party following the 1906 elections that Great Britain tried a significantly different approach. These reforms arose from the work of social reformers like Charles Booth and Joseph Seebohm Rowntree, which suggested that poverty was more likely to be caused by factors such as illness, old age, or a lack of work, rather than by moral failings on the part of the poor. The liberal reforms put a new emphasis on helping the poor find work, rather than on punishments. They also enacted provisions for old-age pensions and assistance to the sick.[44]

Although modest in scope, the liberal reforms of the early 20th century formed the foundation for what would eventually grow into the British welfare state of today.

The United States

We need to pay attention to the history of thinking about poverty in Great Britain because it formed the foundation for American anti-poverty efforts.

Unsurprisingly, the English Poor Law and its subsequent amendments served as the basis for relief programs in colonial America.[45] A clear distinction was drawn between the "deserving" people who were poor—those whose poverty was caused by circumstances beyond their control, such as widows, orphans, and the infirm—and those who were judged "undeserving" because they shirked work or suffered from drinking problems. The able-bodied poor, who were seen as spending their time "idly and unprofitably," could be jailed or impressed into forced labor.[46]

Throughout the 18th and 19th centuries, regardless of whether governments or private charities were providing aid, distinguishing between the deserving poor and "vagrants" or paupers remained popular. As one of the most prominent preachers of early New England, Charles Boroughs, put it, "[Poverty] is an unavoidable evil, to which we are brought from necessity. . . . It is the result, not of our faults, but of our misfortunes. . . . Pauperism is the result of willful error, of shameful indolence, of vicious habit."[47]

At the same time the United States saw a burst of private charity propelled by religious idealism. From shortly after the American Revolution until the mid 1830s, the United States underwent an upsurge in religious fervor known as the Second Great Awakening. This era of religious activism was notable in moving away from Calvinistic notions of predestination toward the ideas of free will and personal responsibility for sin. The combination of religious zeal and emphasis on moral accountability translated directly into greater levels of social activism and charity.

As a result, charitable organizations seemed to bloom in nearly every town or with every church. As Alexis de Tocqueville famously noted, "Americans of all age, all conditions, and all dispositions, constantly form associations," including mutual aid societies or other charitable groups.[48] During this period, more than 1,500 charitable groups operated in New England alone.[49]

But it was not enough merely to tend to the material needs of those who were poor, there was an equal and concomitant need to morally uplift and reform them. A desire to save souls was a part of this, of course. But there was also a belief that vice was the reason behind most poverty. As the mission statement for New York's Society for the Prevention of Pauperism declared, "Intemperance, ignorance, and idleness are the prolific parents of pauperism."[50] The poor were seen as given over to "idleness, intemperance, lottery playing, gambling, truancy, and prostitution."[51]

Alcohol, in particular, was seen as a problem, and probably not without cause. The historian W. J. Rorabaugh, for example, estimated that the average American in the first decades of the 19th century consumed seven gallons of alcohol per year.[52] A Massachusetts government commission, headed by John Quincy Adams, concluded "That of all the causes of pauperism, intemperance, in the use of spirituous liquors, is the most powerful and universal."[53]

The religious zeal for reform carried over into government programs as well. In many cases, the same prominent citizens both sat on the boards of private charities and oversaw local government relief programs, blurring the lines between public and private.

The 20th Century and the Professionalization of Charity

During the latter half of the 19th and the beginning of the 20th century, there was a profound change taking place in attitudes about how to deal with poverty. It was not, strictly speaking, a change in attitudes about the poor themselves or the origins of poverty—that debate continued—but about how the poor could best be helped and by whom.

The term "deserving poor" largely faded from public discourse by the late 19th century, in part because it was considered demeaning to people whose poverty was caused by conditions not of their own making, such as unemployment, illness, or old age. Still, the sentiment prevailed that these unfortunates were worthy of assistance because "in spite of adversity and temptation, most of them, most of the time, made a strenuous effort to provide for themselves and their families."[54] They were seen as very different from "those who will not work" as described in Henry Mayhew's influential survey, *London Labour and the London Poor*, in 1851.[55]

In 1890, Jacob Riis published his survey of the poor in the 1880s and concluded "nearly six and a half percent of all were utterly helpless—orphans, cripples, or the very aged; nearly one-fourth needed just a lift to start them on the road to independence, or to permanent pauperism, according to the wisdom with which the lever was applied. More than half were destitute because they had no work and were unable to find any, and one-sixth were frauds, professional beggars, training their children to follow in their footsteps."[56]

In a similar vein, in 1887 the Charitable Organization Society classified poverty as either "caused by misfortune" or "caused by misconduct."[57] The vast majority of the 28,000 cases surveyed (nearly 63 percent) were deemed unworthy of traditional charity, and very few cases were considered deserving of long-term assistance. Charitable providers considered this differentiation necessary because providing assistance to those whose poverty was perceived to result from their own behavior (rather than outside circumstances) was believed to enable or even encourage such destructive behavior.

However, a few years later, in 1901, Benjamin Seebohm Rowntree catalogued the causes of poverty as (1) death of the chief wage earner; (2) incapacity of the chief wage earner through accident, illness, or old age; (3) unemployment; (4) irregularity of work; (5) too large a family; and (6) low wages. He also saw a secondary set of causes, including (1) drunkenness, (2) gambling, and (3) improvident expenditures.[58] Rowntree's work was particularly influential because, although the list retained its division between deserving and undeserving poor, his emphasis on causes of poverty outside the control of the poor themselves helped shift the debate, for better or worse, toward a more universal form of support, especially toward the elderly, the sick, and the unemployed.[59]

This was also the era of progressivism, when many argued that the problems facing society were so big and complicated that only "experts" could solve them and that only government could provide the needed expertise. For example, according to Unitarian minister and religious writer John Haynes Holmes, poverty was "a problem infinitely bigger than [private charities] can handle—a problem so big that no institution short of society itself can hope to cope with it."[60]

At the same time, the aftermath of the American Civil War had caused the federal government to offer its first welfare programs, notably a series of pensions and other benefits, first for disabled veterans and war widows. State governments also began offering "mother's pensions," small stipends to widows and other impoverished mothers to help them care for their children.[61] The original recipients of these programs were intended to be almost exclusively widows, but the programs quickly expanded to cover women who for a variety of reasons were without the support of the normal breadwinner.[62] By 1930, the mothers of more than 200,000 children, including many divorced or abandoned women, were receiving funds through these programs.[63]

Moreover, this was an era that saw a rising trust in "experts" equipped to handle various problems of society. That was true of philanthropy as well. Simply helping your neighbor was no longer sufficient. Rather, one needed to "improve" and "uplift" him as well—and not just your neighbor, but all of society. Large philanthropic institutions like the Carnegie Corporation, the Ford Foundation, or Rockefeller Foundation, with their benefactors hiring professional social scientists to "maximize charitable giving for social improvement," are good examples of this. Large endowments aside, the enormous task of accomplishing such lofty goals could not be accomplished through traditional charity. It needed a size and expertise that could only be supplied by a much larger enterprise: government.

Still, in 1929, direct transfers to persons from all levels of government were equal to a mere 1 percent of gross national product (GNP). Nearly 80 percent of that amount consisted of veterans' benefits and pensions to retired government employees. Relief for the poor represented just 5 percent of the total.[64]

But the balance between government and civil society was about to change dramatically.

From the Great Depression to the Great Society

The Great Depression established the foundation for the U.S. version of the welfare state. With both private charity and state and local governments overwhelmed by the magnitude of the crisis, the federal government, first under President Herbert Hoover and then under President Franklin Delano Roosevelt, took a much more active role. In 1932, 97.9 percent of all government welfare spending was at the state and local levels. By 1939, only 37.7 percent was.[65]

This centralization was a deliberate policy by Roosevelt who declared:

> We cannot fail to act when hundreds of thousands of families live where there is no reasonable prospect of a living in the years to come. This is especially a national problem. Unlike most of the leading Nations of the world, we have so far failed to create a national policy for the development of our land and water resources and for their better use by those people who cannot make a living in their present positions. Only thus can we permanently eliminate many millions of people from the relief rolls on which their names are now found.[66]

Moreover, for the first time, programs were not directed to the traditional deserving poor—widows, orphans, and the disabled—but to "all needy unemployed persons and/or their dependents," or to "those whose employment or available resources are inadequate to provide the necessities of life for themselves and/or their dependents."[67] By the winter of 1934, 20 million Americans were on the dole.[68]

By 1940, direct transfers to persons had risen to equal 3.2 percent of GNP, although this partly reflects a 6 percent decline in GNP itself. Veterans' benefits and government pensions were only one-third of the total. However, the share of GNP going to direct relief (including the new Aid for Dependent Children [ADC] program) had grown twentyfold, to 1.2 percent, even though the Roosevelt administration had begun in 1935 to move away from cash relief for the poor in favor of social insurance schemes and relief for workers.

The actual amount of aid that the poor received remained quite small. At a time when minimum subsistence was thought to be around $100 per month ($115 by the deflated 1964 official poverty line), the most generous program of the time—the Works Progress Administration (WPA)—was only paying about $55 per month.[69]

Most of Roosevelt's efforts to fight poverty were temporary and focused on putting people into work. The Civil Works Administration, for example, lasted just four months. By 1939, nearly all of Roosevelt's work programs were gone. A few, such as the Works Progress Administration, did limp on through World War II, but with vastly reduced budgets and participation.

Roosevelt much preferred work to cash relief. In speeches, he called continued dependence on relief "a narcotic."[70] The major exception to this approach was the Social Security Act of 1935. This law, of course, created Social Security. But a lesser-known provision also established ADC, a program of matching grants to states to assist poor children (and their mothers). Originally intended as a small program targeted at widows and their families, ADC expanded rapidly. By 1938, 243,000 families with more than 600,000 children were participating in the program. The next year the numbers jumped to 298,000 families and 708,000 children.[71] The modern American welfare state was here.

In the immediate aftermath of World War II, few new programs began, but existing ones continued to grow. The number of Americans receiving government benefits continued to increase steadily. Then, in 1965, President Lyndon Johnson launched the next great leap in the American welfare state.

On January 8, 1964, Johnson delivered his first State of the Union address to Congress, in which he declared an "unconditional war on poverty in America." Johnson's goal was not only to "relieve the symptom of poverty, but to cure it and, above all, to prevent it."[72] Four months later, Johnson amplified his vision in a commencement address at the University of Michigan, in which he called for a "Great Society," which "demands an end to poverty and racial injustice."[73]

A flood of legislation soon followed, establishing many facets of the modern American welfare state. By the time he left office, Johnson had created some 28 new anti-poverty programs, focused on everything from health care to housing and job training to nutrition. Other programs, such as food stamps, were expanded or made permanent. And, this doesn't count broad-based entitlements that also came out of the War on Poverty and Great Society, such as Medicare. Although not directly aimed at poverty, they nonetheless provided increased benefits to the poor.

President Richard Nixon would build on and expand the War on Poverty, expanding eligibility and increasing spending. Nixon started the Supplemental Security Income (SSI) program and significantly expanded Medicaid. He also created several job training and employment programs, including the Comprehensive Employment and Training Act of 1973.[74] At one point, Nixon even unsuccessfully pursued "the development of a universal income supplement program to be administered by the Federal government."[75] Since then, with the possible exception of the Reagan interregnum, the U.S. welfare state has grown steadily under both Democratic and Republican presidencies regardless of which party controlled Congress.

Modern Scholarship: The Debate Renewed

The 1960s were obviously a period of significant legislative activity on poverty, but it was also a time of renewed intellectual debate over the causes of that poverty.

One interesting way to gauge this renewed interest in the causes can be seen in Figure 1.1.[76] References to poverty in books remained relatively flat from the late 1700s until the 1960s, even during the Great Depression. But, from 1960 on, there has been a sharp increase in such references, and they are now at an all-time high. Obviously there are limitations to this methodology, but it does illustrate the emergence of poverty as a topic for academic debate beginning in the 1960s.

The onset of this new debate can perhaps be traced to 1959 when anthropologist Oscar Lewis published *Five Families: Mexican Case Studies in the Culture of Poverty,* which posited that the poor both shaped and

Figure 1.1

Google Books Trends, "Poverty," 1700–2000

Source: Google Books Ngram Viewer.

existed within a "subculture of poverty" that established behaviors, making it harder to escape poverty.[77] As Lewis subsequently explained:

> In anthropological usage the term culture implies, essentially, a design for living that is passed down from generation to generation. In applying this concept of culture to the understanding of poverty, I want to draw attention to the fact that poverty in modern nations is not only a state of economic deprivation, of disorganization, or of the absence of something. It is also positive in the sense that it has a structure, a rationale, and defense mechanisms without which the poor could hardly carry on. In short, it is a way of life, remarkably stable and persistent, passed down from generation to generation along family lines.[78]

Lewis was hardly the first to raise this idea. As we have seen, aspects of the concept had been debated at least since the late Middle Ages. Social science literature had recognized the concentration of social pathologies among the poor for decades. But Lewis gave both popular voice and scientific respectability to the concept.

Lewis found both economic and noneconomic characteristics in this culture. On the economic side, he included such things as (1) unemployment or underemployment; (2) low wages and unskilled occupations; (3) child labor; (4) a lack of savings, chronic shortages of cash, and excessive borrowing, often with high rates of interest; and (5) the reliance on second-hand goods. None of these things should come as a surprise. Indeed, many represent the definition of poverty. However, Lewis also saw noneconomic characteristics to the culture of poverty, including alcoholism, violence, spousal and child abuse, early sexual activity, the abandonment by fathers of wives and children, and a general inability to delay gratification.[79]

Although many criticized Lewis's methodology—his research was often more anecdotal than scientific, and serious social scientists have virtually discarded his assumption that there exists a single universal culture of poverty—there is no doubt that Lewis's work had a substantial influence on the way scholars looked at poverty and laid the groundwork for much of the scholarship on poverty to come.

For example, Lewis's ideas could be considered a forerunner to Daniel Patrick Moynihan's groundbreaking report, "The Negro Family: The Case for National Action," published in 1965.[80]

At the time, Moynihan was assistant secretary of Labor in the Johnson administration. While preparing statistical reports on black poverty, he noticed that rates among African Americans of both unemployment and welfare enrollment were starting to increase relative to other ethnic groups.

The Moynihan report never actually used the term "culture of poverty," although it referred to a "tangle of pathology," and discussed issues such as family disintegration and employment that would become staples of the future debate over culture and poverty.

Moynihan pointed out the unintended consequences of the growing welfare state, particularly as it affected minority families in urban areas. Moynihan spoke about the break-up of the African American family, increased welfare dependency, and high levels of unemployment, all themes that would be replayed in welfare debates to this day. In his view, African Americans, especially youth, were "in danger of being caught up in the tangle of pathology that affects their world, and probably a majority are so entrapped. Many of those who escape do so for one generation only: as things now are, their children may have to run the gauntlet all over again."[81]

Lewis and Moynihan were hardly right-wingers. Moynihan was an old school New Deal liberal, and Lewis was a Marxist, who, for example, praised the Cuban revolution and blamed the culture of poverty on "free enterprise, pre-welfare state capitalism."[82] The Moynihan report specifically referenced America's history of racism, speaking of the "racist virus" that "still infects us." And among the report's conclusions was a call for full employment. Even so, both Lewis and Moynihan were heavily criticized for "blaming the poor."

A different look at poverty was provided by Michael Harrington's 1962 book *The Other America*.[83] Perhaps better than any other writer, Harrington was able to grab the public's attention with his description of poverty coexisting side by side with American prosperity.

While Lewis and Moynihan were excoriated by the left for linking cultural behavior and poverty, Harrington's book was hailed as the gold standard for discussing poverty over the next decade. It was seen by most as providing a far more sympathetic and compelling look at the poor, and it placed more responsibility on society for their plight. Harrington too saw a cultural dimension to poverty, for example writing that the poor often constituted "a separate culture, another nation, with its own way of life."[84] He took notice of such problems as crime, domestic violence, prostitution, and drug abuse in poor communities. In fact, Harrington actually used the term "culture of poverty" repeatedly throughout the book. But Harrington rejected the idea that the poor themselves bore responsibility for their condition. Rather, he argued, the responsibility lay with a larger society that neglected their plight. "Society," he wrote, "must help them before they can help themselves."[85]

The response to Harrington's book reflected a growing academic pushback against the "culture of poverty" hypothesis, a counterargument that the causes of poverty stem from economic and political structures designed to favor particular groups over others on the basis of class, race, gender, and other factors. In other words, the causes of poverty are structural rather than cultural.

Many of the early structural analyses of poverty were Marxist in orientation—or at least anti-capitalist—relying heavily on a class-based critique. But later, the approach came to encompass a much broader critique of political, economic, and social inequities. Structural approaches to poverty would also come to include discussions of technological displacement and globalization.

By 1980, however, when Ronald Reagan was elected president, there had been a significant shift in the average American attitude toward welfare and the poor. The anti-poverty programs of the 1960s and 1970s were widely seen to have failed.

Indeed, a few years before Reagan's election, *Time* magazine published a cover story decrying the emergence of an underclass in America's cities, which it portrayed as rife with drugs, crime, teen pregnancy, and unemployment.[86] This depiction might not have been all that different in substance from the way poor communities had been portrayed by Lewis and Moynihan, or even Harrington, but there was a decided change in moral tone.

One of the best examples of changing attitudes toward the poor can be seen in Ken Auletta's influential book, *The Underclass*, published in 1982. Auletta suggested that as many as 9 million of America's 25–20 million poor people composed a new and deeply troubled underclass, consisting of four types: (1) the passive poor, usually long-term welfare recipients; (2) hostile street criminals and drug addicts; (3) hustlers, who while not violent, had much in common with street criminals and who lived in the underground economy; and (4) the homeless, mentally ill, drunks, and drifters.[87] Such a description would have been instantly recognizable by the authors of the Elizabethan Poor Law. Certainly, it was wildly at odds with Harrington's sympathetic portrayal of poor, unemployed factory workers, driven into poverty by a changing economy.

Some of this change may have been racial. Throughout the 1970s, poverty was increasingly seen as having a black face. The sympathetic white poor of Appalachia and out-of-work factory workers that Harrington portrayed were now the urban, black "welfare queens" of conservative rhetoric. As one scholar of racial attitudes in America explained, "While poor women of all races get blamed for their impoverished condition, African-American women commit the most egregious violation of American values. This storyline taps into stereotypes about both women (uncontrolled sexually) and African-Americans (laziness)."[88]

Martin Gilens examined the racial composition of the poor as portrayed in the three most widely read news magazines of the period—*Time, Newsweek,* and *U.S. News and World Report*—and found that the percentage of African Americans pictured in articles about poverty increased from roughly 25 percent in 1965 (which was roughly in line with their proportion of overall poverty) to more than 60 percent by the late 1970s, although their share of poverty had not increased.[89]

This, of course, leaves open the question of why there was a shift in racial perceptions and portrayals of poverty. The rise of the Civil Rights Movement of the 1960s and the urban riots of the late 1960s undoubtedly played a role. Moreover, as African Americans migrated from the south to the northern cities beginning in 1916 and roughly continuing through the 1970s, black poverty became a less remote experience for many Americans. It may also have been a consequence, rather than a cause, of changing attitudes toward the poor. That is, African Americans have always been perceived as part of the "undeserving poor," and studies show that "images of poor blacks increased when the tone of poverty stories became more critical of the poor and decreased when stories became more sympathetic."[90] Regardless of the reasons, the net effect was to create a vicious cycle in which the association of African Americans with poverty drove more critical media coverage of the poor, which in turn caused more people to associate poverty with African Americans.

But racial stereotypes and antagonism were hardly the only reasons for declining support for welfare. This period was one of economic hardship for large swaths of America that were not part of traditionally poor communities. Unemployment and inflation were rampant, eroding middle-class incomes and opportunities. People who were themselves struggling increasingly resented the cost of programs that redistributed their money to others. Studies of public opinion have consistently shown that Americans are more generous toward the needy during times of economic expansion but react less favorably toward social welfare programs when the economy slows.[91]

Furthermore, a growing cynicism was seen toward government generally. Johnson had launched the War on Poverty amid the optimistic and idealistic residue of the Kennedy era. By the mid 1970s, the climate was very different. The Vietnam War and the Watergate scandal had diminished overall confidence and trust in government. These events were followed in short order by an energy crisis, stagflation, and the Iranian hostage crisis. Polls showed "trust in government" decreasing steadily throughout the decade, with the percentage of Americans expressing trust in government dropping from about 50 percent to only 25 percent.[92]

But most important, the limits of government's ability to fight poverty and the unintended consequences of a growing welfare system were becoming more apparent. As Harvard's James Patterson wrote:

> These limitations [of the War on Poverty programs] stood in cruel contrast to what had been promised. . . . Perhaps no government program in modern American history promised so much more than it delivered. The contrast chastened theorists, who began to reconsider their Utopian notions about the potential for social science and to lead a surge of neoconservative thinking in influential journals. . . . More than any other program in Johnson's so called Great Society, the war on poverty accentuated doubts about the capacity of social science to plan, and government to deliver, ambitious programs for social betterment.[93]

All combined to turn Americans against the war on poverty and the welfare system. A *New York Times*/CBS survey in 1977 found that 54 percent of Americans thought "most people who receive money from welfare could get along without it if they tried." Only 31 percent disagreed. A total of 58 percent disapproved of "most Government sponsored welfare programs."[94]

The conservative critique of welfare received an enormous boost—both political and intellectual—with the publication of Charles Murray's *Losing Ground* in 1984. Murray differed from some earlier cultural poverty theorists in that he did not view the culture of poverty as representing a moral failure on the part of the poor. Rather, he saw the poor as rational actors who respond to the incentives of the welfare system in ways that perpetuate poverty.

Murray argued that the availability of welfare provided an incentive for unmarried childbearing and a disincentive for work. As a result, however well intentioned, welfare programs could prolong or even increase poverty. Murray's thesis became the foundation for modern conservative discussions of the cultural roots of poverty.

That political debate came to a head in 1996 when President Bill Clinton signed the Personal Responsibility and Work Opportunity Reconciliation Act. That bill marked a significant shift away from welfare's previous open-ended entitlement status. Aid to Families with Dependent Children was rechristened Temporary Assistance for Needy Families and returned to greater state control in the form of a block grant. The act established time limits and work requirements.

In the years since welfare reform passed, academic debate over the causes and nature of poverty continued and even intensified, but the issues' political saliency faded rapidly, as concerns about the poor have been largely supplanted by concerns over middle-class stagnation. Even issues of inequality were largely viewed by its impact on the middle class or the working class rather than the poor. As former PBS host Tavis Smiley put it, "There seems to be a bipartisan consensus in this town—and you know how hard that is to do—but a bipartisan consensus that the poor just don't matter, that poverty is just not an important issue."[95]

Even if poverty has fallen off the political radar screen, it remains a critical issue for millions of Americans, and understanding the causes of poverty remains as important as ever. Therefore, let us take a deeper look at the debate over why people are poor. Is poverty the result of personal choices and decisions, a "culture of poverty"? Or does poverty result from structural or institutional forces, outside of an individual's control? The following chapters will look at both sides of this debate.

CHAPTER TWO: THE CULTURAL OR INDIVIDUAL BEHAVIOR THEORIES OF POVERTY

But what if large causes of poverty are not matters of material distribution but are behavioral—bad choices and the cultures that produce them?

—*George Will*[1]

As noted in the previous chapter, we have spent hundreds of years debating why people are poor and who, as a result, deserves help. For most of its history, that debate divided the people who were poor between those who were "deserving" and those who weren't, essentially a division between able-bodied men, who were generally not considered worthy of assistance, and others, such as the children, the elderly, and the infirm, who were found to be poor through no fault of their own and, therefore, deserving of help.

More recently, however, the debate has shifted somewhat. It is now split between two bitterly antagonistic camps, which broadly reflect ideological approaches to poverty. On one side of that debate are those who believe that poverty results from structural factors inherent to the economy or societal institutions beyond the control of individuals. The other camp combines an assignment of responsibility to personal choices and decisions by the poor with a broader critique of a "culture of poverty." To some degree, this debate boils down to the assignment of blame for poverty. But it also reflects an assessment of what interventions will be most successful in dealing with the issue.

Most conservative critiques of welfare suggest that poverty is a result of the behavior of individual poor people and the culture that influences the choices they make. As a result, it is argued, reducing poverty will require changes in the behavior of the poor themselves, and therefore public policy must carefully calibrate the incentives and disincentives that it provides for those choices.[2]

Of course, we should acknowledge up front that culture and unproductive life choices are not the same, although they are often interrelated and mutually reinforcing. I examine them together in this chapter because they are so interwoven in arguments about poverty—and because conservatives so often conflate the two.

To be more precise, "culture" can be described, in the words of Harvard's Orlando Patterson, as "a repertoire of socially transmitted and intra-generationally generated ideas about how to live and make judgments, both in general terms and in regard to specific domains of life."[3] When self-defeating behaviors become the prevailing norms in socially isolated communities, they can reinforce each other in a "culture of poverty" or "culture of dependency" that can trap people in poverty. Moreover, such behaviors can be passed from one generation to the next, increasing the likelihood of multigenerational poverty.

As Patterson also notes, it is incorrect to speak of a single "culture of poverty." People who are poor "adapt to their socioeconomic, physical, and political environments in a wide variety of ways."[4] Moreover, one needs to distinguish behavior from cultural values. Those in poverty may broadly share middle-class values, but acting on those values appears not to offer the same road to upward mobility. Structural impediments may distort the costs and benefits associated with certain behaviors, effectively preventing the poor from acting upon their sincerely held values. For example, surveys show that most poor women recognize the value of marriage and would like to become married themselves, even as marriage rates among the poor decline and births outside marriage increase.[5]

Both cultural and individual behavior theories of poverty have come under criticism in recent years. In some cases, this has been a matter of pure political correctness. As Harvard's William Julius Wilson points out, too many social scientists "avoid describing any behavior that might be construed as unflattering or stigmatizing . . . either because of a fear of providing fuel for racist arguments or because of a concern of being charged with 'racism' or with 'blaming the victim.'"[6] Thus, Wilson warns, "Those who represent traditional liberal views on social issues have been reluctant to discuss openly or, in some instances, even to acknowledge the sharp increase in social pathologies in ghetto communities."[7]

There is reason to be concerned about the stigmatization of people who are poor. And we should be aware that, as Patterson notes, "Some of the cultural traits associated with the ghetto poor (for example, attitudes toward authority, work, violence, parenting, sex and reproduction, school, and crime) closely resemble familiar racist stereotypes about blacks. . . . They smell like racist rationalizations for the status quo."[8]

To acknowledge that agency entails the opportunity to make bad choices as well as good ones, or that the choices of individuals taken as a whole can constitute a culture, is not to suggest that the poor are in some way morally deficient. Rather, it is recognition that, as Oscar Lewis famously wrote, the "culture of poverty" represents "an adaptation to a set of objective conditions of the larger society, [but] once it comes into existence. . . . It tends to perpetuate itself from generation to generation because of its effects on children."[9] For example, as Wilson argues in *The Truly Disadvantaged*, in communities with high levels of joblessness, people may cope by making less than optimal lifestyle choices, such as having children earlier or outside marriage, while larger cultural attitudes begin to drift away from seeing education, work, and marriage as avenues out of poverty.[10]

Wilson also argues the following:

> The exodus of middle- and working-class families from many ghetto neighborhoods removes an important "social buffer" that could deflect the full impact of the kind of prolonged and increasing joblessness that plagued inner-city neighborhoods . . . this argument is based on the assumption that even if the truly disadvantaged segments of an inner-city area experience a significant increase in long-term spells of joblessness, the basic institutions in that area (churches, schools, stores, recreational facilities, etc.) would remain viable if much of the

> base of their support comes from the more economically stable and secure families. Moreover, the very presence of these families during such periods provides mainstream role models that help keep alive the perception that education is meaningful, that steady employment is a viable alternative to welfare, and that family stability is the norm, not the exception.[11]

This idea that the social isolation of the poor reinforces cultural problems is one that we will see frequently recur throughout this book. Some of this social isolation may result from natural sorting processes, but government policy can contribute to social isolation, and its perverse effects, in many ways.

The Success Sequence

There is a robust statistical relationship between individual behavioral characteristics and the likelihood that a person will either escape poverty or rise out of it. These characteristics, including educational attainment, attachment to the labor force, and childbearing only within marriage, are frequently referred to as "the success sequence."

Richard Reeves of the Brookings Institution's Center on Children and Families points out that 73 percent of whites and 59 percent of African Americans reach the middle class or beyond (defined as above 300 percent of the federal poverty line) if they follow three norms of success: (1) graduate from high school, (2) maintain a full-time job or have a partner who does, and (3) have children only while married and after age 21 (should they choose to have children).[12] W. Bradford Wilcox of the American Enterprise Institute and Wendy Wang of the Institute for Family Studies, looking at Americans ages 28–34, arrive at a similar conclusion.[13]

There are, however, a couple of things to keep in mind. First, not every step in the so-called success sequence is equally supported by the evidence. In fact, whether and the degree to which all three factors (education, employment, and marital childbearing) are contributors to exiting or avoiding poverty are much debated by scholars. The evidence mostly consists of correlation studies that may or may not be convincing.

Attributing causation in a complex world is difficult. As we shall see, in some cases the accumulated weight of evidence seems strong, whereas in other cases there is more room for dispute.

Employment and the Work Ethic

The strongest leg of the success sequence is clearly work. Just 2.2 percent of full-time workers are poor. Even part-time work makes a significant difference. Only 13 percent of part-time workers are poor, compared with 21.6 percent of people 16 and older who do not work (Figure 2.1).[14]

No one expects the 21 percent of the poor who are children to enter the labor force, nor should the elderly retired poor be forced back to work. Similarly, the disabled are a special consideration. Still, just 44 percent of poor, able-bodied adults are working full time.[15] That's likely more than commonly believed, but the "working poor" remain a minority of the population in poverty. In fact, a 2016 Harris poll of the

Figure 2.1

Poverty Rate for People 16 and Older, by Work Status, 2016

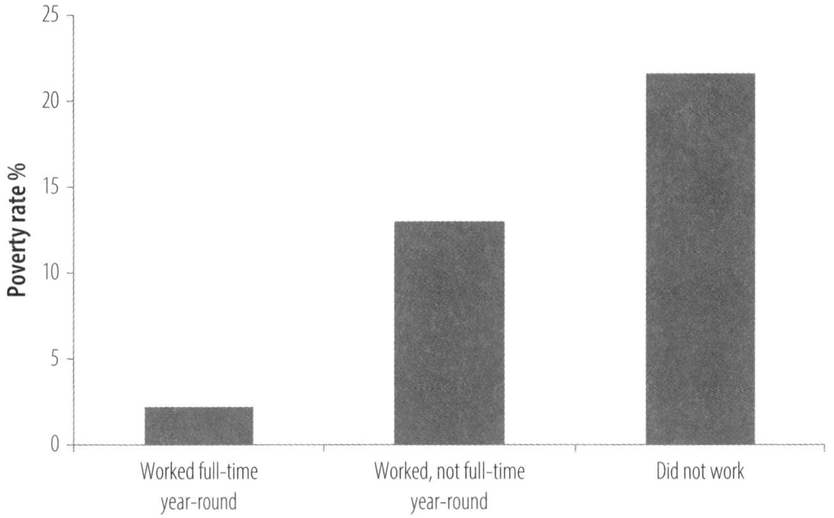

Source: U.S. Census Bureau, "People and Families in Poverty by Selected Characteristics: 2015 and 2016," Table 3, 2016, https://www2.census.gov/programs-surveys/cps/tables/time-series/historical-poverty-people/hstpov25.xls.

unemployed found that most respondents have had no job interviews for two years. And 43 percent agree with the statement, "I've completely given up on looking for a job."[16]

Undoubtedly, structural issues are at work here. Jobs are far from plentiful in most high-poverty areas. Yet even when jobs are available, low-income workers seem less likely to avail themselves of those opportunities to work. It's difficult to deny that at least some of the impoverished seemingly do not show a work ethic that might lead to success.

The available evidence on why people who are poor don't accept jobs raises as many questions as it answers. It's not laziness, despite appearances. As Patterson notes, "There is a strong commitment to the work ethic by working-class black Americans, including those at the poorest end of the spectrum."[17] On the other hand, Patterson does acknowledge a disdain for so-called McJobs among the more disconnected street culture of ghetto youth, who "'proudly prefer unemployment to such seemingly lowly work."[18] Still, Patterson demonstrates that the work ethic remains solid overall among low-income people, particularly African Americans who are poor.

Other observers, while refusing to totally dismiss "negative attitudes toward menial work" as a contributing factor to joblessness in high poverty areas, see little evidence that a loss of work-ethic is a significant problem in poor communities, at least compared to more fundamental issues of economic dislocation.[19]

Surprisingly, there has been little research in the past 20 years about how low-income individuals and welfare recipients feel about work. Older studies indicate that the poor generally expressed a desire to work rather than receive welfare, but that they were not actively seeking work.[20] For this reason, work requirements were central to the welfare reforms enacted in the Personal Responsibility and Work Opportunity Reconciliation Act of 1996.

Why, then, are so many poor people not working or even looking for work? Conventional wisdom says it is a lack of jobs. But data from the Census Bureau suggest that that might not be the sole reason, or even the main one. The Census Bureau's Current Population Survey asks the unemployed why they are not working. Breaking this down by income level and looking at working age population, we can determine broad categories for the reasons behind unemployment. Just 4.4 percent of adults under the poverty line who had not worked or had spent time out of the labor force in the previous year cited an inability to find employment as the reason.[21]

The prominent social scientist Charles Murray points out that, among white men with no more than a high school education, labor force participation declined even during periods of low unemployment.[22] Murray also cites research showing that low-income men increased the amount of time that they devoted to leisure activities, even as high-earning men were decreasing their leisure time and increasing work hours.[23] In short, Murray posits that low-income men were *choosing* to work less.

Further evidence comes from the U.S. Department of Labor's American Time Use Survey, which found that the unemployed spent only about 90 minutes per day, on average, looking for work. At the same time, they spent about 5 hours per day watching television or movies, 2.5 times as much as their employed counterparts. They also slept about 40 minutes more per day.[24] This finding suggests that the unemployed were not making the job search their priority.

The survey also suggested that many unemployed were choosing not to take certain jobs. For example, more than half said they would be unwilling to move to another state to find work. Even more significantly, nearly two-thirds of the unemployed responded that they did not bother to apply for jobs that they perceived as not paying enough. Sixty-six percent agreed with the statement "I don't apply for jobs that offer minimum wage because it's just not enough to pay the bills."[25]

We really don't know why poor people are not more willing to take jobs if they are available. Nevertheless, we can make some guesses.

We know, for example, that some of those currently on welfare are simply reacting to the incentives in the program. Poor people are not lazy; they are behaving rationally. If you pay someone more not to work than they can earn from employment, they will be less inclined to work. So would you or I.

There has been some debate as to how many people face the prohibitively high marginal effective tax rates that act as poverty traps and deter people from working. The Congressional Budget Office examined this question in a recent report, and while it's true that not everyone in or around poverty faces these high rates, many do. The median effective marginal tax rate for households just above the poverty level is almost 34 percent, the highest for any income level. Some households that receive larger benefits or pay higher state taxes have even higher effective rates. For some 10 percent of households just above the poverty line, marginal rates can run higher than 65 percent. For each additional dollar earned in this range, these households would lose almost two-thirds to taxes or lost benefits.[26] If anything, this analysis might understate how steep the effective marginal rates are for some households. The Congressional Budget Office only considers the combined effect of income taxes, payroll taxes, Supplemental Nutrition Assistance Program (SNAP) and the Patient Protection and Affordable Care Act (ACA) exchange subsidies, so households that participate in other programs like Temporary Assistance for Needy Families (TANF) or housing assistance could face even higher rates.

Recent studies have also suggested that the availability of modern technology may have raised the "reservation wage" among young men. What this term means is that relatively cheap sources of digital entertainment have become so pleasurable that the potential labor earnings of lesser-skilled individuals are less appealing in comparison. As such, young men appear to be substituting leisure activities, notably video games, at the expense of work or looking for work. Eric Hurst, a University of Chicago economist, notes that since the mid-2000s the decline in labor force participation by lower-skilled men in their 20s has been accompanied by a nearly 50 percent increase in the amount of time men in that age bracket spend online or playing video games.[27]

There is also some evidence that although people who are poor understand that work is important, they may value other things over work. That seems in line with data that suggest that many low-income people underestimate the value of work for improving their future. In a survey conducted by the Council on Foreign Relations, 46 percent of people in the lowest income quartile agreed with the statement that "hard work offers little guarantee of success," compared with just 23 percent of those in the top quartile who felt that way, and this dynamic was persistent through the first iteration of the survey in 1987.[28]

Finally, there may be a general level of discouragement among individuals who have frequently been rejected for jobs or feel shut out of the larger economy and society. A hint of this is evident in Patterson's research showing that African Americans who are in poverty were more hesitant to recommend job opportunities to their friends and neighbors.[29] This tendency was particularly true of those who were not secure in their own job status.

In addition, the poor must deal with stresses that may interfere with their ability to be employed such as juggling expenses and making stressful trade-offs that higher-income people don't have to worry about. Even when not actually making a financial decision, these preoccupations can be present and distracting.[30]

Attitudes toward work have a multigenerational impact. One study that assesses the relationship between parental and children's attitudes toward work finds that parents and children work similar numbers of hours and that the similarity is only partially accounted for by similar labor market conditions.[31] The authors conclude that there is compelling evidence that parents pass on preferences for work hours to their children, either through their modeling of work behavior or other factors. Another study, by Jens Ludwig and Susan Mayer of the University of Chicago, using data from the National Education Longitudinal Study, concludes that ensuring all eighth graders lived in a household with at least one working adult would lower poverty in the children's generation by as much as 7 percent.[32]

A wide variety of academic literature shows that children who grow up in a family on welfare are more likely to receive welfare themselves at some point.[33] There are many exogenous factors, such as geographic location, economic conditions, structural racism, and the intergenerational educational issues discussed previously that could account for welfare use in the children of welfare beneficiaries. Still, the few studies that directly address the issue show that the relative social acceptability of receiving welfare as an alternative to work also has an intergenerational aspect. That is, children who grow up with their parents on welfare are more likely to view the receipt of welfare as a reasonable choice.

Although there has been little U.S. research, a study based on Australian data found strong support for intergenerational transmission of attitudes toward work and welfare.[34] The study found more opposition to government aid and a stronger work ethic in children from those families in which the mother worked, the family had little or no connection to the welfare system, and the mother had a greater personal opposition to high welfare benefits for the poor. The authors concluded that "young people's attitudes towards work and welfare are shaped by socialization within their families. . . . These results are consistent with—though do not definitively establish—the existence of an intergenerational welfare culture."[35]

Valuing and Pursuing an Education

A substantial body of evidence also supports the importance of successfully pursuing an education. Poverty rates are much higher among those who do not graduate high school than among those who, say, graduate college. Among people age 25 and older, almost a quarter of those without a high school degree are poor, nearly double the percentage for high school graduates, and nearly five times higher than the poverty rate for college graduates (Figure 2.2).

Figure 2.2

Poverty Rate for Persons Age 25 and Older by Educational Attainment, 2016

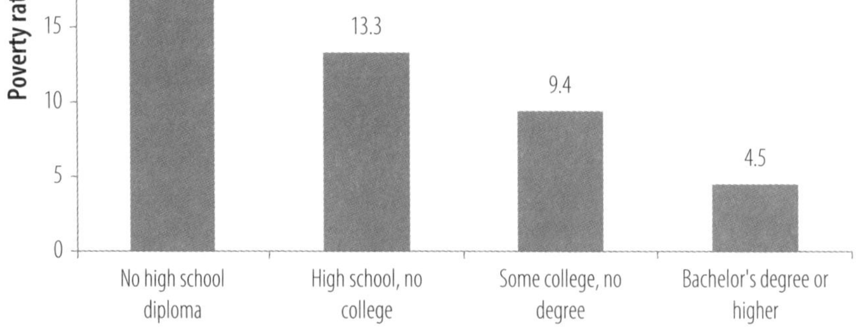

Source: U.S. Census Bureau, "Income and Poverty in the United States: 2016," Table 3, https://www2.census.gov/programs-surveys/demo/tables/p60/259/pov_table3.xls.

Unsurprisingly, the less education people have, the harder it is for them to find a job. The unemployment rate for those without a high school diploma is 50 percent higher than for high school graduates and three times higher than for college graduates. If they do find jobs, their wages are likely to be low. Wages for high school dropouts have declined (in inflation-adjusted terms) by roughly 15 percent over the past 25 years.[36] For adults age 25 and older, earnings for men with a high school diploma (or equivalent) were more than $10,000 higher in 2016 than their counterparts without a degree, while for women this gap was more than $6,200.[37]

Education may help contribute to whether a person will be poor in the first place, but it also matters in economic mobility and the ability to escape poverty. For example, take a child born into a family in the bottom income quintile. Without a college degree, that child has limited upward mobility, with a 45 percent chance of remaining in that quintile and only a 5 percent chance of reaching the highest income quintile. If such children can earn a college degree through hard work and perseverance, they are more likely to reach the top quintile (19 percent) than they are to remain stuck in the bottom quintile (16 percent).[38]

Perhaps even more important, the effect of education on poverty is intergenerational. For example, studies show that a mother's education level has a significant effect on the educational achievement of her children.[39] Researchers at Northwestern University's Joint Center for Poverty Research studied welfare experiments geared toward furthering education rather than providing immediate work. They found that higher levels of educational attainment by mothers substantially increased the school readiness of their children and reduced their children's academic problems.[40] Research by James Heckman of the University of Chicago suggests that the readiness gap attributable to a mother's education is present by the time a child enters school and persists throughout the child's education. "The gaps in cognitive achievement by level of maternal education that we observe at age eighteen," Heckman writes, "are mostly present at age six, when children enter school."[41]

The socioeconomic status of the parents and, at least indirectly, the mother's education level, have a significant effect on a child's readiness to learn. This factor could be due to differences in knowledge about child development; one study found this to be a factor that explains differences in child-directed speech by parental socioeconomic status.[42] The failure, then, of women who are in poverty to complete school and go on to higher education can echo through future generations.

Once children who are impoverished enter school, they are more likely to fall even further behind. Of course, to some degree, the lack of educational achievement among the poor can be chalked up to the failure of public schools and limits on educational opportunities. Certainly, as we will see in chapter 7, schools in low-income areas frequently perform inadequately despite high levels of education spending, and government policies can trap the poor in those failing schools.

We also can't discount the impact of racism and classism on educational opportunity. For instance, African American children, especially African American children who are poor, are more likely to be stereotyped as slow learners. In a review of statewide data from Indiana, the authors found that African Americans made up 13 percent of the students in special education but represented only 8.4 percent of those in general education settings, while they made up 27 percent of those in separate special education classes.[43] Other studies suggest African Americans are less likely to be referred to programs for gifted students.[44]

The attitude of low expectations and harsher judgments is not applied only to African Americans who are in poverty. Surveys suggest that these attitudes extend to poor children more broadly. A study by the Center for American Progress found that "Secondary teachers have lower expectations for students of color and students from disadvantaged backgrounds."[45] Lower expectations can lead teachers to favor less challenging curriculums and to have a general indifference toward a child's academic success. As one low-income child was quoted in a report for the Educational Trust, "What hurts us more is that you teach us less."[46]

However, the attitudes and actions of families who are impoverished themselves cannot be ignored. A study of British school children by Alissa Goodman and Paul Gregg found that roughly one-third of the difference in educational achievement between rich and poor children is attributable to parental attitudes and educational aspirations.[47]

Surveys show that low-income parents believe that there is little they can do to influence their child's educational success. In a study by Nancy Feyl Chavkin and David L. Williams in the *Journal of Sociology and Social Welfare,* low-income parents differed from other income groups on their responses to several statements regarding parental involvement with their child's education. Low-income parents were strongly supportive of parental involvement with their child's education in theory. But 44.7 percent of low-income parents agree with the statement, "I have little to do with my children's success in school," compared with only 11.7 percent of middle-income parents and with only 4.4 percent of high-income parents. Low-income parents also reported a lack of confidence in their ability to make school decisions without further training. More than half agreed with the statement, "I do not have enough training to help make school decisions," a sentiment held by less than 30 percent of middle-income parents, and just 17 percent of high-income parents.[48]

Parents in low-income families may also have lower expectations for their children's success. One study found that only about half of low-income parents (those with annual incomes of $30,000 or less) expect their children to attain a bachelor's degree or higher, compared with seven of nine parents earning $75,000 or more (Figure 2.3). Likewise, low-income parents are more than three times as likely as the wealthiest parents to expect their child to do no more than finish high school.[49]

Figure 2.3

Parental Expectations for Child's Academic Achievement, by Family Income

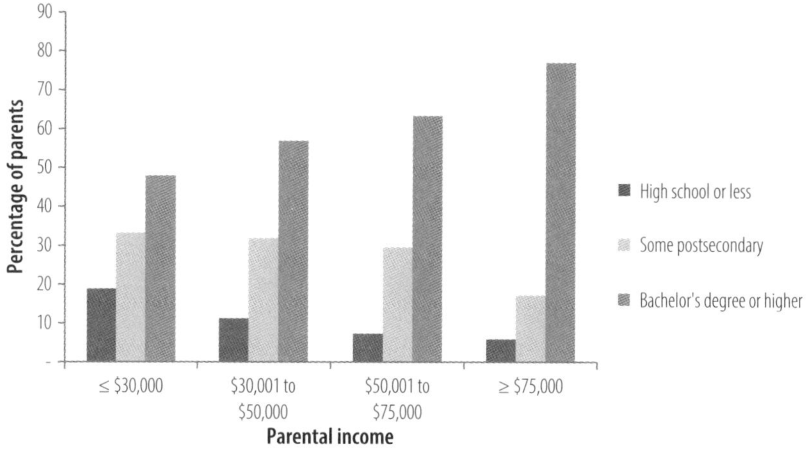

Source: Child Trends Databank, "Parental Expectations for Their Children's Academic Attainment," Child Trends, Bethesda, MD, 2015, http://www.childtrends.org/?indicators=dparental-expectations-for-their-childrens-academic-attainment.

Note: Expectations are for children grades 6 through 12.

Substantial evidence suggests that the culture in the school itself—that is, peer culture—affects student performance. Studies show that peer attitudes, and the associated pressures, can affect academic achievement, educational aspirations, and whether a student goes to college, as well as such issues as truancy, drug use, and other behavioral problems.[50] That makes it particularly concerning that many children who are in poverty, and poor African American children in particular, may undervalue educational excellence. Patterson, for instance, points to "a counterhegemonic, and near nihilistic, rejection of mainstream educational values" as one of the seven core configurations of "street culture" among low-income African American youth.[51] The common shorthand is that a given child is "acting white," and discussion of the problem remains highly controversial. Yet the evidence is strong that there is a cultural resistance to academic achievement among some African American youth.

The late John Ogbu, a professor of anthropology at the University of California–Berkeley, studied attitudes about school among African American students in the Cleveland suburb of Shaker Heights, Ohio. He found that African American students encountered intense peer pressure to "avoid certain attitudes, standard English, and some behaviors because they considered them white." "Acting white" was considered "detrimental to their collective racial identity and solidarity."[52]

For years, academics pushed back against Ogbu and his theory of an "oppositional culture" among black youths. However, Harvard's Roland Fryer Jr. and Paul Torelli used the National Longitudinal Study of Adolescent Health to analyze the friendship patterns in a nationally representative sample of more than 90,000 students entering grades 7 through 12.[53] Even after controlling for other factors that might affect popularity, they find strong evidence that "acting white" is a genuine issue. For students with low grade point averages (GPAs), there is little difference in the relationship between grades and popularity. But once a certain GPA threshold is hit (2.5, a mix of Bs and Cs), the differences start to emerge. Although African Americans with GPAs between 2.5 and 3.5 continue to have more friends than those with lower grades, the rate of increase is no longer as great as among white students. As the GPAs of African American students increase beyond this level, they tend to have fewer and fewer friends. A black student with a 4.0 GPA has, on average, 1.5 fewer friends of the same ethnicity than a white student with the same GPA. Put differently, a black student with straight As is no more popular than a black student with a 2.9 GPA, but high-achieving whites are at the top of the popularity pyramid.

Significantly, while largely applied to the African American community, the "acting white" stigma is not exclusive to black students. Fryer and Torelli's research shows that Latino students displaying academic success lose friends at an even faster rate than do African Americans (Figure 2.4). The decline in popularity starts earlier as well, with a GPA as low as 2.5. From that point on, as their grade point average increases, the authors note, "Hispanic students lose popularity at an alarming rate."[54]

Cultural attitudes toward education matter both among students and parents.

Marriage, Childbearing, and Family Structure

By far, the least-instructive portion of the success sequence is the emphasis on marriage—or particularly on avoiding childbearing outside marriage. Many traditional conservatives value marriage as a positive good in and of itself. This view has led them to overstate the effect that childbearing outside marriage may have on poverty.

That is not to say that motherhood outside marriage is unrelated to poverty in some way. More than 30 percent of people in female-headed households are poor.[55] Fifteen percent of female-headed households had no one in the labor force, and only 56 percent had at least one full-time worker.[56] One-third of families headed by single mothers can be considered "food insecure," and almost 16 percent of people in female-headed families receive more than half of their total income from means-tested assistance programs.[57] Children growing up in a single-parent family are four times more likely to be poor than children growing up in two-parent families.[58] Roughly 63 percent of all poor children reside in single-parent families.[59] Poverty rates for minority single parents are even higher. In 2016, half of all children living in both African American and Hispanic mother-only households were poor.[60]

Figure 2.4

Popularity and Academic Success in Different Ethnicities

A. Spectral popularity and grades by race, raw data.

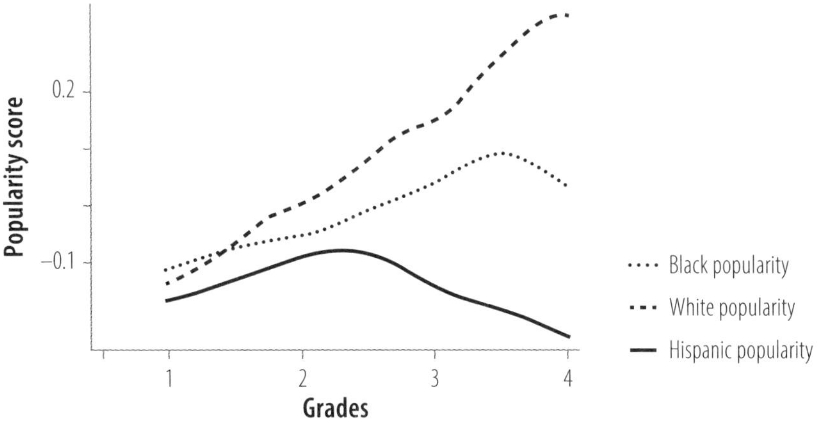

B. Spectral popularity and grades by race, with controls.

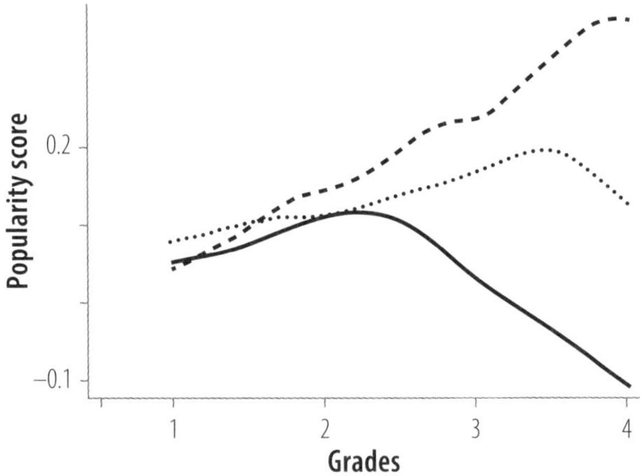

Source: Roland G. Fryer Jr. and Paul Torelli, "An Empirical Analysis of 'Acting White,'" *Journal of Public Economics* 94, no. 5-6 (2010): 380–96, http://www.quantitativesocialscience.com/uploads/5/8/3/3/5833205/fryer_torelli_2010.pdf.

Although single parenthood is widely associated with nonmarital childbearing, slightly more than half of households headed by a single mother are actually the result of divorce.[61] Roughly one of five non-poor women falls into poverty after a divorce. Moreover, as we will see in chapter 4, child support is often meager and frequently unpaid.

Because low-income couples are more likely to divorce than their high-earning counterparts, they (especially the women) are more exposed to the economic consequences.

Divorce-based single parenthood can clearly lead to poverty, but having children outside of marriage in the first place is an even stronger indicator of poverty. Women having a child outside of wedlock are both more likely to be poor and to spend longer in poverty than divorced mothers. The poverty rate for never-married mothers tops 43 percent, compared with roughly 28 percent for previously married mothers.[62] And, while there has been an improvement in the economic status of divorced women since the 1990s, there has not been a comparable improvement for never-married mothers.[63]

Discussions of single parenthood have been increasingly complicated by the rise of cohabitation. Many women who give birth outside marriage are living with their child's father or another partner, even if they are not married. At least part of the growth in nonmarital births is attributable to the increase in cohabitation and the associated rise in births within such unofficial unions.[64] Perhaps as many as one-third of officially single women actually live with the father of their children. Because most poverty measures do not consider cohabiting couples as a single household unit, this may provide a misleading measure of how many single mothers are poor and how deep that poverty may be.

Still, cohabiting relationships tend to be shorter and more fragile than marital ones (Figure 2.5). On average, a cohabitating couple in the United States lives together for just 14 months, and the relationship typically ends without marriage.[65] When children are part of the mix, the relationships do last longer but, even so, two-thirds of women who were unmarried at the time of a birth (roughly half of whom were cohabiting with the child's father at the time) were no longer in a relationship with the father within five years.[66]

Compounding matters, higher-income cohabiting couples who had children together were more likely to form stable long-term relationships than were poor couples. Cohabiting relationships among people who are poor tend to be more frequent, less stable, and shorter term than such relationships among higher-income couples, even when children are involved.[67] In addition, the breakup of cohabitation relationships tends to have greater economic consequences for women than does divorce.

Figure 2.5

Marriage vs. Cohabitation

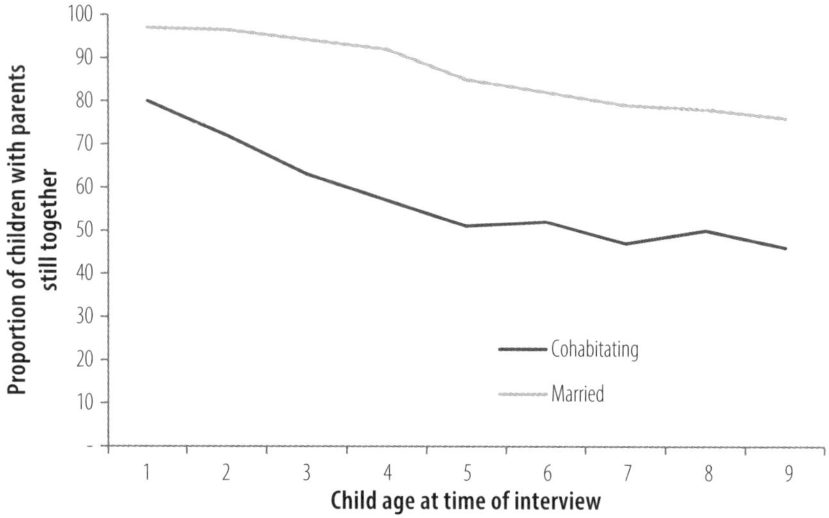

Source: Sheela Kennedy and Larry Bumpass, "Cohabitation and Children's Living Arrangements: New Estimates from the United States," *Demographic Research* 19 (2008): 1685–86, https://www.demographic-research.org/Volumes/Vol19/47/19-47.pdf.

Moreover, while the economic consequences of divorce have been improving in recent decades, the consequences from dissolving cohabitation have grown worse.[68]

The number of children born to unmarried women is far higher than it was in the years before the War on Poverty (Figure 2.6). In 1960, only 5.3 percent of all births were to unmarried women. Among whites, only 2.3 percent of births were out of wedlock, while the out-of-wedlock rate among blacks was 23 percent.[69] Unmarried birth rates peaked around 2008 and have been more or less flat in the decade since. Still, in 2015, 40.3 percent of all births were to unmarried women. The share of nonmarital births among whites had increased to 35.8 percent; among African Americans, it had skyrocketed to an astonishing 70.1 percent. Among Latinos, it is a somewhat smaller, but still concerning 53 percent.[70]

Childbearing outside marriage remains overwhelmingly concentrated at the lowest rungs of the socioeconomic ladder. For example, 88 percent of births to women under age 20 are to unmarried women,

Figure 2.6

Percentage of Births to Unmarried Women

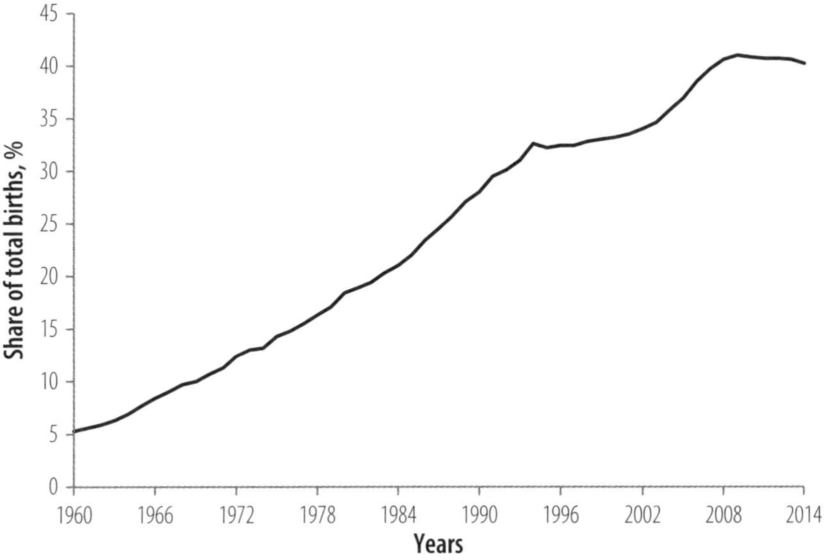

Source: Joyce A. Martin et al., "Births: Final Data for 2015," Centers for Disease Control and Prevention, *National Vital Statistics Reports* 66, no. 1 (January 2017), Table 15, https://www.cdc.gov/nchs/data/nvsr/nvsr66/nvsr66_01.pdf.

representing some 15 percent of the total number of nonmarital births. This fact should not be a surprise, since relatively few women marry before that age. Still, this group is uniquely ill-prepared for the challenges of raising a child on their own. Moreover, 45.5 percent of women giving birth outside marriage had incomes below the poverty level. Fewer than 20 percent had incomes above $50,000 per year.[71]

Whereas the evidence cited previously demonstrates a robust statistical relationship between nonmarital childbearing and poverty, a chicken-or-the-egg problem makes assigning the weight of causality to one or the other unclear. A number of studies suggest that women give birth outside marriage because they are poor rather than that they are poor because they have children outside of marriage.[72]

At least two studies comparing outcomes for nonmarital births among sisters also finds the relationship between such births and poverty to be more complex than earlier studies indicated. For example, a study of teen sisters who timed births differently found that, while there were negative consequences to having a child outside marriage, those consequences were not as significant as previous studies had indicated.[73] Another study, this one of twin sisters, found that the effect of an unmarried birth differed by race, with a significantly negative effect on African American women but no such effect on white women.[74]

The body of scholarship appears to be shifting from a belief that getting pregnant outside of marriage pushes women into poverty to the idea that poverty itself largely causes women to engage in behavior that leads them to become pregnant outside of marriage. Unmarried pregnancy, by itself, appears to contribute little to poverty.

The reasons for the rise in nonmarital childbearing, both in society as a whole and among women who are impoverished, are subject to considerable debate. Studies show that low-income women often believe that they have less to lose financially from an unwed pregnancy than women further up the income ladder. In part, this view is because they see relatively few prospects for their future. If their current prospects are bleak, it is hard for them to foresee those prospects worsening because of a pregnancy.[75] And if they want to have children yet do not foresee that there will be better circumstances in the future, why wait? At the same time, some of the consequences of the pregnancy are ameliorated by the availability of welfare payments.

As early as the 1960s, if not before, it was recognized that welfare had the potential to discourage its recipients from forming traditionally structured families. Aid to Families with Dependent Children (AFDC) included provisions that limited its availability to single women with children. Lured by the prospect of government transfer payments, many women opted not to get married that otherwise would have. As Daniel Patrick Moynihan noted, "What, after all, was the AFDC program but a family allowance for *broken* families." Generally speaking, one became eligible by dissolving a family or by not forming one.[76]

Of the more than 20 major studies of the issue during the 1980s and 1990s, more than three-quarters showed a significant link between benefit levels and nonmarital childbearing.[77] That research was sparked by Murray's seminal book, *Losing Ground*, which first made the issue part of the mainstream welfare reform debate.[78] However, there has been relatively little research on the subject recently.

One of the few recent studies analyzing the issue, published in the *Journal of Political Economy,* found that higher-base welfare benefits (1) lead unwed white mothers to forestall their eventual marriage and (2) lead unwed black mothers to hasten their next birth, although the effects were modest.[79] A second study by Irwin Garfinkle and others also found "generous welfare promotes nonmarital births."[80] Specifically, Garfinkle concluded that decreases in welfare led to a 6 percent decrease in nonmarital births from 1980 to 1996.[81]

Of course, women do not get pregnant just to get welfare benefits. But by reducing the economic consequences for births outside marriage, welfare has removed an important incentive to avoid them. If a teenager sees her friends and neighbors who have given birth out of wedlock and sees that they have suffered few visible consequences, she is less inclined to modify her behavior to prevent pregnancy.

At the same time, a young girl with relatively few prospects for the future may see having a child as an important aspect of her life, someone to love and who will love her back. Surveys show that poor women place a very high value on motherhood as "giving meaning to their lives."[82] As one young unmarried mother told the *New York Times* reporter Annie Lowery in 2013, "I love that [her babies] will always love me, no matter what."[83]

In researching their 2005 book, *Promises I Can Keep: Why Poor Women Put Motherhood before Marriage*, Kathryn Edin and Maria Kefalas lived in a poor neighborhood of Philadelphia for more than two years and interviewed 162 low-income mothers. They concluded that, for many poor women, "Family background, cognitive abilities, school performance, mental health status, and so on . . . have already diminished their life chances so much that an early birth does little to reduce them further." Into a life that often seems meaningless comes a child, "bringing the purpose, the validation, the companionship, and the order, that young women feel have been so sorely lacking."[84] For many poor women, despite the challenges they face daily, or perhaps because of those challenges, Edin and Kefalas found "remaining childless is inconceivable."[85]

While motherhood remains an important part of many poor women's lives, marriage appears to hold a lesser place. That is not to say that most women who are poor do not want to get married. They do.

Women in poverty see marriage as an ideal that they value and aspire to. But whereas many middle-class women see marriage as part of the road to financial stability, many women who are poor (and men who are poor) view marriage as something to look for only after one has sufficient financial resources.

Low-income women also report a particularly high fear of divorce's economic consequences, which may also explain why they tend to postpone marriage until they can be "certain" of their potential spouse.[86] Undoubtedly such fears are heightened by a scarcity of good marriage prospects in many poor communities. As we will see in future chapters, high rates of unemployment and the distortions from over-criminalization can leave poor women with few marriageable men from whom to choose.

It is also notable that, while we are seeing single mothers increasingly cohabit with their baby's father, we are also seeing a decline in postbirth marriages. At one time, the consequences of nonmarital births were softened by the so-called shotgun wedding that often followed. Conservative historian Marvin Olasky estimates that in the 1950s as many as 85 percent of women who were unmarried at the time they gave birth eventually married the father of their child.[87] Although born outside marriage, the child was likely to grow up in an intact two-parent family. Today, only 29 percent of children born nonmaritally experienced their mother marrying their biological father by the time they turned 15.[88]

Social Isolation and the Culture of Poverty

A general "culture of poverty" becomes more plausible when the poor are concentrated in a geographical area and isolated from the rest of society and its middle-class mores. Behaviors, both good and bad, tend to be self-reinforcing.

But economic integration is increasingly rare. Studies have found some evidence that poverty has become more concentrated in recent years. More African American and Hispanic families live in neighborhoods with concentrated poverty (where at least 40 percent of residents are in poverty). While only 5.5 percent of whites who are poor lived in neighborhoods with concentrated poverty, 17.6 percent of Hispanics and 25.1 percent of

African Americans did: African Americans who are poor are almost five times as likely to live in one of those neighborhoods and face the related negative spillover effects as are white people who are poor.[89]

To some extent, the high concentration of black poverty probably reflects housing discrimination along racial lines, but the growing concentration of white poverty suggests that some sort of cultural sorting may also be occurring. Government policy may contribute to poverty concentration as well. Because only certain providers are both qualified and willing to accept payment through many social welfare programs, those who are poor are often forced to live near them, and thus in areas where poverty is concentrated. Government housing programs are among the worst offenders in this regard. Because of its very nature, public housing concentrates a large number of people who are in or near poverty in a small geographic area. As poor people move into a neighborhood, higher-income people move out, leading to an increase in economic segregation. Residents of public housing often have limited interactions with anyone who is not in poverty.

Making matters worse, businesses soon migrate to areas where consumers have more disposable income, reducing both jobs and services in the affected area. Studies have long suggested that high concentrations of poverty make it harder for people who are poor to escape poverty. For example, a 1999 study by Thomas Paul Vartanian used Panel Study of Income Dynamics data to look at the long-term effects that living in concentrated poverty could have on children's future income and poverty (Table 2.1). He found that, compared with otherwise similar

Table 2.1

Long-Term Effects of Neighborhood Poverty Levels on Future Income

Neighborhood poverty (%)	5–15	15–30	>30
Hourly wages (% lower)	—	12	18
Annual labor income (% lower)	13	18	21
Length of poverty (% longer)	16	21	25

Source: Thomas Paul Vartanian, "Adolescent Neighborhood Effects on Labor Market and Economic Outcomes," *Social Service Review* 73, no. 2 (June 1999): 142–67.

Note: — = not applicable.

children, those children growing up in neighborhoods with higher levels of poverty had lower incomes and longer spells of poverty.[90]

A 2004 study used the U.S. Bureau of Labor Statistics' National Longitudinal Survey of Youth to analyze the impact of various neighborhood characteristics on residents' hours of work. The authors found that, controlling for individual characteristics and neighborhood selection effects, there was a growing marginal decline in hours worked associated with increases in neighborhood poverty.[91] And a study in the journal *Social Forces*, looking at the different mechanisms affecting school performance, found "not only that neighborhood characteristics predict educational outcomes but also that the strength of the predictions often rivals that associated with more commonly cited family- and school-related factors."[92] This neighborhood effect is particularly robust for children. Studies suggest there is a particularly strong peer influence on youth when it comes to crime, school attendance, and work.[93]

Researchers from the University of Wisconsin point out that the impact is particularly strong for children. "Children are influenced by the neighborhoods in which they grow up through factors such as the local tax base, the types of role models that are present and via peer group influences. Models of this type can produce poverty traps as poverty among parents is transmitted to children when children are consigned to neighborhoods whose interactions adversely affect their subsequent economic status; poverty among parents, because of its effect on children's neighborhoods, thus transmits economic status across generations."[94]

The Chicago Housing Authority's decision to demolish a number of public housing projects between 1995 and 1998 reveals the extent to which a bad neighborhood can stifle a child's long-run opportunity. Those families residing in public housing were effectively entered into a "lottery," with the "winners" being in buildings set to be demolished. The dislocated families received a housing voucher to move elsewhere, while the remaining families in the buildings left standing served as a control group. An examination of these families by the economist Eric Chyn found that children who remained eventually had annual earnings that were 16 percent lower than those forced to move out of public housing, and they were 9 percent less likely to be employed.[95]

Perhaps the best work on poverty concentration has been done by Raj Chetty of Harvard in his Equality of Opportunity Project. In this experiment, he analyzed the effects of a family moving to a different neighborhood on child outcomes. A random lottery assigned study participants into one of three groups: an experimental voucher group that was offered a subsidized housing voucher that came with a requirement to move to a census tract with a poverty rate below 10 percent, a Section 8 voucher group that was offered a standard subsidized housing voucher, and a control group that was not offered a voucher. For families that used the experimental voucher to move into low-poverty areas, if children moved before their teens, they went on to earn 31 percent more than the comparison group that did not win the voucher and stayed in the high poverty neighborhood. Although preteens in the Section 8 group also experienced gains, these were only about half as large as those that moved into low-poverty neighborhoods. Beyond higher earnings, there were a range of other positive outcomes for these younger children who moved to better neighborhoods: they were more likely to attend college, less likely to become single parents, and more likely to live in better neighborhoods when they grew up.[96]

It is worth noting, however, that a few recent studies have raised questions about the size of the segregation effect. For example, a study by Aaron Yelowitz and Janet Currie for the National Bureau of Economic Research suggested that, after correcting for a variety of factors, public housing might not have the negative impact that has been otherwise suggested.[97] More prominently, the Moving to Opportunity experiment revealed that changing neighborhoods alone may not be sufficient to improve labor market or schooling outcomes for disadvantaged families.[98] One possible reason for the limited effectiveness observed is that participants had already lived much of their formative years in underprivileged neighborhoods. Previously acquired characteristics that limit opportunity may not always be reversible with a simple change in location. For instance, many of the families who moved into less impoverished neighborhoods stayed in the same schools and social networks, limiting the effectiveness of the intervention. In other cases, the disruption associated with moving to a very different environment, especially as an adolescent, could have other adverse effects on child development. Even Chetty's research has indicated that, while there were significant positive effects for younger children, moving to a new neighborhood with lower poverty did not benefit teenagers and actually had some adverse effects.[99]

Still, the preponderance of evidence suggests that living in a high-poverty neighborhood makes climbing out of poverty more difficult. Ironically, there is some evidence that those most ambitious and motivated to escape from the dangers and influences of high-poverty neighborhoods may be held back by their efforts to do so. That is, children may be forced to assume adult responsibilities before they are fully prepared, meaning that they often are forced into low-wage jobs or must forgo education opportunities.[100]

Most research has focused on the isolation of low-income neighborhoods or communities, yet the poor are also more likely to be socially isolated as individuals. For example, a study from the Brookings Institution suggests that the more friends an individual has, the less likely he or she is to be poor. Those with two or more close friends are almost 20 percent less likely to be poor than are those with just one or no close friends. Those with many friendships are even less likely to be poor.[101] Other studies show that the poor, especially poor minorities, receive "useful advice and practical help" from fewer close sources (family, friends, and so forth) than do whites and higher-income individuals.[102] And poor children have fewer school-class friends and are more often isolated than their nonpoor counterparts.[103] All of this means fewer positive role models and more opportunity for negative behaviors to reinforce themselves.

The Limits of Culture and Individual Responsibility

Culture and the individual behavior that both informs it and stems from it can be seen to play a role in poverty. But conservatives frequently overstate how far such arguments can be taken.

Conservative critiques of welfare that emphasize behavior and culture ignore the fact that choices take place within a complex web of influences: cultural, historical, familial, and psychological, as well as incentive structures and interactions with other people. Poor people sometimes make irresponsible decisions. So do people from all walks of life. Being free implies the right to make decisions that others don't approve of, even those that might be deemed self-destructive. Yet the evidence suggests that for the poor, those decisions make their situation much worse than it would be if they had made better choices.

Rational choice models assume that individuals rank priorities by potential outcomes, and then make the choice that is most likely to arrive at the preferred outcome. Actually, however, decisions are the result of a complex process that is influenced at each step by a variety of outside factors as well as internal attitudes and prejudices. Marketers and advertisers have long understood this. The same choice process that applies to, say, deciding to purchase a new car can be ascribed, at least to some extent, to the choices that we make on how we live everyday lives. In fact, even if intellectually we know that a decision is irresponsible for us, we may still make that decision on the basis of other factors.

For those in poverty, the structural factors discussed in chapter 3, notably race, gender, and economic conditions, exert a significant influence on the choices they make.

Should we expect the poor to take responsibility for their own lives and do everything within their power to escape poverty and to help their children escape poverty? That seems self-evident. We should expect the poor to complete school, to work a job, and to avoid nonmarital pregnancy. At the same time, we should also recognize that such behavioral and cultural changes are unlikely to occur in a vacuum. To effectuate a long-term transformation of the culture will require careful attention to the incentive structure of the modern welfare state as well as the societal structures that can underlie culture.

CHAPTER THREE: STRUCTURAL POVERTY: RACE, GENDER, AND ECONOMIC DISLOCATION

. . . poverty is not natural. It is man-made . . .
—*Nelson Mandela*[1]

The biggest problem with ascribing poverty to individual behavior or cultural factors is that it implicitly assumes that everyone in our society is operating on a level playing field. But that is manifestly untrue. Throughout our country's long history of mistreatment of women, people of color, immigrants, and other disadvantaged groups, the choices made by many poor people have been constrained by circumstances outside their control.

Therefore many poverty scholars, especially progressives, argue that we need to pay more attention to the structures of society and how those structures can lead to poverty.

The structural view of poverty rejects, at least to some degree, the popular idea that we live in a meritocracy in which people receive what they deserve or earn and that people receive a reward that directly corresponds to their contribution to the economy. Rather, the structuralist views the relative conditions in which people find themselves to be determined primarily by disparities in political and economic power, tilting the playing field in favor of some, while creating barriers for others. Poverty, therefore, results from factors mostly outside the control of the poor themselves. In essence, a structuralist believes that individuals are poor because of an unlucky draw in the lottery of birth.

Poverty structuralism ultimately serves as a handy grab bag for whatever political issue advocates of bigger government are advancing at the moment. Yet it is also impossible to deny that some groups in our society face barriers that others do not. Further, these barriers may be cumulative. That is, a person may begin life at a disadvantage and then continue to fall further behind as he or she encounters additional discriminatory barriers.

Harvard's William Julius Wilson, one of the nation's foremost researchers on race, class, and poverty, argues that the existence of structural poverty does not mean "that individuals and groups lack the freedom to make their own choices, engage in certain conduct, and develop certain styles and orientations." But, as Wilson continues, "It is to say that these decisions and actions occur within a context of constraints and opportunities that are drastically different from those present in middle-class society."[2]

Given the broad territory covered by structural theories of poverty, it is not surprising that some aspects are stronger than others. Therefore, let us look at some of the most frequently cited structural factors in more detail.

Race

There is no question that African Americans are disproportionately likely to be trapped in poverty.[3] Roughly 26 percent of African Americans live in poverty, compared with just 10 percent of whites. Fully 31 percent of African American children are poor. Poverty rates for African Americans exceed those for whites in all categories of education, work effort, and family structure.[4] Moreover, African American poverty is different from white poverty in substantial ways. For example, a black family that is poor is far more likely than a white one that is poor to live in a neighborhood where most other families are poor, resulting in what sociologists call the "double burden" of poverty. African Americans who are poor are also less likely to escape poverty than are whites who are poor, and their children are more likely to grow up poor. Less than 5 percent of white children will spend half of their childhood in poverty, whereas nearly 40 percent of African American children will do so.[5] There is more likely to be a social estrangement leading to a wide variety of additional pathologies, from crime to poor educational attainment to high rates of unmarried births.

The question is to what degree is this poverty a legacy of past mistreatment or the result of contemporary ongoing racism or both?

It is hard to argue that there is not a connection. As President Lyndon Johnson put it:

> Negro poverty is not white poverty. Many of its causes and many of its cures are the same. But there are differences—radiating painful roots into the community and into the family, and the nature of the individual. These differences are not racial differences. They are solely the consequence of ancient brutality, past injustice, and present prejudice.[6]

In looking at the relationship between racism and African American poverty, we need to consider four factors: (1) the legacy impact of past racism; (2) current racial bias, whether explicit or implicit and internalized; (3) the psychological impact of both past and current racism on individual African Americans and on black culture more generally; and (4) the degree to which racially derived stereotypes continue to influence both government policies and individual social behavior.

In particular, if we want to understand just how the historical oppression of African Americans still affects black poverty today, we need to understand the depths of this sad history. Far too many conservatives minimize the cumulative weight of the African American experience. But even a brief look at that history shows both the extent of that oppression and the myriad ways in which its legacy continues to haunt African Americans to this day.

Slavery is America's original sin. From 1619, when a Dutch ship brought 20 African slaves ashore at Jamestown, until the Act Prohibiting Importation of Slaves was passed in 1807, nearly 600,000 slaves were forcibly brought to this country.[7] At the start of the Civil War, roughly 89 percent of all blacks in America, almost 4 million people, were slaves.[8]

Overall, between the first arrival of those black slaves at Jamestown and 1865 when the 13th Amendment officially outlawed slavery, millions of Africans and their decedents were held in bondage and servitude in the United States.[9]

Initially, slavery and racism were not intrinsically linked institutions. It is neither wholly true that slavery caused prejudice nor that prejudice caused slavery. Racial prejudice predated slavery. Slavery existed in many parts of the world without regard to the race of the enslaved. In the United States, slavery began under conditions that initially had some degree of color blindness. The American colonies were in a hierarchical society where men frequently labored, sometimes involuntarily, for the benefit of others. Servants were common, and many early American settlers were indentured servants. As Lerone Bennett Jr., one of the preeminent African American scholars of early colonial history, put it, "the Colonial population consisted largely of a great mass of white and black bondsmen, who occupied roughly the same economic category and were treated with equal contempt by the lords of the plantations and legislatures."[10] One early visitor to the Colony of Virginia reported that the gentry "abuse their servants with intolerable oppression and hard usage."[11] The need for labor, especially in the agricultural south, led to the use of Native Americans and, in some cases, even white Europeans as slaves before the importation of Africans offered a large scale and relatively inexpensive alternative.

African American slaves were initially more expensive to purchase than white indentured servants were to hire, but shortages were driving up the cost of indenture contracts and, once purchased, black slaves guaranteed a lifetime of labor. Amortized over time, African slaves were quite simply a cost-effective business decision.[12] Furthermore, unlike indentured servants, African slaves were not British citizens and were therefore exempted from even the minimal protections afforded to servants and other lower-class Englishmen. By the mid 1770s, bonded labor had been almost totally supplanted by race-based slavery.

But it was not merely the need for cheap labor that led to black slavery. The early colonists (and, indeed, the English generally) clearly saw Africans as different from themselves. While concepts such as race were not clearly defined, writings from the early colonies clearly differentiated "black" from "white." Second, African culture was seen as uncivilized—inferior to that of Europeans. Like Native Americans, Africans were seen as savages, in many ways less human than whites. Lastly, most Africans were not Christians. Largely animists or Muslims, they were considered heathens. It thus became relatively simple for whites to persuade themselves that blacks were inferior by nature.

Indeed, to justify slavery both to themselves and to the world, those early colonists found an entire ideology of white superiority and black inferiority had to be developed and maintained. After all, slaveholders, for all the wealth and political power, were a minority, even in the south. Slavery simply could not have survived without the support, or at least the acquiescence, of a vast number of fellow citizens who tolerated the institution's existence, despite not owning any slaves personally. And, at the same time, the inherent cruelty of the slave system had to be obvious, even to those who owned slaves.

To build their support among nonslave owners, the planter class offered what some would later call "a racial bribe," extending special privileges to poor whites to keep their interests separate from those of blacks. As a result, slavery was accompanied by both legal and societal strictures designed to enforce racial separatism and white superiority. Blacks, whether slave or free, were to be considered lesser than whites in every aspect of life. "The two great divisions of society are not the rich and the poor," declared South Carolina Senator John C. Calhoun in 1848, "but white and black. And all the former, the poor as well as the rich, belong to the upper class, and are respected and treated as equals."[13] It was made clear to even the poorest of whites that they were better than blacks, thus foreclosing any class-based solidarity between blacks and whites.

This attitude was backed up by a growing body of pseudo-scientific scholarship arguing that differences in physical anatomy meant that blacks and whites were separate species, with different origins, a theory known as polygenesis. In 1839, for instance, Samuel Morton published *Crania Americana*, which divided humankind into five distinct races: American, Caucasian, Ethiopian, Malay, and Mongolian. According to

Morton, whites had larger skulls than other races, allowing for larger brains. Therefore, whites were more intelligent and capable of creating a higher civilization.[14] A few years later, Josiah Nott began publishing a series of essays building on Morton's theories and arguing that there were wide variations in "innate capacity" between races. These differences, Nott claimed, made blacks particularly suited for slavery. Indeed, Nott argued that without the protective role of slavery, blacks were doomed to extinction.[15]

If science were insufficient to persuade people of black inferiority, there was always religion. The prevailing scriptural view of the time, at least in the South, was that blacks were descendants of Ham, the disgraced son of Noah, and were therefore ordained by God to serve. Most popularly articulated by Josiah Priest in his 1851 book, *Bible Defence of Slavery*, the Bible itself said that "the appointment of this race of men to servitude and slavery was a judicial act of God, or, in other words, was a divine judgment . . . and that we are not mistaken in concluding that the negro race, as a people, are judicially given over to a state of peculiar liability of being enslaved by the other races."[16]

By the time of the Civil War, so widespread was the belief in black inferiority and white superiority that it was largely embraced even by abolitionists. Harriet Beecher Stowe, among others, never fully accepted the underlying equality of African Americans.

As for slavery itself, one really cannot overstate its horrors or the lasting long-term impact that such an institution was likely to have on the future development of African Americans. Human beings were *property.* They could be whipped, branded, and otherwise physically harmed with few legal restrictions or consequences. As Edmund Morgan pointed out in his detailed study of colonial slavery, "Slaves could not be made to work for fear of losing liberty, so they had to be made to work for fear of their lives. . . . In order to get an equal or greater amount of work, it was necessary to beat slaves harder than servants, so hard, in fact, that there was a much greater chance of killing them."[17]

As bad as the physical abuse was, the even more insidious aspect of slavery was psychological. As W. E. B. DuBois explained: "It was in part psychological, the enforced personal feeling of inferiority, the calling of another master, the standing with hat in hand. It was the helplessness. It was the defenselessness of family life. It was the submergence below the arbitrary will of any sort of individual."[18]

In what would have a profound influence for generations to come, social customs, family formation, and child-rearing practices were disrupted. This started as early as the Middle Passage (the sea lanes in which the slave trade took place), where Africans, often torn from their families, found themselves mixed with peoples of widely different ethnicities, languages, and cultures under conditions that made it impossible to continue or transmit traditional African family structures.[19]

The physical and emotional suffering only intensified within the bounds of slavery itself. Rape of slaves by their masters, their master's male children, overseers, and sometimes guests was a common practice. It was an inherent part of slavery that a master had a total claim to a slave's body. In addition, an entire ethos was developed to justify the exploitation of slave women. Since the 19th-century ideal for white women was purity and chastity, black women were seen as an all-too-available alternative. They were portrayed as hypersexual, wanton, and anxious to bed their masters. One southern writer defended the rape of slave women by crediting the practice for the "absence of prostitution and the purity of white women."[20]

Forced breeding was also a common practice. Especially after the importation of slaves was banned in 1806, ensuring large numbers of slave children was an economic necessity. [21] Typical was the story told by one former slave to interviewers for the Works Progress Administration Slave Narrative Project in 1937:

> On this plantation were more than 100 slaves who were mated indiscriminately and without any regard for family unions. If their master thought that a certain man and woman might have strong, healthy offspring, he forced them to have sexual relation, even though they were married to other slaves. If there seemed to be any slight reluctance on the part of either of the unfortunate ones, "Big Jim" would make them consummate this relationship in his presence. He used the same procedure if he thought a certain couple was not producing children fast enough.[22]

Beyond the exploitation of women, families were disrupted in other ways. The separation and sale of family members was far too common. It is estimated that as many as one of three husbands or wives was ultimately separated from their spouse and close to half of all children were sold away from at least one parent.[23] Even without sale, slave families were often separated by other circumstances. For example, slaves were frequently hired out to plantations or other employers who were far enough away as to make family visits infrequent or impossible. Even on a single plantation, children might be taken into "the big House," while their parents remained in the fields.[24] Moreover, under slavery there was no legal distinction between legitimate and illegitimate childbearing by slaves. And, slave marriage, although encouraged by slave owners as both a matter of religion and commerce, was not legally recognized.

On paper, of course, the 13th, 14th, and 15th Amendments promised equality. In reality, however, the end of slavery marked the beginning of a century of legally enforced second-class citizenship.

In the aftermath of the Civil War, southern whites acted ruthlessly to preserve their political and economic power through racially targeted violence, discriminatory legal structures, and racially biased social norms.[25] Behind the legal infrastructure of bias lurked the ever-present threat of violence. Peter Kolchin, author of one of the leading histories of slavery, suggests that violence against African Americans actually increased in the aftermath of slavery.[26]

In a particularly damaging way, those African Americans who were most successful, and most important to the future success of the African American community, such as teachers, ministers, landowners, and politicians, were frequently targeted for attacks of all kinds.[27]

By the end of the 19th century, with the last vestiges of Reconstruction firmly buried, racial discrimination and white superiority were deeply entrenched in both law and custom throughout the South. By the 1890s, the term "Jim Crow," derived from the character in a minstrel show famous before the Civil War, had come into popular use to describe a system of "subordination and separation of black people in the South, much of it codified and much of it still enforced by custom, habit, and violence."[28]

In 1896, in perhaps its darkest moment since the *Dredd Scott* case, the Supreme Court, in the case of *Plessy v. Ferguson,* upheld a Louisiana law mandating segregated railroad cars, ruling that public facilities for blacks and whites could be "separate but equal."[29] Two years later, the Court upheld a Mississippi law designed to restrict the right of black men to vote.[30] The second era of Southern racial oppression was at its height.

By 1901, John Knox could open the convention to rewrite Alabama's constitution with the declaration that their job was to "within the limits imposed by the Federal Constitution, to establish white supremacy in this state."[31] As one writer put it, "An uninformed observer of the South in 1910 might well be pardoned if he or she concluded that the Confederates had won the Civil War."[32]

The first decades of the 20th century brought with them a further tide of discrimination and oppression for African Americans. Murder, arson, and mutilation were common practices. In some cases, entire towns of African Americans were slaughtered: Longview, Texas, in 1919, for instance; the black portion of Tulsa, Oklahoma, in 1921; and Rosewood, Florida, in 1923.[33]

By the mid 1920s, the Ku Klux Klan had an estimated membership of more than 4 million and chapters in every state. Its members included governors, congressmen, and senators. In August 1925, some 40,000 Klansmen paraded down Pennsylvania Avenue in Washington, D.C. It wasn't until the 1930s, when the Klan's reputation for violence—and a sex scandal among its leadership—brought about its decline.

Of course, even with the Klan in decline, the subjugation of African Americans continued. Indeed, the more insidious and damaging forms of racial prejudice most frequently took place in the day-to-day interactions of life, in jobs, accommodations, housing, and a thousand other ways that African Americans were denied their full rights as citizens.

For example, despite the fact that most northern states, with the conspicuous exception of Indiana, prohibited explicit school segregation, many local school districts were effectively segregated. Certainly, housing remained segregated even in the North, often enforced through racially discriminatory zoning laws (see chapter 8). In 1920, 36 states had laws against interracial marriage, and nearly half of those laws were in place into the 1950s. Racism and its consequences affected African Americans no matter where they lived.

Eventually, of course, African Americans (and sympathetic whites) organized into a powerful movement for equality and civil rights.

The Civil Rights Era culminated in the passage of the Civil Rights Act of 1964, followed by the Voting Rights Act in 1965. At least on paper, discrimination in both governmental institutions and public accommodations was outlawed, and the right to vote was guaranteed. Jim Crow was illegal, if not exactly dead. But, as we shall see, its legacy lives on.

Obviously, it is difficult if not impossible to draw a straight line between any particular act of racism, past or present, and African American poverty. But as in a criminal trial, the weight of circumstantial evidence can accumulate to where the relationship seems clear beyond a reasonable doubt. The circumstantial case that racism has been—and continues to be—a factor in black poverty is a strong one.

Start with the legacy of past racism. That is to say that, even if overt discrimination has greatly diminished today, the consequences of past discrimination are still with us. You cannot have a race in which one runner is loaded down with weights and chains for half the race, remove them, and suggest that from then on it is a fair contest.

To look at just one example, consider the impact of historical racism on the accumulation of wealth. Wealth is not just an amount of money that can be used to buy things, but, as Melvin Oliver and Thomas Shapiro wrote in their seminal book, *Black Wealth/White Wealth*:

> [I]t is used to create opportunities, secure a desired stature and standard of living, and pass class status on to one's children . . . the command of resources that wealth entails is more encompassing than is income or education, and closer in meaning and theoretical significance to our traditional notions of economic well-being and access to life chances.[34]

African Americans have been systematically deprived of the ability to accumulate wealth. In addition to a deprivation of basic liberty, and all the physical and psychological horrors described above, slavery was also a massive theft of African American labor, wages, and wealth.

Libertarian economist Julian Simon teamed with Larry Neal of the University of Illinois to calculate the value of unpaid wages to slaves (minus maintenance costs such as food and shelter provided by slave owners) at $1.4 trillion. Assuming a 5 percent rate of interest accruing since those wages were earned would yield a debt of roughly $6.5 trillion.[35] Using a slightly different methodology, economic historian James Marketti calculated the value of lost wages at roughly $2.1 trillion, or $10 trillion today assuming accumulated interest.[36] Add in pain and suffering, lost educational and wealth-building opportunities, and we are rapidly approaching numbers that are nearly impossible to comprehend.

One needn't go that far back to see how racism has denied African Americans opportunities to build wealth. For most American families, their house is the largest single component of their savings. Just 41.5 percent of African American families own their own home, the lowest homeownership rate of any racial category, and more than 20 percentage points lower than white homeownership.[37] This is not just the result of chance. Nor is it the consequence of lower incomes among African Americans.

At one time, the National Association of Real Estate Boards actually included in its code of ethics a provision warning realtors against "introducing into a neighborhood . . . any race or nationality . . . whose presence will clearly be detrimental to property values."[38] One brochure issued by the organization listed among the undesirables who should not be able to purchase homes: madams, bootleggers, gangsters, and "a colored man . . . who thought they were entitled to live among whites."[39]

Such private discrimination was backed by the federal government. The Home Owners' Loan Corporation (HOLC), a government agency created as part of the New Deal to provide low-interest mortgages, insisted that any property it covered must include a clause in the deed forbidding the property's resale to nonwhites.[40] The HOLC went so far as to draw up color-coded maps ranking American communities on the basis of which ones had too many "inharmonious racial groups." Areas with large numbers of African Americans were typically outlined in red, hence the term "redlining." [41]

Even the GI Bill, which opened the door to home ownership for millions of whites, failed to have the same effect for African

Americans. Although the law was facially neutral with regard to race, its implementation was so problematic that in her book on the topic, Berkeley historian Kathleen Frydl claims that "black veterans did not experience the same GI bill as white veterans . . . this result did not stem from any direct discrimination in the Bill itself. It was a feature of its implementation – and an intended one."[42]

Long after these more blatant types of discrimination faded or were prohibited, more subtle forms of redlining remained, defined as the practice of denying or limiting financial services to certain neighborhoods based on racial or ethnic composition without regard to the residents' qualifications or creditworthiness.[43] The practice was not formally outlawed until the Fair Housing Act in 1968. As discussed below, housing discrimination continues to be a problem today.

As Oliver and Shapiro point out:

> Locked out of the greatest mass-based opportunity for wealth accumulation in American history, African Americans who desired or were able to afford home ownership found themselves confined to central-city communities where their investments were affected by the "self-fulfilling prophecies" of FHA appraisers: cut off from sources of new investment, their homes and communities deteriorated and lost value in comparison to those homes that FHA appraisers deemed desirable.[44]

This legacy of discrimination still has fallout today. After all, if your family was denied a mortgage in the past because of redlining or other discriminatory practices, then you may not have the family wealth or down payment help to become a homeowner today. The legacy of housing discrimination may also force African Americans into neighborhoods with poor schools or fewer job opportunities, both of which can increase poverty levels.

Similarly, the fact that African Americans were long denied equal employment opportunities means that black families were not able to build either financial or social capital to the same degree as whites. As late as 1960, help wanted ads in major newspapers like the *Washington Post, New York Times, Chicago Tribune,* and *Los Angeles Times* separated job opportunities by race, lumped African American men with boys, and directed African Americans toward menial work. Thus a typical job listing read:

> BOYS—WHITE Age 14 to 18. To assist Route manager full or part-time. Must be neat in appearance. Apply 1346 Conn. Ave. NW.
>
> DRIVERS (TRUCK) Colored, for trash routes, over 25 years of age; paid vacation, year-around work; must have excellent driving record. Apply . . . 1601 W St., N.E.
>
> STUDENTS Boys, white, 14 yrs. and over, jobs immediately available. Apply . . . 724 9th St., N.W.[45]

One study, by Bernadette and Gerald Chachere of Berkeley, estimated that labor market discrimination cost black Americans $1.6 trillion between 1929 and 1969 alone.[46]

It should be obvious that the racism that denied previous generations of African Americans an equal shot at homeownership or high-paying jobs has meant that the current generation has started in a deeper hole than it would absent that history of discrimination.

Finally, consider the impact of discrimination on education. There is a clear gap in education achievement based on race, with African Americans lagging whites on almost all measures of education attainment. There are significant historical roots to this gap.

During slavery, the education of African Americans was actively discouraged where it was not expressly prohibited. From 1835 to 1865, Georgia, North Carolina, South Carolina, and Virginia had laws making it a crime to teach a slave to read or write. Other states had similar laws for short periods, although enforcement was often haphazard.[47]

After slavery ended African Americans were largely confined to segregated schools, often underfunded compared with white schools. It wasn't until 1954 that "separate but equal" was declared unconstitutional in *Brown v. Board of Education*.[48] Moreover, as welcome as the Supreme Court's decision was, it hardly ushered in an age of educational equality. Many southern and border states did everything in their power to resist desegregating the schools.

Human capital, in the form of education, is passed down as an inheritance as surely as financial capital. For example, a sociological study conducted in 1940 by E. Horace Fitchett found that more than half of Howard University students were descended from the small elite group of literate slaves.[49] Similarly, a 1963 study by Horace Mann Bond found that a startlingly large share of black intellectuals and professionals could trace their ancestry to the roughly 10 percent of African Americans who were free in 1860 and were therefore disproportionately likely to be educated.[50] A working paper from the National Bureau of Economic Research found that in a counterfactual world, where school quality was equal across races in the South during the first half of the 20th century, the wage gap between blacks and whites would have been roughly halved.[51]

As much as we may wish to pretend that America is a meritocracy, it is entirely unreasonable to suggest that this legacy of racism has had no impact on the number of African Americans living in poverty.

Second, African Americans continue to deal with racism *today.* Few white Americans use racial slurs in public anymore and "colored only" signs are now museum relics, but African Americans are still not treated with full equality in housing, employment, or the criminal justice system, among other areas. In some cases this bias may be unconscious, a set of stereotypes and other race-based ideas that have been internalized by the white population generally. In other cases, a smaller group of Americans may still possess overtly racist attitudes, even if they tend to hide those beliefs to avoid social censure. For instance, a study by Seth Stephens-Davidowitz uses racially charged Google searches as a proxy for an area's racial animus. An area's racially charged Google search rate strongly predicts the decline in vote share from Democratic Party presidential candidates John Kerry in 2004 to Barack Obama in 2008. Whereas the General Social Survey finds that about 3 percent of Americans would not vote for qualified black candidate because of race, this methodology suggests the true number is closer to 9 percent. The author attributes this discrepancy largely to social desirability bias.[52]

Next let us consider employment, an area in which racial prejudice can rather obviously lead to poverty. By and large, African Americans remain "last hired, first fired." Historically, African American unemployment has been roughly double that of whites since at least the

Figure 3.1

Trends in Black and White Unemployment Rates

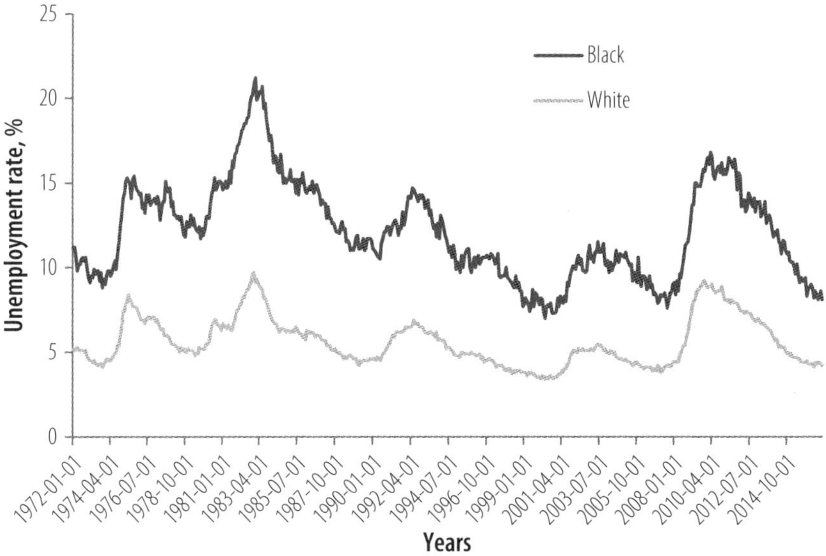

Sources: Federal Reserve Economic Data, "LNS14000006 Unemployment Rate: Black or African American, Percent, Monthly, Seasonally Adjusted," 2016; Federal Reserve Economic Data, "LNS14000003 Unemployment Rate: White, Percent, Monthly, Seasonally Adjusted," 2016.

mid 1950s, when the U. S. Department of Labor first started collecting unemployment data by race.[53] Today, white unemployment is roughly 4 percent, while unemployment for African Americans approaches 8 percent (Figure 3.1).[54]

Studies also show that when hired, African Americans may receive lower wages. Black median weekly earnings are roughly 80 percent of white median weekly earnings.[55] There are many factors that account for this gap, including education, pre-job skills, and previous employment experience. However, one study from Roland G. Fryer Jr. and colleagues estimated that differential treatment, or discrimination, explained at least one-third of the raw black–white wage gap.[56]

A study from the Economic Policy Institute found that such widely cited factors as job preferences and differences in both technical competencies and so-called soft-skills are insufficient to account for the gap in black and white employment.[57] Similarly, a study by the Center for

American Progress found that, holding factors such as age, education, and sex constant, higher unemployment rates for African Americans persist.[58] These findings suggest that some portion of the black–white employment gap is the result of discrimination.

Other evidence comes from a study by Marianne Bertrand and Sendhil Mullainathan in the *American Economic Review*. They replied to advertisements for jobs listed in Boston and Chicago newspapers using resumes that were functionally equivalent except for the applicants' names, which were randomly divided between African American– or white-sounding names. White names received 50 percent more callbacks for interviews across a cross-section of occupations, industries, and employer sizes.[59] A similar study by Michael Gaddis of Pennsylvania State University likewise found that employers were more likely to call back job applicants with white-sounding names than those with black-sounding names even if the black applicant had graduated from an elite university while the white applicant attended a less selective college. Moreover, when black applicants were called back, it was often for jobs with lower starting salaries and lower prestige than white applicants.[60]

Housing is another area where racial discrimination persists. Studies, similar to the correspondence study on employment discussed previously (and subject to the same caveats), show that mortgage loan originators responded less favorably to inquiries from individuals with black-sounding names. In fact, according to one study, having a black-sounding name had the same effect as having a credit score 71 points lower than white applicants for response rates from mortgage loan originators.[61]

A study by the U.S. Department of Housing and Urban Development found that black home buyers were, on average, shown fewer home options than similar white families.[62] A similar investigation, by the National Fair Housing Alliance, tested realtors in a dozen metropolitan areas, including Atlanta, Austin, Birmingham, Chicago, Dayton, Detroit, New York, Philadelphia, Pittsburgh, San Antonio, and the District of Columbia, using African American homebuyers with higher incomes, better credit scores, and more savings for down payments than whites in the study. They found that blacks "were shown fewer homes than their white peers, were often denied information about special incentives that would have made the purchase easier, and were required to produce loan pre-approval letters and other documents when whites were not." This was the case even when the black applicants were "better qualified financially."[63]

But perhaps no segment of American society remains as racially biased as the criminal justice system. As detailed in chapter 6, African Americans encounter disparate treatment at every level, from street-level law enforcement, to arrest, to trial, to incarceration. The treatment of African Americans throughout the criminal justice system is so blatant and so damaging that author Michelle Alexander termed it "the New Jim Crow."[64]

This mistreatment of African Americans by the criminal justice system has profound consequences in terms of black poverty. First, simply removing such a large number of young black men from the community changes the situation. According to the *New York Times*, for every 100 black women ages 25 to 50 and not in jail in America, there are just 83 black men. That amounts to roughly 1.5 million "missing" black men.[65] Premature death accounts for a portion of the difference, but mass incarceration is the single biggest reason. And in inner cities and high poverty areas, this depopulation is even more extreme. Wilson, in particular, has written extensively on how the lack of marriageable men in poor, minority communities pushes women into poverty.

But the racial disparities in the criminal justice system have consequences beyond merely locking up large numbers of young black men. As Alexander points out, even after they are released from jail "they're relegated to a permanent second-class status, stripped of the very rights supposedly won in the civil rights movement—such as the right to vote, the right to serve on juries, the right to be free of legal discrimination in employment, and access to education and public benefits. Many of the old forms of discrimination that we supposedly left behind during the Jim Crow era are suddenly legal again, once you've been branded a felon."[66]

For instance, roughly one-quarter of all nonincarcerated black men have a criminal record.[67] The overwhelming preponderance of the academic literature suggests that employers are, not surprisingly, reluctant to hire those with a criminal history. This includes surveys that track the employment of offenders before and after incarceration,[68] surveys of employer attitudes about hiring job applicants with criminal records,[69] tests of how employers treat applicants with otherwise identical resumes if one has a criminal record,[70] and administrative data comparing employment outcomes for demographic groups with different incarceration rates.[71]

It seems fair to say, then, that the injustices in the criminal justice system have consequences for African American employment. Indeed, as we will see in chapter 6, those consequences extend to education, housing, and even marriage rates.

Third, we need to consider the effect of both past and current racism on African American psychology and culture. The effect shows up both in the economic starting point for black families and psychologically in African American hopes, ambitions, and relationships with larger society. Studies point out that experiencing racism can be akin to other psychologically traumatic experiences.[72] Experiencing racism has been linked to such symptoms as intrusive thoughts, flashbacks, difficulty concentrating, irritability, and jumpiness.[73] Some have even suggested that the psychological response to racism can resemble post-traumatic stress disorder.[74] Others have likened the response of those experiencing acts of racism to the response of rape victims.[75] In particular, victims of racism may experience feelings of powerlessness and hypervigilance, which subsequently affect how African Americans respond in interactions with teachers, the police, and others, making it more difficult to escape poverty and participate in mainstream economic activities.[76]

One need not go that far to realize that there are psychological consequences from racism. As Orlando Patterson of Harvard explains, "Inner city youth live in an all-black world, a world that is completely marginalized economically and socially, and as such, being black is inevitably perceived as being in some critical way the source of their marginality and failure. The stigma of being a young black person is made immediately obvious to them the moment they walk out of their inner city and try to enter mainstream space."[77] Patterson points out that, even though African Americans are not generally inclined to attribute particular failings to racial discrimination, racism still leaves many African Americans with a negative assessment of their own racial identity.[78]

Finally, we should acknowledge that racially based stereotypes may affect both public policy and private behavior in ways that disadvantage African Americans. As discussed earlier, an entire mythology was developed to justify slavery, and many of those ideas were carried forward in slavery's aftermath to justify the continued oppression of black people. Eventually such stereotypes as the oversexed, promiscuous black woman and the dangerous brute black man became ingrained in the popular consciousness.

While recent polling finds that only 7 percent of American voters report having favorable attitudes toward white supremacists, such explicit racial animosity may merely be the tip of the iceberg.[79] For example, according to the General Social Survey, as many whites (27 percent) believe that the disadvantages experienced by African Americans are because blacks "don't have the motivation or will power to pull themselves up out of poverty" as attribute that disadvantage to discrimination.[80]

We should be careful, however, not to present the structural causes of poverty in a way that reduces African Americans to helpless passivity, stripping them of agency, choice, or responsibility. We should recall that even in times of oppression, African Americans raised families, educated themselves, started businesses, and formed charitable societies to care for themselves in hard times. Many became scholars, business owners or executives, politicians, and leaders in all manner of fields.

In fact, black poverty declined during some of the times of greatest racial hostility and discrimination. The National Research Council estimates that in 1939 as many as 93 percent of African Americans were poor, compared with 65 percent of whites.[81] This estimation may somewhat overstate the typical level of black poverty since it represents a point at the end of the Great Depression when poverty was especially high among all groups. Still, it's worth pointing out that by the time that the Civil Rights Act was passed in 1964, black poverty had declined by nearly two-thirds to just 42 percent.[82] That so many African Americans were able to rise above Jim Crow is a testimony to the human spirit that should not be ignored.

Gender

As with racism, America's long history of gender-based discrimination may contribute to poverty. It is a fact that poverty is disproportionately concentrated among women. Since measurement began, women have had higher poverty rates than men in the United States. As far back as 1978, Diana Pearce coined the phrase "the feminization of poverty" and argued that poverty was "rapidly becoming a female problem."[83]

In 2016, 13.4 percent of working-age women lived in poverty, compared with just 9.7 percent of men of similar age.[84] This percentage includes 10.2 percent of non-Hispanic white women, 21.5 percent of black women, and 18.5 percent of Hispanic and Latina women. Poverty is even more endemic among female-headed households. Roughly 26.6 percent of female-headed households with no husband present are poor, compared with less than 13.1 percent for male-headed households with no wife present. Moreover, the combination of being a minority and a woman is doubly associated with poverty. Roughly 31.6 percent of households headed by African American women live in poverty.[85] For every age cohort, women face a higher poverty rate than men, including millennials.[86] At almost every age, adult women have a higher poverty rate than men (Figure 3.2).[87]

Women in our society face a number of disadvantages that can help push them into poverty or make it more difficult to escape poverty. Nor should we forget that historically women have faced legal and social inequality that, if not rising to the level of discrimination against African Americans, nevertheless represents a tremendous injustice that can carry with it lasting consequences.

For much of this country's history, we operated under a legal theory called "coverture" through which "by marriage, the husband and wife are one person in law; that is, the very being or legal existence of the woman is suspended during the marriage."[88] In practice, this gave men nearly complete control over their wives.

For instance, married women were unable to own property on their own. It wasn't until 1839 that Mississippi became the first state to allow married women to own property, including real estate. But even this law specified that, while the wife could own the property, her

Figure 3.2

Poverty Rate by Age, Men and Women, 2016

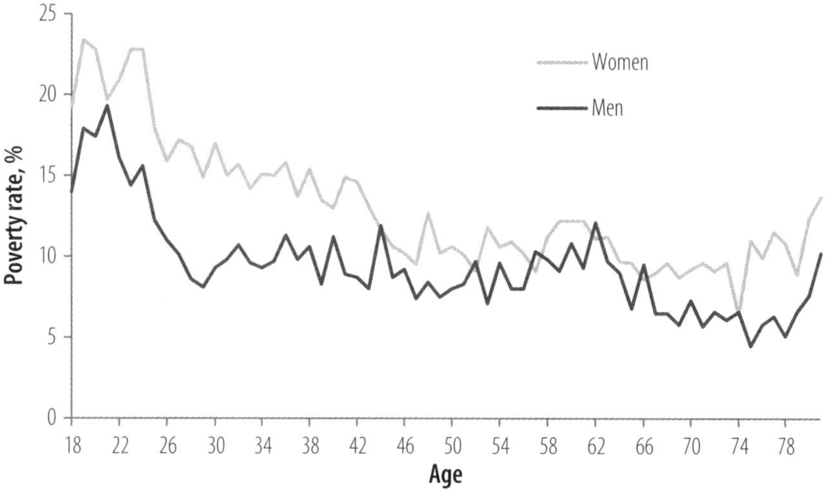

Source: U.S. Census Bureau, POV34, Single Year of Age—Poverty Status, https://www.census.gov/data/tables/time-series/demo/income-poverty/cps-pov/pov-34.html.

husband continued to control its management. It took until 1855 before Massachusetts passed a law giving married women the power to "own real or personal property; sell; contract; sue or be sued; make a will; and have full control over earnings."[89]

States continued to pass laws expanding women's access to property ownership, as well as their employment or ability to contract or to enter into business throughout the end of the 19th century. While there were positive developments—particularly in the Western states where nearly all had dissolved restrictions on women's ability to own property and to conduct business—progress was more hit and miss elsewhere. Even as some restrictions were being lifted, others were being placed on women trying to enter the workplace, as some states enacted laws limiting the workday for women. And South Carolina passed legislation as late as 1887 formally prohibiting married women from business partnerships.[90]

While women were clearly not treated as equal members of society, their treatment did not necessarily consign them to poverty because of their access to the wealth controlled by men. By and large, they were not expected to support themselves on their own, but to rely on support from men. They were effectively expected to trade freedom for security.

This devil's bargain no longer holds for a variety of reasons, some to women's benefit, some at their expense (at least in financial status).

Broadly speaking, there are three primary reasons that so many women are poor. First, women are less likely to be employed, and, when they are, they generally have lower wages than men. Second, they are more likely to be heads of single-parent homes. Finally, the rise of class-based assortative mating in American society means that poor women will likely marry and have children with poor men.

Some researchers suggest the differences in employment are products of unconscious bias—hidden beliefs about women's capabilities that can influence important workplace decisions. For instance, if bosses expect women to be more team oriented and men to be more independent in their jobs, women may be more likely to be shunted into support roles rather than landing the core positions that lead to higher-paying executive jobs. Female employees may internalize and act upon these stereotypes over time, sapping their confidence that they or their female coworkers can handle more demanding positions.[91]

Women also remain far more likely than men to take time off from work for childbirth, childcare, or other family responsibilities. Stay-at-home fathers are still a relative oddity.[92] However, 20 percent of married-couple households with children have a stay-at-home mother. While that is a significant decline from the nearly half of mothers who stayed at home as recently as the 1960s, it still represents some 7.2 million women.[93] As Figure 3.3 shows, the younger the child, the more likely it is that a woman will not be in the labor force. For women with a child age 3 or younger, for instance, only about 60 percent of women are in the labor force. Interestingly as well, the older workers are, the less likely they are to quit their jobs when they become pregnant. Fully 44 percent of those ages 18 to 19 leave their job, while just 12 percent of women age 30 or older do. The reasons for this are unclear, although it may reflect the type of job that women hold at different ages and the availability of paid or unpaid leave. At the same time, younger women are less likely to have resources outside of work that they can rely on, making them more at risk for poverty.

Figure 3.3

Labor Force Participation Rate of Mothers by Age of Youngest Child

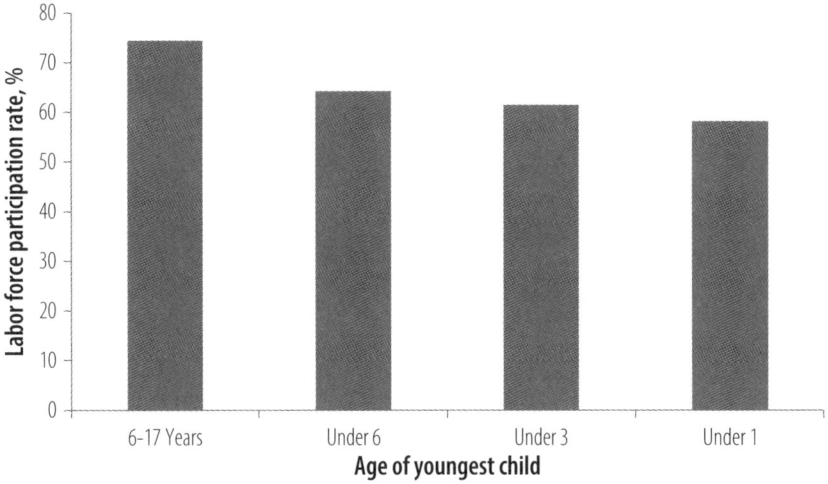

Source: U.S. Bureau of Labor Statistics, "Current Population Survey, March 1975–2015, Annual Social and Economic Supplement," https://www.bls.gov/news.release/archives/famee_04222016.

The vast majority of women, as noted, do not quit their jobs when they have a child, but 93 percent of women take at least *some* time off following a birth. Today, roughly 22 percent of women who have a baby quit their job, about half of what it was 35 years ago. But more women are taking either paid or unpaid leave and then later returning to their job. Overall, workforce participation for women with children is much lower than for men or women without children.

Even after returning to work, women are still likely to take substantial time away from their jobs to deal with family issues. As Figure 3.4 shows, the distribution of chores and childcare is still unbalanced. To some extent, this could reflect choices and preferences of the couples, but it is likely that some of this is explained by other factors.

Women continue to struggle with what sociologist Arlie Hochschild calls the "second shift" impact, in which they come home from a full day of work and still take responsibility for the unpaid labor of housework and childcare. Many women are also effectively working two jobs, but are only being paid for one.[94]

Figure 3.4

Distribution of Chores and Childcare, Responses to McKinsey 2015 Survey

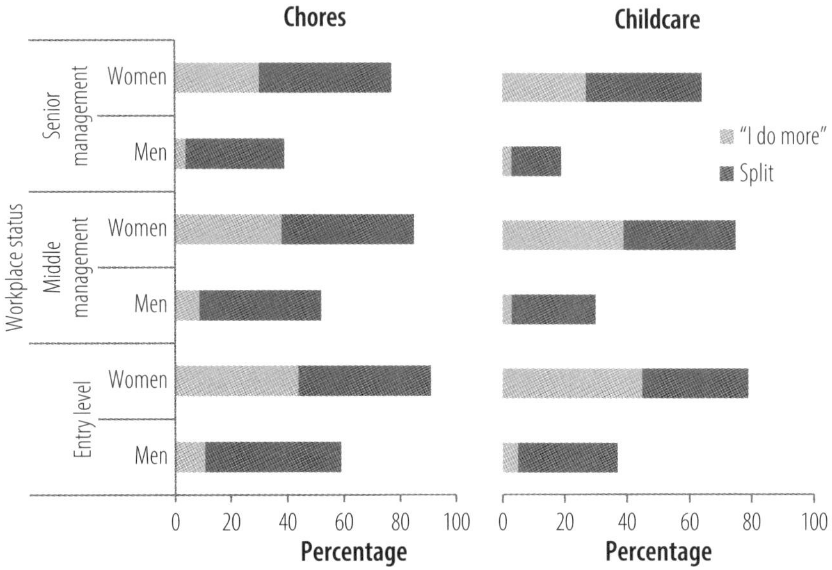

Source: McKinsey and Company, "Women in the Workplace 2015," https://www.mckinsey.com/business-functions/organization/our-insights/women-in-the-workplace.

Compounding these problems, employers may be less likely to approve flexible schedules or give women time off to deal with family problems. One study found that 69.7 percent of employers surveyed said they would approve a request for time off for childcare-related reasons from men, but only 56.7 percent would approve a similar request from a female employee.[95]

These gaps in employment can reduce a woman's "human capital," leading to lower future wages: skills may deteriorate or become dated; contacts and mentorships may be disrupted; opportunities and promotions may be filled by others; supervisors or coworkers may resent having to make alternative arrangements to compensate, and so on. Women may also anticipate employment problems and choose jobs that offer more "family friendly" policies. While this is in many ways good—the market providing choices—such jobs often offer lower pay, substituting other benefits for wages.

Of course, some might argue that pregnancy itself is a choice, especially in this age of modern birth control. And, for many women, it undoubtedly is. But it would be an oversimplification to call it a choice for all women. We should understand that even within marriages and other intimate relationships, the power dynamics are not always equal. Some women may face pressure, overt or otherwise, to have children.[96]

As we saw in the previous chapter, there is a much-debated association between single parenthood and poverty. This relationship holds for both never married mothers and divorced women. Despite the stereotype of women taking men to the cleaners in divorce settlements, on average, men tend to improve their financial conditions after a divorce, while women's financial situations become worse.[97] Fully a quarter of all poverty spells begin after divorce, separation, or other major change in family structure.[98] Roughly 21.5 percent of recently divorced women live below the poverty threshold, compared with only 10.5 percent of recently divorced men.[99] For children, more than a quarter of their transitions into poverty result from divorce or other departure of a male head of household.[100]

Spousal support remains uncommon in divorce cases, and even child support is ordered for custodial mothers in just 75 percent of cases.[101] Even if ordered, the amount is still apt to be quite low. The median award was just $4,370 per year. Bad enough, but custodial parents generally received far less than they were awarded, an average of just $2,260.[102]

If divorce is a risk factor for poverty, giving birth outside of marriage is an even stronger risk factor for poverty. More than 53 percent of women who had their first child while single were in poverty, compared with 33.7 percent of women who were cohabitating and only 12.3 percent of women who were married at the time.[103] Just 1.4 percent of women who were single when they had their first child had a college degree, while 36.3 percent of women who were married at the time had one.[104] Women who were married when they had their first child had earnings almost three times higher than women who were single. These facts do raise something of a chicken and egg question. As Theodora Ooms of the Center for Law and Social Policy asks, "Are single parents poor because they are not married, or are they not married because they are poor?"[105]

As previously noted, the economy and our criminal justice system often leave women in low-income neighborhoods with few marriageable men to choose from. However, a desire for sex, either for pleasure or intimacy, is a part of human nature. Women are going to have sex, and will sometimes become pregnant as a result, even if they can't find a suitable marriage partner. For too many poor women, this is what happens.[106] Several studies have looked at the fathers of children born out of wedlock and found them quite unprepared to support a family. More than a third lacked a high school degree, 28 percent were unemployed, and 20 percent had incomes of less than $6,000 per year.[107] In addition, roughly 38 percent had criminal records.[108] An examination of attempts to collect child support payments from low-income unwed fathers found that a substantial number of them faced serious employment barriers, including criminal records and poor health.[109] Many single mothers may find themselves single precisely because they find their unemployed and undereducated potential partners to be unattractive marriage material.[110]

At the same time, while women may find that suitable marriage partners are scarce, men in these communities have an abundant supply of potential mates and, therefore, don't need to compete as hard to find one. As a result, men are less likely to commit to romantic relationships or to work hard to maintain them.[111]

One final reason for the feminization of poverty stems from the increased economic stratification of our society. That is, people with similar incomes, education, and other attributes increasingly work, live, and socialize with each other.

For much of American history, marriage was an act of upward mobility for women. In 1960, for instance, 75 percent of men with college degrees married a woman without a degree. Such marital pairings are happening with less and less frequency. By 1980, Americans without a high school diploma were three times as likely to be married to one another as compared to the probability with random matching, and by 2007 this had increased to six times as likely.[112] Or, looked at from the woman's perspective, if you have a college degree, your chances of marrying another college graduate are about 65 percent. However, if you only have a high school diploma, your likelihood of marrying someone with a college degree is only about 9 percent.[113]

Ironically, this trend owes a great deal to the progress that women have made overall. Women are more likely to attend college and have high-earning jobs. Roughly 30 percent of women 25 and older now have a four-year bachelor's degree or higher, compared with 26 percent a decade ago.[114]

Growth in women's economic power is likely to continue for the foreseeable future. This growth will provide wealthier and educated men with more marriage options at their own economic class. It should come as no surprise that both men and women prefer mates with similar interests, values, and experiences. As June Carbone and Naomi Cahn, the authors of *Marriage Markets*, note, "the woman likely to make partner at a major law firm no longer thinks seriously about marrying her high school sweetheart—unless they run into each other at the right cocktail party for young lawyers years later."[115]

This trend has become even more pronounced because both men and women are freer to seek sex outside of marriage, meaning they are in less of a hurry to find a spouse. They can more easily wait and be more selective. At least that is true for educated women who are likely to have both knowledge of and ready access to birth control. As Carbone and Cahn put it, "In the 1950s, college women and high school dropouts alike shared the consequences of sex in the backseat of a Chevy."[116] This drove unmarried women to seek at least an implicit promise of marriage in the event of pregnancy as the price of sex. Access to contraception and abortion changed that calculus. For instance, a landmark 2002 study by Claudia Goldin and Lawrence Katz, "The Power of the Pill," found that half of the women born in 1950 who attended college were married by age 23. But for college-educated women born in 1957, who had access to birth control, less than a third were married by age 23. Without the fear of pregnancy to drive them into early marriage, women were free to be more discriminating in their choice of mates.[117]

But as good as this news is for women overall, it is not so good for those less-educated, less-successful women who now have correspondingly fewer marriage options. If the corporate executive no longer marries his secretary, where then does the secretary turn? Her marriage options, as noted, may be particularly unattractive. As we have seen, this has led to a significant increase in unwed pregnancies among low-income women. It also has meant that when those women did marry, they were likely to marry men with similarly meager incomes.

In many ways, we can compare the effect of gender-based discrimination on women to the impact of racism on African Americans (at least in kind, if not necessarily in degree). Throughout most of history, women have been penalized or otherwise treated in ways that left them at an economic disadvantage. While many of the policies and cultural norms that have disadvantaged women arose in response to particular social situations, those discriminatory attitudes and policies frequently persist long after historical conditions have changed.[118]

There is, however, one key difference between the role played by racism on poverty and the role played by gender bias—the question of heritability, which limits the legacy effects of past gender discrimination. Whereas the current generation of African Americans can be seen to suffer from injustices to previous generations, that is less apparent for women, if only because males intervene in their lineage.[119] The fact that a woman was denied the right to own property a generation or two ago is unlikely to lead to poverty today because the intervening generations were less likely to feature direct female to female to female inheritance. Women do, however, continue to suffer from ongoing discrimination. They confront cultural stereotypes that may limit their choices. They may also suffer psychological fallout from discriminatory treatment. All of these factors play into the disproportionate levels of poverty among women (and by extension among children).

Women face one problem that no other group must wrestle with: they give birth to children, and men do not. Children provide an economic benefit to society as a whole (not to mention the important consideration of the survival of the species), but they impose costs on the women who bear them, while the difficult work of bearing and raising children is largely unremunerated. As such, social institutions like marriage that bind individuals' choices for the sake of adequately rearing children are seemingly universal across cultures. Some economists even claim that children meet the technical definition of a public good.[120] Yet in recent years, changes in social dynamics from multiple points of origin (e.g., cultural, technological, market driven, and governmental) have upended the arrangements that have traditionally been used to support women who are raising children.

In the past, for instance, traditional marriage provided an imperfect attempt to solve this problem, a trade of financial security for women's role in having and raising children. In modern society, however, it is increasingly apparent that marriage as an institution no longer serves the same role. Unfortunately, however, as marriage breaks down, we have not yet developed alternative policies or institutions that would, in effect, properly compensate women for their role in reproduction. Until this problem is solved, women will remain at an economic disadvantage.

As with race, it is impossible to tease out how much of female poverty is due to which factor or to trace a direct path between any particular factor and any particular poor woman. Yet the cumulative weight of the evidence suggests that we cannot ignore gender-based discrimination as a contributory factor.

Inequality and Economic Stratification

Beyond those aspects of society that disadvantage particular groups such as women or racial minorities based on their innate characteristics, we should recognize how the larger organization of the economy itself acts as a structural contributor to poverty.

No force in history has lifted as many people out of poverty as free-market capitalism. In addition, as I noted previously, economic growth has dramatically improved the standard of living for the rich and poor alike, growth driven by free-market capitalism. Still, we must acknowledge that the heart of a capitalist economy involves, in Joseph Schumpeter's term, "creative destruction."[121] While markets generate enormous wealth, lifting most, if not quite all, boats, there are also losers. Even the staunchest defenders of capitalism must admit that the benefits are not evenly distributed. Individual workers or even segments of society may be left behind.[122] The economist Thomas Sowell, for example, notes that "During the advance of a capitalist economy, particular groups of workers may suffer not only relative, but absolute impoverishment."[123]

Not too long ago, a man with a high school diploma could expect to provide a middle-class lifestyle for his family on just his income alone. Times have changed. The reasons can be attributed to a confluence of forces, but chief among them are (1) globalization, meaning that workers must differentiate themselves in a global market for labor, and (2) technology and automation, which have displaced tasks previously conducted by labor. While these trends will no doubt affect a broad swath of American workers, the challenges they raise are particularly acute for those from disadvantaged backgrounds because they threaten their ticket into the middle class. As Susan Lund of McKinsey Global Institute (MGI) put it:

> Where are the middle class jobs? U.S. job growth post-2008 is in skilled professions and low-skill, part-time jobs. Thanks to both automation and globalization, jobs in the middle that can be "scripted, routinized, and automated" continue to disappear. What's left, as MGI puts it, are those—both high and low skill—that involve "complex problem solving, experience, and context (e.g., lawyer, nurse)."[124]

Consider the rapidly increasing pace of trade and globalization. Alongside the widespread consumer and economic benefits of expanded trade are significant downsides for those workers in domestic industries that are no longer able to compete. For instance, economists have found that the rise of import competition from China led to the loss of 2.0 to 2.4 million jobs.[125] While the U.S. economy, exporters, and consumers as a whole have benefited significantly from trade with China, the adjustment has been particularly painful in local labor markets where the industries exposed to foreign competition are concentrated.[126]

Whereas trade is easier to demagogue, automation is actually a far larger driver of structural economic dislocation. An analysis by scholars at Ball State University found that automation accounted for 88 percent of manufacturing job loss, with trade accounting for just the remaining 12 percent.[127] More and more, economic activity that was previously human labor is being replaced by robots or computer-assisted technologies.

At least in the short run, this phenomenon can harm wages or employability for individuals who may have invested their entire adult lives into a vocation that is now being threatened with obsolescence. Looking at 722 commuting zones across the continental United States, economists Daron Acemoglu and Pascual Restrepo estimate that one more robot per 1,000 workers in a local economy reduces the employment to population ratio by about 0.18–0.34 percentage points and wages by 0.25–0.5 percent.[128]

Does this mean automation will eventually take away all the jobs? If history is any guide, probably not.[129] Still, it is easy to say in abstract that the displaced factory worker should settle for the lower-wage, lower-prestige job at a fast-food restaurant, but actually doing so is too humiliating for many.

Economic progress has always been difficult. The industrial revolution was certainly difficult for many, but no one today doubts that it eventually led to broad improvements in living standards. On net, these developments have been for the better. Around the globe, countless individuals have been lifted out of deep poverty, and U.S. consumers are able to get more of what they want. Unfortunately, the bulk of recent gains have accrued to the highly educated, with less-skilled Americans absorbing most of the downsides from creative destruction. And the difficulties posed by economic dislocation are unambiguously exacerbated by current government policies in areas such as education and housing (more on these policies in chapters 7 and 8).

With the pace of economic change accelerating and both winners and losers becoming more visible, there has been a growing concern over the unequal distribution of economic gains. It is correctly noted that there is a large gap in the United States between the rich and the poor (although that gap is not as large or growing as rapidly as those like Thomas Piketty contend).[130]

It is suggested, therefore, that the gains of the wealthy have come at the expense of the poor. If the benefits of economic growth had been more widely shared, poverty would be lower.

However, this argument appears to be the weakest area of the structuralist interpretation of poverty. There appears to be little demonstrable relationship between income inequality and poverty. Poverty rates have sometimes risen during periods of relatively stable levels of inequality and declined during times of rising inequality. The idea that gains by one person necessarily mean losses by another reflects a zero-sum view of the economy that is simply untethered to history or economics. The economy is not fixed in size, with the only question being one of distribution. Rather, the entire pie can grow, with more resources available to all.

Comparing the Gini coefficient, the official poverty measure, and two additional poverty measures developed by Bruce Meyer and James Sullivan (the first based on income and accounting for taxes and transfers and the second based on consumption) illustrates that there is no clear relationship among them (Figure 3.5).[131] While the Gini coefficient

Figure 3.5

Changes in the Gini Coefficient and Poverty Rates Since 1980

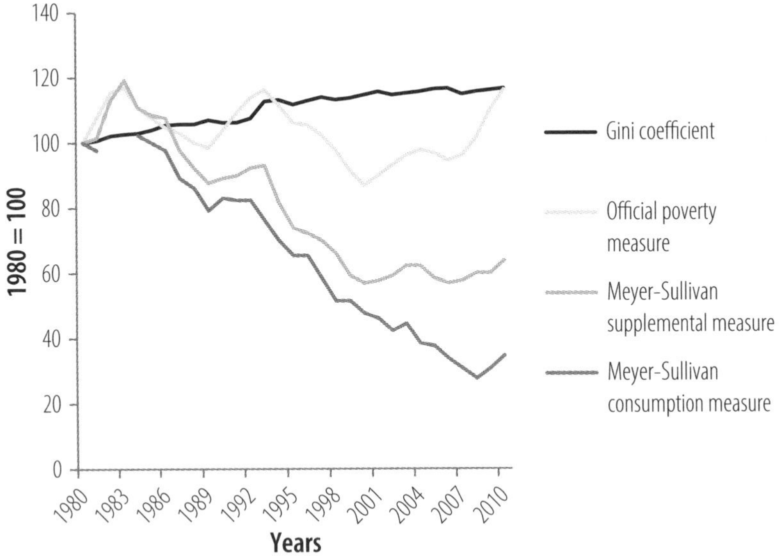

Sources: U.S. Census Bureau, "Historical Poverty Tables: People," Table 2: Poverty Status of People by Family Relationship, Race, and Hispanic Origin: 1959 to 2012; Bruce D. Meyer and James X. Sullivan, "Winning the War: Poverty from the Great Society to the Great Recession," National Bureau of Economic Research Working Paper no. 18718, NBER, Cambridge, MA, January 2013, http://www.nber.org/papers /w18718.

has increased almost without interruption, the official poverty rate has fluctuated mostly in the 13 to 15 percent range, and the two measures from Meyer and Sullivan have both decreased markedly since 1980.[132] Again the mid 1990s are an interesting period, because the inequality was markedly higher than previously, but both the supplemental poverty measure and the official rate saw significant decreases.

The relationship between poverty and inequality remains unclear, in part because the number of confounding variables and broader societal changes make any kind of determination difficult. But what research there is generally finds that poverty cannot be tied to inequality.

For instance, a recent paper by Deirdre Bloome of Harvard finds "little evidence of a relationship between individuals' economic mobility and the income inequality they experienced when growing up . . . over a twenty year period in which income inequality rose continuously, the intergenerational income elasticity showed no consistent trend." While most studies examine these trends at the national level, Bloome delves into state-level variation in inequality and social mobility. Again, she finds no evidence of a relationship, as "the inequality to which children were exposed in their state when growing up provides no information about the mobility they experienced as adults."[133]

That said, it is clear that unless we are prepared to restrict the economy in ways that would ultimately leave us all worse off, there will always be some Americans who fall through the economic cracks through no fault of their own.

Responding to Structural Poverty

There is no honest way to take a look at poverty without seeing that racism, gender-based discrimination, class barriers, and other malign social influences have been contributory factors. As much as we might wish it otherwise, the playing field has not been—and still is not—level. Any effort to combat poverty and increase economic opportunity will need to take a hard look at these issues.

This situation does not mean that individual choices or behavior play no role. No matter their circumstances, individuals always possess agency and have responsibility for their own lives. But we cannot ignore the context in which those choices take place.

In this sense, progressives are more likely to be on the more persuasive side of the argument over the causes of poverty. But diagnosing the problem is only half of the process. As we will see in the following chapter, their preferred remedy—greater redistribution—is not the fix that is needed.

CHAPTER FOUR: THE LIMITS OF REDISTRIBUTION

Insanity is doing the same thing over and over and expecting different results.
—Unknown

Efforts to fight poverty can best described as throwing money at the problem. Contrary to public perception, the American welfare system is far from stingy. Indeed, we already do a great deal of redistribution of wealth.

To start with, U.S. taxes are progressive, significantly so. The top 1 percent of tax filers earned 20.6 percent of U.S. income, but paid 39.5 percent of federal income taxes in 2014.[1] The inclusion of other taxes (payroll, sales, property, and so on) reduces this disparity but does not eliminate it: a report from the Congressional Budget Office (CBO) estimates that the top 1 percent paid 25.4 percent of all federal taxes in 2013, compared with the 15 percent of pre-tax income that they earn.[2] The wealthy pay a disproportionate amount of taxes.

At the same time, lower-income earners benefit disproportionately from a variety of wealth transfer programs. The federal government alone currently funds more than 100 anti-poverty programs, dozens of which provide either cash or in-kind benefits directly to individuals. Federal spending on those programs approached $700 billion in 2015, and state and local governments added another $300 billion.[3]

Figure 4.1

Redistribution by Income Quintile and Top 1 Percent, 2012

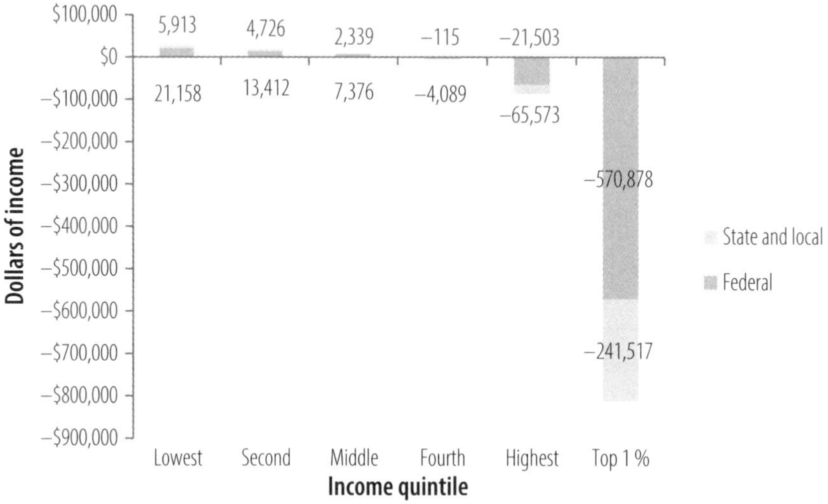

Source: Gerald Prante and Scott A. Hodge, "The Distribution of Tax and Spending Policies in the United States," The Tax Foundation, November 8, 2013, http://taxfoundation.org/article/distribution-tax-and-spending-policies-united-states.

Figure 4.1 shows the amount of redistribution taking place within the current tax and transfer system. In 2012, individuals in the bottom quintile (that is, the bottom 20 percent) of incomes (families with less than $17,104 in market earnings) received $27,171 on average in net benefits through all levels of government, while on average those in the top quintile (families with market incomes above $119,695) pay $87,076 more than they receive. The top 1 percent paid some $812,000 more.[4]

Another way to look at the amount of ongoing redistribution is to consider the impact of redistribution on levels of inequality in our society. According to the CBO, accounting for taxes reduces the amount of inequality in the United States (measured by the Gini coefficient) by more than 8 percent, while including transfer payments reduces inequality by slightly more than 18 percent. By fully accounting for redistribution from taxes and transfers, true inequality is almost 26 percent less than it initially appears.[5] (Figure 4.2)

Figure 4.2

Reduction in Gini Index from Federal Taxes and Government Transfers, 1979–2013

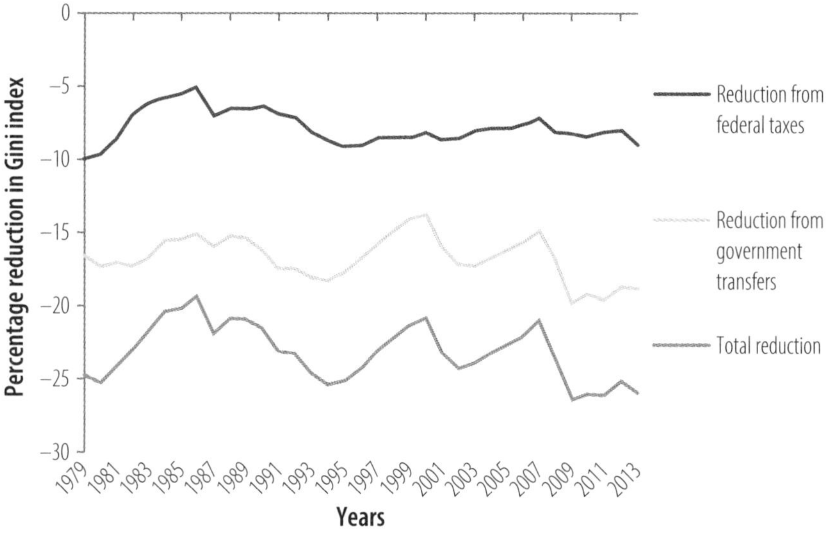

Source: Congressional Budget Office, "The Distribution of Household Income and Federal Taxes, 2013," Figure 15: Reduction in Income Inequality from Government Transfers and Federal Taxes, 1979 to 2013, https://www.cbo.gov/sites/default/files/114th-congress-2015-2016/reports/51361-FigureData.xlsx.
Note: The Gini index, or Gini coefficient, is a common measure of income inequality based on the relationship between cumulative income shares and distribution of the population. The measure typically ranges from 0, which would reflect complete equality, to 1, which would correspond to complete inequality. Some sources, such as the World Bank, use an equivalent range of 0 to 100.

In fairness, it should be pointed out that some of the biggest redistributive programs, such as Social Security and Medicare, are not strictly targeted to the poor, but instead provide most of their benefits to the middle class. It is unfair to blame our country's massive debt on programs for the poor, as some conservatives do. Still, we do have an enormous—and expensive—social welfare (or anti-poverty) system in this country.

When most Americans think of welfare, they think of the cash benefit program known as Temporary Assistance for Needy Families (TANF), formerly known as Aid to Families with Dependent Children (AFDC). In reality, TANF is only a tiny portion of a vast array of federal government social welfare programs designed to fight poverty. Including programs that are means-tested (and therefore obviously targeted to low-income Americans) and programs whose legislative language specifically classifies them as anti-poverty programs, there are currently more than 100 separate federal government programs designed to fight poverty.

Most are means-tested programs that provide aid directly to low-income persons in the form of cash, food, housing, medical care, and so forth, with eligibility based on the recipients' income. The remaining programs are either community-targeted programs, which provide aid to communities that have large numbers of poor people or are economically distressed, or categorical programs, which base eligibility for benefits on belonging to a needy or disadvantaged group, such as migrant workers or the homeless.

Since the start of the War on Poverty in 1965, spending on welfare programs has grown dramatically. This amount is not adjusted for growth in the population, however. A better measure might be to look at welfare spending by per capita, specifically per person in poverty. Measured in this way, federal spending on anti-poverty programs has risen by almost by 302 percent, from $6,972 to $21,113 (Figure 4.3).[6]

Altogether, the United States has spent more than $21 trillion fighting poverty since 1965 (in constant 2014 dollars). In 2015 alone, the federal government spent almost $700 billion, while state and local governments added nearly $300 billion more, for a total of roughly $1 trillion. That is equivalent to more than $21,000 for every person below the poverty level in America, or $63,339 for a family of three.[7] While it is true that a significant portion of the actual money in these "anti-poverty" programs goes to families above the poverty line, the fact remains that we spend enough money on the welfare system to conceivably lift everyone who currently lives in poverty above the poverty threshold, which stood at $19,096 for a single mother with two children in 2015.[8] Not even an entity as inefficient as the federal government can spend this much money without having some impact on poverty.

As noted in the introduction, people who are poor enjoy a much-improved standard of living compared with before most of these programs began, and there is substantial evidence to suggest that welfare programs have reduced the number of people in poverty. They may also be keeping some families with incomes just above the poverty line from falling into poverty. Moreover, they may have helped move some people who are poor closer to the poverty line, meaning that, even if remaining

Figure 4.3
Welfare Spending per Person in Poverty 1973–2013

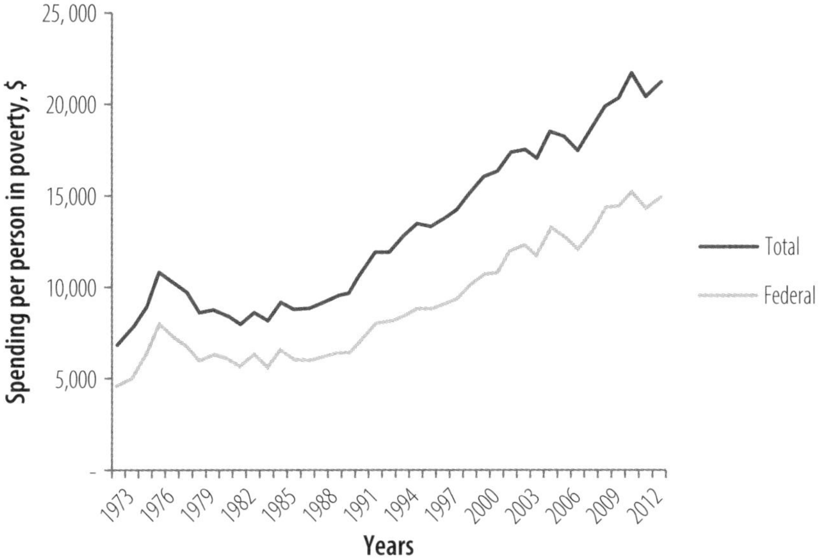

Sources: Michael Tanner, "The American Welfare State: How We Spend Nearly $1 Trillion a Year Fighting Poverty—and Fail," Cato Institute, *Policy Analysis* No. 694, April 11, 2012; Catalog of Federal Domestic Assistance; Gene Falk, "Low-Income Assistance Programs: Trends in Federal Spending," Congressional Research Service report R41823, May 7, 2014, https://fas.org/sgp/crs/misc/R41823.pdf; Congressional Research Service, "Cash and Noncash Benefits for Persons with Limited Income: Eligibility Rules, Recipient and Expenditure Data," report RL33340, 2006, https://www.everycrsreport.com/files/20060327_RL33340_d4430e0a7835d75178354908d415ede687e7f460.pdf; Jeffrey Barnett and Phillip Vidal, "State and Local Government Finances Summary: 2011," U.S. Census Bureau, July 2013; U.S. Census Bureau, "Historical Poverty. Tables: People," Table 2: Poverty Status of People by Family Relationship, Race, and Hispanic Origin: 1959 to 2012.

Note: The figure starts in 1973 because of a lack of uniform, consistent data before that year. State data for 2012 and 2013 are extrapolated, as most recent state data are from 2011. Federal spending for 2013 is extrapolated from 2012 levels using overall federal spending growth rate for 2013.

poor, they are nonetheless better off than they would be in the absence of such aid.

Adjusting the official poverty rate to include tax credits and non-cash benefits such as food stamps, the poverty rate might be as much as 8 percentage points lower in the presence of federal transfer programs—decreasing from 19 percent to 11 percent.[9] That amounts to some 27 million people lifted above the poverty line through those programs, relative to where the rate stood in 1965. There is no dispute that welfare spending reduces poverty to some degree.

However, even as we acknowledge the success of welfare programs in reducing material poverty over the past 50 years, we should consider some important questions:

Have We Reached a Point of Diminishing Returns?

Just because the social welfare spending to date has reduced poverty does not mean that additional welfare spending will yield similar results. In fact, the evidence suggests that the biggest gains from past expenditures occurred in the initial years of the War on Poverty, with decreasing effectiveness more recently.

For example, Bruce Meyer and James Sullivan found that the majority of improvements in the poverty rate occurred before 1972.[10] Less than a third of the improvement has taken place in the past four decades, despite massive increases in expenditures during that time (Figure 4.4).

Similarly, Robert Moffitt and coauthors found that the effect of anti-poverty programs has diminished over time (Figure 4.5).

A plausible conclusion to draw is that the War on Poverty saw early gains because it was picking the low-hanging fruit. For instance, those most likely to benefit from these programs were workers with incomes marginally below the poverty line, such as divorced women with skills and past attachment to the labor force. Meanwhile, those in deep, entrenched poverty were left behind, with myriad welfare programs and trillions of dollars only serving to make their lives marginally more comfortable.

It is also possible the initial gains were due in part to conditions outside the welfare system that no longer apply. For instance, the War on Poverty coincided with both the civil rights movement and second-wave feminism, which increased economic opportunities for African Americans and women. Also, the early years of the War on Poverty coincided with a period of rapid economic growth, while recent years have seen comparatively tepid growth.

Whatever the reasons, the evidence suggests that we may not see the same type of poverty reductions in the future, even if we increase welfare spending. We should therefore be open to other anti-poverty options.

Figure 4.4

Meyer-Sullivan Poverty Rate vs. Combined Welfare Spending

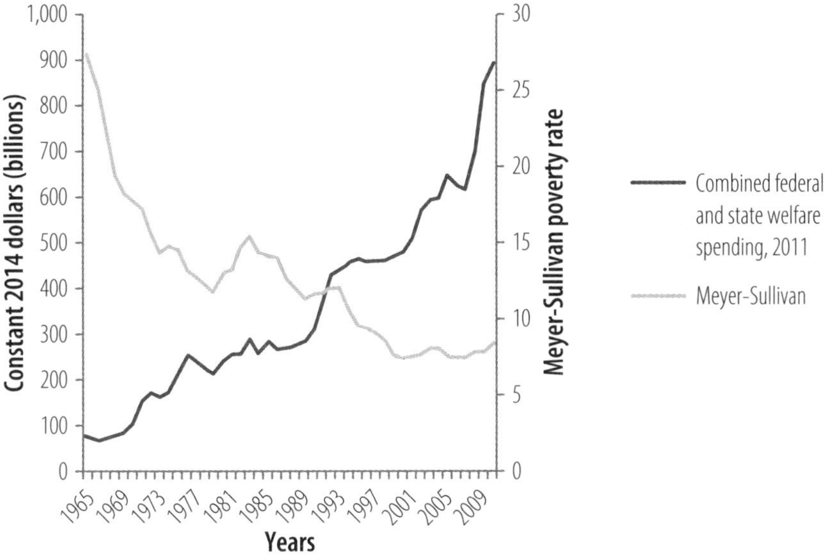

Sources: Bruce Meyer and James Sullivan, "Winning the War: Poverty from the Great Society to the Great Recession," *Brookings Papers on Economic Activity*, Fall 2012; Michael Tanner, "The American Welfare State: How We Spend Nearly $1 Trillion a Year Fighting Poverty—and Fail," Cato Institute Policy Analysis no. 694, April 11, 2012; General Services Administration, Catalog of Federal Domestic Assistance, https://www.cfda.gov/; Gene Falk, "Low-Income Assistance Programs: Trends in Federal Spending," Congressional Research Service report R41823, May 7, 2014, https://fas.org/sgp/crs/misc/R41823.pdf; Congressional Research Service, "Cash and Noncash Benefits for Persons with Limited Income: Eligibility Rules, Recipient and Expenditure Data," report RL33340, 2006, https://www.everycrsreport.com/files/20060327_RL33340_d4430e0a7835d75178354908d415ede687e7f460.pdf; Jeffrey Barnett and Phillip Vidal, "State and Local Government Finances Summary: 2011," U.S. Census Bureau, July 2013, https://www.census.gov/prod/2013pubs/g11-alfin.pdf.

Is the Welfare System Sustainable into the Future?

Given the escalating cost of anti-poverty programs, it is fair to ask, even if those programs provide short-term benefits to the poor, whether they are sustainable into the future without seriously endangering economic growth. After all, one cannot redistribute wealth that doesn't exist.

Economists do not agree on the extent to which transfer income to current beneficiaries is outweighed by the loss of future economic growth or even on a framework that could be used to evaluate such a question. That may ultimately be a question better debated by philosophers than

Figure 4.5

Pre-Transfer vs. Post-Transfer Poverty Comparisons

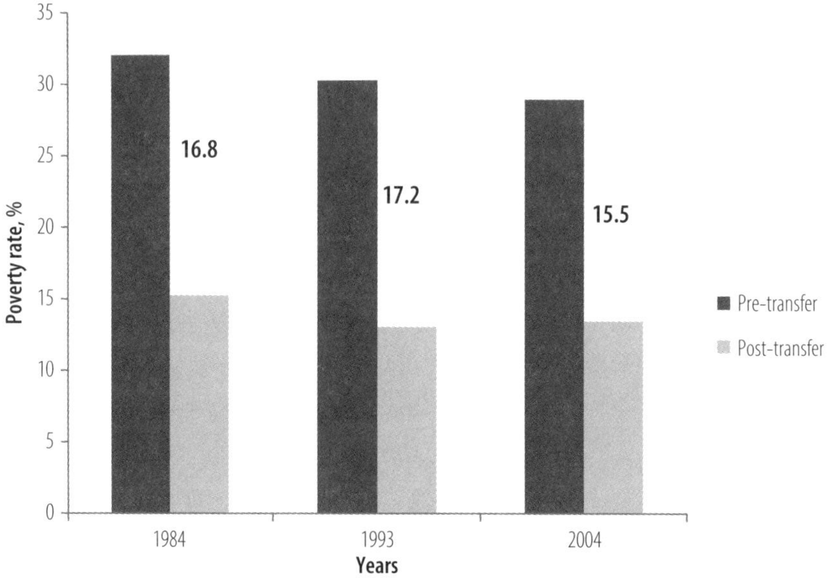

Source: Robert Moffitt, John Scholz, and Yonatan Ben-Shalom, "An Assessment of the Effectiveness of Anti-Poverty Programs in the United States," National Bureau of Economic Research Working Paper 17042, NBER, Cambridge, MA, May 2011.

economists or social scientists. However, to the degree that welfare programs are financed in ways that reduce economic growth, they may do more long-term harm than good. For instance, a transfer from rich to poor often means taking income that would have likely been invested and giving it to someone who is likely to consume it immediately. At first glance, this may seem like the decent thing to do, but over the longer term, the payoff from investments will dominate immediate consumption because of the wealth created, and if history is any guide, this holds true for society's least well-off people as well. (More on this in chapter 9.)

We currently face a national debt of more than $21 trillion.[11] Even if anti-poverty spending is a relatively small portion of overall federal spending, especially when compared with programs for the elderly such as Social Security, Medicare, and a substantial portion of Medicaid, they nonetheless impose a significant burden in the form of taxes or

Figure 4.6
Welfare Spending as a Percentage of GDP

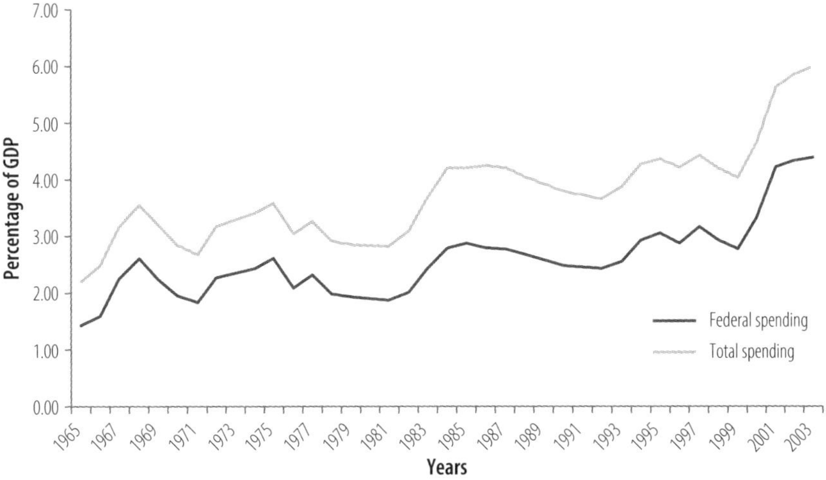

Source: Author's calculations using "Current and Real Gross Domestic Product," Bureau of Economic Analysis, October 27, 2010, http://www.bea.gov/national/xls/gdplev.xls state level welfare spending from "Cash and Noncash Benefits for Persons with Limited Income: Eligibility Rules, Recipient and Expenditure Data," CRS.
Note: GDP = gross domestic product.

debt. Measured as a percentage of gross domestic product (GDP), federal welfare spending increased more than fourfold, from just 0.83 percent of GDP in 1965 to 4.4 percent today (Figure 4.6).[12]

Moreover, even if future welfare spending can be accommodated without increasing debt or taxes, such spending will likely occur at the expense of other forms of government spending that are more likely to lead to economic growth. Most social welfare spending is pure consumption-based spending, rather than anything that could even tangentially be considered an investment.[13] As such, it is far less simulative of future growth.

Finally, if, as discussed below, welfare programs discourage individuals with low earnings potential from entering the labor force, they may similarly reduce future growth. Although the relationship is uneven, studies show that, if productivity remains constant, economic growth is strongly influenced by changes in the size of the labor force. As George

Mason University economist Tyler Cowen points out, both the poor and taxpaying nonpoor will reduce their labor force participation in a welfare state.[14] As a result, future economic growth may be slower than it has been in the past. Any policy that encourages more otherwise able workers to drop out of the labor force would further slow growth.

This slowing of growth means not only more people who are impoverished in the future, but also fewer resources with which to provide those benefits. That, in turn, means higher taxes or debt, which will further slow growth, and so on, in a vicious cycle.

Thus, even if we agreed that our current welfare policies were beneficial and wished to continue them, they might not be economically optimal.

Is Reducing Material Poverty a Sufficient Goal?

Some scholars usefully divide anti-poverty efforts into two categories: "protection," designed to provide palliative assistance, and "promotion," aimed at helping families permanently escape poverty.[15]

Another way to look at this distinction would be to define policy goals as alleviating poverty or as eliminating it. Most welfare programs are aimed at the former, which is entirely understandable. The first goal of any social safety net must be to ensure that people have enough food, shelter, health care, and so forth to survive.[16] Subsistence provisions are insufficient in themselves. Rather, we should be striving to lift people out of poverty, to give them the means and opportunity to become self-sufficient, and to enable the poor to become fully actualized citizens, rising as far as their talents can take them. After all, psychologists have long understood that one aspect of individual happiness or life satisfaction is correlated with the degree to which people feel that they are in control of their own lives.[17] The existing welfare system is failing people in this regard.

One way to measure how well we are doing at helping the poor achieve self-sufficiency is to look at household income in the absence of any form of government assistance, what might be termed self-sufficiency poverty.[18] As Figure 4.7 shows, the rate of self-sufficiency poverty has

Figure 4.7

Material Deprivation and Self-Sufficient Poverty Rates, 1980–2013

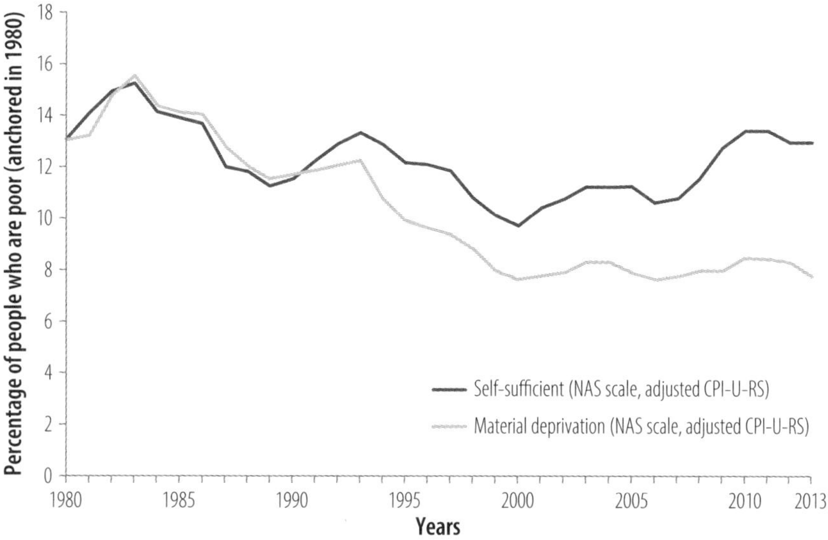

Source: Ben Gitis and Curtis Arndt, "Material Well-Being vs. Self-Sufficiency: How Adjusting Poverty Measurements Can Reveal A Diverging Trend in America," American Action Forum, March 9, 2017, https://www.americanactionforum.org/research/material-well-vs-self-sufficiency-adjusting-poverty-measurements-can-reveal-diverging-trend-america/.

Note: NAS = National Academy of Sciences. The Consumer Price Index research series using current methods (CPI-U-RS) presents an estimate of the CPI for all Urban Consumers (CPI-U) from 1978 to present that incorporates most of the improvements made over that time span into the entire series.

been essentially flat since 1980, even as material poverty has declined. As we have seen, government benefits have helped to raise the standard of living among the poor, yet poor families remain no more able to earn enough on their own to escape poverty than they could 35 years ago. More than 16 million people now fall into that gap, and the number is increasing.

A second measure also suggests that the existing welfare system is failing to help the poor permanently escape poverty. If our anti-poverty efforts were truly successful, we should see increased upward mobility. That is, it should become easier for the children of the poor to escape poverty and reach the middle class. Welfare should be as much a trampoline as a net. The evidence does not suggest this escape is broadly occurring.

There are two different ways to look at economic mobility. The first is "absolute mobility," which measures whether people are better off economically than their parents were at the same point in their lifetimes, and the second is "relative mobility," which measures the chances of upward or downward movement in comparison to other social or economic classes. Relative mobility is a zero-sum process—if you move to a higher economic level, someone else must move down.

For truly helping the poor, absolute mobility should be the ultimate focus. A poverty-stricken society characterized by high levels of relative mobility is clearly inferior to a more segmented one in which everyone is more prosperous. Government attempts at leveling the playing field by regulation or redistribution inevitably run the risk of stemming or even reversing the rising tide of economic growth. This potential outcome is because wealth creation is not an immutable law of nature, but an outgrowth of individuals being rewarded for their services to others in a market economy. A broadly shared upward mobility in absolute terms was the story of the American economy during the 20th century. A paper for the Brookings Institution found that two-thirds of Americans who are age 40 are in households with larger incomes than their parents had at the same age, even after adjusting for changes in the cost of living.[19] Economic growth is what made this absolute mobility possible. A society cannot simply redistribute its way to prosperity. To the extent that improving absolute and relative mobility are in tension, we should favor policies that increase absolute mobility.

Still, libertarians and conservatives often take this preference for absolute mobility too far, ignoring the value of relative mobility altogether. Policies that simultaneously increase absolute and relative mobility ought to be favored doubly so, rather than disparaged as a capitulation to the left. To ignore relative mobility is to tacitly accept the idea of an American caste or class system. While standards of living would rise for both at the top and the bottom of the economic stratification of society, future generations would be locked into the status that their parents currently occupy. That is, if a child is born in the bottom 20 percent of incomes today, that child's great-great-great-grandchildren would still be in the bottom 20 percent. That is fundamentally antithetical to the American experiment. As President Barack Obama pointed out, "the idea that those children might not have a chance to climb out of [poverty] and back into the middle class, no matter how hard they work" is inexcusable.[20]

Indeed, one of the great accomplishments of the development of free-market capitalism is that it shattered the concept that people were born into a hereditary class, noble or serf, but rather could rise or fall according to their own merits. We should never retreat from this world-changing advancement.

However, multiple studies have shown that intergenerational mobility has been stagnant in recent decades, hardly a convincing sign that these welfare programs effectively improve outcomes for children born into poverty. For example, a comprehensive study by Raj Chetty of Harvard that looked at birth cohorts from 1971 to 1993 found that measures of intergenerational mobility have remained extremely stable over time.[21] An earlier paper by Chul-In Lee and Gary Solon that examined cohorts born between 1952 and 1975 also found no major changes in intergenerational mobility.[22] Also, two papers looking at generations that span most of the decades of the War on Poverty find little change in mobility; the introduction of anti-poverty programs did not beneficially affect the earlier generations, while the later generations that felt the full effects of these established programs since birth saw minimal gains. Finally, a report from the U.S. Department of the Treasury found that the degree of intergenerational mobility among income groups from 1996 to 2005 was unchanged from the previous decade.[23] In short, a child born near the beginning of the War on Poverty was about as likely to "climb the ladder" as a child born 13 years and trillions of anti-poverty dollars later.

Obviously, other social forces are at work here. It would be a mistake to attribute this lack of mobility entirely to failures of the welfare system. It is possible that, although mobility was essentially flat, these policies were counteracting other mechanisms that would have led to a decline in mobility. Still, given all the effort and resources dedicated to anti-poverty programs, these results are not encouraging.

If the Welfare System Is Not Helping the Poor Become Self-Sufficient, Could the System Itself Be One Reason for This?

Believing that our existing welfare system can alleviate poverty in the short term while also exacerbating the problem in the longer run does not necessarily constitute a contradiction. Indeed, it is entirely possible to see welfare as helping individuals who are poor while harming the more general community that is poor. In effect, it is possible for welfare to create a sort of prisoner's dilemma, under which each individual is better off because of welfare, but the group as a whole is worse off.[24] This state of affairs seems particularly plausible if we consider human flourishing rather than a simplistic material standard.

One does not need look too far into our welfare system to see ways in which it can contribute to an environment that limits self-sufficiency and mobility.

The current welfare bureaucracy is amazingly convoluted, opaque, and unaccountable. Today, the federal government funds dozens of separate and often overlapping anti-poverty programs. For example, there are 33 housing programs run by four different cabinet departments, including even the Department of Energy. Currently, 21 different programs provide food or food-purchasing assistance.[25] These programs are administered by three different federal departments and one independent agency. There are eight different health care programs, administered by five separate agencies within the Department of Health and Human Services. Six cabinet departments and five independent agencies oversee 27 cash or general-assistance programs. Altogether, seven different cabinet agencies and six independent agencies administer at least one anti-poverty program, and those are just the programs aimed explicitly at poverty.

It can be both demeaning and challenging to navigate these systems. Those applying for benefits must deal with multiple forms, often conflicting eligibility standards, and intrusive program administrators.

Andrea Louise Campbell, a professor at the Massachusetts Institute of Technology, described the struggles of her disabled sister-in-law in the welfare system in her book *Trapped in America's Safety Net*. The professor notes that she found the welfare maze "incredibly complex and confusing."[26] For more typical applicants with far less education and fewer coping skills, the process must be daunting indeed.

The vast majority of benefits are provided not in cash but rather as in-kind benefits. Indeed, direct cash assistance programs, including refundable tax credits, now make up just 24 percent of direct federal transfers.[27] In-kind programs, such as food stamps, housing assistance, and Medicaid, provide the poor with assistance, but only for specific purposes. In most cases, the payments are made directly to providers. The person being helped never even sees the money. The poor are not expected to budget or choose among competing priorities the way individuals who are not on welfare are expected to.

Nearly all programs go even further in limiting the use of benefits to government-approved purchases. For example, the Special Supplemental Nutrition Program for Women, Infants, and Children (WIC) can only be used to buy certain foods determined by government regulation.[28] Even with cash programs like TANF, state lawmakers have enacted a host of restrictions on things such as the locations where electronic benefit transfer cards may be used to access ATMs, or limiting the frequency of withdrawals.[29]

Additionally, many jurisdictions are now adding semipunitive measures such as drug-testing requirements. Fifteen states have passed legislation authorizing drug testing or screening for welfare applicants and recipients, and more states have legislation now pending.[30] Even measures that are likely to benefit recipients in the long run, such as work requirements, add another layer of bureaucratic oversight. Although it is reasonable for taxpayers who are ultimately paying for these benefits to seek accountability for how the funds are used, this paternalism may be both unnecessary and self-defeating.[31]

Perhaps even more important, from the perspective of trying to reduce poverty, the current welfare system sets up an incentive system that can help trap people in poverty.

The 2013 Cato study "The Work versus Welfare Trade-Off" found that a mother with two children participating in seven common welfare programs—TANF; food stamps, or SNAP; Medicaid; housing assistance; WIC; energy assistance, or Low Income Home Energy Assistance Program (LIHEAP); and free commodities—could take home income higher than what she would have earned from a minimum-wage job in 35 states, even after accounting for the earned income tax credit (EITC) and the child tax credit. In fact, in Hawaii, Massachusetts, Connecticut, New York, New Jersey, Rhode Island, Vermont, and Washington, D.C., welfare paid more than a $20-an-hour job, and in five additional states it paid more than a $15-per-hour job.[32] As a result, those who left welfare for work could have found themselves worse off financially.

A report by the Congressional Budget Office looking at the example of Pennsylvania found that marginal tax rates after accounting for the loss of benefits could reach extremely high levels, discouraging labor-force entry and work hours. The report found that unemployed single taxpayers with one child would face an effective marginal tax rate of 47 percent for taking a job paying the minimum wage in 2012, and if their earnings disqualify them from Medicaid, they could face an astonishing marginal tax rate of 95 percent.[33]

Likewise, a 2012 paper in the *National Tax Journal* looked at a similar hypothetical family of a single parent with two children and found that in moving from no earnings to poverty-level earnings, this family faced a marginal tax rate that was as high as 25.5 percent in Hawaii.[34] A study by the Illinois Policy Institute found that a single mother with two children in that state who increased her hourly earnings from the Illinois minimum wage of $8.25 to $12.00 would increase her net take-home wage by less than $400. Even worse, if she further increased her earnings to $18 an hour, supposedly a gateway to the middle class, her net income would actually *decrease* by more than $24,800 because of benefit reductions and tax increases.[35]

Even after the 1996 welfare reform, many programs also include a bias against marriage. Many welfare programs reduce benefits if a single mother gets married, which can work against the formation of stable two-parent households. With traditional welfare, a mother who marries the father of her children may lose a substantial portion of her benefits depending on her new spouse's income. An unmarried parent is better able to meet the income and asset eligibility tests for programs such as TANF and SNAP. For example, if a single mother with a net income of 125 percent of the federal poverty line marries a husband with some income, it could push them over the threshold, and no one in the household would be eligible for SNAP. If they chose instead to cohabitate without marrying, welfare benefits would continue to flow. There is a similar mechanism in the EITC: benefits begin to phase out and are exhausted at lower income levels for married couples.[36]

Finally, as noted in chapter 3, the current welfare system contributes to the geographic concentration of poverty. Because only certain providers are both qualified and willing to accept payment through many social welfare programs, the poor are often forced to live in areas where poverty is concentrated. Often these areas have more crime, fewer economic opportunities, and a lack of social cohesion. Children are often stuck with failing local schools, which leave them less prepared for the job market and limit their opportunities.

It may well be, therefore, that even as existing welfare programs reduce short-term poverty, they help create an environment that leads to increased poverty in the long run.

Can Welfare Be Reformed?

To be sure, there have been attempts to reform welfare, most notably the 1996 Personal Responsibility and Work Opportunity Act. That act and the other legislative acts that closely accompanied it amounted to a shift in the makeup of social assistance from welfare to workfare. Welfare programs were made largely conditional upon work, and the EITC for low-wage workers was dramatically expanded. The net effect of these reforms was to significantly decrease the number of individuals receiving unconditional cash assistance, while transfers increased tenfold to low-income working families in inflation-adjusted terms during the period from 1984 to 1999.[37] However, many studies suggest that the results from these reforms were a mixed bag.

Welfare rolls declined without a commensurate increase in poverty—obviously a welcome development. Indeed, rates of overall poverty, child poverty, black poverty, and black child poverty all fell during the first years following enactment. Poverty rates did edge up following the recession in 2009, but this increase cannot substantially be blamed on the reform rather than the recession. According to Scott Winship, if one includes in-kind welfare benefits and income from cohabiting partners, the numbers of both children in poverty and children in deep poverty were lower in 2014 than at any point since at least 1979.[38] Ron Haskins of the Brookings Institution agrees that "most low-income mothers heading families appear to be financially better off," although he cautions that "work expenses and Social Security taxes consume part of their earnings."[39] Moreover, Moffitt, writing for the Institute for Research on Poverty, also concluded that poverty rates among single mothers declined following welfare reform, while average earnings and family incomes increased.[40]

Welfare reform also increased work participation among single mothers. From 1993 to 2000, the rate of employment among single mothers rose by nearly 30 percent, hitting an all-time high of almost 75 percent. Never-married mothers, formerly the group most likely to end up on long-term welfare, saw their employment rates increase by roughly half, from 44 percent to 66 percent. As Haskins notes, "Employment changes of this magnitude over such a short period for an entire demographic group are unprecedented in Census Bureau records."[41]

We must recognize that gains were not universal. While the overwhelming majority of low-income women and children appear to have benefited from welfare reform (or at least not to have been harmed), most studies indicate that a small group at the bottom of the income distribution appears to be worse off as a result of welfare reform. According to Haskins, this group's members tend to be mothers who live without another adult in their household or who do not have income from cash welfare, employment, or unemployment insurance.[42] In particular, studies suggest that women who did not leave welfare voluntarily—that is, those who were sanctioned off the program because they reached the time limit or failed to fulfill work requirements—were most likely to be pushed further into poverty. These were also women who had other risk factors for poverty, including the lack of a high school education, little previous job experience, substance abuse and mental health problems, and three or more children.[43]

Still, the majority of results were positive. According to a study by Robert Schoeni and Rebecca Blank from the National Poverty Center at the University of Michigan, 98 percent of welfare families with children improved their income in the late 1990s (post-welfare reform) compared with the early 1990s (pre-welfare reform). Even among single-parent households, 92 percent saw gains. The gains do not mean that every single one of these women and their family members escaped poverty, but it does indicate at least incremental improvements in well-being following welfare reform.[44]

The degree to which welfare reform directly caused the subsequent poverty reductions and increases in work effort remains a hotly debated topic among scholars. The 1990s was a period of strong and extended economic growth. Employment increased generally. It should not be surprising, therefore, that employment also increased among welfare recipients. But as Haskins points out, previous economic booms did not result in similar reductions in welfare use, making it likely that welfare reform was at least a contributing factor.[45]

We can still make our existing welfare programs more humane and more efficient. For example, there are several proposals to consolidate current programs and move from in-kind benefits to cash. At its most radical, these minimum income reforms suggest some form of universal basic income (UBI) or, more practically, a negative income tax (NIT).

Either a UBI or an NIT would offer several advantages over the current welfare system. It would obviously be simpler and far more transparent than the hodgepodge of existing anti-poverty programs. With different and often contradictory eligibility levels, work requirements, and other restrictions, our current welfare system is a nightmare of unaccountability that fails to effectively help people transition out of these programs and escape poverty.

Perhaps most important, a UBI or NIT would provide far better incentives when it comes to work, marriage, and savings. As noted previously, because current welfare benefits are phased out as income increases, they create high marginal tax rates that can discourage work or marriage.

Depending upon the form it takes, a UBI could reduce or even eliminate this bias against work. For example, a UBI, unrelated to other income, would by definition not penalize individuals for earning additional income. Whereas some may choose not to work simply because they will have the guaranteed national income, many others may choose to work or increase the amount they work because they no longer will be penalized for doing so. In a British pilot project, for example, recipients of the cash payments were more likely to look for work and believed that the program offered a "better reward for small amounts of work."[46]

An NIT is potentially more of a problem (as will be discussed subsequently), but properly structured it could have a smaller work disincentive than the current system. Work-based income guarantees, such as wage supplements, have been shown to increase work incentives.

Similarly, a guaranteed national income could reduce the bias against marriage that is inherent in many current welfare programs.

For those who believe in getting government out of people's lives, a UBI would also be far less paternalistic, expecting the poor to budget and manage their money like everyone else. It all adds up to a strong theoretical case for supporting some variation of this approach.

Yet theory and practice are two different things, and shifting to either a UBI or an NIT would involve serious trade-offs.[47]

A 2017 study from the American Enterprise Institute suggests that the only way to afford a UBI would be to replace not only anti-poverty programs and unemployment insurance, but also middle-class entitlements, such as Social Security and Medicare. The poor would be big winners under such a shift, the authors conclude, but politically powerful seniors would lose out.[48] That seems like a political nonstarter.

An NIT, which limited the basic income to lower-income people, would be more affordable but would also import all the complexity, fraud, and abuse of the current U.S. tax code. For example, how would an NIT handle someone who had little income but substantial assets? It would also re-create many of the same incentive problems we see in the current welfare system, imposing high effective marginal tax rates, which discourage work.

Moreover, as with other government programs, there would be constant pressure to expand benefits. Once we've established the idea that people are entitled to an income, it becomes much harder to say no in the future. How long would it be before we heard that no one can live on whatever benefit the UBI provides at the moment?

If the concerns discussed here make it impractical and perhaps undesirable to adopt a guaranteed national income at this time, there are a number of smaller steps that could be taken to achieve some of the advantages provided by guaranteed national income schemes. In particular, it may be possible to simplify our current welfare system and substitute cash payments for in-kind benefits.

Representative Paul Ryan (R-WI) has proposed something similar, at least for consolidation. Under Ryan's plan, states would receive a block grant in lieu of funding for 11 current welfare programs.[49] Unfortunately, Ryan's proposal would send the money to the states rather than to the recipients themselves. As noted, state provision of welfare is better than federal provision, but Ryan also includes a host of strings that severely limit the ways in which states may use this money. While that may be politically realistic given the resistance to any reform, it therefore represents a federalist version of the current system. Still, it would simplify the current system, and states could theoretically use the money to provide direct payments to individuals.

Senator Marco Rubio (R-FL) proposes going even further, replacing most current federal welfare programs with a state-run "Flex Fund," under which states could provide benefits the way they want.[50] Rubio specifically urges states to replace in-kind programs with cash benefits, although he would leave the final decision up to the states. For example, although Rubio notes the importance of work requirements as a condition for receiving assistance, he would allow states to decide whether to impose such restrictions. In theory, states would be free to adopt programs that are very close to the sort of guaranteed-income programs discussed here. While cost and implementation issues make a full-fledged move in this direction unlikely, we should nonetheless expect far more state experimentation.

Another way that Congress could move toward a cash payment system would be to encourage states to expand existing cash-diversion programs. These programs, currently in use in 33 states, provide lump-sum cash payments in lieu of traditional welfare benefits, in some cases.[51] These programs are designed to assist families facing an immediate financial crisis or short-term need. The family is given a single cash payment in the hope that if the immediate problem is resolved, there will be no need for going on welfare. In exchange for receiving the lump-sum payment, welfare applicants in most states—but not all—give up their eligibility for TANF for a period ranging from a couple of months to as long as a year.[52]

Cash diversion programs are not a guaranteed national income, but these programs do share two important characteristics: both are cash payment programs, and there are few restrictions on the use of the money in either, putting the onus on the recipient to behave responsibly with it. The evidence suggests that they do. Several studies indicate that for individuals who had not previously been on welfare, diversion programs significantly reduced their likelihood of ending up there.[53] Studies also suggest that diversion participants are subsequently more likely to work than become recipients of traditional welfare.[54] However, the effect was far less pronounced for those who had previously been part of the welfare system.

Obviously these programs are extremely limited, but they do shift welfare toward cash payments and away from in-kind benefits. In doing so, they offer some of the advantages of universal income on a much smaller scale. They make the welfare system somewhat more transparent and treat recipients more like adults. They reduce bureaucracy and create better incentives.

Yet any welfare reform is likely to have a limited impact. Quite simply, we may have reached the limits of what can be achieved through redistribution.

A Libertarian Alternative

Anyone who spends much time reading contemporary poverty scholarship realizes that the dirty little secret among many scholars, as well as many of those who work directly with the poor, is that they do not believe that every person who is poor can thrive on his or her own. To put it somewhat crudely, they think that some people are incapable from the start of picking up the skills that would allow them to produce enough value to rise above poverty. Technology and competitive displacement will mean that a certain number of people will always be detached from the workforce and incapable of gaining the skills necessary to reinvent themselves.[55]

Others are sufficiently dysfunctional for a wide variety of reasons that they will never be able to fully participate in the economy in a way that would make them self-sufficient. The evidence from the programs discussed above certainly seems to give weight to that conclusion.

This pessimistic view entails that much contemporary scholarship appears to focus on the most efficient mechanism for redistribution: How can the poor be provided with sufficient resources in a way that does the least harm to the larger economy and that creates the fewest behavioral distortions? The necessity of continued government support for the poor is presupposed from the beginning. One might call this approach a custodial welfare state, in which some people will forever be incapable of caring for themselves and must, perforce, be cared for by the state.

However, I believe such pessimism is misplaced, at least in part, for two reasons.

First, the common ingredient of all the interventions that I have described is that they are top-down, outside interventions. They are designed to impose solutions on the poor. But such centrally planned initiatives are flawed from the outset. We should not be surprised that they have limited success.

In contrast, the types of policies that I describe in the following chapters are designed to establish conditions that would encourage an organic, internal change that would have a much better chance for long-term success. They are not top-down, imposed solutions that strip the poor of agency and expect outsiders to consider the costs or benefits to the poor in the same way that the poor themselves might. Nor are they simple calls for the poor to change their behavior and pull themselves up by their bootstraps. Instead, they seek to modify the economic and cultural environment within which the poor make choices, thereby empowering the poor to more directly benefit from their efforts to escape poverty and become self-sufficient.

History is replete with examples of such organic shifts and how they have lifted huge numbers of people from poverty. These broad cultural, political, and economic shifts lifted millions from poverty, but none stemmed from top-down, centrally planned interventions. They came from internal, self-generated changes in attitudes, beliefs, and behavior.[56] They were the natural outgrowth from an economic climate that made social change something that was in the poor's self-interest.

A second reason to reject pessimism is that even if there is a population that, for a variety of reasons, is likely to remain poor regardless of what policies we pursue, there is no reason to believe that this population makes up a majority of the poor. Utopia is not an option, and no one is seriously suggesting that we can eliminate poverty completely.[57] It is almost certain that, even if all the policies and programs that I discuss in the chapters that follow are successful, there will remain a group of people that will continue to need financial assistance. But it is my hope that there will be far fewer.

Moreover, even if the reform proposals that follow have only a small-scale immediate impact (in many cases, it may be too late to undo the damage that current institutions have already wrought), we should expect that an altered landscape would have a substantial influence on future generations. Thus what would begin as a small wedge of increased self-sufficiency would steadily widen as the children of the poor have an opportunity to grow up under very different circumstances. Ideally, intergenerational mobility would also increase. The curve may start to bend today, but the biggest effect will be on future generations. The portion of people in need of government assistance, we hope, will be much smaller than it is today.

Here are five specific areas where we can help the poor by enhancing freedom:

1. *Reform the criminal justice system and curtail the War on Drugs.*
2. *Reform education to give more control and choice to parents and break up the public school monopoly.*
3. *Eliminate zoning and land-use restrictions and reduce property taxes to lower the costs of housing and rents.*
4. *Reduce barriers to saving by the poor, including asset tests for public assistance, excessive banking regulations, and barriers to nonbanks.*
5. *Reduce taxes and regulations to stimulate economic growth and to make it easier for the poor to become full participants in a growing economy.*

Taken as a whole, I believe that these reforms would give far more people the opportunity to partake in the prosperity that they seek. Now, let us take a look at these proposals in more detail.

CHAPTER FIVE: FIGHTING POVERTY THROUGH CRIMINAL JUSTICE REFORM

Imprisonment has become the response of first resort to far too many of our social problems.

—*Angela Davis*[1]

One of the most consequential steps that the government could take to reduce poverty has little to do with what we traditionally think of as an anti-poverty program. Yet reforming our criminal justice system is essential to any serious effort to fight poverty.

The United States incarcerates more people than any other developed nation. At any given time, roughly 2.2 million Americans are in jail or prison, with another 4.7 million on probation or parole, a population that has grown substantially over the past 30 years (Figure 5.1).[2] Another 5 million are on parole or probation. With an incarceration rate of 690 per 100,000 residents, we have the world's second highest incarceration rate, trailing only the tiny African archipelago of Seychelles.[3] We incarcerate more people than such authoritarian regimes as Russia and China. In fact, roughly 22 percent of all the world's prisoners are jailed in the United States (Figure 5.2).[4] The only other nations that potentially rival us are dictatorships like North Korea that do not publish credible or useful data on incarceration rates.

Obviously, some people do belong in jail. Yet since the 1990s, there has been a significant drop in crime rates. The reason for that decline

Figure 5.1
Trends in Correctional Population

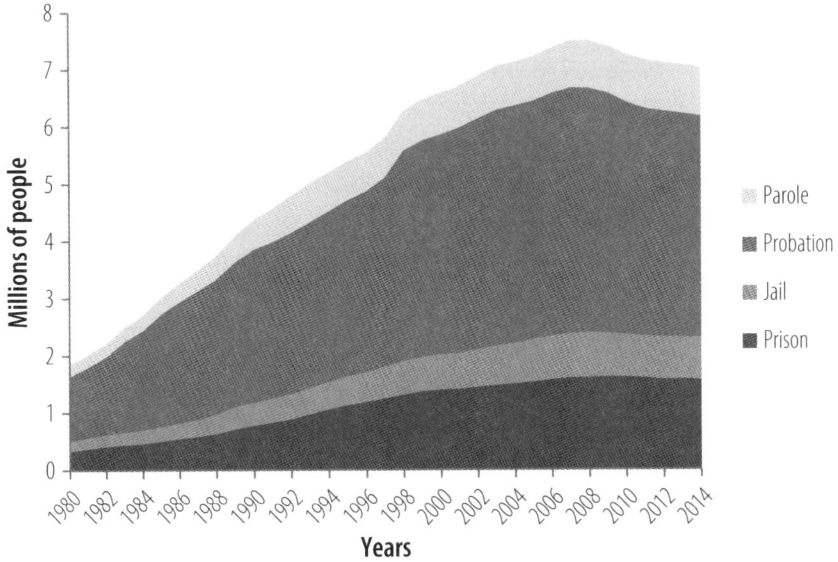

Sources: Danielle Kaeble et al., "Correctional Populations in the United States, 2014," NCJ 249513, U.S. Department of Justice, Bureau of Justice Statistics, Table 1: Estimated Number of Persons Supervised by U.S. Adult Correctional Systems, by Correctional Status, 2000, 2005–2010, and 2013–2014, January 2016, http://www.bjs.gov/content/pub/pdf/cpus14.pdf; Bureau of Justice Statistics, "Correctional Populations in the United States, 1992," January 1995, http://www.bjs.gov/content/pub/pdf/cpus92.pdf; Bureau of Justice Statistics, "Census of Jails: Population Changes, 1999–2013," NCJ 248627, December 2015, http://www.bjs.gov/content/pub/pdf/cjpc9913.pdf.

is much debated. Among the factors that scholars suggest to be contributing factors are economic growth, changing demographics (notably a declining youth population), an increase in the number of police and improved policing strategies, the receding of the crack cocaine epidemic, increased incarceration, and even increased availability of abortion. Steven Levitt of the University of Chicago, author of *Freakonomics*, attributes as much as one-third of the decline in crime to a rising prison population.[5] Conversely, given how large the U.S. prison population already is, the incremental gains from further increases in incarceration are likely to be minimal.[6] A review of the literature for the National Bureau of Economic Research concludes that a 10 percent increase in incarceration results in less than a 2 percent reduction in crime.[7]

Figure 5.2

Incarceration Rates across OECD Countries

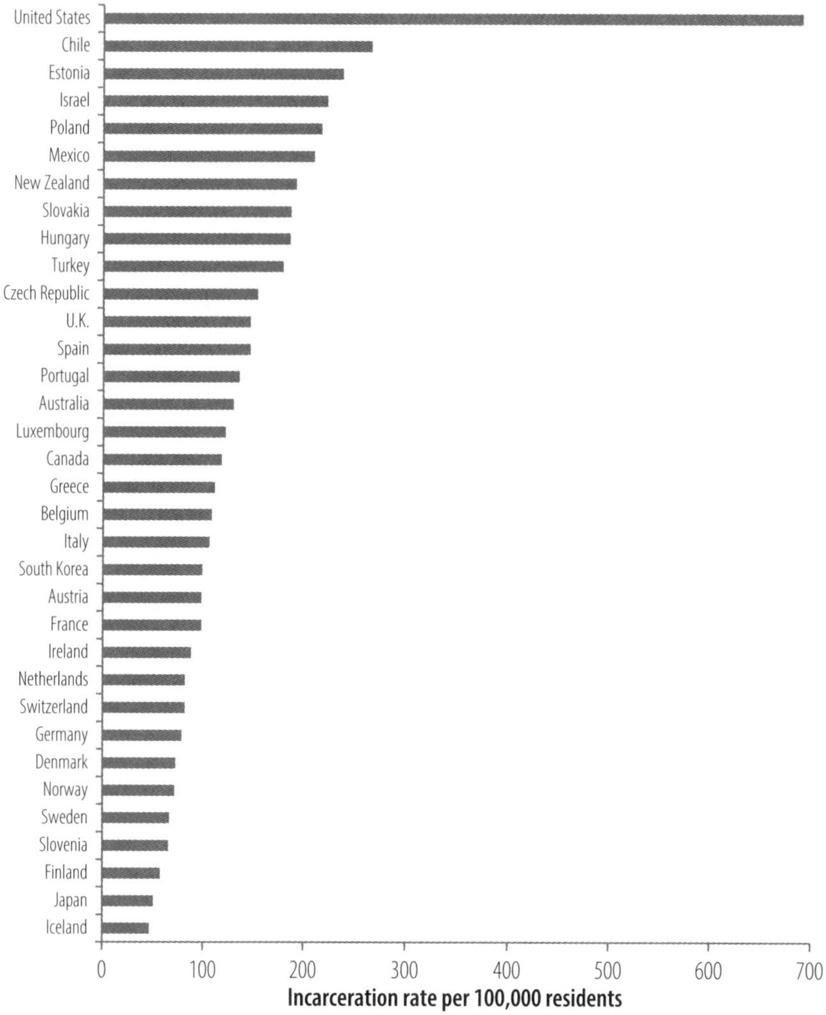

Source: Roy Walmsley, "World Prison Population List," World Prison Brief, Institute for Criminal Policy Research, http://www.prisonstudies.org/sites/default/files/resources/downloads/world_prison_population_list_11th_edition.pdf.

Note: OECD = Organisation for Economic Co-operation and Development.

Of course, even if mass incarceration does contribute to a small reduction in crime, it does not automatically follow that this would be an efficient use of resources. To start with, putting and keeping this many people in jail is not cheap. Governments at all levels spend more than $274 billion per year on criminal justice.[8] Roughly half of that is spent by local governments, with state governments spending about a third, and the rest attributable to the federal government. This outlay represents a 74 percent increase since 1993.[9]

While policing is the largest single criminal justice expense, incarcerating all those prisoners is also hugely expensive. The average annual cost of keeping someone in prison varies widely depending on the type of facility, but estimates range from $14,000 to $60,000 per inmate.[10]

But the question we are considering here is not whether mass incarceration is a wise use of resources or even whether it helps reduce crime rates, but instead, its effect on poverty. As the Council of Economic Advisers has pointed out:

> The costs of criminal justice policies are not limited to direct government expenditures. Individuals who obtain a criminal record or serve a prison sentence often face difficult circumstances when they return to society. Having a criminal record or history of incarceration is a barrier to success in the labor market, and limited employment or depressed wages can stifle an individual's ability to become self-sufficient. Beyond earnings, criminal sanctions can have negative consequences for individual health, debt, transportation, housing, and food security. Further, criminal sanctions create financial and emotional stresses that destabilize marriages and have adverse consequences for children.[11]

Politicians love to portray themselves as tough on crime. But there are real consequences in terms for poverty. A study by scholars at Villanova University concluded that mass incarceration has increased the U.S. poverty rate by an estimated 20 percent.[12] Another study found a family's probability of being poor is 40 percent greater if the father is imprisoned.[13] Since an estimated 5 million children have a jailed parent, this is an enormous problem. Minority children are particularly at risk. Rates of parental incarceration are two to seven times higher for black and Hispanic children than for white children. An African American child whose father does not have a high school diploma faces a roughly 50-50 chance that his or her father will be in prison by the time of the child's 14th birthday.

Children of incarcerated parents are highly at risk for a number of adverse life outcomes, including anti-social and violent behavior, mental health problems, dropping out of school, and unemployment. Robert Putnam points out that there is a spillover effect in areas of high incarceration that affects even children whose own parents are not incarcerated.[14]

As discussed in chapter 3, the high level of incarceration in poor communities, especially poor minority communities, reduces the pool of marriageable men, leading to increases in the number of women having children outside of marriage, with all the consequences it carries for poverty. Incarceration also increases divorce rates. Unsurprisingly, the longer the sentence, the more likely that the couple will divorce. One influential study showed that every year that a spouse spends in jail increases the likelihood that a couple will divorce by 32 percent.[15] But even shorter prison stays make it more likely that a couple will get divorced. Moreover, even after a spouse's release from prison, there remains a much-heightened risk of divorce.[16] Without rehashing all the arguments from chapters 2 and 3, it is easy to see that the failure of the criminal justice system contributes enormously to the prevalence of single parenting in low-income communities, with all the problems that this entails.

Issues of child custody are also likely to arise when women go to prison. In most instances when a mother is imprisoned, no one is available to care for the child (fathers are most often absent in these cases), so the child is likely to end up in foster care. Ernest Drucker, senior researcher at the John Jay College of Criminal Justice, points out that when children are put into foster care, they not only lose contact with their parents, but also with an entire family support system of grandparents, siblings, aunts, uncles, and cousins. They may be forced to change schools or move to different neighborhoods, disrupting friendships and other attachments.[17] A further reason for concern is the well-documented failure of some state and municipal child services agencies to protect children in the foster care system.[18]

The federal Adoption and Safe Families Act of 1997, which streamlined the adoption process, has also increased terminations of parental rights for prisoners. Even a relatively brief period of imprisonment can now be used to permanently deprive parents of not only custody of their children, but all other legal rights, including contact and visitation, information on the child's development, and any input into important decisions in the child's life.[19] Evidence suggests that this forced family breakup harms children, increasing their risk for a variety of social problems. Having an incarcerated parent increases the likelihood of being incarcerated oneself, increases anti-social behavior, and reduces potential lifetime earnings for children.[20] And the mothers themselves are more likely to re-offend and to have other problems readjusting to society after release.[21] If you are concerned about reducing poverty, destroying families—even flawed and fragile families—is unlikely to make the situation better.

Even if the family remains intact, when the principal breadwinner is incarcerated, resources available to that family are reduced. Estimates suggest that if a father goes to jail, the likelihood increases by 38 percent that his family will fall into poverty while he is incarcerated.[22] Also, incarceration permanently lowers wages. Someone who has been to prison can expect to earn roughly 40 percent less than someone who has avoided jail. And the effects are long-lasting. A Pew Charitable Trust survey found that inmates released in 1986 were still in the bottom 20 percent of incomes in 2006, 20 years after having served their sentence.[23]

Of course, that assumes that the previously incarcerated can find jobs at all. Recent job application experiments find that applicants with criminal records were 50 percent less likely to receive an interview request or job offer, relative to otherwise identical applicants with no criminal record, and these disparities were even more significant for African American applicants.[24] A study by the National Institute of Justice found that being arrested at any point in a person's life was a bigger barrier to finding a job than any other employment-related stigma, including long-term unemployment, being on welfare, or having a GED instead of a high school diploma.[25] Another study of recently released prisoners in New York City found that just 9 percent had jobs paying more than minimum wage. More than half were unemployed.[26]

Among those with a criminal record, the combination of greater difficulty in finding a job and lower wages does not consign merely themselves to poverty. It also makes it much harder for them to provide for their families, either directly or through paying child support. That is one reason states report that as many as 40 percent of child-support cases that are considered hard to collect involve a parent with a criminal record.[27] This combination often creates a vicious circle, since failure to pay child support can result in arrest and imprisonment, making future payment even more difficult.[28]

Of course, incarceration is not the only reason for low wages and increased unemployment among those possessing a criminal record. The people most likely to go to prison are disproportionately likely to experience other markers of socioeconomic disadvantage, including low educational attainment, weak attachment to the workforce, and substance abuse or mental health problems. Approximately 65 percent had not completed high school, and 14 percent have less than an 8th-grade education.[29] Many were unemployed before prison, or at least not employed in traditional jobs, and pre-incarceration incomes for this group were already far below their nonincarcerated peers.[30] After all, educated, financially stable individuals with few social problems are less likely to commit crimes in the first place.

Prison exacerbates every one of the problems we have just discussed.[31] So what can we do to reform the criminal justice system in ways that will not only make it fairer but will also help reduce poverty? This effort would involve virtually every level of the criminal justice system and every step of the criminal justice process, including the following:

1. Look hard at over-criminalization and victimless crime laws;
2. Improve police tactics and the way in which police enforce laws;
3. Make the justice process fairer, including reforming the bail system, limiting the abuse of prosecutorial discretion, and ensuring fairness in sentencing; and
4. Make it easier for ex-offenders to reenter society and participate in the economy.

No single proposal will correct such systematic bias in the criminal justice system on its own. More significant oversight and review are needed at every stage. As we respond to the consequences of the involvement in the criminal justice system for the poor and minorities, we also need to be aware of how structural inequities produced such involvement to begin with.

Meaningful reform needs to start right at the beginning of the criminal justice process, not just with policing practices but with the laws that the police enforce. Far too many "crimes" are designed to protect us from ourselves, to impose a value judgment against vices or other conduct that a majority disapproves of, or to turn errors of judgment into illegal activities, even in the absence of intent. Too often, criminal law is used as a blunt instrument against a broad range of societal issues.

When researchers at the Congressional Research Service were asked to compile a list of federal crimes, they were unable to do so because they ran out of time and money before they could complete the project. But they did manage to find at least 4,000 criminal infractions.[32] On average, Congress creates 50 new crimes every year, and that is just federal crimes. There is no way to come up with even a reasonable guess at the total number of state and local crimes that a person could commit. Many, of course, are the sorts of things we hope would be illegal—robbery, rape, murder, and so on—but many are trivial actions that should never be illegal in the first place.

Most Americans are unlikely to run afoul of this excess of criminalization. And, if they are charged with breaking some obscure federal or state statute, we can expect the police to treat them respectfully and their sentences to be light. The same is not necessarily the case for the poor and minorities.[33]

Remember that Eric Garner, who died after a police officer applied what may or may not have been an illegal chokehold, was arrested for the crime of selling "loosies," that is, single cigarettes from packs without a tax stamp.[34] In fact, the Garner case illustrates many of the inequities in the criminal justice system: a trivial offense, an arrest rather than a ticket or summons, and the violent conduct of that arrest. Does anyone truly believe that this situation would have unfolded the same way if Garner had been a middle-class white man from the suburbs?

Or consider the 2016 case of Philando Castile, a Minnesota school cafeteria worker who was shot and killed during a traffic stop. Castile, 32, had been pulled over by police 46 times since he was 18, accumulating more than $6,000 in fines. Reports indicate that only six of the stops were for offenses that were noticeable outside of the car.[35]

Some jurisdictions use the criminal code as a revenue source. We are all familiar with the stereotype of the speed trap, with a police officer lurking behind a billboard, ready to ticket an unwary traveler. Studies have found that such practices are widespread and often target the poor and minorities. One study, looking at more than 9,000 cities, found that those jurisdictions with more black residents consistently collected unusually high amounts of fines and fees—even after controlling for differences in income, education, and crime levels.[36]

The federal report on law enforcement in Ferguson, Missouri, illustrates how these practices work. Court fees and fines were Ferguson's second biggest source of revenue in 2013.[37] The Ferguson city government was fully aware of this. In 2010, for instance, the city's finance director wrote to the city's police chief that "unless ticket writing ramps up significantly before the end of the year, it will be hard to significantly raise collections next year. . . . Given that we are looking at a substantial sales tax shortfall, it's not an insignificant issue."[38] Police officers were even disciplined for failure to bring in enough revenue. Evaluations and promotions were in part based on the number of citations issued.[39] And senior police officials made it clear that procedural and constitutional concerns were not to stand in the way of revenue collection. Moreover, the Justice Department found that once an arrest was made or a citation was issued, the municipal court was complicit in the revenue raising scheme, using its authority to extort as much money as possible from defendants.[40] The number of arrests and citations in Ferguson was staggering. In 2013, Ferguson police issued 32,975 arrest warrants for a city with a population of just 21,000 people.[41]

At the heart of over-criminalization in America is the failed and counterproductive "War on Drugs." There were 1.5 million arrests for drug violations in 2012. Cumulatively, there were roughly 21.8 million arrests for drug violations from 2000 through 2012.[42] Although many of those arrests may involve repeat offenders, the War on Drugs clearly results in the arrest of millions of Americans—and those Americans are more likely to be poor or minorities.

Studies have repeatedly shown little variation in rates of drug use by race. For instance, according to the 2014 National Survey on Drug Use and Health, 53.8 percent of whites have used drugs at some point in their lives, compared with 47.6 percent of African Americans and 38.9 percent of Latinos. The rate of survey subjects who reported having used drugs the previous month was slightly higher for African Americans: 12.4 percent for blacks, 9.5 percent for whites, and just 8.9 percent for Latinos. Studies also show that drug users tend to purchase their drugs from members of the same race, suggesting that there is also little racial variation among dealers, at least at the lower levels of the drug chain.[43] The drug-related arrest rate is significantly higher for the black population, at 870 arrests per 100,000 residents compared with 332 for whites.[44] Lest one assume that this disparity stems from a propensity of African Americans to consume harder drugs, blacks are 3.7 times more likely than whites to be arrested for marijuana possession.[45] In some states, such as Alabama, Illinois, Iowa, Kansas, Kentucky, Minnesota, Nebraska, Nevada, New York, Pennsylvania, and Wisconsin, the marijuana arrest rate is at least six times higher for blacks than whites.[46] African Americans, especially those who are poor, are the biggest victims of the War on Drugs.[47]

Of course, drug laws are not the only laws against victimless crimes that adversely affect the poor. For instance, laws against sex work are especially damaging for women who are poor. Those sex workers most likely to engage in outdoor work (such as street walkers as opposed to escorts, who practice "indoor work") and are therefore more likely to be arrested, are more likely to come from low-income backgrounds and suffer from other social problems, such as substance abuse and lack of education. Such arrests, of course, further limit their future options. In the same way that young black men are often penalized for life because of a minor drug arrest, young women may be permanently burdened from a prostitution arrest. Every year, some 24,400 women (and 11,100 men) are arrested for "prostitution and commercialized vice."[48]

While laws against drugs, sex work, gambling, and other vices are obvious examples of over-criminalization, they are by no means the only areas of criminal justice overreach. That means that efforts to decriminalize society should be much broader, encompassing everything from tax offenses to occupational code violations. Politicians should realize that every time they make something illegal, they are empowering the police to enforce that law through the use of force, with all that entails for the criminal justice system. A law is not merely an advisory opinion; it is a mandate for the use of force, arrest, trial, imprisonment, and all the rest.

The second step in criminal justice reform requires greater efforts at every stage of the system, from policing to prosecuting, to ensure that suspects and defendants are treated fairly and equally.

Start with policing. In recent years, media attention has focused heavily on the unnecessary deaths of young black men at the hands of police. The actual evidence is mixed as to whether or not police shoot African Americans at disproportionate rates, but those same studies also show that police treat African Americans differently and more harshly in other regards. For example, research by Harvard's Roland Fryer showed that African Americans were far more likely to be the victims of other forms of police misconduct.[49] As we have seen, African Americans and the poor are more likely to be stopped, questioned, and arrested.

Once an arrest occurs, the biases in the criminal justice system only become more pronounced for the poor and minorities accused of a crime. Fixing this requires several changes to the way the system operates today.

We should reform the bail system so that it fulfills its intended goal of ensuring that a defendant appears for trial and of protecting society from a defendant who is liable to re-offend while awaiting trial. In recent years, bail has been required of more and more defendants. In some jurisdictions, an expensive bail fee can be applied to even minor offenses like traffic tickets.[50] As a result, on any given day, more than 730,000 Americans are in jail *awaiting* trial. Some will be held only briefly, but many will be held for months or sometimes even years.[51]

Nor is bail applied in an even-handed manner. There is no uniform bail schedule nationwide, and most states likewise leave bail decisions up to individual prosecutors and judges. This can make bail awards capricious and arbitrary. Moreover, judges generally consider factors such as employment, finances, community ties, character references, and family, as well as offense, criminal history, and appearance record at past court proceedings.[52] These criteria naturally work to the disadvantage of the poor. In addition, surveys show that African Americans and Latinos are far more likely to be held on bail and are typically assigned higher bail costs than white defendants charged with similar crimes.[53]

Bail is particularly burdensome for those with lower incomes. Even when poor individuals manage to post bail, they often end up depleting their savings or credit as a consequence. Sometimes they lack the resources to pay even relatively inexpensive bails. For example, in Virginia, 92 percent of those being held on bond had bail set at $5,000 or below. And a 2010 study from New York City found that only 21 percent of those assigned bail as low as $500 were able to make bail.[54] Recall that Sandra Bland, who died in police custody in Waller County, Texas, following a traffic stop, was in jail because she couldn't come up with the roughly $500 she needed to pay the bail bondsmen to post her bail.[55]

An inability to post bail can be devastating for the poor, even if they are eventually acquitted. Even a short pretrial detention often results in the loss of a job. And the removal of defendants from already fragile families is a recurrent theme in the criminal justice system.

Another step in reforming criminal justice is to ensure meaningful legal representation at every stage of the judicial process. As anyone who has ever watched a police procedural television show knows, a person accused of a crime has the right to consult with an attorney and to have that attorney present during questioning, and if she is indigent, an attorney will be provided at no cost to represent her.[56] In practice, however, the poor often lack access to adequate counsel.

As many as 80 percent of criminal defendants cannot afford to pay a lawyer, or cannot pay for one over the extended period of a criminal case.[57] Except on rare occasions, indigent defendants tend to receive their counsel through one of two methods: public defenders or assigned counsel. The exact mechanism varies significantly from state to state. Just 24 states have statewide public defender programs.[58] In other states, responsibility for establishing and funding such programs is the responsibility of counties or municipalities, which may or may not follow through. Nationwide, only about 15,000 public defenders are available to represent millions of criminal suspects before trial, defendants at trial, and those convicted but appealing their cases.[59] The burden on each attorney is mind-boggling. In Miami-Dade County, Florida, for instance, the average public defender handles 500 felonies and 225 misdemeanors per year.[60] In Kentucky, for example, two-thirds of defendants accused of misdemeanors appeared in court without an attorney.[61]

Where public defenders are not available, defendants may be "assigned counsel" from a list of attorneys available to the court, case by case.[62] Often, these attorneys are whoever is hanging around the courtroom with some free time. Some attorneys even make a career of waiting for assigned cases. Even when low-income defendants do have counsel, the quality of legal representation is extremely uneven. Although much maligned, public defenders actually do a fair job, roughly on par with private counsel. But assigned counsels have a far worse record. Defendants with assigned counsel are 5.2 percent more likely to be convicted on the most serious charge in the indictment and end up with a sentence an average of 3.4 months longer than defendants with other counsel.[63]

We also need to limit the abuse of prosecutorial discretion. After all, prosecutors have enormous leeway regarding whether to charge someone, what to charge them with, and when to accept a plea bargain. As Michelle Alexander points out in *The New Jim Crow*:

> Few rules constrain the exercise of prosecutorial discretion. The prosecutor is free to dismiss a case for any reason or no reason at all, regardless of the strength of evidence. The prosecutor is also free to file more charges against a defendant than can realistically be proven in court, so long as probable cause exists. Whether a good plea deal is offered to a defendant is entirely up to the prosecutor. And, if the mood strikes, a prosecutor can transfer drug defendants to the federal system, where the penalties are far more severe. Juveniles, for their part, can be transferred to adult court, where they can be sent to adult prison.[64]

Prosecutorial decisions are entirely discretionary and mostly unreviewable, making the prosecutor perhaps the most pivotal player in the entire criminal justice system. Even if there were not a hint of racial or other animus in a prosecutor's decisions, there is still constant pressure and systemic incentives to obtain convictions. Seldom are prosecutors praised for failing to bring a case or letting someone get off. Conversely, high conviction rates are often viewed as a mark of success.

Plea bargaining places an enormous amount of power in the hands of prosecutors. It has been estimated that 94 percent of all state criminal cases end in a plea bargain.[65] Unfortunately, studies have repeatedly shown that prosecutors tend to offer the poor and minorities either a harsher deal or no deal at all. One study of 700,000 criminal defendants conducted by the *San Jose Mercury News* found that "at virtually every stage of pretrial negotiations, whites were more successful than non-whites."[66] Prosecutors also routinely charge African Americans with more severe offenses for the same underlying act.[67] African American juveniles are also more likely to be tried by prosecutors as adults than their white counterparts. A 2014 analysis by the National Center for Juvenile Justice found that although African American youths compose 17 percent of the total juvenile prison population, they account for 31 percent of juvenile arrests and 43 percent of juveniles sentenced to adult prisons.[68]

If African Americans go to trial and are convicted, they tend to be sentenced to longer prison terms than whites who are convicted of the same offense and with similar criminal histories.[69] One study estimates that an African American has a roughly 30 percent higher probability of imprisonment than a white defendant charged with the same crime.[70] Another study by the U.S. Sentencing Commission found that, on average, sentences for African American men were 20 percent longer than for similar white defendants.[71]

We should review sentencing to ensure that the punishment fits the crime and is being applied equally. It is a fundamental principle of criminal justice that the sentence should be proportionate to the offense. The necessity of reform is not merely a matter of fairness, but an essential check on untrammeled government power. This reasoning is deeply rooted and frequently repeated in common-law jurisprudence.[72] But it is a principle that our criminal justice system has increasingly lost sight of.

In particular, mandatory minimum sentences have led to punishments that cannot be justified as "fitting the crime."[73] Today more than 55,000 Americans are serving mandatory minimum sentences for drug offenses alone.[74] On average they are serving a sentence of more than 11 years.[75]

So-called three strikes laws are also a problem. These are laws that automatically enhance sentences if the defendant has a previous conviction. A third conviction can result in a mandatory life sentence. While this can help take dangerous career criminals off the street, these laws seldom differentiate between serious and petty offenses. To cite just one example, more than 2,000 people have received a life sentence without parole under Alabama's Habitual Felony Offender Act, often because of earlier convictions for minor crimes such as writing bad checks, simple drug possession, and nonviolent theft of property.[76]

Even under traditional sentencing guidelines, there is often a disparity in penalties that results in discriminatory outcomes. The penalty for crack cocaine, used mostly by the poor and minorities, is several times as severe as the penalty for the powdered cocaine that is more often used in wealthier communities and by whites.[77]

While fines are often employed as an alternative to prison, they can also create problems. For example, fines are not generally tied to ability to pay. The collection of criminal debt can often add 40 percent or more in interest and processing fees. As a result, fines can pose an enormous and disproportionate hardship on the poor.[78]

No one is suggesting that the punishment for a crime should be means-tested. But penalties should be proportional, and judges should keep in mind the practical effect of the penalties that they impose. A traffic ticket or citation for marijuana possession may be a modest annoyance for a middle-class individual. For the poor, this same penalty can amount to financial ruin. In some cases, failure to pay fines or fees can even result in jail time. When fines are included as an additional punishment on top of jail time, the accumulated debt can make re-entry into society that much more difficult. The U.S. Justice Department has warned that excessive fines mean that "Individuals may confront escalating debt; face repeated, unnecessary incarceration for nonpayment despite posing no danger to the community; lose their jobs; and become trapped in cycles of poverty that can be nearly impossible to escape."[79]

Finally, we should do everything we can to make it easier for ex-offenders to reenter society and to support themselves and their families. One should think of prisoners who are released as having served their time. Yet difficulties involved in dealing with parole or probation are just the tip of the iceberg for many former inmates. As one former inmate put it, "My sentence began the day I was released."[80]

Ex-offenders face a wide variety of barriers to reintegrating into society. These barriers make it far more difficult for returning prisoners to find jobs, support their families, and move into the mainstream of productive society. As a result, they will either be pushed back to crime or end up living in poverty.

Part of making it easier for ex-offenders to reenter society would entail greater efforts to ensure that those in prison receive the education and training that will prepare them for their release and that adequate post-release services be available. On the positive side, nearly all prisons now offer some form of education or training services. Still, participation and success rates are low. For example, about 20 percent of inmates participate in GED classes, but only about half of those actually achieve a high school diploma. Studies show that completion of a prison education program can increase post-release wages by roughly 15 percent, and improving participation in these programs may reduce rates of both criminal recidivism and post-release poverty.[81]

In addition to academic education programs, nearly all federal prisons also offer instruction in vocational or work-related skills. However, only about 57 percent of state prisons do.[82] There are also prison work programs, and, for some minimum-security inmates, work release programs.[83] Sadly, participation in all these programs has either stagnated or declined over the past decades. To illustrate, the percentage of prisoners participating in prison work assignments fell from 74 percent in 1970 to 66 percent in 2014.[84] This suggests that prisons should undertake considerable efforts to encourage participation in such programs. After release, intensive job search programs have shown success in reducing recidivism for nonviolent offenders. The "intensive" adjective is particularly important here. For instance, a randomized controlled trial reviewed by economists Christopher Bollinger and Aaron Yelowitz and others found that only 39 percent of parolees in the intensive job search program were rearrested, with an average of 2.9 charges, compared with 46 percent of the parolees in a more standard program, who had an average of 5.9 charges.[85]

But none of these policies are likely to be entirely successful unless we deal with the legal and structural barriers to reintegrating ex-offenders into the economy. For example, roughly 70 percent of employers currently conduct criminal background checks on job applicants. That's nearly double the rate from as recently as 20 years ago.[86] Nor are criminal background checks merely a formality. Roughly 60 percent of potential employers say that they would not consider an ex-offender for a job.[87] Other surveys show that barely a quarter of businesses would consider hiring someone with a drug-related conviction on their record, while only 7 percent would consider someone previously convicted of a property related crime like burglary or auto theft, and barely 1 percent would even consider someone with a conviction for a violent crime.[88] Even when not dismissed outright, job applicants with criminal records will almost certainly find themselves at a disadvantage throughout the application process.

There is also reason to be concerned about the accuracy and interpretation of information in criminal background checks. Most such checks on prospective employees use data that may contain not only convictions, but arrests for which charges were eventually withdrawn or dismissed. The data are often difficult to understand, leading employers to assume a conviction where there may not be one. For instance, when prosecutors in Maryland drop a case it goes into the record as *nolle prosequi* (unwilling to pursue).[89] What is a prospective employer to make of that obscure legal jargon?

In other cases, the final outcome may not be part of the data at all. In Pennsylvania, for example, a background check through the state police system will generate only a generic arrest code, with details to follow separately. That additional information can take up to four weeks. Will potential employers really wait a month to find out whether an arrest ended in a conviction?[90]

Even when employers are willing to hire ex-offenders, they are often barred by state laws from many professions. Individuals with a criminal record may be denied occupational licenses or prohibited from working in many occupations. According to an article in *Criminology and Public Policy*, there could be as many as 800 occupations nationwide that automatically disqualify people with felony convictions for life.[91] Not only do these restrictions extend to jobs with public safety or fiduciary concerns, which might be understandable, but also to such careers as cosmetologist, plumber, and even funeral director.[92]

It's not just employers who rely on criminal background checks. Nearly 80 percent of landlords, for instance, run checks on potential tenants. There is no evidence that a criminal record makes a potential renter less likely to be a good tenant.[93] Still, many landlords fear not only dangers from the tenant themselves, but also a possible reaction from other tenants, as well as potential lawsuits should something happen. A blanket refusal to rent to ex-offenders can run afoul of the Fair Housing Act, but even so, many landlords continue to make it more difficult for ex-offenders to rent. Moreover, the U.S. Department of Housing and Urban Development has said that the Fair Housing Act does not apply in cases of renters convicted of the manufacture and distribution of illegal drugs.[94]

A criminal record also limits future educational opportunities. For example, federal law imposes a lifetime ban on participation in some tuition assistance programs, such as the American Opportunity Tax Credit, for anyone convicted of a drug-related felony.[95] Whatever the problems with federal tuition assistance—and there are many—there is no doubt that such a blanket ban has a disparate impact on the poor and minorities. Also, roughly two-thirds of colleges and universities ask about criminal histories or conduct background checks as part of the application process.[96] While colleges are less likely than employers or landlords to consider a criminal record as an absolute bar to admission, it cannot help but be a barrier, a problem exacerbated by the fact that less than half of colleges have a written policy on the question, and just 40 percent train admissions personnel on how to handle it.[97]

If ex-offenders cannot transition back into productive society, it should come as no surprise that they re-offend. Roughly two-thirds of those released from state prisons are rearrested within three years.[98] Half of those released from federal prison are rearrested within eight years following their release. Even former inmates who successfully stay out of jail often struggle to become productive, self-supporting citizens. Creating barriers to employment, education, and housing is unfair, and it is likely to condemn millions to a life of poverty.

Several states have begun to recognize the problem. Since 2009, 11 states (California, Colorado, Connecticut, Delaware, Illinois, Maryland, Massachusetts, Nebraska, New Mexico, Minnesota, and Rhode Island) and the District of Columbia have enacted variations of so-called ban the box legislation, limiting the use of criminal history in employment decisions. In addition, Hawaii has offered such protections to ex-offenders since 1998.[99] But a criminal history is still a barrier to employment in most states, and federal legislation has so far been blocked by congressional Republicans.

Even purging criminal records may not solve the deeper, underlying problem: a tendency on the part of some employers to associate young minority men with criminality. This ongoing racial stereotyping means that prohibitions on employer consideration of criminal records in hiring may actually increase racial discrimination as employers may use race as a proxy for criminal history.[100] A study by Jennifer L. Doleac of the University of Virginia and Benjamin Hansen of the University of Oregon, for instance, found that "banning the box" actually decreased the likelihood that a young black man would be hired by 5.1 percent and a young Latino man by 2.9 percent.[101]

The best answer to the criminal history dilemma may simply be to stop arresting people for things that shouldn't be crimes in the first place and to ensure that those detained for legitimate crimes are treated fairly throughout the criminal justice system. No one is suggesting that crime is not a legitimate government concern. Indeed, poor communities suffer disproportionately from high crime rates. In 2016, blacks made up 15 percent of violent crime victims despite accounting for only 13 percent of the total population.[102] There are economic consequences too. Businesses are naturally reluctant to locate in high crime areas, exacerbating the joblessness, poverty, and urban blight in those neighborhoods.

Criminologists debate whether our current approach is an effective response to the dangers of crime. What is indisputable, however, is that it adds to poverty. We will not be able to significantly reduce poverty in America unless we reform our criminal justice system.

Fortunately, this is one area where there has been some bipartisan progress. In 2010, Congress passed, and President Obama signed, the Fair Sentencing Act, which reduced, but did not eliminate, the disparity between crack and powdered cocaine sentences.[103] The independent U.S. Sentencing Commission has moved to amend federal sentencing guidelines to reduce the penalties for certain drug crimes.[104] While good news, those changes will affect only a small number of federal prisoners.[105]

Of greater concern, under President Donald Trump and Attorney General Jeff Sessions, there appears already to be serious backsliding on reform. Sessions has repeatedly called for a return to the worst days of the War on Drugs, seeking to reinstate mandatory minimum sentencing, to strengthen asset forfeiture, and to implement other draconian policies.[106] He has also sought to weaken federal oversight of police departments found to engage in racial profiling or other improper conduct.[107] Those concerned about basic fairness in our criminal justice system should resist these efforts to turn back the clock. Those who are concerned about reducing poverty in America should join them.

CHAPTER SIX: IMPROVING HUMAN CAPITAL: THE IMPORTANCE OF EDUCATION FREEDOM

It is doubtful that any child may reasonably be expected to succeed in life if he is denied the opportunity of an education.

—*Brown v. Board of Education (1954)*[1]

If anti-poverty policy is to move away from simple redistribution to better preparing people who are poor to take charge of their lives and become self-sufficient, we need to place greater emphasis on building "human capital."

However, "human capital" is an amorphous term that can be, and has been, distorted to encompass almost anything that a proponent of government programs wants. Perhaps the best definition comes from Nobel laureate Gary Becker, who described it as the abilities and qualities of people that make them productive. Knowledge is the most important of these, but other factors, from a sense of punctuality to the state of someone's health, also matter.[2]

Historically, efforts to improve human capital for the poor have focused on job training. The federal government oversees some 47 job training programs, and there are many more at the state and local level. Study after study has found little evidence that such programs deliver cost-effective improvements on wages or the ability to be employed. Those few programs that are successful in raising long-term prospects are both intensive and expensive. Promising results collected from small-scale trials do not scale well at all, demonstrating the limits of decisions made by far-away bureaucrats. In the case of specialized training, just because a particular skill has been shown to be useful for a particular set of disadvantaged workers, it does not necessarily mean the training will generalize well for all workers or can be applied on a broader scale.[3]

A handful of public training programs show some effectiveness, albeit in a modest way. However, none can promise to move people out of poverty cost-effectively.[4] Worse, sometimes even the most intensive and expensive are not only inefficient but also can actually hurt those that they intend to help.[5]

One popular theory is that if disadvantaged youths or displaced adults were merely given a job, the rest would shake itself out.[6] In contrast to training programs, temporary jobs programs that put low-skilled workers directly into jobs are far less costly, but they often fail to offer sustained benefits to the temporary employees. As an example, the employment and earning effects tend not to persist long after the job program.[7] The jobs most likely to require government subsidies to fill are hard to fill for a reason. People don't want them because they are mostly dead-ends; they offer little room in terms of promotion or career development. In some cases, putting individuals in temporary-help jobs through government placement programs may even diminish earnings in the long run.[8]

The concept of human capital encompasses far more than hard skills like the ability to write software code or knowledge of how to operate a crane. Indeed, James Heckman, a leading economist in the area of human capital development, points out that not all skills are cognitive.[9] They include factors such as such as perseverance, motivation, and reliability.

Private and charitable organizations that try to prepare individuals who are poor for future employment—organizations as varied as the Doe Fund in New York City and the Milton Hershey School in Pennsylvania—report a common concern that many poor individuals need to learn such soft employment skills as showing up for work on time every day, taking instructions, and getting along with bosses and coworkers.[10]

Corroborating this concern is research from the journal *Review of Economic Studies*, which found that the wage premium for high school graduates compared with dropouts in both semiskilled and skilled occupations can be traced to the same perseverance that led the graduates to stay in school.[11] The study by Heckman and others found that noncognitive skills are almost as predictive as cognitive ones in determining wages.[12]

Because we either cannot or do not know how to teach noncognitive skills reliably, expectations of our ability to raise low-skilled individuals' human capital need to be somewhat tempered. Government interventions designed to increase soft skills have generally been no more successful than have efforts to build hard skills. For example, the mayor of New York City, Michael Bloomberg, experimented with cash incentives, but those programs yielded few long-term gains.[13] The cash benefits raised beneficiaries' incomes, but incomes declined again as soon as the grants ended. School attendance increased, but educational outcomes did not improve. Nonprogram employment and incomes did not improve.

All this has led many poverty experts to conclude that there may be only a limited ability to change human capital for adults. By the time a person who is poor reaches adulthood, the damage (whether one considers that damage to have structural or cultural causes) may already have been done. Certainly, a relatively consistent finding in the literature on human capital is that the potential return on investment declines gradually with age, even aside from the number of productive years available to an individual before retirement.[14]

We might conclude, therefore, that we would see far higher returns by focusing our efforts on children, especially very young children. For this reason, many progressives have advocated increased spending for Head Start and other preschool programs for the youngest children.

In practice, most government preschool programs have little lasting effect. In particular, studies show that although children participating in Head Start and other preschool programs *do* show modest improvements in academic achievement while the child is in preschool, those gains fade out rapidly once the child enters school. By the end of first grade, nearly all the gains have evaporated.[15]

For example, the Head Start Impact Study found statistically significant, although modest, improvements in both reading and math for children in Head Start. However, these positive results did not survive the child's first year of school. By the end of first grade, there was no discernable difference between Head Start participants and other children.[16] A study of Tennessee's statewide preschool program also found modest academic gains for students while they participated in pre-kindergarten, but those gains faded by the end of the kindergarten year to the point where differences between participants and nonparticipants were no longer statistically significant.[17]

These two studies are particularly noteworthy because of their rigorous methodology. They are randomized control trials. That is, they randomly assigned children to either a treatment group—in this case attending pre-K—or a control group—in this instance, no pre-K. Then researchers followed them for several years to see if the pre-K children showed greater achievement gains than children without pre-K.[18] Studies of this type reduce the possibility of "selection bias" that may distort other studies, by ensuring comparisons between "like" and "like." These studies also benefited from massive population samples. The Head Start Impact Study included 2,600 children in the preschool group and 1,800 students in the control group.[19] The Tennessee study evaluated 3,000 students between the treatment and control groups.[20] All of this makes the results especially noteworthy.

There are, however, two important exceptions to this record of preschool failures that deserve some additional discussion: (1) the Perry Preschool Program experiment and (2) the Abecedarian Project, both of which showed significant long-term benefits for the students who participated. One should be careful about generalizing from two programs that educated a handful of children more than 40 years ago. Still, the results were impressive. The Abecedarian Project, for instance, produced a measurable gain in IQ (slightly more than four points), as well as more than a full year's worth of educational gain by age 21. Program participants were more likely to attend college and to be employed than were similar individuals who did not go through the program. The benefits seem to hold in follow-up research as long as 40 years after students completed the program[21] The Perry Preschool Program also generated long-term positive outcomes, not just in academic performance, but also in increased college attendance, higher employment levels, lower crime rates, and other factors, compared with similar children who did not attend the preschool program.[22]

However, before using these studies to justify universal preschool, we should understand that both programs may be hard to scale. They were far more intense—and costly—than traditional preschool programs. These programs were outliers precisely because they were unlike other preschool programs.

Equally important, both programs included a level of intervention that would be difficult to reproduce nationwide. Some estimates put the cost of Abecedarian-style preschool at nearly $90,000 per child (in today's dollars).[23] The Perry Preschool model is less expensive, roughly $20,000 per child, but still enormously costly if implemented universally.[24]

Moreover, even if we could replicate the conditions in these programs, there is no guarantee that we would produce the same results. Indeed, an attempt to replicate the Abecedarian method on a national basis, a program known as Early Head Start, failed to achieve the same results as the original experiment. Follow-up studies of Early Head Start participants found few significant long-term benefits, especially for poor and disadvantaged children.[25]

Hopes that early childhood education and other childhood interventions would provide a significant victory against poverty appear to be misplaced.

The Key to Human Capital: Reforming a Broken Educational System

All is not lost, however. There is one area where reforms can significantly improve human capital for the poor: education reform at the K–12 level.

As we saw in chapter 3, education is one of the fundamental determinants of income. Failure to finish school vastly increases the chances that someone will end up in poverty. At the same time, public schools are doing an increasingly poor job of educating children, especially children who grow up in poverty. The consequences are stark and grow steadily worse with each successive generation. We are not going to see inclusive prosperity and economic mobility without addressing these underlying educational disparities.

For reasons of race and geography, our schools are increasingly segregated along class lines. Nationwide, about 40 percent of students in low-income families (10 million) attend high-poverty schools—that is, schools where more than 75 percent of students come from low-income families. Only about 6 percent of students in low-income families attend low-poverty schools, where less than 25 percent of students come from low-income families.[26] At the same time, only about 6 percent of students from families that are not low income attend high-poverty schools.[27] It is impossible to deny the extent to which educational opportunities divide our society.

Studies have consistently found that students from schools attended mostly by poor children have lower levels of academic achievement than those from schools attended by more affluent students. Of course, some might blame this disparity on the many other social problems facing poor children, problems that no school, no matter how good, can remedy. Many teachers complain that they are expected to make up for missing parents, poor nutrition, neighborhood violence, and other issues outside their control. They cannot be expected to do so. Nonetheless, the fact that those same poor children, facing those same social problems, perform better in schools from high-income neighborhoods is "one of the most consistent findings in research on education," according to Gary Orfield and Susan Eaton of Harvard.[28]

In fact, some studies show that a student's educational achievement correlates at least as strongly with his or her classmates' family income as with that of their own family.[29] A dismal 18 percent of children nationwide from low-income families score "proficient" on scholastic achievement tests, compared with roughly 48 percent of the rest of the student population. However, in schools with high concentrations of low-income students, just 7.8 percent of low-income students, less than half as many, score "proficient."[30] As Robert Putnam writes in *Our Kids: The American Dream in Crisis*, "there's no denying that rich and poor kids in this country attend vastly different schools," a fact that he blames in part for "the growing youth class gap."[31]

If class divides our government school system, so too does race. Sixty years after *Brown v. Board of Education*, our schools are once again becoming segregated by race. From 2000 to 2014, the number of schools with an enrollment of more than 75 percent African American or Latino students has nearly doubled, from 9 percent to 16 percent.[32] The connections between race and class have already been discussed.

The consequences of being trapped in a bad school can be lifelong. In one study, students in Tennessee and their teachers were randomly assigned to classrooms within their schools from kindergarten to third grade. Students who were randomly assigned to higher quality classrooms in grades K–3 (according to classmates' end-of-class test scores) had higher earnings, college attendance rates, and other outcomes.[33]

Proponents of public education have long argued that increased spending provides the solution to our growing education crisis, particularly for schools in low-income neighborhoods. However, the case that increasing the money spent on public schools will lead to increased educational performance is weak at best.

Spending by the U.S. Department of Education (DOE) rose from $27.25 billion in 1970 to $79.00 billion in 2016, in constant 2016 dollars.[34] That actually understates federal education spending, since many agencies outside the DOE also spend money on education programs. Moreover, while federal spending accounts for a growing piece of the overall pie, state and local governments contribute most of the spending for public education. Nationally, education spending by government has risen by more than 250 percent since 1970 (in inflation-adjusted terms).[35] On average, public schools spend roughly $12,300 per student per year.[36] Per pupil, that is more money than any country besides Luxembourg spends.[37] It is hard to make a serious case that education is underfunded.

Moreover, as Figure 6.1 shows, increases in education spending have done nothing to improve national performance scores in math, reading, and science.

Figure 6.1

Trends in American Public Schooling since 1970

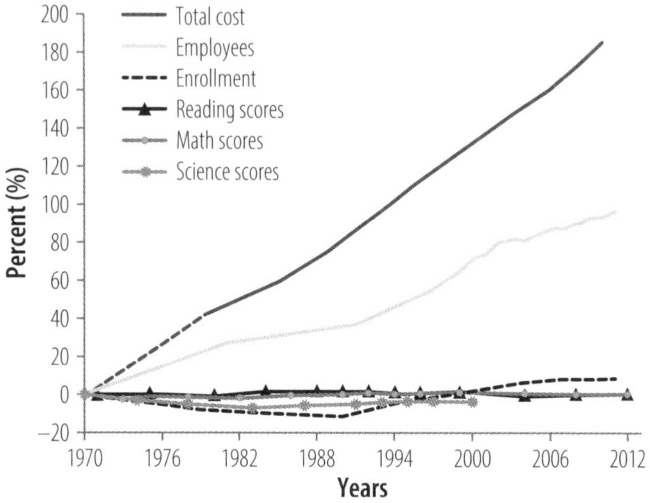

Sources: Andrew J. Coulson, "State Education Trends Academic Performance and Spending over the Past 40 Years," Cato Institute Policy Analysis no. 746, March 18, 2014, http://object.cato.org/sites/cato.org/files/pubs/pdf/pa746.pdf; based on data from U.S. Department of Education, "Digest of Education Statistics"; National Assessment of Educational Progress, "Long Term Trends, 17-Year-Olds."

The evidence of a lack of correlation between expenditures and results is clear at the aggregate level, yet this evidence does not necessarily mean that increased spending will not bring improvements in particular local school systems. Here, the evidence is more ambiguous. Eric Hanushek, perhaps the leading expert on this issue, has studied the effect of per-pupil expenditures on academic outcomes, finding either no relationship or a relationship that is weak or inconsistent, while other scholars have found benefits in specific cases, depending on how the money was used.[38] Despite the lack of consensus, leading researchers in the area agree that any effect of per-pupil expenditures on academic outcomes depends on how the money is spent, not on how much money is spent.

For example, Hanushek concludes, "Few people . . . would recommend just dumping extra resources into existing schools."[39] From the other side of debate, Larry Hedges and Rob Greenwald note, "The results do not provide detailed information on the educationally or economically efficient means to allocate existing and new dollars."[40]

In fact, some of the worst-performing public school systems have some of the highest levels of per pupil spending. Baltimore, for example, ranks fourth among the major cities in per-pupil expenditures for districts with more than 40,000 students, and it spends $16,578 a year per pupil—roughly 52 percent above the national average. The majority of that money comes not from the city itself but from the state and federal governments. Yet 70 percent of Baltimore public school students did not score high enough on their High School Assessment test to meet the national standard, and more than half failed to reach that bar on the English exam. SAT scores for Baltimore students are more than 100 points below the national average.[41]

Similarly, Detroit spends nearly $14,860 per pupil, but also has the nation's worst graduation rate among major school districts.[42] A quarter of Detroit's students fail to graduate.[43] On the 2015 National Assessment of Educational Progress tests, 93 percent of Detroit students were rated not proficient in reading, and an astounding 96 percent were not proficient in math.[44]

Moreover, Washington, D.C., spends an astonishing $26,670 per student, making it the biggest spending public school system in the nation.[45] On the latest round of standardized testing, fully 83 percent of the eighth graders in the District's schools were not proficient in reading, and 81 percent were not proficient in math.[46] Obviously, those school districts have other problems that are going to make educating children more difficult. Still, it is hard to look at those results and argue that money alone can solve the problem of educating poor children.

Efforts to federalize education, both in teaching standards and in funding, have been no more successful. Take the most recent federal education initiatives, No Child Left Behind, Race to the Top, and Common Core.[47]

Under No Child Left Behind (NCLB), small improvements were made in math and reading scores for children who were poor.[48] That

Figure 6.2

National Assessment of Educational Progress: Average Math and Reading Scores for Age 17

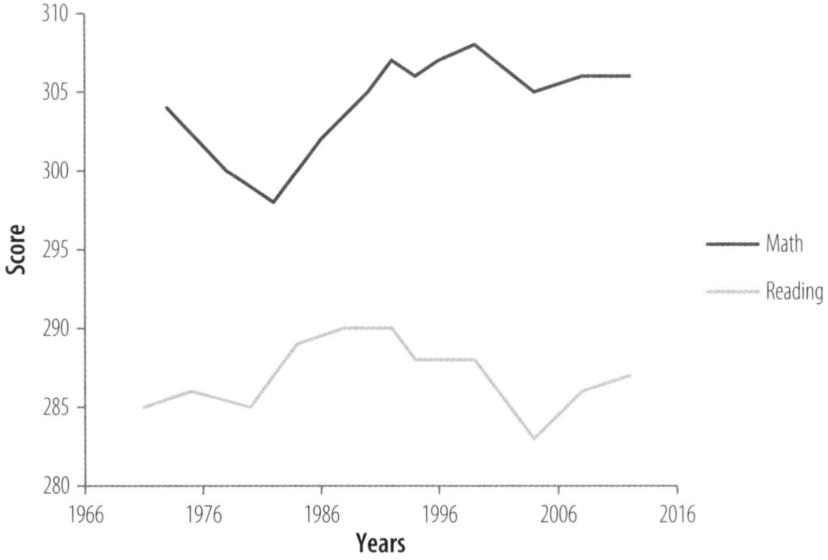

Source: National Center for Education Statistics, "The Condition of Education 2016," U.S. Department of Education, NCES 2016-144, https://nces.ed.gov/pubs2016/2016144.pdf.

sounds like modestly good news. However, there is little evidence that these improvements can be traced to NCLB, because similar levels of improvement can be found in the years immediately before its implementation.

Race to the Top and Common Core are newer initiatives, so we have less data on success. However, so far, there is little evidence that either program has significantly influenced the trajectory of education in this country. (Figure 6.2).[49] This lack of progress is particularly disturbing because these programs focused both students and teachers on standardized tests in ways that they were not previously, including teaching to the test and employing more strategies to exploit test designs and rules.

Our public schools were failing before the recent rise in federal intervention. They continue to fail in the aftermath of federalization.

And, the biggest losers from that failure are likely to be the children who are poor and otherwise disadvantaged.

Incremental Reforms

That federal efforts have mostly been ineffective does not mean incremental steps cannot be taken to improve education, even within the confines of the public school system.

For example, we can make it easier to fire bad teachers. Numerous studies have shown that teacher quality is key to student performance. For example, a study of Los Angeles students by Thomas Kane of Harvard found that those students who had a teacher in the bottom 5 percent of competence for just one year lost the equivalent of 1.0 to 1.5 months of learning compared with students with an average teacher.[50] Other studies show that simply one semester's improvement in math teacher quality raises student math scores by roughly one-fifth of average yearly gains.[51]

Even more alarming, a study by Raj Chetty and John Friedman of Harvard and Jonah Rockoff of Columbia found that replacing a teacher who is in the bottom 5 percent with an average teacher increases the present value of the students' lifetime income by $250,000.[52] That is a potential financial windfall that low-income students cannot afford to forgo. Clearly, the quality of teachers matters.

Unfortunately, the teachers' unions continue to resist any changes to the current system of tenure, a system that protects even the worst teachers. In California, the nation's largest school system, a teacher can earn tenure after just 16 months in a classroom. In Mississippi, tenure can be awarded in just a year. South Carolina and Vermont also provide tenure in two years or less. Another 32 states grant tenure in three years.

Once a teacher receives tenure, it becomes difficult and costly to fire, or even to reassign the teacher. For instance, in California it can take at least 2 years, and possibly as long as 10, to dismiss a poorly performing teacher.[53] The cost of the dismissal action can run to more than $450,000.[54] As a result, many school administrators report that they do not pursue dismissals even in egregious cases. Nationwide, there are 187 teachers per district on average, but roughly only 0.2 tenured teachers per district are dismissed as a result of poor performance each year.[55] Children who are poor cannot continue to be saddled with incompetent or underperforming teachers.

Along similar lines, school districts should not use seniority as the most important criteria in determining which teachers to lay off as part of staff reductions or in making teacher assignments. Eleven states currently require that, when layoffs are necessary because of either budgetary or enrollment considerations, teachers must be laid off in accordance with seniority, *regardless of performance evaluations*.[56]

Although it should be easier to fire bad teachers, it should also be easier to reward good teachers. That means merit pay and other ways to differentiate and reward high-performing teachers. Currently, virtually all teachers in a given school district receive the same pay based on their seniority, regardless of outcomes in their classrooms. This system occurs in few other professions. There's no real consensus about how teachers would be chosen to receive merit pay bonuses. Most likely it would be some combination of test scores, teacher evaluations, or other more intangible parameters. One particular benefit of merit pay is that it helps draw more qualified teachers to poorly performing schools, especially those in low-income neighborhoods.[57]

States should also consider ending teacher certification requirements altogether. One reason private and charter schools have good teachers but don't necessarily pay them more is that they lack worthless certification requirements. Studies show that teachers without a "college of education" background perform as well, or in many cases better, than those with certification gained by taking education college courses.[58] One can look at highly successful nonprofit organizations like Teach for America to see that certification or graduation from a college of education is unnecessary.[59]

The above proposals would undoubtedly improve public schools. Ultimately, however, there are limits to how much change can take place in the current system. The deeper problem lies, not with tenure or pay scales or federal bureaucracies, but with the very nature of the government-run education monopoly.

As even Albert Shanker, the near-legendary former president of the American Federation of Teachers, once admitted,

> It's time to admit that public education operates like a planned economy, a bureaucratic system in which everybody's role is spelled out in advance and there are few incentives for innovation and productivity. It is no surprise that our school system doesn't improve: it more resembles the communist economy than our own market economy.[60]

Choice and Competition

The only way to force truly meaningful change in education is to break up the monopolies themselves, creating more competition and giving more power to parents. That means parents must be free to send their children to whatever school they choose. Injecting competition, market forces, and parental choice into education will improve education for all Americans. However, the most significant effect will be in the inner cities and among low-income parents. Instead of being forced to send their children to underperforming schools, parents who are poor will have the choice of a wide variety of competing schools—Montessori, religious, Afrocentric, vocational, and traditional. Some children will still be born into poverty, but they will have a far better opportunity to get a good education, which has always been one of the best tickets out of poverty.

In general, students attend the school closest to where they live, but there are exceptions, depending on the state. Parents with the resources to do so choose neighborhoods with schools thought to provide better outcomes. For instance, a study by Sandra Black of the Brookings Institution used house prices to estimate the value parents place on school quality. After correcting for a variety of factors, she found that parents were willing to pay 2.1 percent more for a house if that added cost returned a 5 percent increase in elementary school test scores.[61] Children whose parents are poor and lack the resources to move to those better neighborhoods are left behind.

Forty-seven states and Washington, D.C., *do* offer some degree of public school choice (the exceptions are Alabama, Maryland, and Illinois), but many programs are limited. For example, students may only be able to transfer to other schools within their overall district. In other cases, transfers must be approved by district school administrators and may be limited to maintain diversity balances within schools.[62]

Under NCLB, students from underperforming schools could transfer to another school, but only within their district.[63] In practice, however, this right to transfer may be little more than window dressing. Given the roadblocks put in parents' way, fewer than 5 percent of parents affected ultimately move their children to a better school.[64]

Generally, the ultimate decision on where a child will attend school lies with the state, a proposition that has been upheld by the courts. In 2015, for instance, the Eighth U.S. Circuit Court of Appeals held that parents do not have a fundamental right to decide where to send their children to school.[65] It can, in fact, be a crime—a felony even—to lie about your address or to fail to inform the school district about a change of address in order to send your child to a better or safer school. In Washington, D.C., parents can get 90 days in jail for providing false documentation, and in Oklahoma, parents can go to jail for up to a year.[66] Some school districts employ private investigators to spy on parents and children to ensure they live at the correct address.[67] Boston, Massachusetts, schools maintain a tip line, offering rewards for parents to inform on children they think do not belong in their school.[68] Bayonne, New Jersey, offers a $200 bounty to anyone who provides credible evidence that a child is illegally enrolled.[69] In nearly every case where charges are brought, the case involves a child who is poor attempting to enroll in a school in a wealthy district. It is almost as if the children existed for the benefit of the public schools rather than the other way around.[70]

America's poor are the biggest losers of district-based education. Wealthy and middle-class parents can send their children to private schools or, at least, move to a district with better public schools. Low-income families are trapped, forced to send their children to public schools that often fail to educate.

It is time to give parents the right to decide what schools their children will attend. This action is achievable through a variety of ways, from charter schools to educational vouchers to tuition tax credits. Whatever the exact way, returning control to parents is essential to meaningful education reform.

Let's look more closely at the various options.

Perhaps the most common attempt to create more educational options is the establishment of charter schools. Charters have operated since at least the 1980s, when Philadelphia established a number of "schools within schools" and designated them as charters. Minnesota followed suit shortly after that and passed the first state charter school law in 1981. Today, 41 states have established charter schools, although, in some cases, the restrictions are so severe that few charters exist in practice.[71] Nationally, roughly 6.6 percent of public schools are charter schools, approximately 6,500 schools nationwide. The District of Columbia enrolls the largest proportion of public school students in charter schools, an astounding 42 percent, followed by Arizona at almost 18 percent.[72] Alabama, Kentucky, Mississippi, Montana, Nebraska, North Dakota, South Dakota, Vermont, Washington, and West Virginia do not have charter schools.

Charter schools are public—that is, government—schools. Some raise funds privately, but they do not charge tuition, and the overwhelming majority of their financing comes from taxpayers. They also must accept all students, including those with disabilities, and must participate in their state's testing and accountability systems. However, the school operates under a charter, a contract between the school and the state or local government, giving it greater autonomy over matters such as curriculum, personnel, and budgeting than traditional public schools. Because most charters operate independently from school districts, parents can enroll their children regardless of their home address. Some charters have a specific programmatic focus, such as STEM (science, technology, engineering, and math) or the arts, whereas others simply provide a mainstream education with a different academic approach.

According to the Center for Research on Education Outcomes, urban charter schools provide significantly higher levels of annual growth in both math and reading compared to traditional public schools.[73] These gains are largest for African American, Latino, low-income, and special-needs students. This is not to say that charter schools are uniformly excellent. There have been more than a few fly-by-night charter operations that have essentially defrauded taxpayers, parents, and students. The quality also varies significantly. For example, students attending urban charter schools in the District of Columbia, Boston, Newark, and Memphis gained as much as 50 school days' worth of advantage over their peers in traditional schools, while charter students in Fort Worth or Phoenix lost ground compared to more traditional public schools.[74] In general, charters work best in densely populated areas such as large cities where there are enough customers and suppliers to create a functioning market.[75]

On the other hand, the quality of charters appears to be improving. Inferior charters shut down, something that seldom happens to poor-performing traditional schools. Roughly 3 to 4 percent of charter schools close every year.[76] That is, after all, what markets are supposed to do, reward success and punish failure. As a result, charter schools have shown steadily improving results over the past decade. For instance, a study of charter schools in Texas concluded: "Our analysis clearly indicates that charter school quality has improved over time." The authors found the following: "This improvement is the result of three consistent changes. First, schools that close are drawn disproportionately from the least effective charter schools. Second, schools that open during the period of study far outperform those that close; the average value-added for new charters is roughly equal to the average among existing charters. Third, charter schools remaining open throughout the decade from 2001 to 2011 exhibit increases in average school value-added."[77]

While charter schools offer an alternative to traditional public schools, they are still, in the end, government-run schools. Government oversight puts limits on how innovative they can be. Therefore, an approach that is liable to yield even greater fruit for poor and disadvantaged students is to open up America's large and thriving private education sector to them.

Because private schools charge tuition, it can be difficult—if not impossible—for children from low-income families to attend them. The average cost of attending a private elementary school is $7,770 per year, and the cost of attending a private secondary school is approximately $13,000 annually, although in some states it can be more than twice as high.[78] As a result, only about 6 percent of students enrolled in private schools are poor, and another 9 percent are from "near poor" families.[79]

One way to rectify this disparity of opportunity is to provide parents with financial assistance if they wish to send their child to a private school. Essentially, the idea is that education funding should follow the child regardless of where that child attends school. And, in general, there are two mechanisms that are offered for accomplishing this: vouchers and tuition tax credits.

The most frequently discussed method is school vouchers. Vouchers provide parents a roughly equal amount of money to what would have otherwise been used to educate their child in a public school. Parents can then use that money to pay tuition at private schools (and in some cases public schools in another school district). In most cases, the money is paid directly to the school, and, depending on the program and the school, the voucher may or may not cover the full cost of tuition.[80] In addition, most legislative proposals are means-tested, available only to low-income parents or made otherwise conditional. This generally avoids what would effectively be a cash windfall for wealthier families that are already sending their children to private schools.

The city of Milwaukee, Wisconsin, established the first voucher program for the 1990–1991 school year. It provided financial assistance to low-income parents to send their children to nonsectarian private schools and was later expanded to include religiously affiliated ones as well.[81] Currently, 14 states and the District of Columbia operate voucher programs. However, in most cases, these programs are strictly limited in scope. For instance, in eight states, vouchers are limited to special-needs students. Five states (Indiana, Louisiana, North Carolina, Ohio, Wisconsin) plus Washington, D.C., have more extensive programs, covering low-income students or students from underperforming public schools. Roughly 170,000 students participate in voucher programs.[82]

Research shows that students usually benefit from voucher programs, particularly those from minority and poor backgrounds. There have been 18 empirical studies examining academic outcomes for school choice programs using random assignment, the gold standard of social science. Of those, six found improved student outcomes for all participating in the voucher program, while eight other studies found benefits accrued primarily to poor and minority students.[83] For instance, a study by Matthew Chingos of the Brookings Institution and Paul Peterson of Harvard University found that participation in a voucher program increased college admission rates for African Americans by 20 percent.[84] Similarly, earlier work from the Brookings Institution found that African American students that opted to receive a voucher had combined reading and math scores substantially higher than the control group after two years.[85]

Minority and poor students are most likely to show significant gains because they are moving out of far worse schools. For a middle-class student, however, shifting from a public to a private school is likely shifting from one decent school to another.

Despite these apparent benefits, there remain limitations to the usefulness of vouchers as an anti-poverty tool. To start with, it may be legally and politically difficult to enact voucher programs. Although critics of school vouchers allege that they unconstitutionally subsidize religious schools, the U.S. Supreme Court has upheld the constitutionality of vouchers in the landmark 2002 case of *Zelman v. Simmons-Harris*.[86] However, legal barriers remain in place at the state level. In particular, many states have historically anti-Roman Catholic "Blaine Amendments" as part of their state constitutions.[87] Response by the courts to these amendments has been decidedly mixed, and several state courts have relied on them to strike down voucher programs.[88]

Because vouchers are public funds from a legal standpoint, they inevitably come with strings attached. For example, schools that accept vouchers may have to agree to accept all students that apply, including those with special needs, disciplinary problems, or poor educational skills. Schools taking vouchers may also have to revamp their curriculum according to government standards, and teachers may have to meet government requirements. Most states also require schools that accept vouchers to participate in statewide testing.[89]

These regulations have serious consequences. Louisiana, for example, is one of the few states where studies have shown little improvement in academic outcomes from its voucher program.[90] However, Louisiana's program is also highly regulated. Voucher-accepting schools in Louisiana may not set their own admissions criteria, cannot charge families more than the value of the voucher (a meager $5,311 on average in 2012), and must participate in state testing programs, among other requirements.[91] As a result, many of the state's best private schools were scared away from the program. Barely a third of Louisiana private schools accept voucher students, a considerably lower rate than in most other states.[92]

Moreover, one of the purposes of establishing private schools as an alternative to public schools is to spur innovation. We want schools that will try to educate children in different ways. Education, after all, is one of the few areas of society that has remained virtually unchanged over the past 200 years. Forcing private schools to conform to the existing education model does little to change this. In fact, it is for this reason that some private schools refuse to accept school vouchers.

More recently interest has been growing in an alternative way to assist parents who are poor with paying private school tuition, one that avoids many of the shortcomings of school vouchers: tuition tax credits or educational savings accounts (TTC/ESA). These programs provide a tax credit to individuals and corporations that contribute to a scholarship fund, operated by a private, charitable foundation. The scholarship is then offered to parents for tuition, fees, and other expenses to send their children to private school, or, in some cases, public schools from another district. In this way, the scholarship operates much like a voucher. The critical difference is that the money contributed to the scholarship fund never passes through the state treasury or any other publicly managed account.[93] As a result, courts have generally held that Blaine amendments do not apply.[94] Today, 17 states operate tuition tax credit programs, and roughly 225,000 students have received scholarships through those programs.[95]

A second noteworthy consequence of avoiding the public funds label is that tax credits bypass many of the regulations that afflict vouchers. If one goal of educational choice is to spur innovation through competition, we should want to sidestep restrictions that merely turn private schools into replicas of the cookie-cutter public schools that have already failed.

Because tuition tax credit programs are new, there has not yet been much evaluation of their effectiveness. One study of Arizona's TTC/ESA program did show that parents used the funds to send their children to a wide variety of schools, including Montessori academies, parochial schools (Roman Catholic, Protestant, and Jewish), single-sex schools, Waldorf academies, and schools that specialize in students with autism. Parents also used TTC/ESA funds for nontuition educational expenses such as textbooks, tutoring, counseling, and online education programs. Some students also appear to have saved a portion of the money for future education expenses.

Either vouchers or tuition tax credits (or even charter schools) would represent a step forward. But tuition tax credits go much further to establishing an actual market in education, while reducing government regulation and putting parents in charge. They should be the preferred option.

Regardless of which legislative approach is ultimately pursued, expanding parental control over educational choices would potentially offer families who are needy several benefits.

First, and perhaps most important from the standpoint of alleviating poverty, expanded parent control would enable low-income families to take advantage of better schools. Although the quality of private schools is far from uniform, the evidence from more than 30 years of studies has shown that private schools outperform public schools in test scores, graduation rates, future income, lower violence levels, parental satisfaction, and so on.[96] For example, a survey of the literature by Andrew Coulson compared the performance of public and private schools across different metrics of success like student academic achievement, efficiency, and parental satisfaction. He found 106 studies presented evidence of a significant advantage for private schools relative to public schools, compared with 37 studies finding no statistically significant difference and 13 studies finding an advantage for public schools. Moreover, after controlling for individual and job characteristics, private nonsectarian high school graduates earn 2.6 percent more than their public school counterparts. Graduates of Roman Catholic high schools do even better, earning 13.6 percent more than comparable students from public high schools.[97]

Second, the process of opening up educational choices generates incentives for increased parental involvement in their child's education, improving both the quantity and quality of information available to parents. For example, a study of the D.C. Child Opportunity Scholarship program by Georgetown University found that one of the most significant consequences of the school choice program was that parental involvement for all levels of schooling—elementary, junior high school, and high school—improved dramatically.[98] And, a study by Michael Lovenheim and Patrick Walsh for the National Bureau of Economic Research concludes that not only do school choice programs result in parents searching for more information on schools, the increased parental involvement creates a virtuous cycle, generating more and better information for parents.[99]

And, third, educational choice is based on the idea that a true free market in education can provide the same innovation and improvement in services that markets provide in other goods and services.[100] Today, we still use a model of schooling that largely dates to 18th-century Prussia. This model is not just a question of educational technology—computers are omnipresent in schools today—but in the entire pedagogical method.[101] Moreover, parents will be able to better match available options to their child's needs. Children have vastly different talents and needs. Not every child learns the same way or needs the instruction in the same skills. A changing world, and a changing population of students, will require a changing way of teaching and learning.

There are few things we could do that would have more of an effect on poverty than reforming our education system. Indeed, failure to graduate—or to receive a solid education—is one of the best predictors of future poverty.

Over recent decades, we have dramatically increased spending on education at federal, state, and local levels. We have given the federal government greater control over school operations and school curriculums. Yet more money and more government have done little to improve educational outcomes. There is no reason to believe that more of the same will yield any measurable differences.

Instead, it is time to break the monopoly of public schools. Only by freeing the market in education, liberating schools, students, and parents, can we achieve the type of innovation that will bring improved education to impoverished children. Charter schools, vouchers, and tuition tax credits all can move us in that direction. Also, they can help break up the ossified education establishment and challenge the power of teachers' unions.

Education reform—in particular, educational choice—should be considered a vital component of any successful anti-poverty policy.

CHAPTER SEVEN: REDUCING THE COST OF HOUSING THROUGH DEREGULATION

Housing is absolutely essential to human flourishing. Without shelter, it all falls apart.

—Matthew Desmond[1]

It has long been a rule of thumb that families should spend no more than 30 percent of their income on housing. The reality, however, is that most people living in poverty spend even more. Indeed, in 2014 Americans in the lowest third of incomes spent on average 40 percent of their income on housing—and renters in that third spent nearly 50 percent of their income on housing.[2]

Contrary to popular belief, homeownership rates are actually quite high among low-income American families. Roughly 40 percent of poor households own their home.[3] In many ways, the prevalence of homeownership among families who are otherwise poor illustrates the difficulties in defining poverty in America.[4]

However, simply looking at the levels of homeownership among the poor implies a level of affluence that is misleading. Many have little equity in their homes, and often the homes would be difficult to turn into income. Others purchased homes before they were poor, yet subsequently saw their incomes plummet. These individuals can be described as "house poor," with mortgage and upkeep consuming substantial portions of their income, leaving them unable to meet other financial needs. Moreover, the homes may be in disrepair, with nearly 5 percent of people who are poor reporting a leaking roof and almost 10 percent reporting pests in the house in one survey.[5] Furthermore, one study estimated that more than half of low-income housing suffered from three or more of "exposure-related" problems such as mold, combustion by-products, second-hand smoke, chemicals, pests, or inadequate ventilation.[6]

Nor is homeownership evenly distributed across all categories of the poor. The elderly poor are more likely to own their homes than young families and to have a low or no mortgage if they do own. Whites are more likely to own than African Americans, and their homes are typically more valuable as well.[7] A Brookings Institution study concluded that lower-income white neighborhoods had more home value compared to income than low-income minority neighborhoods.[8]

Despite the nation's high rate of homeownership, it is still true that the majority of low-income households rent, and here the problems are easier to see.[9] Rents have risen far faster than incomes since the 1990s. Among low-income families who rent their homes, more than 50 percent spend more than half of their income on rent and other housing costs such as utilities, with nearly a quarter of such tenants spending more than 70 percent.[10] Roughly 1 in 10 poor Americans report that they cannot pay their rent and an equal number are worried that they might not be able to in the future.[11] High rents are an even bigger problem in some states and cities. In San Francisco, a one-bedroom apartment averages an astounding $3,460.[12] In New York, the average rent is over $3,000, and it's more than $2,000 in Boston and Washington, D.C. In America's opportunity-rich cities, most rental units are out of reach for the poorest families.

Stable and affordable housing is critical to fighting poverty on several levels. A home located in a safe neighborhood that is close to jobs and other opportunities can serve as a gateway to economic success. Oftentimes, those families who cannot afford to live in these communities are relegated to dangerous neighborhoods with few employment prospects.[13]

Unsurprisingly, poor people move far more often than those with better housing options. In part, this may be an attempt to move from neighborhoods with high crime, poor schools, and few resources to better areas.[14] However, moves are also frequently precipitated by circumstances beyond their control, including an inability to pay rent, changes in family circumstances such as birth of a child or loss of a job, or the unsuitability of the conditions of the rental unit itself (i.e., lack of heat, plumbing problems, vermin infestations, and so on).

An analysis of data from the American Housing Survey shows that 55 percent of children in families that are poor move each year, compared with less than a third of children from nonpoor families.[15] Another study found that roughly 20 percent of low-income families had moved more than six times in six years.[16] Families that spend more than half their income on rent were more likely to move than those with lower income shares spent on rent.

Studies also show that a lack of stable housing often brings about other forms of instability that help trap families in poverty. Results from the Milwaukee Area Renters Study found that workers who involuntarily lost their housing were roughly 20 percent more likely to subsequently lose their jobs, compared with similar workers who did not.[17] Similarly, a 2015 study by Matthew Desmond and Carl Gershenson of Harvard found that workers who had been forced to move were significantly (11 to 22 percent) more likely to be laid off compared with observationally identical workers who did not.[18]

Likewise, frequently uprooting children from their schools can make learning more difficult. A study by the Urban Institute found the following:

> Children experiencing residential instability demonstrate worse academic and social outcomes than their residentially-stable peers, such as lower vocabulary skills, problem behaviors, grade retention, increased high school drop-out rates, and lower adult educational attainment . . . residential instability is related to poor social development across age groups.[19]

According to the Center for Housing Policy, families that move involuntarily face a higher risk of adverse educational outcomes following the move, such as increased difficulty in school and excessive school absenteeism among children.[20] Thus, housing instability can lead indirectly to poorer academic performance, which, as we saw in the previous chapter, can translate into an increased likelihood that children who are poor will become adults who are poor.

Evictions are frequent, often setting in motion a cascade of additional problems. In Milwaukee, for example, a city with just 105,000 rental units, landlords evict roughly 16,000 people from 6,000 units every year.[21] This is hardly surprising. If rents are high, poor people will have difficulty paying the rent, and if they don't pay rent, they are likely to be evicted.[22] This provides yet another entry point to a host of problems for the poor.

There are many reasons for the troubles the poor face in finding stable, low-cost housing. However, government policies, from land use and zoning to building codes and property taxes, do not make their lives any easier. As with education, the government is a big part of their problem.

Zoning and Land Use

Los Angeles is commonly credited with enacting the first large-scale municipal zoning and land-use plan in 1908.[23] The goal was to protect the city's residential areas from rapidly encroaching industrial use. The U.S. Supreme Court upheld Los Angeles's zoning policy in the 1915 case of *Hadacheck v. Sebastian*, the first of a long line of cases in which the court sanctioned various zoning laws.[24] The court's jurisprudence culminated in the 1926 case of *Village of Euclid v. Ambler Realty Corporation*, generally considered the court's definitive expression of support for the role of government's police power in regulating land use.[25]

While initially justified on the grounds of protecting property values, many cities—mostly in the south, but also including northern cities such as Chicago—quickly seized on zoning as a mechanism for enforcing racial segregation.[26] Baltimore was the first. In 1910, it passed a zoning ordinance that, among other provisions, prohibited anyone from purchasing a home or renting on a block where more than half the residents were of a different race. It also required builders to specifically designate, in the permit application, what race could buy their property.[27] In signing the law, Baltimore Mayor J. Barry Mahool said that "Blacks should be quarantined in isolated slums in order to reduce the incidents of civil disturbances, to prevent the spread of communicable disease into nearby White neighborhoods, and to protect property values among the White majority."[28]

Several other cities—including Atlanta, Georgia; Birmingham, Alabama; Louisville, Kentucky; and Richmond, Virginia—quickly followed suit. As one historian noted, "racial zoning in southern cities was as much a foundation for overall land-use regulation as were regulation of the garment industry in New York City or encroaching industrial uses in Los Angeles."[29]

The courts generally took an unfavorable view of race-based zoning, relying on concepts of property rights to invalidate the laws in what became a running battle with local governments. Finally, the Supreme Court made a definitive ruling in *Buchanan v. Warley* (1917), striking down Louisville's racial zoning law, holding that race was an insufficient basis for violating the right to contract.[30] Thus it was the same economic liberties that are often derided by advocates of racial equality that formed the legal basis for a major victory against racism.

Unfortunately, racism is extremely resilient. In the wake of *Buchanan v. Warley*, some cities simply ignored the court's ruling. Others, however, began to develop more wide-ranging urban development plans, ostensibly predicated on issues such as neighborhood preservation, land use, the location of civic improvements, building codes, and other race-neutral policies. These measures nevertheless served to push African Americans into isolated, segregated enclaves. As a 1925 Birmingham city plan noted, its intent was to "protect the property holders against the manufacturing plants and corner grocery stores which tend to spring up promiscuously about the city *and to restrict the negroes to certain districts*" (emphasis added).[31]

Having found a tool for keeping so-called undesirables out of white middle-class neighborhoods, cities quickly learned to apply these measures to other groups such as newly arrived immigrants, Jews, and the poor more generally. Cities also used planning and zoning laws to push manufacturing plants, especially those whose operations constituted a particular nuisance, and those that polluted heavily, into poor and African American neighborhoods, what we refer to today as environmental racism.[32]

Zoning continues to play a major role in maintaining racial segregation in housing. The Civil Rights Act of 1968 forbids explicitly race-based exclusionary zoning, but zoning and land-use laws still force the poor and minorities into clearly segregated neighborhoods. By pricing the poor out of specific locations, these laws effectively make those communities inaccessible to many people. For example, a study of zoning regulations such as minimum lot size requirements and restrictions on the permitting of multifamily housing in Massachusetts showed that such regulations tended to steer minorities into particular neighborhoods.[33] Moreover, a Brookings Institution study of zoning laws, in particular anti-density regulations, suggests that they effectively amount to "institutionalized segregation."[34]

Regardless of intent, however, zoning laws and land-use ordinances have a detrimental impact on the poor by making housing prohibitively expensive. Zoning and land-use laws restrict the availability of housing/rental stock in a given neighborhood. Housing prices, like the prices of other goods, are products of the law of supply and demand. That is, housing prices reflect both the demand in terms of consumer preferences for certain types of housing in a certain location as well as the physical supply of such housing. Harvard's Edward Glaeser and his coauthors argue that the price of a house consists of three elements: construction costs, the value of the land, and the value of the right to build on the property.[35] Zoning and land-use laws drive up the value of the right to build on the property both directly and indirectly, by constricting the supply of land available for housing of various types.

There are five primary mechanisms through which zoning/land-use rules limit the supply of housing:[36]

Minimum lot sizes, which specify the smallest permissible area a structure can be built on. These laws are designed to reduce housing density, that is, the total number of units in any given area. Perhaps the first such regulation was in Wayne Township, New Jersey, which set a minimum square footage for new housing at 768 square feet, which at the time was larger than 30 percent of the township's existing housing stock.[37]

Minimum parking requirements are often a less explicit way to limit housing density. They require that a certain number of parking spaces be provided for every home or apartment. Since available parking areas are often limited by spatial constraints, especially in urban areas, they effectively limit the number of units that can be built. These regulations might seem trivial at first glance, but they can have a significant impact on home prices, especially in cities where land is expensive. For example, one estimate suggests that San Francisco's parking requirements add as much as $104,000 to the cost of each apartment in the city.[38]

Smart growth and urban growth boundaries tend to be found in more suburban or rural areas. They are designed to limit encroachment on farm or greenspace, and they restrict building in specific areas, especially of high-density projects like apartment complexes.[39]

Historic preservation is designed to protect both individual buildings and sometimes entire neighborhoods deemed to be of historic, architectural, or artistic importance. This may be a worthwhile goal, but when abused can serve as a back-door mechanism for limiting development. In Manhattan, for instance, fully 27 percent of buildings are designated for historic preservation.[40]

Inclusionary zoning, while designed to increase low-cost housing by forcing developers to set aside a certain percentage of new development to lease or sell at below-market rates, can often make development projects financially untenable, again limiting the total availability of housing.[41]

A 2017 Cato Institute study using state and federal court decisions on zoning or land use as a proxy for the number and strength of housing regulation in a state shows that the impact of such regulations is growing.[42] Looking at the strength and pervasiveness of regulation on a state-by-state basis, Ohio, Connecticut, Maine, Delaware, and Vermont augmented land-use regulation most quickly, while Oklahoma and Texas increased land use most slowly, between 2000 and 2010. Turning to zoning regulation, we see a similar pattern, with Ohio, Connecticut, Maine, Missouri, and Delaware increasing zoning regulation most quickly between 2000 and 2010, and Mississippi and Texas increasing regulation most slowly (Figures 7.1 and 7.2).[43]

Figure 7.1

Land-Use Regulation

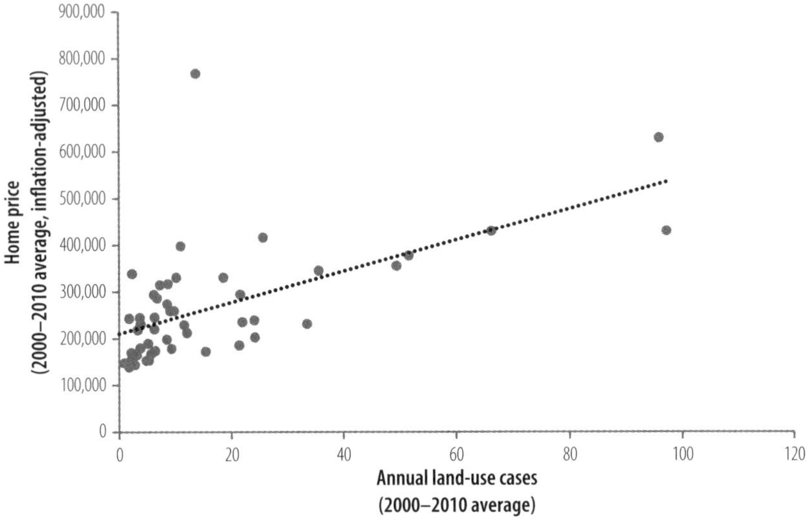

Source: Vanessa Brown Calder, "Zoning, Land-Use, and Housing Affordability," Cato Institute Policy Analysis no. 823, October 18, 2017, https://www.cato.org/publications/policy-analysis/zoning-land-use-planning-housing-affordability.

Figure 7.2

Zoning Regulation

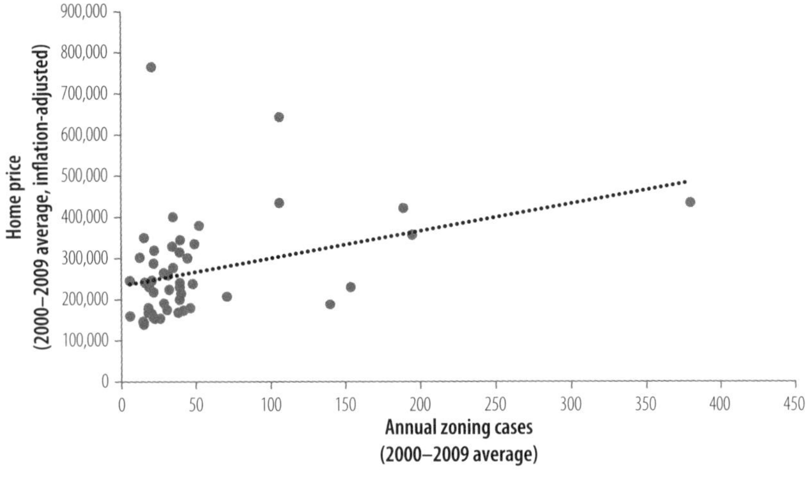

Source: Vanessa Brown Calder, "Zoning, Land-Use, and Housing Affordability," Cato Institute Policy Analysis no. 823, October 18, 2017, https://www.cato.org/publications/policy-analysis/zoning-land-use-planning-housing-affordability.

The exact degree varied from state to state, but 44 states showed a positive relationship between increasing land-use regulation, as identified by the annual increase in land-use decisions, and the increase in real average home cost. The exceptions to the rule are Alaska, Illinois, Missouri, North Dakota, Oklahoma, and Oregon. As one of the states with the lightest zoning and land-use burden, it seems reasonable that Oklahoma may not see a positive relationship between additional regulation, which remains minimal in absolute terms, and home price increases. Most of the remaining states are small states, which may explain why they were outliers.

The aforementioned Cato study is hardly an outlier. Other studies have demonstrated that zoning and land-use regulations can add as much as 20 percent to the cost of a home in Baltimore, Boston, and Washington, D.C.; more than 30 percent in Los Angeles and Oakland; and more than 50 percent in Manhattan, San Francisco, and San Jose.[44] Another study by Salim Furth of the Heritage Foundation estimated that residents of high-cost coastal cities "would pay 9 percent less in rent and 20 percent less for the costs of homeownership if the city adopted regulatory policies that are typical of the rest of the country."[45] A study by John Quigley and Steven Raphael for the American Economic Association estimates that every new zoning measure leads to a 3.0 percent to 4.5 percent increase in the prices of owner-occupied housing, and a 1.0 percent to 2.3 percent increase in the price of rental housing.[46]

The immediate beneficiaries of higher housing prices are, naturally, existing homeowners, who see their equity rise commensurately, as well as landlords, who can charge correspondingly higher rents. Municipalities also benefit from both increased property values and limits on low-income housing.[47]

At the same time, because lower-income households spend on average a more significant portion of their income on housing than higher-income households, the costs of these regulations disproportionately burden low-income households. Zoning and land-use policies not only increase housing insecurity, but also exacerbate economic inequality.

Moreover, the problems that such policies are designed to remedy are more likely to be concerns of higher-income Americans.[48] Families who are poor and who are struggling to put a roof over their children's heads are less likely to be concerned about whether there are sufficient "green spaces" or if new construction obstructs their view. Such regulations represent the preferences of the wealthy and come at the expense of low-income households.[49] Similarly, the dynamics of zoning winners and losers mean that municipalities often fail to consider the full costs of restrictive zoning. As Roderick Hills and David Schleicher point out, "On any given zoning vote, the supporters of restrictive zoning have an advantage over the supporters of additional housing supply even when less restrictive zoning across a given local government might be preferred by city residents."[50]

Property Taxes

Property taxes are the primary revenue mechanism for most local governments. As such, they generally finance local government functions including education, police and fire protection, local road maintenance, and so forth. Rates vary widely across jurisdictions, but typically run between 0.5 and 2.0 percent of a building or home's value, on the basis of two components: (1) the value of the land on which the building sits and (2) physical improvements on that land, meaning the building itself.[51]

Illinois, New Hampshire, New Jersey, and Vermont have the highest average property tax rates, and Alabama, Hawaii, Louisiana, and Wyoming have the lowest. However, because the actual tax paid is a combination of both the property tax rate and housing values, the most onerous property tax burden is actually in states like Connecticut, New Jersey, New York, and Vermont, which have both high rates and high home values.[52]

Property taxes often vary according to the type of property as well. The nationwide average property tax for single-family, owner-occupied homes is just 0.90 percent of valuation, whereas large (five units or more) rental complexes are assessed an average of 1.14 percent and small (4 units or fewer) rental properties face the highest rate, 1.20 percent on average.[53]

Because the wealthy tend to have bigger and more expensive houses, they pay higher absolute levels of property tax. However, as noted previously, people who are poor spend a much larger proportion of their income on housing. As a result, property taxes are effectively regressive.[54] Some estimates suggest that the poor pay as much as a 25 percent higher effective tax than do the rich.[55]

A substantial portion of the tax assessed on rental properties is passed through to renters in the form of higher rents. One study suggests that even an increase of one standard deviation in property taxes increases rents by roughly $400 per year.[56] Other studies indicate that the property tax burden falls more heavily on apartment renters than on homeowners of similar incomes.[57]

Because the poor are more likely to rent, this hits them the hardest. Making matters worse, property taxes tend to fall hardest precisely on those types of small, less expensive rental properties that the poor occupy. Property taxes account for about 24 percent of the annual operating budget of the average rental unit. However, as noted above, smaller rental properties pay a somewhat higher effective tax rate. In addition, property taxes tend to make up a slightly higher proportion of operating costs for lower-rent units, 27 percent compared with 21 percent for high-rent flats.[58] Because property taxes are a fixed cost of operation, they also may make it harder for low-cost apartments to offset those costs. When they do so, the offsets are likely to come in the form of less upkeep, fewer services, or other mechanisms that negatively affect renters.

Ironically, while property taxes adversely affect low-income tenants, the government subsidizes home ownership for higher-income individuals through the mortgage-interest tax deduction on federal income taxes. Poor Americans pay property taxes—directly or indirectly—but most do not pay income taxes, and even those low-income families that do seldom itemize their deductions to allow them to take advantage of the tax break. Besides, wealthier families are more likely to own their home, have more expensive houses, and can take on more debt, meaning they pay more interest. Fully 75 percent of the benefit from the mortgage interest deduction goes to Americans in the top 20 percent of incomes, and nearly all the benefit goes to families with incomes over $100,000 per year.[59]

At the same time, while the mortgage interest deduction reduces the cost of housing for homeowners, it increases the price of homeownership for nonhomeowners.[60] After all, demand-side subsidies can increase the cost of the goods being subsidized when supply is restricted. The poor get hit coming and going.

Rent Control

Ironically, one of the policies making it difficult for the poor to find affordable housing is a policy designed to reduce rental costs—rent control.

There were some early attempts at rent control following World War I, but rent control began in earnest in the 1940s when returning GIs faced a housing shortage, especially in New York and other cities, that drove rents to astronomical heights. Currently, 35 states have laws prohibiting rent control, while some of the most populous states with the most expensive rental markets—California, Maryland, New Jersey, and New York, along with Washington, D.C.—have some form of rent control.[61] In some cases, the restrictions apply to all rentals, in others only to certain types of units, and in still others only to existing tenants, allowing for increases for new renters.

The logic of rent control is superficially enticing. If rents are too expensive and rising too fast for poor people to afford, then lower them. If market forces can't do that, then do it artificially. In reality of course, as Adam Davidson wrote in the *New York Times Magazine*, rent control "has become a standard part of many Econ 101 courses, because it is such a clear example of public policy that achieves the near opposite of its goals."[62]

In a well-functioning housing market, a process known as "filtration" occurs. As people become wealthier, they tend to exchange their current living arrangements for better, more costly homes. They may move to a bigger apartment in a better neighborhood or buy instead of renting. In doing so, they make their previous, less expensive location available for new occupants. As everyone moves up the scale, units at the bottom open up for those with limited incomes. Rent control disrupts this filtering process by encouraging families to remain in place even when they might otherwise move. Older couples stay in multi-bedroom apartments even after their children move out, while other families make do in smaller apartments despite the birth of a child. One study found that rent control nearly tripled the time that occupants remained in apartments in New York City.[63] If nonpoor individuals fail to move up and out of low-cost apartments, those apartments remain off the market and unavailable to those new, low-income renters searching for them.

At the same time, rent control discourages the construction of new rental units, further reducing the availability of housing stock. This unintended consequence applies especially to so-called first-generation rent-control policies, which established a hard ceiling on rents. Other forms of rent control that limit but still permit rent hikes have a lesser effect on new building. A review of the literature on rent-control economics concluded, "It is self-evident that textbook first-generation rent controls will have negative effects on construction. The size of the effect depends on the elasticity of supply. With second- and third-generation controls, where landlords are allowed cost coverage for new dwellings, the effect on construction is less clear."[64] Even when overall housing construction appears relatively unaffected, there is a tendency by developers to shift away from rental units and toward co-ops or other owner-occupied construction.[65] As a result, vacancy rates in cities with rent control are extremely low.

At the same time, many, and by some accounts most, beneficiaries of rent control are not poor. A study of rent control in Cambridge, Massachusetts, for example, concluded that "the poor, the elderly, and families—the three major groups targeted for benefits of rent control—were no more likely to be found in controlled than uncontrolled units."[66] Similarly, an analysis of San Francisco's rent control showed that beneficiaries earning more than $107,000 annually outnumbered those earning less than $35,000, 29 percent to 27 percent.[67] According to data from New York University's Furman Center for Real Estate and Urban Policy, barely more than half of the tenants in rent-stabilized or controlled apartments in Manhattan are classified as low income.[68]

Moreover, rent control effectively creates two different rental markets. Rent-controlled apartments remain underpriced (and scarce) while non-controlled units become more expensive than they otherwise would be. In some ways, housing becomes a lottery with winners and losers. Unfortunately, the losers too often turn out to be the poor and disadvantaged.

The Futility of Subsidies

Having made housing both scarce and expensive through its counterproductive policies, the government has responded with a variety of programs designed to subsidize housing costs for the poor and other lower-income Americans. The federal government funds 33 different housing programs, the largest and most prominent of which is known as Section 8 housing vouchers.[69]

Anyone earning less than 80 percent of the median income is theoretically eligible for a voucher, but priority goes to the poorest applicants. By law, 75 percent of vouchers must go to households earning 30 percent or less of median family income in the housing area. Currently, 2.2 million households, composed of more than 5 million individuals, receive housing subsidies through the Section 8 program.[70]

Far too often, Section 8 vouchers act as a trap, locking a recipient into poverty. As we saw in chapter 5, the phaseout of poverty programs can create high marginal tax rates for those leaving welfare for work. Section 8 housing is a particular problem in this regard. Under Section 8, rent is pegged at 30 percent of a recipient's adjusted household income. Therefore any increase in a recipient's wages above that amount leads to a steep rent increase. As a result, Section 8 creates a strong disincentive for individuals to expand their market earnings and seek personal advancement.

Section 8 vouchers have also failed in their goal of breaking up concentrations of poverty. Public housing failed in part because by concentrating the poor in one area, it aggravated and magnified the social pathologies of poverty. Section 8 vouchers were supposed to spread low-income families more widely throughout the community. However, because only a small fraction of landlords are willing to accept Section 8 vouchers, tenants have become concentrated in particular buildings and certain areas of cities. As Senator Barbara Mikulski (D-MD) said, Section 8 replaced "vertical ghettos with horizontal ones."[71]

Some landlords specialize in Section 8, becoming experts at its complex regulations, and they skillfully work the system to their financial advantage. With Section 8 tenants, landlords do not have to worry about nonpayment, because the government deposits its share of the rent—the lion's share—directly into the property owner's bank account. For many buildings, the government-paid rent is more than the market rent would be because the program allows voucher holders to pay up to the average rent in their entire metropolitan area. Landlords in lower-income neighborhoods, where rents are below average, simply charge voucher holders precisely that average rent.[72]

As a result, Section 8 contributes to the creation of what might be called "frozen cities." Subsidized tenants remain stuck in Section 8 buildings for years, even decades. The actual buildings inhabited by subsidized tenants remain tied to one particular low-value use, which prevents the affected areas of cities from enjoying the natural changes and upgrading over time that other neighborhoods experience. Neighborhoods with subsidized housing do not get renewed, and they offer fewer opportunities for individuals to improve their lives and their surroundings.[73]

At the same time, Section 8 vouchers do not address the cause of rising rents, and they may exacerbate affordability problems overall. Like many subsidies, they may actually be passed through, leading to higher rental prices. Worse, the availability of housing subsidies may encourage many of the destructive policies discussed above. It is notable that those states with the most restrictive zoning and land-use policies are those that receive the most federal housing subsidies.[74] This suggests that housing policy is at least partially chasing its own tail.

Inexpensive and stable housing is critical to any effort to reduce poverty over the long term. That means first and foremost, that government at all levels, federal, state, and local, should examine their policies to remove impediments to low-cost housing.

CHAPTER EIGHT: SAVINGS AND THE ACCUMULATION OF WEALTH

For the vast majority of households, the pathway out of poverty is not through income and consumption, but through saving and accumulation.

—*Michael Sherraden*[1]

Too often, the importance of savings and wealth accumulation gets neglected in the context of poverty discussions. The logic behind this omission is obvious: immediate needs for food, shelter, and so on must be met before other, more long-term goals can be addressed. Yet even a relatively small amount of savings can make a significant difference in the short term, enabling the poor to pay a car repair or health care bill and preventing such unanticipated expenses from forcing a family into a cycle of debt and poverty.

Over the longer term, savings is even more critical. For example, studies show that single mothers with savings are significantly more likely to keep their families out of poverty than other single mothers, even after correcting for a variety of social and economic factors.[2] Other studies show that families with assets have greater household stability, are more involved in their community, demonstrate greater long-term thinking and planning, and provide increased opportunity for their children.[3] Clearly, the ability to save and accumulate assets offers a wide array of benefits.

Some observers suggest that the whole definition of poverty should be revised to consider the accumulation of assets or the lack of them. One common definition of "asset poverty" would define people as "asset poor" if they lack sufficient savings or other assets to survive for three months at the poverty level. This form of poverty can be measured two ways: (1) by net worth, that is, the value of all assets (e.g., car, home, savings account, etc.) minus debts or (2) liquid assets, meaning cash or assets that can easily be converted to cash.[4]

Studies have long shown that levels of asset poverty exceed levels of income poverty in the United States. Using the first measure, net worth, roughly one of five Americans can be considered asset poor. Looking at liquid assets measurements, the picture is even worse: more than a third of Americans can be regarded as asset poor.[5] However, even these measures may understate the severity of the lack of savings or assets among lower-income Americans. For instance, according to the Federal Reserve, 46 percent of adults say they either could not cover an emergency expense costing $400 or would cover it by selling something or borrowing money.[6] It should be no surprise that asset poverty is a much bigger problem for the poor. Using a liquid assets measure, more than 80 percent of Americans in the lowest quintile of incomes can be considered asset poor.[7]

The consequences of asset poverty for poor households are substantial. Most obviously, a lack of savings or other assets leaves a family more vulnerable to unanticipated expenses or a sudden change in their economic circumstances. Events like job loss, divorce, or a health crisis can cause financial difficulties for all families. For those without savings to fall back on, the problems can become a full-blown crisis.[8]

For example, 16 percent of Americans who lost their job reported that it created severe material hardships for their family, but that rose to 44 percent among the asset poor. Health-related work limitations caused material hardship for 19 percent of the general population, but 40 percent of the asset poor. And divorce or other circumstances where a parent left the family resulted in such hardship for 11 percent of Americans overall, but it did so for a third of asset-poor families.[9]

Lack of savings and assets also makes it harder for the poor to invest in those things that can help them escape from poverty, such as relocating, purchasing a house or car, starting a business, or pursuing education either by themselves or for their children.[10] This fact makes it particularly troubling that so many government policies make it more difficult for the poor to save and accumulate assets and wealth.

Banking and the Unbanked

Roughly 1 of every 13 U.S. households does not have a bank account.[11] The poor, minorities, young people, and the unemployed were most likely to be "unbanked." More than 20 percent of African American households, for instance, are unbanked.[12] Nearly a quarter of those with incomes below $18,900 lack an account.[13] About half of those without accounts had one at some point in the past, but about half have never had a bank account.[14] Usually, the reason for dropping an account is an outside intervening event, especially the loss of a job.[15]

Without a traditional bank, the unbanked are often forced to rely on alternative financial arrangements, such as check cashing services and short-term lenders, although these services can have high transaction costs.[16] They also may keep large amounts of cash in their homes or on their persons, making them a target for both crime and police harassment.

There are numerous reasons why the poor go unbanked. The most commonly cited reason—and the most obvious—is a lack of money.[17] It is hard for the poor to save what they don't have. Those living in severe poverty often manage day-to-day, with little discretionary income and very little left over at the end of the week. The poor also express a lack of confidence in the banking system.[18] This may stem from a lack of experience with banks (they may not have previously had an account or even know someone who does) or from a general suspicion of institutions. Either way, it makes them reluctant to open an account.

There are barriers to savings that are even further outside the control of many individuals. For starters, poor and minority neighborhoods are far less likely to have bank branches, a problem that has grown worse in the wake of the Great Recession and the mortgage crisis. Since 2008, banks have shut 1,826 branches, with 93 percent of those closings in neighborhoods where the household income is below the national median.[19]

As such, transportation and time issues can make for significant obstacles to banking by the poor. This may become less of a problem in the future given advances in mobile banking technology, but for now, the inconvenience of banking with few branches can discourage low-income people from opening accounts.

Banks make very little money from small savings or checking accounts. Therefore, many banks don't provide financial services for customers with limited resources. While some states have responded by requiring banks to offer a low-cost basic banking service, they don't force banks to advertise or promote those services.[20] Given that businesses would already do so voluntarily if it was profitable, the resulting regulatory burden associated with such a mandate would almost certainly be counterproductive.

Unsurprisingly, high bank fees can also be a barrier to banking by the poor. Traditional banking methods involve a host of such fees and other associated costs, including account opening fees, minimum balance requirements, and withdrawal fees.[21] Some of these practices are unavoidable and necessary to the profitable operation of a bank, but many stem from misguided government policies.

The 2010 banking and financial services regulatory reform known as Dodd-Frank, for example, has been blamed for imposing significant costs on small and community banks, precisely the type of banking institution most likely to service high-poverty communities. This increased regulatory burden has led small banks to reconsider their product and service offerings. These changes in product offerings will hurt small and community bank consumers, who may have difficulty locating convenient alternatives. For example, smaller banks also have begun to cut back on overdraft protection.[22]

Other banking regulations that limit the ability of the poor to bank include anti-money laundering or so-called "know your customer" laws. These laws require banks to ask for identification documents (including proof of name, date of birth, address, and Social Security number) from anyone opening a bank account.[23] However, as has frequently been pointed out in other contexts such as voter ID cases, many poor people lack such identification. Roughly 4 percent of adults from households earning less than $25,000 per year lack legally acceptable identification.[24] Young people, African Americans, Latinos, and undocumented immigrants in particular are more likely to lack such identification.

In an age of identity theft, it seems hard to get around the need for identification, particularly when it comes to withdrawing funds. Banks have sought to address the problem by accepting alternative forms of identification. According to a survey by the Federal Deposit Insurance Corporation (FDIC), 58 percent of banks accepted a non-U.S. passport, 40 percent accepted an ID from a foreign consulate, and 73 percent accepted an Individual Taxpayer ID Number (ITIN) as an alternative to a Social Security number at account opening.[25] Yet these are not necessarily common forms of identification among the poor.

There is evidence that a lack of identification either directly blocks or indirectly discourages low-income people from opening bank accounts. One study of undocumented immigrants, for example, found that the distribution of identification cards to migrant workers increased the likelihood that they would open a bank account by 38 percent.[26]

With traditional banking options costly and inconvenient, many low-income people turn to alternative financial arrangements. Yet here again, they often encounter government regulations that block their efforts.

For example, many poor people use commercial check cashing services. Nationwide there are some 13,000 of these stores, almost all located in poor neighborhoods.[27] One small chain alone, RiteCheck, with 12 check cashing centers in New York City, reports serving more than 30,000 people each month.[28] Surveys suggest that the customers are likely to be low income (although roughly 85 percent are employed at least part time), with low levels of education. They are also somewhat more likely to be single, male, and African American or Latino.[29]

For individuals with no bank account, these centers may be the only way that they can access banking services, such as cashing a paycheck, getting a money order, paying bills, purchasing or reloading a prepaid debit card, or wiring money out of state or overseas. The immediacy of payout is also important for poor people who live day to day and cannot wait for a check to clear with traditional banking.

However, such convenience can come at a steep price. Fees for many services are high and are creeping upward. Generally this is a reflection of the risk being assumed by the centers operating in an environment with a high default rate. Some states have reacted by capping fees, but that has merely served to reduce access, forcing the poor to use even riskier, costlier, and less-regulated services.

The answer, then, is not greater regulation of nonbank alternatives, but increasing the ease of access to banks for the poor.

Welfare and Asset Limits

Even when poorer Americans can make banking arrangements, they often run into government policies deliberately designed to limit asset accumulation.

Specifically, many welfare programs impose eligibility requirements that disqualify potential recipients if they have too many assets. This makes a certain amount of intuitive sense. Someone with substantial assets but low income should not be eligible for welfare benefits. Many seniors, who are far from poor, fit this definition. However, too strict a rule against asset accumulation can prevent people from getting off of welfare and out of poverty.

Although there are exceptions, such as unemployment insurance and Supplemental Security Income (SSI), for the most part, asset limits are set by the states. In many of these programs, the asset limit is set at or about $2,000. Significantly, asset limits are typically not indexed to inflation. Therefore they have declined substantially in inflation-adjusted terms and are expected to continue to do so in the future.[30]

In addition to effectively imposing a high marginal implicit tax on saving, asset tests can be arbitrary, capricious, and confusing, treating similar assets differently depending on the state, program, or even the attitude of investigators. As the Federal Reserve Bank of Boston pointed out in a study, while one family may be able to retain its retirement savings when it applies for a means-tested program, another similar family that uses a different retirement saving vehicle or lives in a different state may be ineligible for the same program unless it depletes its retirement savings.

Also, a household may qualify for some programs but not for others solely on the basis of different rules for the various programs.[31]

- *Temporary Assistance for Needy Families (TANF):* States have complete discretion over their TANF asset limits and the types of assets that count toward them. Currently 43 states limit the value of total assets a family can have and still be eligible for TANF, the principal cash welfare program. The exact limit varies widely from state to state, but in some instances, the asset threshold can be as low as $1,000, although in some cases specific items such as retirement funds or the value of a car may be excluded from this amount.[32]
- *Supplemental Nutrition Assistance Program (SNAP):* Although most states have eliminated asset tests for food stamps, or SNAP, 16 states still have such limits in place, including such states as Louisiana, Missouri, Texas, and Virginia, which have large numbers of recipients.[33] The food stamp asset limit is usually $2,000 ($3,000 if at least one household member has a severe disability or is age 60 or older). Most employer-based retirement plans, including defined-benefit plans and 401(k) plans, are excluded from the asset limit.
- *Medicaid and the Children's Health Insurance Program (CHIP):* Nearly all states have eliminated the Medicaid asset test for children, but the majority of states continue to apply an asset test when evaluating Medicaid eligibility for parents, and most of these states count 401(k) plans and IRAs toward the asset limit. States could dispense with their Medicaid asset tests for both children and parents, or if they wish to retain an asset test for either group, they could exclude retirement accounts from the asset test. Also, by excluding retirement accounts from the Medicaid asset test applied to working-age people with disabilities, states could encourage them to save for their old age.[34]
- *Low Income Home Energy Assistance Program (LIHEAP):* Eleven states, including New York, have asset limits for the LIHEAP fuel subsidy.[35]
- *Supplemental Security Income (SSI):* The federal government also imposes a nationwide asset limit of $2,000 per person, $3,000 per family for SSI.[36]

Studies confirm that these restrictions mean that poor families consume more and save less. A study by the Massachusetts Institute of Technology's Jonathan Gruber and Aaron Yelowitz of the University of Kentucky looked at changes to asset limits under Medicaid in the 1980s and 90s and found evidence that social insurance programs contribute to the skewed distribution of assets in the United States by reducing the savings of eligible low-income households.[37] Similarly, a study in the *Journal of Political Economy* concluded that "means-tested social insurance has a disproportionate impact on saving behavior of lower-lifetime-income households."[38]

Not only do asset thresholds discourage savings and wealth accumulation by the poor, but they are administratively inefficient. Studies in those states that have eliminated asset tests suggest that the administrative savings more than exceed the cost of any potential caseload increase.[39] Eliminating them would save taxpayer money. Notably, however, only the elimination of the asset test in its entirety, not merely raising the limit or allowing the exclusion of certain assets, resulted in substantial administrative savings.

Enable the Poor to Build Wealth

Although removing existing barriers to savings would provide immediate benefit to the poor, there are three other steps that the government could take that might have an even more significant long-term effect.

First, we should reform and better use a little-known program known as Individual Development Accounts (IDAs). The 1996 federal welfare reform allowed states to establish and fund IDAs for TANF recipients. These trust accounts may be opened by individuals or a nonprofit sponsor on behalf of individuals who are eligible for assistance under TANF or other state welfare programs. Funds in the accounts must be used to accumulate capital for postsecondary education, for a first-time home purchase, or to start up a business. Individuals can contribute to IDAs from earned income, from matching funds coming from 501 (c) 3 nonprofit organizations, or from state or local government agencies. Funds in an IDA will be disregarded for purposes of any asset tests for TANF or welfare programs.[40]

States never took full advantage of this program, although there was some success in limited applications. However, in 1998, Congress authorized the Assets for Independence IDA program, and appropriated $19 million to fund demonstrations.[41] The average IDA participant in the study saved $935 after three years in the program, a net savings rate of 1.2 percent of earnings. Although this sounds like a tiny amount, it nonetheless appears to have increased the likelihood that participants would purchase a home, start a business, or pursue further education.[42]

Certainly, programs like IDAs are not going to solve the savings problem among the poor. But when so many government programs and regulations work directly against savings, even a tiny step in the right direction should be welcomed.

Second, we should simplify our current tangled knot of overlapping savings and retirement vehicles in a way that would make it easier for low-income people to access them. Currently, the higher an individual's income, the more likely they are to use vehicles such as IRAs, 401(k) plans, or Education Savings Accounts. In part, of course, that is because poor people have less discretionary income and because the tax advantages of such accounts mean less to individuals who pay little or no federal income tax. However, studies also show that low-income families avoid specialized savings programs because they fear the penalties for withdrawals outside the accounts' specified purposes. Since low-income families have little liquidity, unexpected expenses are more likely to cause them to need the funds put away in a retirement or education account. It should be no surprise that they are reluctant to risk high penalties for doing so.

Additionally, the sheer complexity of our savings programs may overwhelm individuals with little financial acumen or education. Financial advisory services are often difficult to access for needy families. Studies have shown that low-income African American families in particular may have less financial information, in part because of segregated social networks and a legacy of discrimination by financial institutions.[43] Studies also show that this lack of financial literacy can have negative consequences for savings and other financial behavior.[44]

One approach to fixing this problem would be to borrow an idea from the British and Canadians to establish a single unified savings option.[45] This single account would replace a host of existing tax-preferred savings options, including traditional IRAs, Roth IRAs, Coverdell Education Savings Accounts, 529 Education Plans, Simplified Employee Pension (SEP) IRAs, and Savings Incentive Match Plan for Employee Individual Retirement Accounts (SIMPLE IRAs), among others. IDAs, personal accounts for Social Security, and Health Savings Accounts (HSAs) could also be integrated into the new savings vehicle.

The new savings plan should be available to anyone, have a high annual contribution limit, invest in a broadly diversified, privately managed portfolio of bonds and equities (similar to the Federal Thrift Savings Program), and grow untaxed. Most important, individuals should be able to withdraw funds at any time for any purpose, without paying taxes or penalties.[46]

By simplifying savings options, a unified savings plan would make it easier for low-income Americans to take advantage of saving opportunities. And, by eliminating the paternalism and penalties that accompany most current tax-advantaged vehicles, it would increase liquidity for low-income households, thereby encouraging them to save more. As Glenn Hubbard, former chairman of President George W. Bush's Council of Economic Advisers put it, "With no withdrawal penalties, the account's greater liquidity will encourage individuals to save, particularly moderate-income households worried about tying up funds for long periods of time."[47]

The British and Canadian experience with unified savings vehicles shows that they do boost savings for the poor. For example, in the United Kingdom, 55 percent of those with Individual Savings Accounts (ISAs) have incomes below £20,000 (about $25,000 in 2018 U.S. dollars). In Canada, more than half of all Tax-Free Savings Account (TFSA) holders earn less than US$37,500. Even better, low-income TFSA account holders actually save more relative to their incomes than do high-income Canadians.[48]

Finally, one of the reforms that could do the most to boost saving and wealth accumulation for the poor would be to allow them to save and invest a portion of their Social Security payroll taxes through personal accounts.[49] A detailed discussion of Social Security's finances, its looming insolvency, and the benefits of personal accounts is far beyond the scope of this book. Yet low-income workers, who are otherwise constrained in their saving and investment options, would be among those with the most to gain from personal Social Security accounts.[50]

That's because Social Security payroll taxes are particularly burdensome for poor workers. The combined employer-employee tax is 12.4 percent, starting with the first dollar earned, with no deductions or exemptions.[51] For poor workers, this is by far the highest tax they pay, far higher than federal or state income taxes. This tax burden helps squeeze out private savings options, even if those private options would yield a much higher return. Personal accounts would not require additional savings by the poor but would allow them to divert a portion of *what they are already paying* to higher returning investments, providing them with a chance to earn capital returns currently only available to those with higher incomes.

Moreover, unlike Social Security benefits, personal accounts would be inheritable. This means that, instead of being forced to effectively annuitize their wealth, those groups in our society with shorter life expectancies, such as the poor and African Americans, would have the opportunity to pass this wealth to their children rather than simply losing it. This intergenerational wealth transmission would have a significant impact on poverty and inequality.

Harvard economist Martin Feldstein reaches a similar conclusion. A larger proportion of a high-income worker's wealth is in fungible assets. Since fungible wealth can be inherited, while Social Security wealth is not, this has led to a stable concentration of fungible wealth among a small proportion of the population. Feldstein's work suggests that the concentration of wealth in the United States would be reduced by as much as half if low-income workers were able to substitute investment wealth for Social Security wealth. [52]

This is especially significant for African Americans. At every age and every income-level, African Americans have shorter life expectancies than do whites. Roughly one of every three African American men will pay into Social Security but die before they can collect benefits. Think of this, again, in the context of forced annuitization. Jeffrey Brown of the University of Illinois has suggested that a college-educated white male would be best served by converting about 92 percent of his retirement savings into an annuity. Conversely, an African American man with less than a high school education should only be annuitizing about 69 percent of his retirement income. Yet given the likelihood that Social Security will provide all, or nearly all, of his retirement income, he will effectively be forced to annuitize almost 100 percent of his retirement funds.[53]

In *Capital in the Twenty-First Century*, Thomas Piketty makes much of the accumulation of capital by the wealthy that have disproportionate access to investment.[54] The answer to that problem is not to deprive the wealthy of the opportunity to invest intergenerationally, but to extend that opportunity to the poor. Few policy changes would do more to expand capital ownership, both for this generation of poor people and their children, then allowing low-income workers to save and privately invest a portion of their Social Security taxes through personal accounts. Social Security reform will undoubtedly be debated on other grounds.[55] However, the benefits that personal accounts offer for low-income wealth accumulation should not be forgotten.

We naturally think of wealth as being something for the wealthy. It shouldn't be. If we truly want to help the poor become self-sufficient and give them the opportunity to invest in both their own and their children's futures, we need to make it easier for those currently in poverty to accumulate wealth. That means removing existing regulatory barriers to saving while expanding savings options that allow the poor to tap into the same wealth-building opportunities that are available to wealthier Americans.

CHAPTER NINE: INCLUSIVE ECONOMIC GROWTH

> *[T]he free market is the greatest producer of wealth in history—it has lifted billions of people out of poverty.*
>
> —*Barack Obama*[1]

As President Barack Obama was saying, the past 300 or more years of history have shown us that economic growth can do more to improve the lives of the poor than any government program ever could. As Figure 9.1 shows, for most of recorded history, humankind was desperately poor. Then, coinciding with the advent of modern free-market capitalism, human wealth suddenly began to increase exponentially. And while those at the top of the income ladder undoubtedly saw major gains, those who benefited the most from this increase in wealth were those at the bottom.

In her groundbreaking book *Bourgeois Equality*, Deirdre McCloskey points out that in the era before modern free-market capitalism, great civilizations, such as Periclean Greece or Song Dynasty China, sometimes saw a temporary doubling of national income per capita. Such gains were considered extraordinary. But compare that to the fact that since 1800, developed countries like Sweden or Japan have seen a 3,200 percentage growth in per capita income. And with that growth came all sorts of associated benefits, including longer life expectancies,

Figure 9.1

Economic Growth in Major World Regions

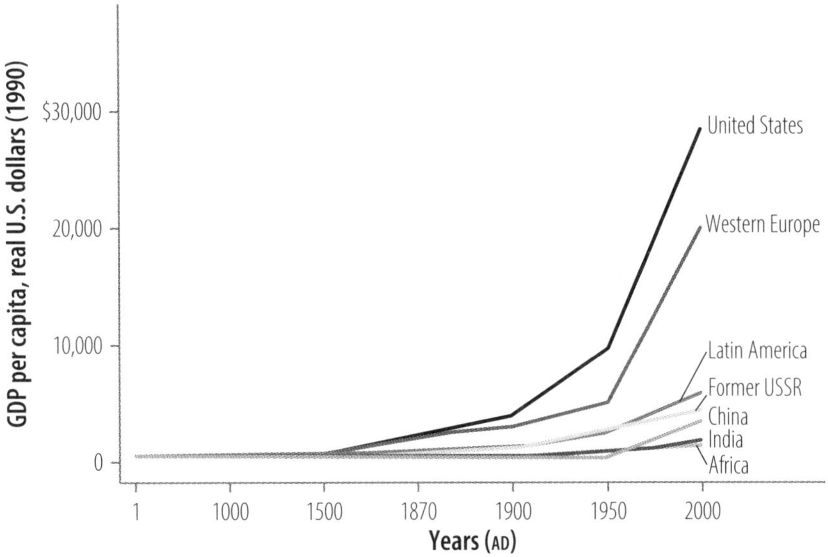

Source: Angus Maddison, *Contours of the World Economy: 1–2030 AD* (Oxford, U.K.: Oxford University Press, 2007).
Note: Time line is not to scale. GDP = gross domestic product.

a better-educated citizenry, expanded civil and political rights, and reduced poverty.[2] Studies measuring inequality over time against indexes of economic freedom (adjusted to exclude exogenous factors such as educational levels, climate, agricultural share of employment, and so forth) show a small but statistically significant *reduction* in inequality in countries with high economic freedom scores.[3]

What has been true worldwide has been true for the United States as well. Consider that by most measures nearly all Americans were poor at the start of the last century. Indeed, if we use a definition corresponding to today's poverty measures, 60 to 80 percent of the U.S. population was poor at the start of the 20th century. By 1948, despite an interruption during the Great Depression, the poverty level had fallen to under 33 percent. Poverty continued to decline steadily, and by the start of the War on Poverty in 1965, was down to just 17.3 percent (Figure 9.2).[4]

Similar improvements can be seen for key subgroups as well. For instance, African American poverty declined from more than 75 percent

Figure 9.2

Projected Poverty Rates for Persons, 1900–1946

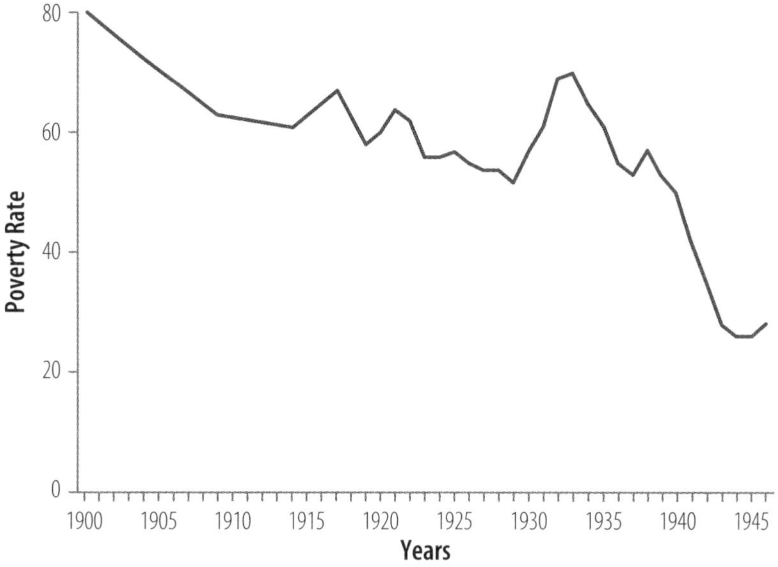

Source: Computations based on mean personal income data from U.S. Census Bureau, 1975.

in 1959 to under 35 percent by 1965.[5] The poverty rate for female-headed households also fell by roughly 10 percent over that period.[6]

Much of this decline took place in the absence of major federal anti-poverty programs. True, Social Security likely played a role for the elderly poor, and other small-scale anti-poverty programs came and went, but there was nothing close to the massive federal welfare state that exists today. Clearly, some other factor played an enormous role, and nearly all economists would agree that that factor was economic growth. As Tyler Cowen puts it, "As a matter of empirical fact, it is economic growth that lifts most people out of poverty, not transfer payments."[7] McCloskey refers to this succinctly as The Great Fact.[8]

Of course, it is not necessarily true that a rising tide lifts all boats. Many poor people have far too many holes in their boat. Others lack a boat at all. Still, it seems hard to visualize a way to reduce poverty that does not involve a rising tide of some sort. A vigorous and growing economy might not be sufficient to reduce poverty, but it is necessary. You cannot redistribute wealth if there is no wealth to redistribute. Nor can you expect the poor to work and support themselves and their families in the absence of good-paying jobs. Whether on the left or right, whatever your preferred approach to fighting poverty, a growing economy should be a key component to any comprehensive anti-poverty strategy.

Not only do we know the benefits of economic growth, but also we know what leads to it. Most economists would agree that there are three component ingredients of economic growth: (1) growth in the labor supply, (2) improvements in the quality of labor participation, and (3) policies that increase innovation and productivity.[9] It is really fairly simple. More workers will produce more output. So will smarter or more skilled workers. Likewise, growth comes from making workers more efficient by providing them with better equipment, materials, or ways to do things. That comes from innovation, which is, in turn, supported and sustained by investment and entrepreneurship.

Unfortunately, however, current trends make all three of these factors problematic, suggesting that future growth could be far slower than we would like. Moreover, our ability to significantly improve at least two of these factors may be limited.

First factor. Consider first the growth of the labor force, either in the size of the overall workforce or the number of hours worked per capita. Simply put, the more workers or the longer they work, the more that they can produce. Over the past 50 years, nearly half of the U.S. growth rate can be attributed to a growing labor force.[10]

However, the trends for U.S. growth have been going in the opposite direction. For the past two decades, the U.S. labor force has been growing by only 1.2 percent annually, down significantly from the 2.6 percent annual growth we saw in the 1970s.[11] The future looks even bleaker. The Bureau of Labor Statistics projects a labor force growth rate of just 0.5 percent over the next decade, and little to no improvement beyond that. Since 1948, the work rate (employment to population ratio) for U.S. men 20 and older fell from 85.8 percent to 68.2 percent. For "prime-age" men—the 25-to-54 age group that historically is the most likely to be employed—work rates fell from 94.1 percent in 1948 to 84.3 percent in 2015. And just since 2000, the work rate for all Americans age 20 and older has fallen by 4 percentage points.[12] It is not just that the growth in the number of workers has slowed, but that the number of hours worked (per worker) has declined. Since 1920, total hours worked by Americans has fallen by more than 20 percent. This decline in the workforce makes it much harder to maintain economic growth.[13]

Some of the policies discussed in previous chapters would help increase the labor supply by bringing more poor and disadvantaged people into the workforce. For instance, changes to the criminal justice system will make it easier for those with a criminal record to find work. In addition, some kind of welfare reform that dealt with the implicitly high marginal tax rate conundrum and encouraged recipients to move into the workforce would also improve labor force participation. And increased immigration would help. Indeed, without current immigration levels, we would not be seeing even the small growth in the workforce that we are. Some estimates suggest that increasing immigration by even an additional 1 million immigrants per year could increase economic growth rate by 15 percent going forward.[14]

Realistic gains from any or all of these policies, at least in the current political environment, is likely to be marginal. The big gains in the labor force from the baby boom and the civil rights revolution that moved women and minorities into the labor force have already been absorbed, and there is nothing of a similar magnitude on the horizon. Immigration policy under the Trump administration appears to be moving in a distinctly nativist direction. Therefore we should not expect significant gains in growth from increases in the labor supply.

Second factor. This brings us to the second factor in economic growth: human capital. If you can't increase labor participation, another way to increase economic growth is to make the workers you do have more productive by developing their skills. But, here too, barring some unforeseen innovation in technology or vocational methods, there appears to be little room for improvement. The low-hanging fruit has been picked for now.

We saw big gains from increased educational attainment in the 1950s and 1960s, but that growth has all but disappeared in recent years, especially for men. High school graduation rates have actually declined slightly from their peak in the late 1960s, and college graduation rates have been largely flat since 1980.[15] We have already achieved the easiest gains from widespread education. As Ryan Avent writes in *The Economist*, "[I]t's much easier to teach the median kid to read, write, and do algebra than it is to teach the median kid graduate engineering." And it is much easier to "teach the median kid to read, write, and do algebra than it is to teach the underperforming student from a household in the lowest income decile to do the same thing."[16] As a result, James Heckman and Dimitriy Masterov estimate that productivity growth from education will be only half of what it was before 2000.[17]

As we saw in chapter 7, efforts by the government to improve the ability of low-skilled workers to be employed have largely been ineffective. At the same time, public schools have largely failed to prepare students for future jobs. The education reforms suggested in chapter 7 may well have a positive impact, but any short-term gains will likely be on the margins.

Third factor. If the ability to extract greater growth from both increased labor force participation and improved human capital are limited, we are then left with the third factor for economic growth, improving the institutional environment that enables productivity in the private sector. This results in increased economic output via greater entrepreneurship, innovation, and investment. A more efficient economy means that we can produce more output from each unit of input.

In 1908 it took nearly two years' wages for a typical worker to purchase a Model T. Today, a worker can buy a car with technology and luxuries that Henry Ford could hardly have conceived of for less than six months of wages.[18] That is a tangible improvement in the lives of millions of Americans that is directly attributable to the increased productivity resulting from innovation. Looking into the future, it is estimated that the continued growth in artificial intelligence will create nearly $3 trillion in new wealth over the next decade, a substantial proportion of which will accrue to the United States.[19] While there is always attention paid to the big technological breakthroughs, it is the little, everyday improvements and innovations that compound to bring increased growth and improve our standards of living.

The United States has long been considered nearly synonymous with innovation. Yet that edge has been steadily eroding. New firms now compose a smaller share of total firms than they did during the previous four decades. Business deaths now exceed business startups. And while some of this can be traced to the Great Recession, the decline in entrepreneurship has actually been going on since the 1970s.[20] There are undoubtedly many causes for this change, not the least of which is that many of the big-government policies that we have pursued over the past half century have been inimical to innovation and economic growth.

Innovation doesn't occur in a vacuum. It requires political institutions and a legal environment that is conducive to entrepreneurship and encourages investment. Those institutional factors are generally considered to include, in the broadest sense, "governmental stability, the enforceability of contracts and property rights, tax and fiscal policies, trade policies, regulatory policies," and so on.[21]

Essentially, this is economic liberalism in the classical sense. Policies that expand economic liberty provide an environment that leads to increased economic growth. Conversely, policies that restrict economic freedom, such as high taxes, out-of-control spending, and excessive regulation, slow economic growth. Even policies that have only a small immediate impact on economic growth can compound significantly over time. If America's economic growth rate had been just 1 percentage point lower between 1870 and 1990, the U.S. economy today would be no larger than that of Mexico.[22]

Figure 9.3 illustrates the relationship between generally recognized components of economic liberty and economic growth.

Overall, the quartile of countries rated most economically free by the Fraser Institute's annual Index of Economic Freedom had an average Gross Domestic Product (GDP) per capita of $39,899. The least free quartile averaged just $6,253. Economic growth among the freest economies averaged 3.4 percent, compared with just 2.6 percent for those ranked least free. Freer countries also perform better on measures ranging from life expectancy to the amount of income earned by the poorest citizens.[23]

Unfortunately, the United States is becoming less economically free, and therefore less hospitable to investment, entrepreneurship, and innovation. Every year a consortium of research organizations from more than 90 countries ranks countries on their level of economic freedom. As recently as 2000, the United States was considered to have the

Figure 9.3

Prosperity and Economic Freedom, 2014

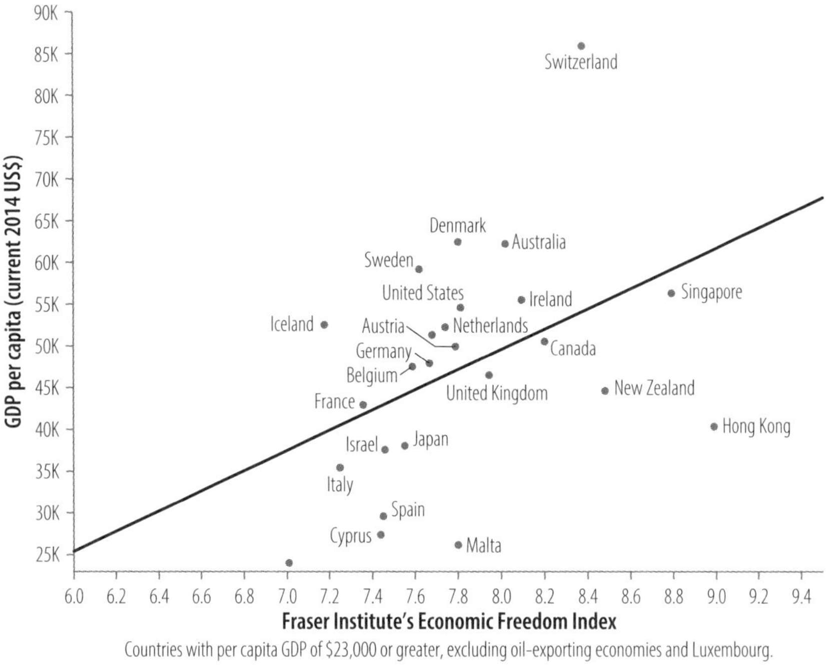

Sources: James Gwartney, Robert Lawson, and Joshua Hall, *Economic Freedom of the World: 2017 Annual Report*, Fraser Institute, September 28, 2017, https://www.fraserinstitute.org/studies/economic-freedom-of-the-world-2017-annual-report; World Bank, "GDP per capita (current US$) 2014," World Development Indicators, World Bank, Washington, https://data.worldbank.org/indicator/NY.GDP.PCAP.CD.
Note: GDP = gross domestic product; k = 1,000.

second-freest economy in the world, trailing only Hong Kong. But in the most recent report, we have fallen all the way to 16th, squeezed between 15th-ranked Taiwan and number 17, Romania.[24] Nor is this report the only indication that our economy is far from free. For example, the United States is 51st in the World Bank's rankings of how easy it is to start a business.[25] And Transparency International ranks the United States 18th on its Corruption Perceptions Index.[26]

To increase economic growth, the United States needs to reverse this trend toward declining economic freedom. This means pursuing policies that will reduce the burden of excessive debt, taxes, and regulations, while liberalizing labor markets and remaining open to trade. In short, we must reduce the size, cost, and intrusiveness of government.

The corporate tax cuts that passed Congress in December 2017 were helpful in reducing the bias in the U.S. tax code against investment and increasing U.S. firms' global competitiveness. The corporate rate cuts and movement toward a territorial, as opposed to global, tax regime increased incentives for firms to remain located in the United States.

Despite these improvements, there is still work to be done. The tax code remains opaque and complex. Before 2017's tax legislation, tax compliance constituted a serious drag on the U.S. economy.[27] While the 2017 tax bill trimmed a number of deductions, some potentially pernicious new provisions were added. We don't yet know whether, on net, the tax overhaul actually reduced or increased the code's complexity in practice. In particular, the creation of a lower rate for so-called "pass-through" businesses opens up a number of opportunities for gaming by creative tax advisers.[28] Furthermore, some of the tax expenditures most criticized by economists have also been the most stubbornly hard to kill. Among the largest of these are the tax exclusion for employer-provided health insurance, the mortgage interest deduction, the deduction for state and local taxes, and the deductions for charitable contributions. Disguised as tax relief and guarded by well-financed lobbying efforts, these distort economic activity in a number of pernicious ways.[29]

Like taxes, excessive government debt also drives down economic growth. Our official national debt now tops $21 trillion, and the inclusion of unfunded liabilities for programs like Social Security and Medicare bring the nation's total indebtedness to nearly $100 trillion.[30] Our official debt exceeds 100 percent of GDP, and total debt tops 500 percent.

Although scholars differ on the point at which debt becomes an encumbrance to growth, most agree that there is some point at which debt cannot be sustained. The Congressional Budget Office suggests that because of our current debt, our children will be $3,000 to $5,000 poorer than they would otherwise be.[31]

Excessive regulation can also be a barrier to economic growth. Every year the federal government issues some 3,500 to 4,800 new regulations, the vast majority of which fall on business.[32] While some of these rules may have contributed to health and safety as well as a cleaner environment, there is no doubt that they have also raised the cost of hiring and made it more difficult to start a new business. One report estimates that the total cost of regulatory compliance is $1.88 trillion each year.[33]

No one is suggesting that all regulations should be eliminated. But there needs to be recognition that excessive regulation brings with it a cost. This cost includes not just the direct cost of complying with the regulations, but the indirect costs as well. General Electric alone employs roughly 1,000 accountants and lawyers in order to comply with federal regulations.[34] As costly as this is for large corporations, it can be a devastating burden for a small business.

Above all, we should recognize that economic growth is not a separate issue from fighting poverty. It is not either one or the other. A robust, growing economy can make it easier for those in poverty to find jobs, improve wages and working conditions, and ultimately lead to a broader distribution of resources. Poverty, after all, is the natural condition of humanity. Throughout most of human history, we have existed in the most meager of conditions. Prosperity, on the other hand, is something that is created.

We know that the best way to create wealth is not through government action, but through the power of the free market. Our anti-poverty policies should reflect this.

Making Growth More Inclusive

While the poverty-reducing power of economic growth is impossible to deny, it is also true that over the past few decades the amount of poverty reduction from economic growth has been smaller and less steady than expected. During the 1960s, for instance, a 1 percent increase in the annual growth of real GDP was typically accompanied by a 0.4 percentage-point reduction in the poverty rate. In the 1970s, however, the effect of GDP growth on poverty reduction was slightly more than half that amount, and this weaker relationship persisted throughout the 1980s.[35] This trend has persisted to the present day. It is critically important to understand why this has happened and take steps to rectify it.

There have been three broad theories as to why economic growth has not automatically reduced poverty in recent years. Those ideas are not mutually exclusive, and all are likely to have played a role, although experts differ on the relative weight to assign each component.

First, some suggest that growth has simply been too slow and uneven. Rebecca Blank of the University of Wisconsin, one of the nation's leading poverty researchers, for example, notes that the years "between 1970 and 1982 contained four business cycles . . ., five years of negative GNP [gross national product] growth, and a rapid increase in both inflation and unemployment. It is perhaps not surprising that poverty is less responsive to short and sequential upturns and downturns in the economy."[36] Since 2000, we have also had two recessions, and the current recovery has been tepid at best.

Second, the weaker relationship may be something of an illusion, reflecting changes in the composition of welfare benefits and poverty measurement. Poverty measures may have become less useful and accurate as Medicaid and other in-kind benefits began to account for a greater share of transfers to low-income families. Elizabeth Powers of the University of Illinois argues the following:

> [A] first look at the consumption poverty data suggests at the very least that the picture of increasing inequality and the failure of the 1980s' "rising tide" to lift all boats may be exaggerated. The poor appear to benefit from a vigorously expanding economy now as much as before. After considering this new evidence, it is not at all clear that a policy to promote overall growth (and hence to expand aggregate consumption opportunities) is of declining interest to Americans below the poverty line.[37]

Finally, some suggest that external factors like changing demographics, stagnating education quality, slower wage growth for unskilled workers, and the growth in the number of female-headed households may have worked together to offset the reduction in poverty that would have otherwise occurred because of economic growth. In an article in the *Journal of Economic Literature*, Isabel Sawhill explains that "[e]conomic growth does produce (small) declines in poverty among the non-aged once other variables are controlled for. However, other variables have been operating to offset the effects of growth."[38] She claims that absent these external changes—if the age, race, and sex composition of household heads in 1980 had been the same as that in 1950—the poverty rate would have been 23 percent lower at the end of the period.[39]

Whereas each of these theories may offer a partial explanation for the weakening of the relationship between growth and declining poverty in the United States, there is another explanation that must be considered: government policies themselves may have prevented the poor from fully participating in the growth that we have seen. To be truly effective as an anti-poverty instrument, policies must encourage not just generalized economic growth, but inclusive growth.

Chapters 6 through 9 have laid out a number of policy changes that would enable the poor to take better advantage of the opportunities generated by growth. By reforming the criminal justice system, we can remove barriers to employment and education, as well as increase opportunities for stable family formation. By reforming the education system to promote innovation and competition, thereby giving parents greater choice and control, we can build human capital for those who need it most. By reducing zoning restrictions and other regulations that inflate the cost of housing, we can both lower the financial burden of housing and make it easier for the poor to locate in areas that offer greater opportunity. And by making it easier for the poor to save and accumulate assets, we give them opportunities to invest in their future (or that of their children).

There are also some specific steps that can be taken to remove regulatory and policy obstacles that unduly limit the ability of the poor to join in the broader enrichment of society.

The Minimum Wage

It has become fashionable among progressives to suggest that an increase in the minimum wage is an effective way to reduce poverty. In reality, minimum wage laws prevent many low-skilled individuals from getting a start on the first rung of the ladder to economic success and self-sufficiency.

The current federal minimum wage is $7.25 per hour, although 29 states and the District of Columbia actually have higher minimums under state law, and as much as $11.50 in the District.[40] Several cities also have much higher minimum wages. The federal minimum has not been raised since 2009, and there has been a growing push to increase it to $12 or even $15 per hour. Efforts at the state and municipal level to increase minimum wages have been even more vigorous.

One can certainly understand why some people believe that increasing the minimum wage would help reduce poverty. If a single mother with two children worked 40 hours a week at the current minimum of $7.25 per hour, she would earn $15,080 per year. That would leave her $4,450 below the poverty line. Conversely, a minimum wage of $12.50 per hour would lift her $6,470 above poverty.

However, the hypothetical woman in the example is *not* the typical minimum wage earner. Fewer than 5 percent of minimum-wage earners are adults working full time trying to support a family. Minimum-wage earners might not be college kids earning summer beer money anymore, but neither are they typically hard-pressed single parents. In fact, the average family income for a minimum-wage worker is $53,000 a year.[41]

One study found that even increasing the minimum wage to $15 would help only 12 percent of Supplemental Nutrition Assistance Program (SNAP, or food stamps) recipients and 9.7 percent of working-age Medicaid recipients. For smaller increases, almost no welfare recipients would be affected: less than 1 percent of Temporary Assistance for Needy Families (TANF) recipients, barely 2 percent of those eligible for Special Supplemental Nutrition Program for Women, Infants, and Children (WIC), and just over 1 percent of working age housing assistance recipients.[42] Another study, by Jeffrey Clemens, found that the $2.05 minimum wage increase of 2009 had no significant effect on the receipt of welfare benefits.[43] It has been estimated that an increase to $15 an hour would give only 12 percent of the associated rise in incomes to families below the poverty line, while 38 percent would go to middle-class families well above the poverty level.[44] Still, even a poorly targeted effort to raise wages might be worthwhile if it did more good than harm. But the preponderance of the evidence suggests otherwise.

At one time, there was a nearly universal consensus among economists that artificially increasing the minimum wage almost inevitably led to job loss. The amount of compensation a worker receives is more or less a function of his or her productivity. As Greg Mankiw, chairman and professor of economics at Harvard, explains, "Economic theory says that the wage a worker earns, measured in units of output, equals the amount of output the worker can produce."[45] This explanation somewhat oversimplifies the issue, of course. There are other factors involved. However, one can't just arbitrarily declare a worker's value. Raising wages above any productivity gains from that worker means that the employer would be losing money on that worker. In many cases that will result in the loss of the job.

However, in the 1990s, a new wave of research began to challenge this economic orthodoxy. Led by David Card of the University of California at Berkeley and Alan Kruger of Princeton University, researchers used state minimum wage variations to compare workers in states that raised the minimum wage to workers in contiguous states that did not. They did not find the expected job losses in those states that increased the minimum wage.[46]

The revisionism of Card, Kruger, and others provided academic support to those who argued that factors such as increased employee satisfaction and retention lead to increases in productivity that offset increased wage costs. Not only did this mean it was unnecessary to eliminate jobs, but some employers might even be better off after a minimum wage hike. Moreover, it is possible that productivity gains have outpaced wages, meaning that small increases in the minimum wage would simply be playing catch up.

More recently, however, a third wave of research suggests that Card, Kruger, and their followers are wrong, and the original consensus was correct. Some such as David Neumark of the University of California at Irvine have criticized the Card-Kruger methodology, suggesting that the adjustments for preexisting trends and comparison counties or states were poorly chosen. Using different controls, they find job losses similar to those predicted in the earlier literature.[47]

Perhaps more significantly, a new body of literature has developed that looks at different channels of effects of minimum wage hikes. These studies suggest that previous research, which largely focused on the immediate aftermath of a minimum wage hike, failed to capture the full effect of the change over time. Such long-term studies are far more likely to show job loss, or perhaps more accurately, reduced job creation, as a result of increases in the minimum wage.[48] These studies also show that both the size and speed of the increase matter. If the minimum wage increase is temporary because in real terms inflation and wage growth will erode the increase in a few years, fewer firms will adjust to the increase, and their adjustments will be smaller. However, more permanent increases in the minimum wage would result in even greater job losses. For instance, a study by Jonathan Meer and Jeremy West found that, while we may not see an immediate hit from raising the minimum wage, "minimum wage reduces job growth over a period of several years."[49]

It can safely be said, therefore, that the consensus on the relationship between job loss and the minimum wage is shakier than it used to be. Small increases in the minimum wage, or those with very long phase-in periods, may have little impact on jobs, especially in the short term. It is also worth noting that even economists who are supportive of modest increases in the minimum wage are concerned over the effect of larger increases. For example, Harry Holzer, who served as chief economist in the U.S. Department of Labor for President Bill Clinton, explained that he had "serious worries about a $15 an hour minimum wage" and described an increase of this magnitude as "extremely risky [because in] job markets where young or less-educated workers already have difficulty finding jobs and gaining important work experience, such mandates will likely make it much harder."[50] For this reason, even Card's colleague Alan Krueger warns against a national $15 minimum wage, saying it would "put us in uncharted waters, and risk undesirable and unintended consequences."[51]

Finally, raising the minimum wage effectively forces low-skilled workers to compete with the higher-skilled for the same scarce employment resources. It can also put them at a disadvantage against labor situated in other countries, and more recently, increasingly capable machines. President Obama's Council of Economic Advisers reported that the jobs most susceptible to being replaced by automation are concentrated at the low end of the wage scale—precisely those jobs that would be adversely affected by a mandated increase in labor costs.[52]

Perversely, hiking the minimum wage could keep low-skilled workers trapped at minimum wage levels rather than moving up the income scale. A study by Jeffrey Clemens and Michael Wither found that as a result of state minimum wage increases in the second half of the 2000s, workers ages 16 to 30 with no high school degree saw their income fall by as much as $100 in the first year after the increase and $50 in the following two years. The combination of reduced earnings and employment had adverse effects on this group's economic mobility, as these targeted workers experienced a 5 percentage point decline in their medium-run probability of reaching earnings greater than $1,500 per month.[53] The authors warn that the minimum wage increases reduced these workers' "short-run access to opportunities for accumulating experience and developing skills."[54]

Similar issues apply to efforts to mandate other forms of compensation, such as paid family leave, paid sick leave, fixed work schedules, vacation time, and so on. Any increase in the cost of hiring a worker will have to be offset elsewhere. That can take many forms, inducing reduced wages or lower future pay increases, cutbacks in other nonmandated benefits, or lower levels of employment, whether layoffs of current works or reduced future hiring. An inclusive and market-oriented policy would avoid this tradeoff.

Occupational Licensing

An even more pernicious barrier to economic inclusiveness is the proliferation of occupational licensing laws. Five times as many professions today require a license or certification of some kind than in the 1950s. Overall, more than 1,100 different professions require a license in at least one state, from florists to funeral attendants, from tree trimmers to make-up artists.[55] In fact, according to both the Brookings Institution and the president's Council of Economic Advisers, roughly 25 percent to 30 percent of the workforce is currently covered by some form of occupational licensing.[56]

Although in some cases licensing requirements can be a mere formality, the education, training, and financial burden is often substantial. Iowa, Nebraska, and South Dakota, for instance, require 16 months of training to become a beautician or hairdresser. One study found that on average, obtaining a license for a low-skilled job required at least 8 months of training.[57] Such training courses are far from free. Nor is it just the time and money spent in training that poses a hurdle for the poor. In Louisiana, to become a florist, you must pass a state-administered test. The application fee for that test is $150, but, more significantly, it is only delivered in the state capital, Baton Rouge, meaning that people from other areas of the state must travel there at their own expense.[58] This effectively puts those professions off limits for those Americans who lack the time or money to complete the training requirements.

Economists broadly agree that occupational licensing tends to increase wages for those with licenses, while simultaneously reducing wages for those without licenses. The size of this gap varies widely depending on the profession and the difficulty of obtaining a license. In general, though, estimates suggest that wages for licensed workers could be as much as 10 percent to 15 percent higher relative to unlicensed workers with similar characteristics.[59]

Unsurprisingly, licensed workers also find it easier to get a job. Again, there is a wide variation from profession to profession, but in general, licensing requirements are a barrier to entry within a field. As such, they tend to create a labor shortage for licensed professionals, with fewer workers competing for each job. At the same time, they create increased "crowding" in unlicensed occupations, with the larger number of unlicensed workers competing for a shrinking pool of unlicensed jobs. A study by the Institute for Justice found a strong correlation between occupational licensing laws for low-skilled jobs and a state's unemployment rate.[60]

In addition to making it harder to find a job, occupational licensing also makes it more difficult to create your own job, that is, start a business. Such entrepreneurial activity is especially important to poor communities. As Kelly Edmiston, an economist with the Federal Reserve

Bank of Kansas City points out, "Entrepreneurship may yield a double dividend in low- and moderate-income communities. Many of the retail and services establishments available in higher-income areas, such as grocery stores, often are not available to low- and moderate-income people . . . [who also] face transportation challenges. Entrepreneurial activity not only provides income to the entrepreneurs and perhaps others in the community, but it also provides needed goods and services."[61]

Studies show lower rates of entrepreneurship and new business starts in states with extensive occupational licensing requirements. For example, a study by the Goldwater Institute concluded that "States that license more than 50 percent of the low-income occupations had an average entrepreneurship rate that was 11 percent lower than the average for all states."[62] The poor, who lack financial resources, the skills to maneuver through the bureaucracy, and access to legal reputation, are the least likely to be able to start a business. "[T]he higher the rate of licensure of low-income occupations, the lower the rate of low-income entrepreneurship," according to the Goldwater Institute's study.[63]

Finally, the lack of mutual licensing recognition between states makes it much harder to move from state to state in search of a better opportunity. It tends to keep licensed professionals within the state of their licensure, as well as to prevent those without licenses from moving into a state where they may not be able to practice their profession.[64] This can force poor people to remain in areas with low economic growth, poor schools, high crime rates, and few amenities. Traditionally, moving to start a new life has been a way to escape poverty. By reducing that mobility, occupational licensure limits that opportunity.

Given the many ways that occupational licensing laws harm the poor and minorities, it is worth noting that many licensing requirements and other restrictions were initially developed to prevent African Americans from fully participating in the free market.[65] Near the beginning of the 20th century, as African Americans began to move into trades such as plumbing and carpentry, trade unions began to advocate occupational licensure laws to keep them out. Often those licensing statutes contained testing and other requirements only tangentially related to the job in question. An examination of union journals and newspaper accounts at the time many of those laws were passed leaves little doubt as to their racist intent. Typical was this letter in the January 1905 edition of the *Plumbers, Gas, and Steam Fitters Official Journal*: "There are about 10 Negro skate plumbers working around here [Danville, VA], doing quite a lot of jobbing and repairing, but owing to the fact of not having an examination board it is impossible to stop them, hence the anxiety of men here to organize."[66]

African Americans were not the only targets of discriminatory regulations. Regulations were also used to limit the access of other minorities to the economy. For example, one of the nation's earliest zoning laws was an 1885 Modesto, California, ordinance aimed at Chinese immigrants: "[It is] unlawful for any person to establish, maintain, or carry on the business of a public laundry . . . within the City of Modesto, except that part of the city which lies west of the railroad track south of G street."[67]

Occupational licensing continues to have a disproportionate impact on the poor and minorities today.[68] For example, Florida requires interior decorators to have a college degree. Because African Americans are less likely to have a degree than whites, they are more often blocked from the profession. Consider that nationally, two-thirds of white interior decorators have a college degree, but less than half of African American or Latino decorators do.[69] That means many well-trained and successful African American interior decorators are barred from practicing their trade in Florida.

We saw in chapter 6 that many states prohibit anyone with a criminal record from obtaining a license for many professions, a restriction that disproportionately hurts African Americans. In addition, many states prohibit anyone who was ever cited for practicing a profession without a license from ever receiving a license for that profession.[70]

Adding all this together, we see a system that makes it that much harder to get out of poverty. An Arkansas study, for instance, found that a two-thirds reduction in the number of jobs which required a license would reduce poverty among African Americans by 15.6 percent.[71]

When considering the impact of regulations, we should consider the trade-offs involved, especially their impact on those most in need.

The List Goes On

The minimum wage and occupational licensure are good examples, but hardly the only regulations that make it harder for the poor to participate in a growing economy. For instance, chapter 8 explored how zoning laws price the poor out of affordable housing, but zoning laws also cost them jobs. According to the U.S. Census Bureau, 52 percent of all businesses are "operated primarily from somebody's home."[72] While many of these jobs may provide small amounts of secondary income for middle-class families, home-based employment may also be particularly well suited for low-income single parents, who lack the resources for childcare or transportation. Yet many cities limit or ban home-based businesses. Others impose onerous regulations on such businesses, such as prohibiting signs, imposing parking restrictions, or forbidding the business owner from receiving clients or bringing nonfamily employees into the home.[73]

We are all familiar with stories about how such famous businesses as Amazon and Microsoft started in someone's garage. In many American cities, they would have been illegal. Far more often, the type of businesses outlawed through zoning and other land-use regulations are those that can be started with minimal capital investment or by those with limited skills, including day care, beauticians, caterers, bakers, auto repair, and so on. Nashville, Tennessee, even bans giving piano lessons in your home.[74]

In addition, making even modest alterations to a home for accommodating business needs may run into zoning, land use, and construction code challenges. Where not prohibited outright, such changes can require a costly, often labyrinthine, approval process, involving architects and lawyers. The process itself can block the poor from being able to start a home business.

Government regulations that prohibit or restrict ride-sharing companies like Uber and Lyft also limit opportunities for the poor. Studies show that ride-sharing companies consistently provide better and more reliable services to poor and minority neighborhoods than traditional taxi services.[75] By offering convenient and affordable transportation options to poor households, ride-sharing companies make it easier for the poor to work in areas outside their immediate neighborhoods. Given the scarcity of high-paying jobs in many neighborhoods that are poor, which also frequently lack easily accessible public transportation, ride-sharing companies can make the difference between working or not.

Ride-sharing companies also offer an entry-level job opportunity for poor people. Roughly three-quarters of poor families have a car.[76] Because a car and a functioning knowledge of the city are the only real requirements for being a driver for these companies, they are often the ideal starting job for those with few skills or resources. That's one reason why so many new immigrants take jobs as drivers. Moreover, drivers can generally set their own hours, making driving attractive for those with other responsibilities, such as family obligations or seeking other income.[77]

Meanwhile, traditional taxis are subject to strict regulations, including limits on the number of operators, which create effective monopolies and force would-be drivers to pay exorbitant rents. Yet many states and localities have attempted to impose tax-like regulations on those operations or even prohibited ride-sharing altogether. Such regulations protect entrenched existing interests, but it is often the poor who pay most of the cost.

Regulations can also make it harder for single parents who are poor to work by restricting their childcare options. In most states, it is illegal to operate an unlicensed childcare center, with a handful of exceptions for small churches or home-based services. Few would oppose local regulations designed to ensure the health and safety of children in these settings. But a growing number of regulations have nothing to do with such concerns.

Regulations often have more to do with protecting large institutional childcare providers or increasing the salary of professional child educators than they do with protecting children. For example, many states require such things as both basic and continuing teacher training for childcare workers, impose English language proficiency for workers (even if the children being cared for are not English speakers), limit child-to-staff ratios, and cap the number of children per center.[78]

These unnecessary regulations can substantially drive up the cost of childcare. For example, decreasing the staff to child ratio by just one child can increase the cost of care by as much as 20 percent.[79] With childcare costs averaging more than $10,000 per year per child, even a small increase can pose an insurmountable burden for a poor family.

And, while much of the recent public policy debate has focused on subsidizing childcare to reduce costs, those subsidies are often accompanied by strings that limit parental choices. Surveys have shown that many low-income parents prefer the type of informal childcare that is least likely to be eligible for subsidies.[80] Rather than chase rising costs with more and more subsidies, we should be examining those regulations that make it hard for the poor to find the childcare arrangements that they both want and need.

The previous examples are by no means an exhaustive list of regulatory hurdles for the poor. But these few examples demonstrate how even well-intentioned regulations often harm the poor. The wealthy, powerful, and well connected are much better situated to absorb or avoid these costs. In many cases—occupational licensure being a prime example—the powerful directly benefit from regulations that penalize the poor. All this means that when calculating the cost of regulation, we should pay special attention to how those rules affect those who are already struggling to get a foothold.

CHAPTER TEN: LOOKING AHEAD

Some men see things the way they are and say why;
I dream things that never were and say, why not?
—Robert F. Kennedy[1]

It is easy to become pessimistic about efforts to fight poverty. Despite myriad programs and trillions of dollars in anti-poverty spending, millions of Americans remain left behind. We have managed to make poverty less miserable for some and lifted others above an arbitrary poverty line, but we have done little to help people become self-sufficient or to take charge of their own lives. Nor can we promise that their children and grandchildren will not be similarly trapped in poverty.

Redistribution has limits and appears to be reaching a point of diminishing returns. Government programs that try to provide the poor with more and better skills have had modest success at best, while public schools leave millions of poor children unprepared for the future. Some government efforts to fight poverty may even be counterproductive, setting incentives that actually make it harder for people to get out of poverty over the long term.

Meanwhile, Washington, D.C., remains trapped in a sterile debate about whether funding for program A should be increased by $1 billion or program B should be cut by $1 billion. We can't even agree on what causes poverty. Is it any wonder that even poor people themselves believe that there is little that we can do to fight poverty?[2]

Compounding the policy difficulties are the political realities. Bipartisanship is almost impossible to find. We recently completed one of the most divisive presidential campaigns in modern history, and both political parties are being driven to the extremes.

Yet I remain an optimist.

The term "the American dream" was first coined by the writer and historian James Truslow Adams in his 1931 book, *The Epic of America*. Adams defined it as "a land in which life is richer and fuller for everyone, with opportunity for everyone according to his ability or achievement. . . . It is not a dream of motorcars and high wages merely, but a dream of a social order in which each man and each woman shall be able to attain the fullest stature of which they are innately capable, and be recognized by others for what they are, regardless of the fortuitous circumstances of birth or position."[3] In short, the American dream is about human flourishing.

That should be the ultimate goal of anti-poverty policy: to make the American Dream a part of everyone's life and expectations.

Will we ever eliminate poverty in America? Certainly not in my lifetime, and perhaps never. But I believe that we can make a difference. We can reduce the number of people unable to care for themselves and their families. We can create more opportunity. We can enable the poor to become full participants in the economy. We can do better than we do today.

To achieve this goal, both the left and right will have to abandon long-held positions. Progressives will have to understand that merely spending more money or creating new programs will not fundamentally alter the equation. Conservatives will need to recognize that poverty is not a moral failure and that incentives matter. Simply blaming the poor for failure to "pull themselves up by their bootstraps" is not an actual policy for fighting poverty.

We need to recognize the role that racial oppression and gender discrimination has played—and continues to play—in creating the conditions that lead to poverty. And we should recognize that the "creative destruction" of a capitalist economy, while creating wealth and reducing poverty in the aggregate, nonetheless results in disruptions that can leave some people behind. We must also recognize that people always have choices and control over their own lives and decisions. Ultimately, people must be responsible for themselves and their families. Anything else deprives them of their place as full human beings. The poor are neither helpless victims of the lottery of life nor the sole architects of their own condition.

But whether poverty results from our checkered history and the current structures of society, from cultural influences, from individual choices, or from some combination of all of these, the government is much more part of the problem than part of the solution. Rather than continuing to throw money at the problem, we must instead create the conditions that enable people to become self-sufficient and to lift themselves out of poverty.

For decades we have essentially pursued the same anti-poverty strategy—creating more and more government programs and spending more and more money without visible improvement in the lives or opportunities of the poor and vulnerable.

It should be apparent that ending—or even reducing—poverty will not be achieved through more small tweaks to the existing social welfare system. It is not a question of spending slightly more or less money, tinkering with the number of hours mandated under work requirements, or rooting out fraud, waste, and abuse. We need a new debate, one that moves beyond our current approach to fighting poverty to focus on what works rather than noble sentiments or good intentions.

Throughout this book, I have tried to outline a series of reforms that offer an opportunity to open up a new and different debate over poverty. Each of them should draw support from across the political spectrum.

1. *Reform the criminal justice system and curtail the War on Drugs.* The criminal justice system is discriminatory against the poor and minorities at every level. That would be a problem regardless of context. But in the context of poverty, it is even more of an issue. It leaves large numbers of the poor burdened with a criminal record that makes it far more difficult for them to find jobs. By dragging large numbers of poor and minority youth into the

criminal justice system, we severely limit the pool of marriageable men, and further the wave of fatherlessness that afflicts poor communities. An effective anti-poverty policy should remove barriers to work and family formation.

2. *Reform education to give more control and choice to parents and break up the public school monopoly.* The days when it was possible to drop out of school and still find a job that enabled a person to support a family are long gone. Education is now vital to escaping poverty. At the same time, despite our spending more and more money on education, our public schools are failing many poor and minority students. The type of innovation necessary to turn this around is unlikely to occur under a system dominated by a government-run monopoly. Instead, our education system needs to be opened up to greater competition and choice.
3. *Bring down the cost of housing.* Restrictive housing regulations primarily benefit the wealthy who own homes, while they drive up rents for the poor. Rather than chase rising housing costs with ever higher subsidies, we should focus on lowering the cost of housing and of rents in particular.
4. *Make it easier for the poor to bank, save, borrow, and invest.* Income is critical to dealing with the immediate needs of the poor, but savings are vital to long-term prosperity. Yet too many poor people find it difficult to access the banking system. We should review banking regulations that primarily harm the poor, while also easing access to nontraditional banking alternatives. At the same time, we should review welfare eligibility requirements to ensure that they do not unnecessarily discourage the poor from accumulating savings.
5. *Increase economic growth and make it more inclusive.* Economic growth does more to reduce poverty over time than any government intervention. Therefore, any effective approach to fighting poverty should include policies that encourage economic growth. But that growth must be inclusive. Thus, we should also make it easier for the poor to find work today by reforming or abolishing regulations that make it harder for the poor to find jobs or start a business.

These proposals are not top-down, government-imposed solutions that treat the poor like helpless children. Nor are they simple calls for the poor to change their behavior and "pull themselves up by their bootstraps." Instead, these proposals aim to reimagine both the structures and cultures within which the poor make choices, to make it possible for the poor to benefit from the actions that can help both them and their children escape poverty and become self-sufficient.

Is there a guarantee that the proposals outlined in this book will work? Of course not. Even if every one of my recommendations were to be enacted in full, some people would still fall between the cracks. Utopia is not an option.

However, the policies we are pursuing today have failed. We may not know whether new policies will work, but we know that existing policies do not. As a result, people are suffering now—today. To stick with a system that we know has failed is to prolong their suffering.

Free markets and individual liberty have done more to reduce poverty than any force in history. Argue as we will about economic inequality, we should recognize that being equally poor is far worse than being unequally rich. Our goal, therefore, should not be to kill the goose that lays the golden eggs, to mindlessly pursue economic equality, or to redistribute wealth regardless of the consequences.

But neither can we adopt a narrow and legalistic program, even a libertarian one, that worries only about process while ignoring outcomes. We should not be satisfied as long as even one person is left behind. We must constantly try to do better, to ensure that every American has the opportunity to be all that they can be. We must challenge those forces that have contributed to poverty, whether they be government policies or racial and gender oppression.

Good intentions and noble desires are never enough. We owe the poor real, tangible, and lasting results.

That should be something that we all agree on.

NOTES

Introduction

[1]Antoine de Saint-Exupéry, *Citadelle* [*The Wisdom of the Sands*] (Paris: Gallimard, 1948), sec. 75, p. 687.

[2]Michael D. Tanner, "The American Welfare State: How We Spend Nearly $1 Trillion a Year Fighting Poverty—and Fail," Cato Institute Policy Analysis no. 694, April 11, 2012, https://www.cato.org/publications/policy-analysis/american-welfare-state-how-we-spend-nearly-%241-trillion-year-fighting-poverty-fail.

[3]Rachel Sheffield and Robert Rector, "The War on Poverty after 50 Years," The Heritage Foundation, September 15, 2014, http://www.heritage.org/poverty-and-inequality/report/the-war-poverty-after-50-years.

[4]Tyler Cowen, "Does the Welfare State Help the Poor?" *Social Philosophy and Policy* 19, no. 1 (2002): 36–54, sec. 2.

[5]Citizens' Board of Inquiry into Hunger and Malnutrition in the United States, *Hunger, USA: A Report by the Citizens' Board of Inquiry into Hunger and Malnutrition in the United States* (Boston: Beacon Press, 1968).

[6]The "very low food security" category identifies households in which food intake of one or more members was reduced and eating patterns disrupted because of insufficient money and other resources for food. Households classified as having *low food security* have reported multiple indications of food access problems and reduced diet quality, but typically those households have reported few, if any, indications of reduced food intake. Those classified as having *very low food security* have reported multiple indications of reduced food intake and disrupted eating patterns because of inadequate resources for food. In most, but not all, households with very low food security, the survey respondent reported that he

or she was hungry at some time during the year but did not eat because there was not enough money for food.

[7]Alisha Coleman-Jensen, Christian Gregory, and Anita Singh, "Household Food Security in the United States in 2013," U.S. Department of Agriculture, Economic Research Report no. 173, September 2014, https://www.ers.usda.gov/webdocs/publications/45265/48787_err173.pdf?v=42265.

[8]John Quigley and Steven Raphael, "Is Housing Unaffordable? Why Isn't It More Affordable?" *Journal of Economic Perspectives* 18, no. 1 (2004): 191–214, http://urbanpolicy.berkeley.edu/pdf/QRJEP04PB.pdf. Their data for households in severely inadequate housing are divided by total number of households found in the U.S. Census Bureau, "Table HH-1. Households, by Type: 1940 to Present," https://www.census.gov/data/tables/time-series/demo/families/households.html.

[9]Nicholas Eberstadt, *The Poverty of "The Poverty Rate": Measure and Mismeasure of Want in Modern America* (Washington: American Enterprise Institute, 2008), http://www.aei.org/files/2014/03/27/-the-poverty-of-the-poverty-rate_102237565852.pdf.

[10]U.S. Energy Information Administration, "2009 Residential Energy Consumption Survey (RECS) Data," http://www.eia.gov/consumption/residential/data/2009/#undefined.

[11]U.S. Census Bureau, "Table 2: Poverty Status of People by Family Relationship, Race, and Hispanic Origin: 1959 to 2009," https://www2.census.gov/programs-surveys/cps/tables/time-series/historical-poverty-people/hstpov2.xls; Carmen DeNavas-Walt, Bernadette Proctor, and Jessica Smith, "Income, Poverty, and Health Insurance Coverage in the United States: 2012," U.S. Census Bureau, Current Population Reports, September 2013, http://www.census.gov/prod/2013pubs/p60-245.pdf. The official poverty measure (OPM) in the United States uses a set of income thresholds that vary by family size and composition to determine who is in poverty. The threshold income is set at three times the cost of a minimum food diet in 1963, updated annually for inflation using the Consumer Price Index for all Urban Consumers. In 2016, the poverty threshold for an individual living alone was $12,228; for a single adult with two children it was $19,337, and for a two-parent household of four it was $24,339. The OPM is badly flawed, counting only money income. In recent years the role of cash assistance has diminished while other programs have become more prominent in the War on Poverty, especially since the welfare reform of 1996. Therefore, the official poverty rate actually measures the number of people living in poverty before taking into account the effect of most government welfare programs. For purposes of this book, most references to poverty refer to the official Census Bureau definition because that is the measurement used in most of the available research. To repurpose Donald Rumsfeld, sometimes you go to print with the research you have, not the research you want. Where other

measures are used, they are identified as such. None are perfect, and we should always be aware of the bias reflected in any specific measure. However, I continue to believe that poverty actually extends beyond material measure. Therefore, when I write about poverty outside of the context of academic studies or government statistics, I am referring to a broader state that denies people the ability to be self-sufficient and fully in control of their lives. It may not be possible to measure this type of poverty precisely, but I believe it best reflects the aspirations for those of us who seek an end to poverty.

[12]Bruce D. Meyer and James X. Sullivan, "Winning the War: Poverty from the Great Society to the Great Recession," National Bureau of Economic Research Working Paper no. 18718, Cambridge, MA, January 2013, http://www.nber.org/papers/w18718.

[13]Ibid.

[14]Christopher Wimer et al., "Trends in Poverty with an Anchored Supplemental Poverty Measure," CPRC Working Paper 1-25, December 5, 2013, Columbia Population Research Center, New York, https://www.gc.cuny.edu/CUNY_GC/media/LISCenter/Readings%20for%20workshop/Madrick2.pdf. Critics of the study point out that the inflation adjustment may overstate the actual reduction in poverty. While questions remain about the magnitude of poverty reduction over time, their study shows a shift away from traditional cash assistance, toward in-kind assistance and programs that operate through the tax code, neither of which show up in the official poverty rate, and it notes that this shift has grown more pronounced in recent years.

[15]Arloc Sherman, Danilo Trisi, and Sharon Parrott, "Various Supports for Low-Income Families Reduce Poverty and Have Long-Term Positive Effects on Families and Children," Center on Budget and Policy Priorities, July 30, 2013, Washington, http://www.cbpp.org/research/various-supports-for-low-income-families-reduce-poverty-and-have-long-term-positive-effects.

[16]Trudi Renwick and Liana Fox, "Table 5b. Effect of Individual Elements on the Number of Individuals in Poverty, 2015," *The Supplemental Poverty Measure: 2015*, U.S. Census Bureau, Current Population Reports, 2016, https://www.census.gov/content/dam/Census/library/publications/2016/demo/p60-258.pdf.

[17]Ibid.

[18]Charles Murray, *Losing Ground: American Social Policy, 1950–1980* (New York: Basic Books, 1984); Robert Moffitt, "Welfare Reform: The U.S. Experience," Institute for Research on Poverty, Discussion paper no. 1334-08, February 2008, http://www.irp.wisc.edu/publications/dps/pdfs/dp133408.pdf.

[19]Moffitt, "Welfare Reform: The U.S. Experience."

[20]Michael Tanner and Charles Hughes, "The Work versus Welfare Trade-Off: 2013," Cato Institute White Paper, August 19, 2013, https://www.cato.org/publications/white-paper/work-versus-welfare-trade.

[21]Rebecca M. Blank, *It Takes a Nation: A New Agenda for Fighting Poverty* (Princeton, NJ: Princeton University Press, 1997), p. 135.

[22]Tyler Cowen, "Does the Welfare State Help the Poor?" *Social Philosophy and Policy* 19, 1 (2002): 36–54, sec. 2. https://philpapers.org/rec/COWDTW.

[23]"DC Neighborhood Cluster Profile, Cluster 39," NeighborhoodInfoDC, http://www.neighborhoodinfodc.org/nclusters/Nbr_prof_clus39.html; D.C. Government Office of Planning, "ACS Profile report, 2015: Social," https://planning.dc.gov/sites/default/files/dc/sites/op/page_content/attachments/2015%20ACS%201-Year%20Districtwide_0.xls.

[24]Jeremey Ashkenas et al., "A Portrait of the Sandtown Neighborhood in Baltimore," *New York Times*, May 3, 2015, https://www.nytimes.com/interactive/2015/05/03/us/a-portrait-of-the-sandtown-neighborhood-in-baltimore.html.

[25]"Students Meeting or Exceeding Grade-Level Standard in English Language Arts (CAASPP), by Grade Level," Lucile Packard Foundation for Children's Health, 2018, http://www.kidsdata.org/topic/127/readingproficiency/table#fmt=133&loc=357&tf=88&ch=1249,1250,623,1251,624,1252,1253,1255&sortColumnId=0&sortType=asc; Mackenzie Mays, "Report: Fresno County's Racial Equality Is among the Worst in the State," *Fresno Bee*, November 2017, http://www.fresnobee.com/news/local/article186907188.html.

[26]Mackenzie Mays, "Poverty Nothing New to Fresno County, but It's Especially Tough for Kids, Report Says," *Fresno Bee*, November 15, 2016, http://www.fresnobee.com/news/local/education/article114766498.html.

[27]Kevin Williamson, "The White Ghetto," *National Review*, January 9, 2014, http://www.nationalreview.com/article/367903/white-ghetto-kevin-d-williamson.

[28]For a good overview of the day-to-day lives of the poor—or near poor—see Susan E. Mayer, *What Money Can't Buy: Family Income and Children's Life Chances* (Cambridge, MA: Harvard University Press, 1998).

[29]S. M., "Are We Helping the Poor?," *The Economist*, December 18, 2013, http://www.economist.com/blogs/democracyinamerica/2013/12/anti-poverty-programmes.

[30]Lyndon B. Johnson, "Special Message to the Congress on the State of the Union," January 8, 1964, http://www.lbjlib.utexas.edu/johnson/archives.hom/speeches.hom/640108.asp.

[31]Ibid.

[32]American Enterprise Institute and *Los Angeles Times,* "Views on Poverty: 1985 and Today," August 14, 2016, http://www.latimes.com/projects/la-na-pol-poverty-poll-interactive/.

[33]Ibid.

[34]Peter Lipton, "Inference to the Best Explanation," in *A Companion to the Philosophy of Science,* ed. W.H. Newton-Smith (Hoboken, NJ: Blackwell, 2000), pp. 184–93.

[35]James M. Buchanan, "The Justice of Natural Liberty," *Journal of Legal Studies* 5, no. 1 (January 1976): article 2, p. 16.

Chapter One

[1]Emil Munsterberg, "The Problem of Poverty," *American Journal of Sociology* 10, no. 3 (1904): 335–53.

[2]Matthew 26:11 (New International Version [NIV]).

[3]Shadi Hamid, "An Islamic Alternative? Equality, Redistributive Justice, and the Welfare State in the Caliphate of Umar," *Renaissance: Monthly Islamic Journal* 13, no. 8 (August 2003).

[4]Asaf Goldschmidt, *The Evolution of Chinese Medicine, Song Dynasty, 960–1200* (New York: Routledge, 2009), pp. 58–59.

[5]Glenn Sunshine, "The Church and the Poor: Historical Perspectives," Institute for Faith, Work & Economics, June 6, 2012, https://tifwe.org/part-7/.

[6]John Winthrop, "A Modell of Christian Charity (1630)," Collections of the Massachusetts Historical Society (Boston, 1838), 3rd series 7, pp. 31–48.

[7]Matt. 25:40 (NIV).

[8]Luke 11:41 (NIV).

[9]Gary A. Anderson, "Redeem Your Sins by the Giving of Alms: Sin, Debt and the 'Treasury of Merit' in Early Jewish and Christian Tradition," *Letter & Spirit* 3 (2007): 39–69, https://www.jstor.org/stable/j.ctt284w2x.

[10]Richard Ely et al., *Outline of Economics Third Revised Edition* (New York: The MacMillan Company, 1919), p. 743.

[11]Matt. 19:24 (NIV).

[12]Michael Mollatt, *The Poor in the Middle Ages: An Essay in Social History* (New Haven, CT: Yale University Press, 1986), p. 29.

[13]Rabanus Maurus Magnentius, *Commentariorum in Ecclesiasticum* libri decem 1.11, PL 109, accessed via Documenta Catholica Omnia at http://www.documentacatholicaomnia.eu/04z/z_0788-0856__Rabanus_Maurus__Commentariorum_In_Ecclesiasticum_Libri_Decem__MLT.pdf.html.

[14]Talmud, Baba Batra 9a, Sefaria, https://www.sefaria.org/Bava_Batra.9a?lang=bi; also quoted in Malkie Janowski, "Why Is Charity the Greatest Mitzvah?" Chabad.org, http://www.chabad.org/library/article_cdo/aid/580598/jewish/Why-is-Charity-the-Greatest-Mitzvah.htm.

[15]Quran 9:60 (Oxford World's Classics).

[16]Rather of Verona, Praeloquia, ed. by P. Reid, in *Corpus Christianorum continuatio mediaevalis* (CCCM) 46A (Turnhout: Brepols, 1984), pp. 3-196.

[17]Mollatt, *The Poor in the Middle Ages*, p. 290.

[18]Quoted in Jeremy Seabrook, *Pauperland: Poverty and the Poor in Britain* (New York: Oxford University Press, 2013), p. 44.

[19]Ibid., p. 45.

[20]Prepared by Nassau W. Senior, *Poor Law Commissioners' Report of 1834* (London: H. M. Stationery Office, 1905), Library of Economics and Liberty, 27 Henry VIII. c. 25, http://www.econlib.org/library/YPDBooks/Reports/rptPLC1.html.

[21]Ibid.

[22]Ibid., 5 Elizabeth, c. 3.

[23]Ibid., 14 Elizabeth, c. 5.

[24]Quoted in Seabrook, *Pauperland*, p. 45.

[25]Henry Walker Parker, *A Digest of the Law Relating to the Relief of the Poor; Containing the Statutes with the Adjudged Cases under Titles Alphabetically Arranged* (London: Shakespeare Press, 1849), p. 44.

[26]John Brewer and Susan Staves, eds., *Early Modern Conceptions of Poverty* (New York: Routledge, 1996), p. 55.

[27]Thomas William Heyck, *A History of the People of the British Isles: From 1688 to 1914* (London: Routledge, 2002), p. 49.

[28]Jean-Jacques Rousseau, "On Wealth," in *Collected Writings*, ed. Christopher Kelly and trans. Christopher Kelly and Judith Bush (Hanover, NH: Dartmouth College Press, 2005), 11: pp. 6–17.

[29]Sharon K. Vaughan, *Poverty, Justice, and Western Political Thought* (Lanham, U.K.: Lexington Books, 2008).

[30]Jean-Jacques Rousseau, "Considerations on the Government of Poland and on Its Proposed Reforms," April 1772, http://www.css.ethz.ch/en/services/digital-library/publications/publication.html/125482.

[31]Jean-Jacques Rousseau, "Constitutional Project for Corsica," 1765, http://www.constitution.org/jjr/corsica.htm.

[32]John Locke, *Two Treatises of Government*, ed. Thomas Hollis (London: A. Millar et al., 1764), http://oll.libertyfund.org/titles/222#lf0057_label_074.

[33]Ibid.

[34]Adam Smith, *An Inquiry into the Nature and Causes of the Wealth of Nations* (London: J.M Dent & Sons, Ltd., 1947), p. 69.

[35]Ibid., p. 10.

[36]Ibid., pp. 75, 83.

[37]Prepared by Nassau W. Senior, *Poor Law Commissioners' Report of 1834* (London: H.M Stationery Office, 1905), Library of Economics and Liberty, "Part I. Progress of the Law," http://www.econlib.org/library/YPDBooks/Reports/rptPLC1.html.

[38]Marian Bowley, *Nassau Senior and Classical Economics* (New York: Augustus M. Kelley, 1949), pp. 272, 293.

[39]Senior, *Poor Law Commissioners' Report of 1834*.

[40]Ibid., "Part I, Section 1 Administration of the Law, Chapter IV Parish Employment."

[41]Ibid., "Chapter 2, Out-Door Relief of the Able-Bodied in Money."

[42]Gertrude Himmelfarb, *Poverty and Compassion: The Moral Imagination of the Late Victorians* (New York: Alfred Knopf, 1991), p. 7.

[43]Paul Smith, *Disraeli: A Brief Life* (Cambridge, U.K.: Cambridge University Press, 1996), p. 77.

[44]J. R. Hay, "The Origins of the Liberal Welfare Reforms 1906–1914," in *Studies in Economic and Social History*, ed. M. W. Flinn and T. C. Smout (London: Macmillan Education LTD, 1975).

[45]Michael Katz, *In the Shadow of the Poorhouse: A Social History of Welfare in America* (New York: Basic Books, 1986), pp. 13–14.

[46]John Iceland, *Poverty in America: A Handbook* (Berkeley: University of California Press, 2013), pp. 12–13.

[47]Quoted in Katz, *In the Shadow of the Poorhouse*, p. 6.

[48]Alexis de Tocqueville, *Democracy in America* (Cambridge, U.K.: Sever and Francis, 1863), p. 129

[49]Seth Rockman, *Welfare Reform in the Early Republic: A Brief History with Documents* (Long Grove, IL: Waveland Press, 2003), p. 12.

[50]Quoted in Rockman, *Welfare Reform in the Early Republic*, p. 15.

[51]Ibid.

[52]W. J. Rorabauch, *The Alcoholic Republic: An American Tradition* (New York: Oxford University Press, 1979).

[53]Quoted in Katz, *In the Shadow of the Poorhouse*, p. 16.

[54]Himmelfarb, *Poverty and Compassion*), pp. 12, 122–128.

[55]Henry Mayhew, *London Labour and the London Poor* (Hertfordshire, U.K.; Wordsworth Editions Limited, 2008).

[56]Jacob A. Riis, *How the Other Half Lives* (1890; repr., New York: Seven Treasures Publications, 2009), p. 145.

[57]Linda Gordon, *Pitied but not Entitled: Single Mothers and the History of Welfare* (New York: Free Press, 1994), p. 176.

[58]Benjamin Seebohm Rowntree, *Poverty: A Study of Town Life* (London: Macmillan, 1902), pp. 119–20, 141–42.

[59]Peter Townsend, *Poverty in the United Kingdom* (London: Allen Lane and Penguin Books, 1979), pp. 64–65.

[60]Quoted in Paul Ringenbach, *Tramps and Reformers, 1973–1916: The Discovery of Unemployment in New York* (Westport, CT: Greenwood, 1973), p. 168.

[61]Children's Bureau, *First Annual Report of the Chief, Children's Bureau to the Secretary of Labor* (Washington: Government Printing Office, 1914).

[62]*Proceedings of the Conference on the Care of Dependent Children* (Washington: Government Printing Office, 1909), p. 123.

[63]Katz, *In the Shadow of the Poor House*, p. 128.

[64]Robert Plotnick et al., "The Twentieth Century Record of Inequality and Poverty in the United States," Institute for Research on Poverty, Discussion Paper no. 1166-98, July 1998, http://www.irp.wisc.edu/publications/dps/pdfs/dp116698.pdf.

[65]Michael Katz, *Improving Poor People: The Welfare State, the Underclass, and Urban Schools as History* (Princeton, NJ: Princeton University Press, 1995), p. 56.

[66]Franklin Delano Roosevelt, "Message to Congress Reviewing the Broad Objectives and Accomplishments of the Administration," June 8, 1934, http://www.ssa.gov/history/fdrstmts.html#exec.

[67]U.S. Senate Subcommittee on Manufacturing, Relief for Unemployed Transients: Hearings on S 5121, 72nd Congress, 2nd session.

[68]Plotnick et al., "The Twentieth Century Record of Inequality and Poverty"; Francis Fox Piven and Richard Cloward, *Regulating the Poor: The Functions of Public Welfare* (New York: Vintage Books, 1971), p. 75.

[69]Plotnick et al., "The Twentieth Century Record of Inequality and Poverty."

[70]Franklin D. Roosevelt, "Annual Message to Congress," January 4, 1935, http://www.presidency.ucsb.edu/ws/?pid=14890.

[71]Blanche Coll, *Safety Net: Welfare and Social Security, 1929–1979* (New Brunswick, NJ: Rutgers University Press, 1995), pp. 104, 199.

[72]Lyndon B. Johnson, "Annual Message to the Congress on the State of the Union," January 8, 1964, http://www.presidency.ucsb.edu/ws/?pid=26787.

[73]Lyndon B. Johnson, "University of Michigan Commencement, 1964," May 22, 1964, http://bentley.umich.edu/exhibits/lbj1964/.

[74]Sheldon Danziger, "Welfare Reform from Nixon to Clinton: What Role for Social Science?," conference paper prepared for "The Social Sciences and Policy Making," Institute for Social Research, University of Michigan, March 13–14, 1998.

[75]The President's Commission on Income Maintenance Programs, "Poverty amid Plenty: The American Paradox," November 1969, p. 57.

[76]Google Books Ngram Viewer, https://books.google.com/ngrams/graph?content=poverty&year_start=1700&year_end=2000&corpus=15&smoothing=3&share=&direct_url=t1%3B%2Cpoverty%3B%2Cc0.

[77]Oscar Lewis, *Five Families: Mexican Case Studies in the Culture of Poverty* (New York: Basic Books, 1975), p. 2.

[78]Oscar Lewis, *The Children of Sanchez* (New York: Penguin Books, 1965), p. xxiv.

[79]Ibid., pp. xxiv–xxvii.

[80]Office of Policy Planning and Research, "The Negro Family: The Case for National Action," United States Department of Labor, March 1965, https://www.dol.gov/oasam/programs/history/webid-meynihan.htm. Interestingly, the report was never intended for the public, but only as an internal government document. Moynihan originally produced only 100 copies and circulated just one.

[81]Office of Policy Planning and Research, "The Negro Family: The Case for National Action."

[82]Oscar Lewis, "The Culture of Poverty," *Scientific American*, October 1, 1966, https://www.scientificamerican.com/magazine/sa/1966/10-01/#article-the-culture-of-poverty.

[83]Michael Harrington, *The Other America: Poverty in the United States* (New York: Touchstone, 1997).

[84]Michael Harrington, "Our Fifty Million Poor: Forgotten Men of the Affluent Society," *Commentary Magazine*, July 1, 1959.

[85]Ibid., p. 162.

[86]"Minority Within a Minority: The Underclass." Cover. *TIME Magazine*, August 29, 1977.

[87]Ken Auletta, *The Underclass*, (Woodstock, NY: The Overlook Press, [1982] 1999).

[88]Franklin D. Gilliam Jr., "The 'Welfare Queen' Experiment," *Nieman Reports* 53, no. 2 (1999): 49–52.

[89]Martin Gilens, "How the Poor Became Black: The Radicalization of American Poverty in the Mass Media," in *Race and the Politics of Welfare Reform*, ed. Sanford F. Schram, Joe Soss, and Richard C. Fording (Ann Arbor: University of Michigan Press, 2003), p. 108.

[90]Ibid.

[91]Saundra K. Schneider and William G. Jacoby, "Elite Discourse and American Public Opinion: The Case of Welfare Spending," *Political Research Quarterly* 58, no. 3 (September 2005): 367–79; Robert Durr, "What Moves Policy Sentiment?," *American Political Science Review* 8, no. 7 (1993): 158–70; Randolph Stevenson, "The Economy and Policy Mood: A Fundamental Dynamic of Democratic Politics," *American Journal of Political Science* 45 (2001): 620–33.

[92]Beyond Distrust: How Americans View Their Government," Pew Research Center, November 23, 2015, p. 18, http://www.people-press.org/2015/11/23/beyond-distrust-how-americans-view-their-government/.

[93]James Patterson, *America's Struggle against Poverty in the Twentieth Century* (Cambridge, MA: Harvard University Press, 2003), p. 147.

[94]Cited in Patterson, *America's Struggle against Poverty in the Twentieth Century,* p. 196.

[95]Leigh Ann Caldwell, "Cornel West and Tavis Smiley: Poverty in America Threatens Democracy," *CBS News*, April 22, 2012, http://www.cbsnews.com/news/cornel-west-and-tavis-smiley-poverty-in-america-threatens-democracy/.

Chapter Two

[1]George Will, "Listen Up, Millennials. There's Sequence to Success," *Washington Post,* July 5, 2017.

[2]Perhaps the best current iteration of this view can be found in Charles Murray, *Coming Apart: The State of White America, 1960–2010* (New York: Crown Forum Books, 2012).

[3]Orlando Patterson, "Taking Culture Seriously: A Framework and Afro-American Illustration," in *Culture Matters: How Human Values Shape Human Progress,* ed. L. E. Harrison and S. P. Harrington (New York: Basic Books, 2001), p. 208, http://scholar.harvard.edu/files/patterson/files/takingcultureseriously.pdf?m=1360040736.

[4]Orlando Patterson, *The Cultural Matrix: Understanding Black Youth* (Cambridge, MA: Harvard University Press, 2015), p. 4.

[5]John Iceland, *Poverty in America: A Handbook* (Berkeley: University of California Press, 2013), p. 50.

[6]William Julius Wilson, *The Truly Disadvantaged: The Inner City, the Underclass, and Public Policy*, 2nd ed. (Chicago, IL; University of Chicago Press, 2012).

[7]Ibid., p. 187.

[8]Patterson, *The Cultural Matrix*, p. 521.

[9]Oscar Lewis, *La Vida: A Puerto Rican Family in the Culture of Poverty—San Juan and New York* (New York: Random House, 1966) pp. xliii–xlv.

[10]Wilson, *The Truly Disadvantaged.* To be sure, Wilson ultimately believes that "structure trumps poverty," but his work clearly demonstrates that the impact of culture cannot be ignored.

[11]Ibid., p. 56.

[12]Richard V. Reeves, Edward Rodrigue, and Alex Gold, "Following the Success Sequence? Success Is More Likely if You're White," Brookings Social Mobility Papers no. 12, August 6, 2015, http://www.brookings.edu/blogs/social-mobility-memos/posts/2015/08/06-following-success-sequence-race-reeves.

[13]W. Bradford Wilcox and Wendy Wang, "The Millennial Success Sequence: Marriage, Kids, and the 'Success Sequence' among Young Adults," report, American Enterprise Institute and Institute for Family Studies, Washington, June 14, 2017, http://www.aei.org/publication/millennials-and-the-success-sequence-how-do-education-work-and-marriage-affect-poverty-and-financial-success-among-millennials/.

[14]U.S. Census Bureau, "'Historical Poverty Tables–People,' Table 25, Work Experience and Poverty Status for People 16 Years Old and Over," https://www2.census.gov/programs-surveys/cps/tables/time-series/historical-poverty-people/hstpov25.xls. This statistic is based on the Official Poverty Measure, so it doesn't include transfer income. As a result, it likely understates the effect of work on poverty rates.

[15]Elise Gould, "Poor People Work, A Majority of Poor People Do," Employment Policy Institute, May 19, 2015. It is worth noting that by work, I am referring to formal employment. Many poor people work in the underground or informal economy. We know this from consumption patterns that far outstrip reported

income. In *Off the Books: The Underground Economy of the Urban Poor*, Sudhir Alladi Venkatesh reports on a vast and intricate network of economic exchange, barter, and trade, both legal and not, that frequently replaces traditional employment in poor communities. Sudhir Alladi Venkatesh, *Off the Books: The Underground Economy of the Urban Poor* (Cambridge, MA: Harvard University Press, 2008).

[16]Express Employment Professionals, "New Poll Explores Plight of the Unemployed," June 8, 2016, https://www.expresspros.com/Newsroom/America-Employed/New-Poll-Explores-Plight-of-Unemployed.aspx.

[17]Patterson, *The Cultural Matrix,* p. 72.

[18]Ibid.

[19]Wilson, *The Truly Disadvantaged*, pp. 160–61.

[20]Dan Bloom, *After AFDC: Welfare-to-Work Choices and Challenges for States* (New York: Manpower Demonstration Research Corporation, 1997), pp. 24–25, http://www.mdrc.org/sites/default/files/full_17.pdf; Robert Plotnick, Marieka Klawitter, and Mark Edwards, "Do Attitudes and Personality Characteristics Affect Socioeconomic Outcomes? The Case of Welfare Use by Young Women," Institute for Research on Poverty, no. 1161–98, April 1998, http://www.irp.wisc.edu/publications/dps/pdfs/dp116198.pdf; Lyndelia Burch Wynn, "The Attitude of AFDC Recipients Towards Work," *Sociation Today* 1, no. 2 (Fall 2003), http://www.ncsociology.org/sociationtoday/v2/wynn.htm.

[21]U.S. Census Bureau, "Annual Social and Economic Supplement (ASEC) of the Current Population Survey (CPS)," May 8, 2017, https://www.census.gov/programs-surveys/saipe/guidance/model-input-data/cpsasec.html.

[22]Murray, *Coming Apart*, p. 183.

[23]Ibid., p. 184.

[24]U.S. Bureau of Labor Statistics, *American Time Use Survey* (Washington: U.S. Bureau of Labor Statistics, 2014), https://www.bls.gov/news.release/atus.tn.htm.

[25]Express Employment Professionals, "New Poll Explores Plight of the Unemployed."

[26]Congressional Budget Office, "Effective Marginal Tax Rates for Low- and Moderate-Income Workers in 2016," November 19, 2015.

[27]Erik Hurst, "Video Killed the Radio Star," *Chicago Booth Review*, September 1, 2016, http://review.chicagobooth.edu/economics/2016/article/video-killed-radio-star. Article based on Mark Aguiar, Mark Bils, Kerwin Kofi Charles, and Erik Hurst, "Leisure Luxuries and the Labor Supply of Young Men," working paper 23552, NBER, Cambridge, MA, 2017."

[28]Andrew Kohut and Michael Dimock, "Resilient American Values: Optimism in an Era of Growing Inequality and Economic Difficulty," Council on Foreign Relations, May 2013, http://www.cfr.org/united-states/resilient-american-values/p30203.

[29]Patterson, *The Cultural Matrix*, p. 72.

[30]Andandi Mani et al., "Poverty Impedes Cognitive Function," *Science* 341, no. 6149 (August 2013): 976–80, http://science.sciencemag.org/content/341/6149/976.abstract.

[31]Joseph Altonji and Thomas Dunn, "An Intergenerational Model of Wages, Hours and Earnings," *Journal of Human Resources* 35, no. 2 (2000): 221–58, http://www2.econ.iastate.edu/classes/econ520/Huffman/documents/AnIntergenerationalModelofWagesHoursandEarnings.pdf.

[32]Jens Ludwig and Susan Mayer, "'Culture' and the Intergenerational Transmission of Poverty: The Prevention Paradox," *Future of Children* 16, no. 2, (Autumn 2006): 175–96, http://www.jstor.org/stable/3844796.

[33]Ludwig and Mayer, "'Culture' and the Intergenerational Transmission of Poverty"; Altonji and Dunn, "An Intergenerational Model"; Gordon B. Dahl, Andreas Ravndal Kostøl, and Magne Mogstad, "Family Welfare Cultures," *Quarterly Journal of Economics* 129, no. 4 (2014): 1711–52, http://qje.oxfordjournals.org/content/129/4/1711; Greg Duncan and Martha Hill, "Welfare Dependence within and across Generations," *Science*, January 29, 1988, pp. 467–71; Karin Edmark and Kajsa Hanspers, "Is Welfare Dependency Inherited? Estimating Causal Welfare Transmission Effects Using Swedish Sibling Data," *European Journal of Social Security* 17, no. 3 (2015), http://www.ejss.eu/pdf_file/ITS/EJSS_17_03_0338.pdf.

[34]Juan Barón, Deborah Cobb-Clark, and Nisvan Erkal, "Cultural Transmission of Work-Welfare Attitudes and the Intergenerational Correlation in Welfare Receipt," Institute for the Study of Labor (IZA) Decision Paper Series no. 3904, IZA, Bonn, December 2008, http://ftp.iza.org/dp3904.pdf.

[35]Ibid. As with education, as discussed in the previous endnote, fathers appeared to have less impact.

[36]U.S. Census Bureau, "Historical Income Tables, People: Table P-16 Educational Attainment—People 25 Years Old and Over by Median Income and Sex," https://www2.census.gov/programs-surveys/cps/tables/time-series/historical-income-people/p16.xls.

[37]Ibid.

[38]Michael Greenstone et al., "Thirteen Economic Facts about Social Mobility and the Role of Education," The Hamilton Project policy memo, June 2013, http://www.brookings.edu/research/reports/2013/06/13-facts-higher-education. It is worth noting that this relationship is far stronger for whites than for African Americans. We should be careful, however, about assigning the blame for this difference entirely to conscious racism. Racism may play a role, but it is also possible that the "skills/learning" of a college degree does not raise an individual's wages as much as it acts as a signal. Under this interpretation, whites' higher probability of being embedded in affluent social networks enables them to access better jobs,

and the college degree acts more like "box checking," https://d3n8a8pro7vhmx.cloudfront.net/yicare/pages/141/attachments/original/1403804069/Closing_the_Race_Gap_Ntnl_6.25.14.pdf?1403804069.

[39]The father's level of education appears to have little effect, perhaps because there is less father-child interaction during the child's formative years, or because in so many poor households the father is absent.

[40]Katherine Magnuson and Sharon McGroder, "The Effect of Increasing Welfare Mothers' Education on their Young Children's Academic Problems and School Readiness," report, Northwestern University Joint Center for Poverty Research, Evanston, IL, 2002, http://www.jonescollegeprep.org/ourpages/auto/2013/1/17/61972839/Effect%20of%20Increasing%20Welfare%20Mothers%20Education%20on%20their%20Young%20Childrens%20Problems%20and%20School%20Readiness.pdf.

[41]James J. Heckman, "Promoting Social Mobility," *Boston Review*, September 1, 2012, http://www.bostonreview.net/forum/promoting-social-mobility-james-heckman. Studies show that by age 6, children from high-income families will have spent about 1,300 more hours in nonroutine contexts than children from low-income families, with a similar gap between white children and African American children. Upon entering school, high-income or white children will have spent more than 400 more hours in literacy activities than their low-income or African American peers, and this disparity has important implications for their development of human capital and school readiness. Meredith Phillips, "Parenting, Time Use, and Disparities in Academic Outcomes," in *Whither Opportunity? Rising Inequality, Schools, and Children's Life Chances*, ed. Greg J. Duncan and Richard J. Murnane (New York: Russel Sage Foundation, 2011), pp. 207–28. Other studies suggest that low-income parents spend, on average, half an hour per day less in direct face-to-face time with their children than do parents in higher-income families. As a result, by the time a low-income child reaches age 5 and is ready to start school, he or she will have heard as many as 30 million fewer words than peers from wealthier families. Betty Hart and Todd. R. Risley, "The Early Catastrophe: The 30 Million Word Gap by Age 3," *American Educator*, Spring 2003, pp. 4–9, http://www.aft.org//sites/default/files/periodicals/TheEarlyCatastrophe.pdf. Because they hear fewer words from parents and caregivers, children from low-income families learn fewer words.

[42]Meredith L. Rowe, "Child-Directed Speech: Relation to Socioeconomic Status, Knowledge of Child Development and Child Vocabulary Skill," *Journal of Child Language* 35 (2008): 185–205, http://www.education.umd.edu/HDQM/labs/Rowe/LDPL/Publications_files/Rowe_JCL_2008.pdf.

[43]R. J. Skiba et al., "Disparate Access: The Disproportionality of African American Students with Disabilities across Separate Educational Environments," *Exceptional Children* 72 (2006): 411–24.

[44]David Card and Laura Giuliano, "Can Universal Screening Increase the Representation of Low Income and Minority Students in Gifted Education?," National Bureau of Economic Research Working Paper no. 21519, NBER, Cambridge, MA, September 2015, http://www.nber.org/digest/nov15/w21519.html. There are also disparities in disciplinary practices. Black students are suspended and expelled at a rate three times greater than white students. On average, 5 percent of white students are suspended, compared with 16 percent of black students. Although more sophisticated analyses indicated that this does not seem to be the main explanation of the broader pattern, there are certainly individual cases of discrimination. Joshua Kinsler, "Understanding the Black-White School Discipline Gap," *Economics of Education Review* 30, no. 6 (2011): 1370–83.

[45]Ulrich Boser, Megan Wilhelm, and Robert Hanna, "The Power of the Pygmalion Effect: Teacher Expectations Strongly Predict College Completion," K–12 Education Report, Center for American Progress, October 6, 2014, https://www.americanprogress.org/issues/education/report/2014/10/06/96806/the-power-of-the-pygmalion-effect/.

[46]Kati Haycock, "Educational Leadership: Helping All Students Achieve: Closing the Achievement Gap," Association for Supervision and Curriculum Development, *Educational Leadership* 58, 6 (March 2001): 6–11, http://www.ascd.org/publications/educational-leadership/mar01/vol58/num06/Closing-the-Achievement-Gap.aspx.

[47]Alissa Goodman and Paul Gregg, "Poorer Children's Educational Attainment: How Important Are Attitudes and Behaviour?," Joseph Roundtree Foundation, March 29, 2010, https://www.jrf.org.uk/report/poorer-children%E2%80%99s-educational-attainment-how-important-are-attitudes-and-behaviour.

[48]Nancy Feyl Chavkin and David L. Williams Jr., "Low-Income Parents' Attitudes toward Parent Involvement in Education," *Journal of Sociology and Social Welfare* 16, no. 3 (1989): article 3, http://scholarworks.wmich.edu/jssw/vol16/iss3/3.

[49]Child Trends Databank, "Parental Expectations for Their Children's Academic Attainment," Child Trends Databank Indicator, Bethesda, MD, 2015, http://www.childtrends.org/?indicators=parental-expectations-for-their-childrens-academic-attainment.

[50]Robert Putnam, *Our Kids: The American Dream in Crisis* (New York: Simon and Schuster, 2015), p. 169, citing Gregory Palardy, "High School Socioeconomic Segregation and Student Attainment," *American Educational Research Journal*, August 2013, http://journals.sagepub.com/doi/abs/10.3102/0002831213481240; Robert Crosnoe, *Fitting In, Standing Out: Navigating the Social Challenges of High School to Get an Education* (New York: Cambridge University Press, 2011).

[51]Patterson, *The Cultural Matrix*, p. 78.

[52]John Ogbu, *Black American Students in an Affluent Suburb: A Study of Academic Disengagement* (New York: Routledge, 2003), pp. 24–25. Although the subjects of

Ogbu's research were mostly middle-class students, the same attitudes have been observed in African American students from lower-income households, under circumstances where the behavior could be even more self-destructive.

[53]Roland G. Fryer Jr. and Paul Torelli, "An Empirical Analysis of 'Acting White,'" *Journal of Public Economics* 94, no. 5-6 (2010): 380–96, http://www.quantitativesocialscience.com/uploads/5/8/3/3/5833205/fryer_torelli_2010.pdf.

[54]Ibid., p 6.

[55]Carmen DeNavas-Walt and Bernadette D. Proctor, "Income and Poverty in the United States: 2014," Table B-3, https://www.census.gov/content/dam/Census/library/publications/2015/demo/p60-252.pdf.

[56]U.S. Department of Health and Human Services, *Welfare Indicators and Risk Factors* (Washington: U.S. Department of Health and Human Services, 2015), p. 80 (Table WORK 1a. Percentage of Persons in Families with Labor Force Participants by Selected Characteristics: 2012), https://aspe.hhs.gov/sites/default/files/pdf/116161/FINAL%20Fourteenth%20Report%20-%20FINAL%209%2022%2015.pdf.

[57]Ibid., Table IND 1a and Table ECON 7a.

[58]Federal Interagency Forum on Child and Family Statistics, "America's Children: Key National Indicators of Well-Being 2015," https://www.childstats.gov/pdf/ac2015/ac_15.pdf; Alysse ElHage, "For Kids, Parental Cohabitation and Marriage Are Not Interchangeable," *Institute for Family Studies* (blog), May 7, 2015, http://family-studies.org/for-kids-parental-cohabitation-and-marriage-are-not-interchangeable/.

[59]Michelle Chau, Kalyani Thampi, and Vanessa R. Wight, "Basic Facts about Low-Income Children, 2009: Children under Age 18," National Center for Children in Poverty, October 2010, http://www.nccp.org/publications/pub_975.html.

[60]National Center for Education Statistics (NCES), "Family Characteristics of School-Age Children," *The Condition of Education* (Washington: NCES, U.S. Department of Education, 2016), p. 7 (Figure 7. Percentage of Children under Age 18 in Families Living in Poverty, by Race/Ethnicity and Family Structure: 2014), https://nces.ed.gov/programs/coe/pdf/coe_cce.pdf.

[61]Single parenthood is overwhelmingly a female experience. Of approximately 12 million single-parent households in the United States, more than 80 percent are headed by women. U.S. Census Bureau, "'America's Families and Living Arrangements: 2016: Family Groups,' Table FG10. Family Groups: 2016," https://www2.census.gov/programs-surveys/demo/tables/families/2013/cps-2013/tabfg10-all.xls. Given the many other factors increasing the likelihood that women will be poor (see chapter 4 of this book), single parenthood adds to their burdens. Single mothers are far more likely to be poor than are single fathers.

[62]U.S. Department of Health and Human Services, *Welfare Indicators and Risk Factors*, p. 75, "Figure ECON 6. Poverty Rates for Custodial Mothers by Marital Status and Receipt of Child Support: 2011."

[63]Laura M. Tach and Alicia Eads, "Trends in the Economic Consequences of Marital and Cohabitation Dissolution in the United States," *Demography* 52, no. 2 (April 2015): 401–32, http://www.ncbi.nlm.nih.gov/pubmed/25749487.

[64]Child Trends Databank, "Births to Unmarried Women: Indicators of Child and Youth Well-Being," Child Trends Databank Indicator, Bethesda, MD, October 2016, https://www.childtrends.org/wp-content/uploads/2015/12/75_Births_to_Unmarried_Women.pdf.

[65]Andrew J. Cherlin, "Demographic Trends in the United States: A Review of Research in the 2000s," *Journal of Marriage and Family* 72, no. 3 (June 2010): 403–19, 408.

[66]Sheela Kennedy and Larry Bumpass, "Cohabitation and Children's Living Arrangements: New Estimates from the United States," *Demographic Research* 19 (2008): 1685–86, https://www.demographic-research.org/Volumes/Vol19/47/19-47.pdf.

[67]Putnam, *Our Kids*, pp. 67–68.

[68]Tach and Eads, "Trends in the Economic Consequences of Marital and Cohabitation Dissolution in the United States."

[69]Stephanie J. Ventura et al., "Nonmarital Childbearing in the United States, 1940–99," *National Vital Statistics Reports* (from the Centers for Disease Control and Prevention) 48, no. 16 (October 2000), https://www.cdc.gov/nchs/data/nvsr/nvsr48/nvs48_16.pdf.

[70]Joyce A. Martin et al., "Births: Final Data for 2015," *National Vital Statistics Reports* (from the Centers for Disease Control and Prevention) 66, no. 1 (January 2017), Table 15, https://www.cdc.gov/nchs/data/nvsr/nvsr66/nvsr66_01.pdf.

[71]U. S. Census Bureau, "Annual Social and Economic Supplement (ASEC) of the Current Population Survey (CPS)," May 8, 2017, https://www.census.gov/programs-surveys/saipe/guidance/model-input-data/cpsasec.html. The fathers of these children are no better economically situated. Roughly 37 percent were high school dropouts, while another 39 percent had only a high school diploma. Like the mothers, unmarried fathers are generally poor.

[72]For example, one study looks at women who miscarried. Because miscarriage is close to a random event, these women provide an ideal control group. Starting from this base, the authors conclude that women who give birth outside marriage are the same women who would have been poor regardless of the birth. Moreover, the study suggests that births to unmarried women are not purely random exogenous events, but they may reflect choices and decisions by the mothers that need to be accounted for. Joseph Hotz, Susan Williams McElroy, and Seth G. Sanders, "Teenage Childbearing and Its Life Cycle Consequences: Exploiting a Natural Experiment," *Journal of Human Resources* 40, no. 3 (2005): 683–715.

[73]Arline T. Geronimus and Sanders Korenman, "The Socioeconomic Consequences of Teen Childbearing Reconsidered," National Bureau of Economic Research Working Paper no. 3701, NBER, Cambridge, MA, May 1991.

[74]Stephen G. Bronars and Jeff Grogger, "The Economic Consequences of Unwed Motherhood: Using Twin Births as a Natural Experiment," *American Economic Review* 84, no. 5 (December 1994): 1141–56, http://www.jstor.org/stable/2117765.

[75]Kathryn Edin and Maria Kefalas, *Promises I Can Keep: Why Poor Women Put Motherhood before Marriage* (Berkeley: University of California Press, 2005).

[76]Daniel Patrick Moynihan, *Family and Nation: The Godkin Lectures* (New York: Harcourt Brace Jovanovich, 1985), p. 8.

[77]Ron Haskins, "Does Welfare Encourage Illegitimacy? The Case Just Closed. The Answer Is Yes," American Enterprise Institute, January 1996. http://www.pbs.org/thinktank/transcript102.html. It should be noted that, while out-of-wedlock birthrates are far higher among African Americans, the studies showed a stronger correlation for white women than for African Americans.

[78]Charles Murray, *Losing Ground: American Social Policy, 1950–1980*, (New York: Basic Books, 1984).

[79]Jeff Grogger and Stephen G. Bronars, "The Effect of Welfare Payments on the Marriage and Fertility Behavior of Unwed Mothers: Results from a Twins Experiment," *Journal of Political Economy* 109, no. 3 (2001): 529–45, http://www.jstor.org/stable/pdfplus/10.1086/321016.pdf.

[80]Irwin Garfinkel et al., "The Roles of Child Support Enforcement and Welfare in Nonmarital Childbearing," *Journal of Population Economics* 16, no. 1 (February 2003): 55–70, http://link.springer.com/article/10.1007%2Fs001480100108.

[81]Ibid.

[82]John Iceland, *Poverty in America: A Handbook* (Berkeley: University of California Press, 2013), p. 110.

[83]Quoted in Phil Harvey and Lisa Conyers, *The Human Cost of Welfare: How the System Hurts the People It's Supposed to Help* (Santa Barbara, CA: Praeger, 2016), p. 30.

[84]Edin and Kefalas, *Promises I Can Keep.*

[85]Ibid., p. 205.

[86]Iceland, *Poverty in America: A Handbook*, p. 110.

[87]Marvin Olasky, *The Tragedy of American Compassion* (Washington: Regnery, 1992), p. 186.

[88]Christina Gibson-Davis, "Magic Moment? Maternal Marriage for Children Born Out of Wedlock," *Demography* 51, no. 4 (2014): 1345–56, https://doi.org/10.1007/s13524-014-0308-7.

[89]Elizabeth Kneebone and Natalie Holmes, "U.S. Concentrated Poverty in the Wake of the Great Recession," Brookings Institution, March 31, 2016, http://www.brookings.edu/research/reports2/2016/03/31-concentrated-poverty-recession-kneebone-holmes.

[90]Thomas Paul Vartanian, "Adolescent Neighborhood Effects on Labor Market and Economic Outcomes," *Social Service Review* 73, no. 2 (June 1999): 142–67.

[91]Bruce Weinberg, Patricia Reagan, and Jeffrey Yankow, "Do Neighborhoods Affect Work Behavior? Evidence from the NLSY79," *Journal of Labor Economics* 22, no. 4 (2004): 891–924. http://www.journals.uchicago.edu/doi/pdfplus/10.1086/423158.

[92]James Ainsworth, "Why Does It Take a Village? The Mediation of Neighborhood Effects on Educational Achievement," *Social Forces* 81, no. 1 (2002): 117–52.

[93]Anne Case and Lawrence Katz, "The Company You Keep: The Effects of Family and Neighborhood on Disadvantaged Youths," Working Paper 1555, Harvard Institute of Economic Research, 1991, p. 2.

[94]William A. Brock and Steven N. Durlauf, "Multinomial Choice with Social Interactions," in *The Economy as an Evolving Complex System, III: Current Perspectives and Future Directions,* ed. Lawrence E. Blume and Steven N. Durlauf (Oxford: Oxford University Press, 2006), http://www.nber.org/papers/t0288.pdf.

[95]Eric Chyn, "Moved to Opportunity: The Long-Run Effect of Public Housing Demolition on Labor Market Outcomes of Children," Working Paper, October 12, 2016, http://ericchyn.com/files/Chyn_Moved_to_Opportunity.pdf.

[96]Raj Chetty, Nathaniel Hendren, and Lawrence F. Katz, "The Effects of Exposure to Better Neighborhoods on Children: New Evidence from the Moving to Opportunity Experiment," *American Economic Review* 106, no. 4 (April 2016), https://www.aeaweb.org/articles?id=10.1257/aer.20150572.

[97]Aaron Yelowitz and Janet Currie, "Are Public Housing Projects Good for Kids?," National Bureau of Economic Research (NBER) Working Paper no. 6405, NBER, Cambridge, MA, December 1997, http://www.nber.org/papers/w6305.

[98]Jens Ludwig et al., "Long Term Neighborhood Effects on Low-Income Families: Evidence from Moving to Opportunity," *American Economic Review Papers and Proceedings* 103, no. 3 (May 2013): 226–31.

[99]Chetty, Hendren, and Katz, "The Effects of Exposure to Better Neighborhoods on Children."

[100]Stephanie Deluca, Susan Clampet-Lundquest, and Kathryn Edin, *Coming of Age in the Other America* (New York: Russell Sage Foundation, 2016), pp. 146–81.

[101]Richard Reeves and Emily Cutty, "Poverty, Isolation, and Opportunity," Brookings Institution Social Mobility Memo, March 31, 2015, https://www.brookings.edu/blog/social-mobility-memos/2015/03/31/poverty-isolation-and-opportunity/.

[102]Markus Schafer and Nicholas Vargas, "The Dynamics of Social Support Inequality: Maintenance Gaps by Socioeconomic Status and Race?," *Social Forces* 94, 4 (June, 2016): 1795–1822, http://sf.oxfordjournals.org/content/94/4/1795.

[103]Simon Hjalmarsson and Carina Mood, "Do Poorer Youth Have Fewer Friends? The Role of Household and Child Economic Resources in Adolescent School-Class Friendships," *Children and Youth Services Review* 57 (October 2015): 201–11, http://www.sciencedirect.com/science/journal/01907409/57/supp/C?sdc=1.

Chapter Three

[1]Nelson Mandela, "Make Poverty History" address, London, February 3, 2005, http://www.mandela.gov.za/mandela_speeches/2005/050203_poverty.htm.

[2]William Julius Wilson, *When Work Disappears: The World of the New Urban Poor* (New York: Vintage Books, 1996), p. 55.

[3]The concept of race is itself a problematic one. In reality, race is largely a social construct. Racial categories may be drawn in different ways at different times and in different places. For example, under the "one drop" rule prevalent in the pre–Civil Rights era southern United States, a person could be defined as black based on a single African American ancestor, regardless of whether the person displayed any physical characteristics associated with African Americans. Nor do racial classifications necessarily reflect racial discrimination or oppression. They may be nothing more than classification linked to biological descent or an easy description of physical appearance. However, in practice, they are too often linked to disparities in treatment and injustice, especially when different groups have different degrees of access to the levers of power. For purposes of this book, African Americans are generally defined as those perceived as African American and subject to social and legal treatment as such.

[4]The link between race and poverty may seem so pervasive that it could seem as if the term African American is almost being used as a synonym for poverty. That is not my intent. The majority of poor Americans are white—by a large margin. Roughly 17.8 million whites are poor. There are almost 8 million more poor whites than poor African Americans and 5.5 million more poor whites than poor Latinos. See U. S. Census Bureau, "Income and Poverty in the United States: 2015," Table 3, People in Poverty by Selected Characteristics, http://www2.census.gov/programs-surveys/demo/tables/p60/256/pov_table3.xls. More important, most African Americans are not poor and are not suffering from any of the dysfunctions discussed in this book. As Marc Morial, president of the National Urban League, put it, "Black America has deep problems—deep economic problems—but black America also has a large community of striving,

successful, hardworking people; college educated, in the work force." Quoted in Richard Fausset, Alan Blinder, and John Eligon, "Donald Trump's Description of Black America Is Offending Those Living in It," *New York Times*, August 24, 2016, https://www.nytimes.com/2016/08/25/us/politics/donald-trump-black-voters.html. That said, there is no doubt that people of color are disproportionately likely to be poor. This fact means it is difficult to disentangle the issue of poverty from this country's long history of racial discrimination. It also means African American poverty has been a particular focus of much poverty research. For both good reasons and bad, debates over poverty policy in this country have long been viewed through a racial lens.

[5]Carolyn Ratcliffe, "Child Poverty and Adult Success," brief, Urban Institute, September 2015, https://www.urban.org/sites/default/files/alfresco/publication-pdfs/2000369-Child-Poverty-and-Adult-Success.pdf.

[6]Lyndon B. Johnson, "Commencement Address at Howard University: 'To Fulfill These Rights,'" Washington, June 4, 1965, http://www.presidency.ucsb.edu/ws/?pid=27021.

[7]Act Prohibiting Importation of Slaves of 1807, Pub. L. No. 9-22, 2 Stat. 426.

[8]Inter-university Consortium for Political and Social Research and Michael R. Haines, "Historical Demographic, Economic, and Social Data: The United States, 1790–1970," Inter-university Consortium for Political and Social Research, 1997, https://assets.nhgis.org/original-data/historical-census/HISTseries-ICPSR0003.pdf; U.S. Census Bureau, "Historical Statistics of the United States, Colonial Times to 1970," Bicentennial Edition, Part 2, September 1975, https://www.census.gov/history/pdf/histstats-colonial-1970.pdf.

[9]A precise estimate of the number of people who were enslaved is almost impossible to make given the imprecision of records. Most likely, we are talking about 7–9 million people. See U.S. Census Bureau, "A Century of Population Growth," XIV, Statistics of Slaves, https://www2.census.gov/prod2/decennial/documents/00165897_TOC.pdf.

[10]Lerone Bennett Jr., *The Shaping of Black America* (Chicago: Johnson Publishing Company, 1975), p. 62.

[11]Quoted by Ta-Nehisi Coates, "The Case for Reparations," *Atlantic*, June 2014, http://www.theatlantic.com/magazine/archive/2014/06/the-case-for-reparations/361631/.

[12]Robert W. Fogel, *Without Consent or Contract: The Rise and Fall of American Slavery* (New York: W. W. Norton, 1989).

[13]Ibid.

[14]Samuel George Morton, *Crania Americana; or, A Comparative View of the Skulls of Various Aboriginal Nations of North and South America. To Which Is Prefixed an Essay on the Varieties of the Human Species* (Philadelphia: J. Dobson, 1839).

[15]Josiah C. Nott, *An Essay on the Natural History of Mankind, Viewed in Connection with Negro Slavery, Delivered before the Southern Rights Association, December 14, 1850* (Mobile, AL: Dade, Thompson, 1851), https://archive.org/details/essayonnaturalhi00nott.

[16]Josiah Priest, *Bible Defense of Slavery: or, The Origin, History, and Fortunes of the Negro Race, as Deduced from History, both Sacred and Profane, Their Natural Relations—to the Other Races of Mankind Compared and Illustrated—Their Future Destiny Predicted, etc.* (Louisville, KY: J. F. Brennan, 1851), p. 98.

[17]Edmund Morgan, *American Slavery, American Freedom: The Ordeal of Colonial Virginia* (New York: Octagon Press, 1975), p. 312, quoted in William Julius Wilson, *The Declining Significance of Race: Blacks and Changing American Institutions* (Chicago: University of Chicago Press, 1978), p. 29.

[18]William H. Turner, Edward J. Cabbell, and W. E. B. DuBois, *Blacks in Appalachia* (Lexington: University Press of Kentucky, 2015), p. 152.

[19]E. Franklin Frazier, *The Negro Family in the United States* (New York: Free Press, 1979).

[20]William Harper, Thomas Roderick Dew, James Henry Hammond, and William Gilmore Simms, *The Pro-Slavery Argument, as Maintained by the Most Distinguished Writers of the Southern State, Containing the Several Essays on the Subject, of Chancellor Harper, Governor Hammons, Dr. Simms, and Professor Dew* (Philadelphia: Lippincott, Grambo, & Co., 1853); cited in Peter Kolchin, *American Slavery, 1619–1877* (New York: Hill and Wang, 1993), p. 124. The status of slave women also made them vulnerable to sexual abuse by their fellow slaves. Although the rape of a white woman by a black man was a capital offense, black-on-black rape was not a crime under most state laws. Kolchin, p. 125.

[21]Yale University Avalon Project, "An Act to Prohibit the Importation of Slaves into any Port or Place Within the Jurisdiction of the United States, From and After the First Day of January, in the Year of our Lord One Thousand Eight Hundred and Eight," http://avalon.law.yale.edu/19th_century/sl004.asp.

[22]"On Slaveholders' Sexual Abuse of Slaves: Selections from the 19th and 20th century Slave Narratives," in *The Making of African American Identity: Vol 1, 1500–1865*, National Humanities Center Resource Toolbox (Durham, NC: National Humanities Center, 2007), http://nationalhumanitiescenter.org/pds/maai/enslavement/text6/masterslavesexualabuse.pdf.

[23]Kolchin, *American Slavery, 1619–1877*, pp. 125–26, citing research by Michael Tadman.

[24]Ibid., p. 125.

[25]Avidit Acharaya, Matthew Blackwell, and Maya Sin, "The Political Legacy of Slavery," *Journal of Politics* (2016), http://scholar.harvard.edu/msen/cations/american-slavery-political-legacy.

[26]Kolchin, *American Slavery, 1619–1877*, pp. 234–35.

[27]Ibid., p. 235.

[28]Gail Lumet Buckley, *The Black Calhouns: From Civil War to Civil Rights with One American Family* (New York: Atlantic Monthly Press, 2016), pp. 46–47.

[29]Plessy v. Ferguson, 163 U.S. 537 (1896).

[30]Williams v. Mississippi, 170 U.S. 213 (1898).

[31]Quoted in "Lynching in America: Confronting the Legacy of Racial Terror," Equal Justice Initiative, Montgomery, AL, 2015.

[32]Kolchin, *American Slavery, 1619–1877,* p. 236.

[33]Coates, "The Case for Reparations."

[34]Marvin Oliver and Thomas Shapiro, *Black Wealth/White Wealth: A New Perspective on Racial Inequality* (New York: Rutledge, 1996), p. 2.

[35]Julian Simon and Larry Neal, "A Calculation of the Black Reparations Bill," *Review of Black Political Economy* 4, no. 2 (1974): 75–86, http://link.springer.com/article/10.1007%2FBF03040655. Compounding this injustice, and making racial inequality more pronounced, is the amount of white wealth that was accumulated on the backs of slaves. Numerous private companies profited substantially from the slave trade. This includes insurers such as Aetna, New York Life, and AIG that sold insurance on the value of slaves; banks that made loans against and for the purchase of slaves; and even companies like Brooks Brothers that started by selling clothes for slaves to plantation owners. And although we think of slaves being used primarily for agriculture, companies like Norfolk Southern Railroad used slave labor at various times. Newspapers ran advertisements for slave auctions. It is impossible to put a dollar value to the amount of white wealth that can trace its origins back to slavery, yet it is hard to deny that as a group whites are better off because slavery existed.

[36]James Marketti, "Estimated Present Value of Income Diverted during Slavery," in *The Wealth of Races: The Present Value of Benefits from Past Injustices*, ed. Richard F. America (Westport, CT: Greenwood Press, 1990).

[37]U.S. Census Bureau, "Residential Vacancies and Homeownership in the First Quarter 2016," CB 16-62, Table 7, Homeownership Rates by Race and Ethnicity of Householder: 2012 to 2016, https://www.census.gov/housing/hvs/files/currenthvspress.pdf.

[38]Jon C. Teaford, *The Metropolitan Revolution: The Rise of Post-Urban America* (New York: Columbia University Press, 2006), p. 64.

[39]National Association of Real Estate Boards, *Fundamentals of Real Estate Practice,* 1943, cited in Thomas Guglielmo, *White on Arrival: Italians, Race, Color, and Power in Chicago, 1890-1945* (New York: Oxford University Press, 2004.)

[40]Kenneth T. Jackson, *Crabgrass Frontier: The Suburbanization of the United States* (New York: Oxford University Press, 1985), pp. 199–201.

[41]Emily Badger, "Redlining: Still a Thing," *Washington Post*, May 28, 2015, https://www.washingtonpost.com/news/wonk/wp/2015/05/28/evidence-that-banks-still-deny-black-borrowers-just-as-they-did-50-years-ago/.

[42]Kathleen Frydl, *The G. I. Bill* (Cambridge: Cambridge University Press, 2009), p. 7.

[43]Brentin Mock, "Redlining Is Alive and Well–and Evolving," *CityLab*, September 28, 2015, http://www.citylab.com/housing/2015/09/redlining-is-alive-and-welland-evolving/407497/.

[44]Oliver and Shapiro, *Black Wealth/White Wealth*.

[45]William A. Darity Jr. and Patrick L. Mason, "Evidence on Discrimination in Employment: Codes of Color, Codes of Gender," *Journal of Economic Perspectives* 12, no. 2 (1998): 63–90, http://www2.econ.iastate.edu/classes/econ321/rosburg/Darity%20and%20Mason%20-%20Evidence%20on%20Discrimination%20in%20employment%20(Color,%20Gender).pdf.

[46]Bernadette Chachere and Gerald Chachere, "An Illustrative Estimate: The Present Value of the Benefits from Racial Discrimination, 1929–1969," in *The Wealth of Races: The Present Value of Benefits from Past Injustices*, ed. Richard America (Westport, CT: Greenwood Press, 1990).

[47]Kolchin, *American Slavery, 1619–1877,* pp. 126–27.

[48]Brown v. Board of Education of Topeka, 347 U.S. 483 (1954).

[49]Cited in Brent Staples, "Why Slave Era Barriers to Black Literacy Still Matter," *New York Times*, January 1, 2006, http://www.nytimes.com/2006/01/01/opinion/why-slaveera-barriers-to-black-literacy-still-matter.html.

[50]Ibid.

[51]Celeste K. Carruthers and Marianne H. Wanamaker, "Separate and Unequal in the Labor Market: Human Capital and the Jim Crow Wage Gap," National Bureau of Economic Research Working Paper no. 21947, NBER, Cambridge, MA, January 2016, http://www.nber.org/papers/w21947.pdf.

[52]Seth Stephens-Davidowitz, "The Cost of Racial Animus on a Black Candidate: Evidence Using Google Search Data," *Journal of Public Economics* 118 (October 2014): 26–40.

[53]Drew Desilver, "Black Unemployment Is Consistently Twice That of Whites," *Fact Tank New in the Numbers*, Pew Research Center, August 21, 2013, http://www.pewresearch.org/fact-tank/2013/08/21/through-good-times-and-bad-black-unemployment-is-consistently-double-that-of-whites/.

[54]U.S. Bureau of Labor Statistics, "Unemployment Rate: Black or African American [LNS14000006]," retrieved from FRED, Federal Reserve Bank of St. Louis, March 27, 2018, https://fred.stlouisfed.org/series/LNS14000006; U.S. Bureau of Labor Statistics, "Unemployment Rate: White [LNS14000003]," retrieved from FRED, Federal Reserve Bank of St. Louis, March 27, 2018, https://fred.stlouisfed.org/series/LNS14000003.

[55]U.S. Bureau of Labor Statistics, "Table 3. Median Usual Weekly Earnings of Full-Time Wage and Salary Workers by Age, Race, Hispanic or Latino Ethnicity, and Sex, Third Quarter 2016 Averages, Not Seasonally Adjusted," economic news release, http://www.bls.gov/news.release/wkyeng.t03.htm.

[56]Roland G. Fryer Jr., Devah Pager, and Jörg L. Spenkuch, "Racial Disparities in Job Finding and Offered Wages," *Journal of Law and Economics* 56 (August 2013): 663–89.

[57]Darrick Hamilton, Algernon Austin, and William Darity Jr., "Whiter Jobs, Higher Wages: Occupational Segregation and the Lower Wages of Black Men," Economic Policy Institute (EPI) Briefing Paper no. 288, EPI, Washington, February 11, 2011, https://www.epi.org/publication/whiter_jobs_higher_wages/.

[58]Christian Weller and Jaryn Fields, "The Black and White Labor Gap in America: Why African-Americans Struggle to Find Jobs and Remain Employed Compared to Whites," issue brief, Center for American Progress, Washington, July 25, 2011, https://www.americanprogress.org/issues/economy/reports/2011/07/25/9992/the-black-and-white-labor-gap-in-america/.

[59]Marianne Bertrand and Sendhil Mullainathan, "Are Emily and Greg More Employable Than Lakisha and Jamal? A Field Experiment on Labor Market Discrimination," *American Economic Review* 94 (September 2004): 991–1013.

[60]S. Michael Gaddis, "Discrimination in the Credential Society: An Audit Study of Race and College Selectivity in the Labor Market," *Social Forces* 93, no. 4 (2015): 1451–79, http://sf.oxfordjournals.org/content/93/4/1451. One caveat: while this study claims to control for naming on the basis of social class, it also included just 12 names in total, thereby leading some to be wary of its methodology.

[61]Andrew Hanson et al., "Discrimination in Mortgage Lending: Evidence from a Correspondence Experiment," *Journal of Urban Economics* 92 (March 2016): 48–65.

[62]U.S. Department of Housing and Urban Development, *Housing Discrimination against Racial and Ethnic Minorities 2012* (Washington: U.S. Department of Housing and Urban Development, Office of Policy Development and Research, 2012), p. xiv, "Exhibit Es-4: Inspect Available Rental Units," https://www.huduser.gov/portal/Publications/pdf/HUD-514_HDS2012.pdf.

[63]"How Discrimination Destroys Black Wealth," *New York Times*, editorial, September 15, 2015, http://www.nytimes.com/2015/09/15/opinion/how-segregation-destroys-black-wealth.html?_r=0.

[64]Michelle Alexander, *The New Jim Crow: Mass Incarceration in the Age of Colorblindness* (New York: The New Press, 2012).

[65]Justin Wolfers, David Leonhardt, and Kevin Quillers, "1.5 Million Missing Black Men," *New York Times*, April 20, 2015, http://www.nytimes.com/interactive/2015/04/20/upshot/missing-black-men.html.

[66]Michelle Alexander, interview with National Public Radio, January 17, 2012, http://www.npr.org/2012/01/16/145175694/legal-scholar-jim-crow-still-exists-in-america.

[67]Sarah Shannon et al. "The Growth, Scope, and Spatial Distribution of People with Felony Records in the United States, 1948–2010." Conditionally accepted for publication in *Demography* 54, no. 5 (2017), http://users.soc.umn.edu/~uggen/former_felons_2016.pdf.

[68]See, for example, Bruce Western and Catherine Sirios, "Racial Inequality in Employment and Earnings after Incarceration," unpublished paper, Harvard University, Cambridge, MA, February 2017, https://scholar.harvard.edu/files/brucewestern/files/racial_inequality_in_employment_and_earnings_after_incarceration.pdf; Harry Holzer, "Collateral Costs: The Effects of Incarceration on the Employment and Earnings of Young Workers," IZA Discussion Paper no. 3118, October 2007, Institute for the Study of Labor, Bonn, http://ftp.iza.org/dp3118.pdf.

[69]Harry Holzer, Steven Raphael, and Michael Stoll, "Employment Dimensions of Reentry: Understanding the Nexus between Prisoner Reentry and Work," Urban Institute Reentry Roundtable Discussion Paper, New York University Law School, May 19–20, 2003.

[70]Devah Pager, Bruce Western, and Naomi Sugie, "Sequencing Disadvantage: Barriers to Employment Facing Young Black and White Men with Criminal Records," *Annals of the American Academy of Political and Social Sciences* 623, no. 1 (May 2009): 195–213, http://scholar.harvard.edu/pager/publications/sequencing-disadvantage-barriers-employment-facing-young-black-and-white-men.

[71]Harry Holzer, Paul Offner, and Elaine Sorenson, "Declining Employment among Black Less-Educated Men: The Role of Incarceration and Child Support," research report, Urban Institute, April 2004, https://www.urban.org/research/publication/declining-employment-among-young-black-less-educated-men. However, some studies, which use administrative data, show a much more moderate and short-lived effect. Holzer reviewed a number of these studies and argues that "a number of problems plague all of these studies based on administrative data . . . [unemployment insurance] records only capture earnings in formal jobs . . . [and] would automatically exclude public sector jobs, any employment that occurs in another state, any self-employment, and most importantly—any casual and informal work for cash . . . " He notes that the employment rates, both before and after incarceration, tend to be "dramatically lower" in the administrative-data studies than they are in the National Longitudinal Surveys of Youth studies. He continues: "Another problem arises from the absence of a clear control or comparison group of non-offenders in at least some of these studies. Simple pre-post incarceration comparisons of employment and earnings outcomes may tell us little about the counterfactual situation that would have existed in the absence

of incarceration." He concludes that, "These considerations suggest that the studies based on administrative data might well understate the negative impacts of incarceration on subsequent earnings or employment." Harry Holzer, "Collateral Costs: Effects of Incarceration on Employment and Earnings among Young Workers," in *Do Prisons Make Us Safer?: The Benefits and Costs of the Prison Boom* (New York: Russell Sage Foundation, 2009), p. 254.

[72]Robert T. Carter and Jessica M. Forsyth, "A Guide to the Forensic Assessment of Race-Based Traumatic Stress Reactions," *Journal of the Academy of Psychiatry and Law* 37, no. 1 (March 2009): 28–40.

[73]Monnica Williams, "Can Racism Cause PTSD? Implications for DSM-5," *Psychology Today*, May 20, 2013, https://www.psychologytoday.com/blog/culturally-speaking/201305/can-racism-cause-ptsd-implications-dsm-5.

[74]Ibid.

[75]Therma Bryant-Davis and Carlota Ocampo, "Racist Incident Based Trauma," *Counseling Psychologist* 33 (July 2005): 479–500.

[76]Ibid.

[77]Orlando Patterson, *The Cultural Matrix: Understanding Black Youth* (Cambridge, MA: Harvard University Press, 2015), p. 117.

[78]Ibid., pp. 116–17.

[79]Morning Consult and Politico, "National Tracking Poll #170809," August 17–19, 2017, Table POL14_9, p. 127, http://www.politico.com/f/?id=0000015e-0bfc-d354-abfe-abfe66d70000.

[80]General Social Survey, 2017, National Opinion Research Center at University of Chicago, https://gssdataexplorer.norc.org/variables/vfilter.

[81]Gerald Jaynes and Robin Williams Jr., *A Common Destiny: Blacks and American Society* (Washington: National Academy Press, 1989), p. 278.

[82]U.S. Census Bureau, "Historical Poverty Tables: People and Families—1959 to 2015," Table 3, Poverty Status of People by Age, Race, and Hispanic Origin," http://www2.census.gov/programs-surveys/cps/tables/time-series/historical-poverty-people/hstpov3.xls.

[83]Diana Pearce, "The Feminization of Poverty: Women, Work, and Welfare," *Urban and Social Change Review*, Special Issue on Women and Work, 11, no. 1 and 2 (1978): 28–37.

[84]U.S. Census Bureau, "Annual Social and Economic Supplement (ASEC) of the Current Population Survey (CPS)," May 8, 2017, https://www.census.gov/programs-surveys/saipe/guidance/model-input-data/cpsasec.html.

[85]U.S. Census Bureau, "Historical Poverty Tables: People and Families—1959 to 2016," HSTPOV02, Poverty Status of People by Family Relationship, Race, and Hispanic Origin, https://www2.census.gov/programs-surveys/cps/tables/time-series/historical-poverty-people/hstpov2.xls.

[86]"Status of Women in the States: Poverty and Opportunity," Institute for Women's Policy Institute, April 8, 2015, https://iwpr.org/publications/the-status-of-women-in-the-states-2015-poverty-opportunity/.

[87]U.S. Census Bureau, "Historical Poverty Tables: People and Families—1959 to 2016," HSTPOV15, Age Distribution of the Poor, https://www2.census.gov/programs-surveys/cps/tables/time-series/historical-poverty-people/hstpov15.xls.

[88]William Blackstone, *Commentaries on the Laws of England*, vol. 1, (Philadelphia: J. B. Lippencott Co. [1753] 1893), pp. 442–45, accessed via Liberty Fund, http://files.libertyfund.org/files/2140/Blackstone_1387-01_EBk_v6.0.pdf.

[89]Ian Millhiser, "When Redefining Marriage Meant That Women Had to Be Treated as Human Beings," *Think Progress*, October 7, 2014, http://thinkprogress.org/justice/2014/10/07/3573438/three-ways-america-redefined-marriage-long-before-the-supreme-court-got-involved/.

[90]Ava Baron, "Protective Labor Legislation and the Cult of Domesticity," *Journal of Family Issues* 2, no. 1 (March 1981): 25–38, http://jfi.sagepub.com/content/2/1/25.extract.

[91]Rachel Emma Silverman, "Gender Bias at Work Turns Up in Feedback," *Wall Street Journal*, September 30, 2015, http://www.wsj.com/articles/gender-bias-at-work-turns-up-in-feedback-1443600759.

[92]D'Vera Cohn, Gretchen Livingston, and Wendy Wang, "After Decades of Decline, A Rise in Stay-at-Home Mothers," Pew Research Center, *Social and Demographic Trends*, April 8, 2014, http://www.pewsocialtrends.org/2014/04/08/after-decades-of-decline-a-rise-in-stay-at-home-mothers/.

[93]Bureau of Labor Statistics, "Table 4. Families with Own Children: Employment Status of Parents by Age of Youngest Child and Family Type, 2015–2016 Annual Averages," http://www.bls.gov/news.release/famee.t04.htm.

[94]Arlie Russell Hochschild, *The Second Shift*, (New York: Viking Penguin, 1989).

[95]Christin L. Munsch, "Flexible Work, Flexible Penalties: The Effect of Gender, Childcare, and Type of Request on the Flexibility Bias," *Social Forces* 94, no. 4 (June 2016): 1567–91, http://sf.oxfordjournals.org/content/early/2016/01/08/sf.sov122.abstract.

[96]Remember that marital rape only became widely recognized as a crime in the 1980s. (North Carolina was the last state to criminalize marital rape in 1993.) And eight states still include exceptions. For example, Ohio does not include the use of a "drug, intoxicant, or controlled substance" to incapacitate a victim as rape for a spouse, although it does for other victims. Similarly, Oklahoma specifically requires spousal rape to include the use of "force or violence" if the victim is the "spouse of the perpetrator." The law also deems penetration to be rape in instances when "the victim is at the time unconscious," but specifically not when the victim

is the perpetrator's spouse. South Carolina still doesn't even recognize marital rape, but rather "spousal sexual battery," and requires "the threat of use of a weapon" or "physical violence of a high and aggravated nature" to prosecute. Samantha Allen, "Marital Rape Is Semi-Legal in 8 States," *Daily Beast*, June 9, 2015. Apart from marital rape, women often experience more subtle forms of coercion. These subtle forms of coercion can include culture, religion, and psychological pressure. Women are often acculturated from an early age to believe that having children is their highest aspiration. As they grow up, women who choose not to have children are frequently looked down on. Even if they are otherwise employed, the primary role of women is still often seen to be wife, mother, and homemaker. The income they provide is an extra. The constant repetition of such messages does affect, even if they do not determine, the choices that women make.

[97]Raquel Fernández and Joyce Cheng Wong, "Free to Leave? A Welfare Analysis of Divorce Regimes," *American Economic Journal: Macroeconomics* 9, 3 (2017): 72–115.

[98]Ann Huff Stevens, "Transition into and out of Poverty in the United States," University of California–Davis, Center for Poverty Research, http://poverty.ucdavis.edu/policy-brief/transitions-out-poverty-united-states.

[99]Diana B. Elliot and Tavia Simmons, "Marital Events of Americans: 2009," American Community Survey Reports, U.S. Census Bureau, ACS-13, Table 2, Characteristics of Those Married, Divorced, and Widowed in the Last 12 Months, by Sex: 2009, August 2011, https://www.census.gov/prod/2011pubs/acs-13.pdf.

[100]Stevens, "Transition into and out of Poverty in the United States."

[101]Mona Chalabi, "Are Moms Less Likely Than Dads to Pay Child Support?" *FiveThirtyEight*, February 26, 2015, https://fivethirtyeight.com/features/are-moms-less-likely-than-dads-to-pay-child-support/.

[102]Timothy Grall, "Custodial Mothers and Fathers and Their Child Support: 2013," Current Population Reports, Series P60-255, U.S. Census Bureau, https://www.census.gov/content/dam/Census/library/publications/2016/demo/P60-255.pdf.

[103]Sara McLanahan, "Fragile Families and the Reproduction of Poverty," *Annals of the American Academies of Political and Social Sciences* 621, no. 1 (January 2009): 111–31, http://www.ncbi.nlm.nih.gov/pmc/articles/PMC2831755/.

[104]Ibid.

[105]Theodora Ooms, "Marriage and Government: Strange Bedfellows?," Policy Brief no. 1, Couples and Marriage Series, Center for Law and Social Policy, Washington, August, 2002, p. 3, http://research.policyarchive.org/13927.pdf.

[106]See, for example, Wilson, *When Work Disappears: The World of the Urban Poor*; William Julius Wilson and Kathleen Neckerman, "Poverty and Family Structure: The Widening Gap between Evidence and Public Policy Issues," in *The Truly*

Disadvantaged: The Inner City, The Underclass, and Public Policy (Chicago: University of Chicago Press, 1987); Kathryn Edin, "Few Good Men: Why Poor Mothers Don't Marry or Remarry," *American Prospect*, June 2, 2000.

[107]McLanahan, "Fragile Families and the Reproduction of Poverty"; Irwin Garfinkle et al., eds., *Fathers Under Fire: The Revolution in Child-Support Payments* (New York: Russell Sage Foundation, 1998).

[108]McLanahan, Sara, et al., "Fragile Families and Child Wellbeing Study," Robert Wood Johnson Foundation, Program Results Report, January 28, 2014, https://fragilefamilies.princeton.edu/sites/fragilefamilies/files/rwjf_program_results_report.pdf.

[109]Cynthia Miller and Virginia Knox, "The Challenge of Helping Low-Income Fathers Support Their Children: Final Lessons from Parents' Fair Share," Manpower Demonstration Research Project, New York, 2001.

[110]Ooms, "Marriage and Government: Strange Bedfellows?," p. 3.

[111]Wolfers, Leonhardt, and Quillers, "1.5 Million Missing Black Men."

[112]Lasse Eika, Magne Mogstad, and Basit Zafar, "Educational Assortative Mating and Household Income Inequality," Federal Reserve Bank of New York, Staff Report no. 682, August 2014 (revised March 2017), https://www.newyorkfed.org/medialibrary/media/research/staff_reports/sr682.pdf.

[113]Christine Schwartz and Robert Mare, "Trends in Assortative Marriage from 1940 to 2003," University of California–Los Angeles, California Center for Population Research, July 2005.

[114]Kurt Bauman and Camille Ryan, "Women Now at the Head of the Class, Lead Men in College Attainment," *Census Blogs*, U.S. Census Bureau, October 7, 2015, https://www.census.gov/newsroom/blogs/random-samplings/2015/10/women-now-at-the-head-of-the-class-lead-men-in-college-attainment.html.

[115]June Carbone and Naomi Cahn, *Marriage Markets: How Inequality Is Remaking the American Family* (Oxford: Oxford University Press, 2014), p. 43.

[116]Ibid., p. 38.

[117]Claudia Goldin and Lawrence F. Katz, "The Power of the Pill: Oral Contraceptives and Women's Career and Marriage Decisions," *Journal of Political Economy* 110, no. 4 (2002): 730–70, https://dash.harvard.edu/bitstream/handle/1/2624453/Goldin_PowerPill.pdf?sequence=4. While this study remains the gold standard for discussion of the impact of a woman's reproductive control on marriage and nonmarital birth, it is worth noting that a 2017 paper by Caitlin Myers raises questions about whether the availability of contraception has a significant impact on motherhood and marriage, especially when compared to the effect of legally available abortion. See Caitlin Myers, "The Power of Abortion Policy: Re-Examining the Effects of Young Women's Access to Reproductive Control," *Journal of Political Economy* 125, no. 6 (December 2017): 2178–224.

[118]See Paola Giuliano, "Gender: An Historical Perspective," National Bureau of Economic Research Working Paper no. 23635, NBER, Cambridge, MA, July 2017.

[119]Moreover, statistical poverty among women is disproportionately driven by high levels of poverty among African American women. For black women who are poor there is no way to determine the relative impacts of racial versus gender bias, or the ways in which the two intersect. It seems clear, however, that African American women face barriers that white women do not.

[120]For example, see Nancy Folbre, "Children as Public Goods," *American Economic Review* 84, no. 2 (May 1994): 86–90.

[121]W. Michael Cox and Richard Alm, "Creative Destruction," in *The Concise Encyclopedia of Economics*, http://www.econlib.org/library/Enc/CreativeDestruction.html.

[122]See Claudia Goldin and Lawrence F. Katz, *The Race between Education and Technology* (Cambridge, MA: Belknap Press, 2008); Daron Acemoglu et al., "Import Competition and the Great US Employment Slag of the 2000s," *Journal of Labor Economics* 34, S1 (2016): S141–S198.

[123]Thomas Sowell, *Marxism: Philosophy and Economics* (New York: William Morrow & Co., 1985), p. 137.

[124]Susan Lund, McKinsey Global Institute, cited by James Pethokoukis, "Where Are US Jobs Being Created? Not in the Middle," *AEIdeas* (blog), May 22, 2014, http://www.aei.org/publication/where-are-us-jobs-being-created-not-in-the-middle/.

[125]Daron Acemoglu et al., "Import Competition and the Great US Employment Slag of the 2000s," *Journal of Labor Economics* 34, S1 (2016): S141–S198.

[126]David H. Autor, David Dorn, and Gordon H. Hanson, "The China Shock: Learning from Labor Market Adjustment to Large Changes in Trade," *Annual Review of Economics* 8, no. 1 (2016): 205–40. Economists consider this so-called China shock caused by this surge of imports to be a one-off occurrence. China had been effectively cut off from the rest of the world under the Mao era, and 800 million new workers essentially entering the global economy at once was bound to cause large readjustments. Still, China is just an extreme example of how economic dynamics outside a worker's control may expose that worker to poverty.

[127]Michael J. Hicks and Srikant Devaraj, "The Myth and Reality of Manufacturing in America," Ball State University, Muncie, IN, https://projects.cberdata.org/reports/MfgReality.pdf.

[128]Daron Acemoglu and Pascual Restrepo, "Robots and Jobs: Evidence from US Labor Markets," National Bureau of Economic Research Working Paper no. 23285, NBER, Cambridge, MA, March 2017, http://www.nber.org/papers/w23285.

[129]Ronald Bailey, "Are Robots Going to Steal Our Jobs?" *Reason*, July 2017, http://reason.com/archives/2017/06/06/are-robots-going-to-steal-our.

[130]Thomas Piketty, *Capital in the Twenty-First Century* (Cambridge, MA: Belknap Press, 2014).

[131]Bruce D. Meyer and James X. Sullivan, "Winning the War: Poverty from the Great Society to the Great Recession," National Bureau of Economic Research Working Paper no. 18718, NBER, Cambridge, MA, January 2013, http://www.nber.org/papers/w18718; Bruce D. Meyer and James X. Sullivan, "Winning the War: Poverty from the Great Society to the Great Recession," Brookings Papers on Economic Activity, Fall 2012, https://www3.nd.edu/~jsulliv4/BPEA2.0.pdf.

[132]U.S. Census Bureau, "Historical Income Tables: Income Inequality," Table H-4 Gini Ratios for Households, by Race and Hispanic Origin of Householder, https://www.census.gov/data/tables/time-series/demo/income-poverty/historical-income-inequality.html; U.S. Census Bureau, "Historical Poverty Tables—People," Table 5, Percent of People by Ratio of Income to Poverty Level, https://www.census.gov/data/tables/time-series/demo/income-poverty/historical-poverty-people.html; Meyer and Sullivan, "Winning the War," Brookings; Meyer and Sullivan, "Winning the War," NBER.

[133]Dierdre Bloome, "Income Inequality and Intergenerational Income Mobility in the United States," *Social Forces* 93, no. 3 (2015): 1047–80, http://sf.oxfordjournals.org/content/93/3/1047.

Chapter Four

[1]Scott Greenberg, "Summary of Latest Federal Income Tax Data, 2016 Update," Tax Foundation, February 1, 2017, https://taxfoundation.org/summary-latest-federal-income-tax-data-2016-update/.

[2]Congressional Budget Office, "The Distribution of Household Income and Federal Taxes, 2013," Supplemental Data, Tables 2–3, June 8, 2016, https://www.cbo.gov/sites/default/files/114th-congress-2015-2016/reports/51361-SupplementalData.xlsx.

[3]Michael Tanner, "The American Welfare State: How We Spend Nearly $1 Trillion a Year Fighting Poverty—And Fail," Cato Institute Policy Analysis no. 694, April 11, 2012, http://www.cato.org/publications/policy-analysis/american-welfare-state-how-we-spend-nearly-$1-trillion-year-fighting-poverty-fail. See the paper's appendix for a complete list of these programs.

[4]Gerald Prante and Scott A. Hodge, "The Distribution of Tax and Spending Policies in the United States," Special Report no. 211, The Tax Foundation, November 8, 2013, http://taxfoundation.org/article/distribution-tax-and-spending-policies-united-states.

[5]Congressional Budget Office, "The Distribution of Household Income and Federal Taxes, 2013," Figure 15, "Reduction in Income Inequality from Government Transfers and Federal Taxes, 1979 to 2013," https://www.cbo.gov/sites/default/files/114th-congress-2015-2016/reports/51361-FigureData.xlsx.

[6]Author's calculations using U.S. Census Bureau, "Table 7: Number of People in Poverty by Sex," http:// www.census.gov/hhes/www/poverty/data/historical/people.html; General Services Administration, Catalog of Federal Domestic Assistance, https://www.cfda.gov/; Congressional Research Service, "Cash and Noncash Benefits for Persons with Limited Income: Eligibility Rules, Recipient and Expenditure Data," Report RL33340, March 2006. Welfare spending also increased when measured as a percentage of gross domestic product (GDP). Federal spending more than doubled from just 1.8 percent of GDP to 3.9 percent, while total welfare spending also doubled from 2.7 percent of GDP to 5.6 percent between 1965 and 2011.

[7]Michael Tanner, "The American Welfare State: How We Spend Nearly $1 Trillion a Year Fighting Poverty—And Fail," Cato Institute Policy Analysis no. 694, April 11, 2012, http://www.cato.org/publications/policy-analysis/american-welfare-state-how-we-spend-nearly-$1-trillion-year-fighting-poverty-fail.

[8]U.S. Census Bureau, "Poverty Thresholds by Size of Family and Number of Children," http://www2.census.gov/programs-surveys/cps/tables/time-series/historical-poverty-thresholds/thresh15.xls.

[9]Arloc Sherman, "Official Poverty Measure Masks Gains Made over Last 50 Years," Center on Budget and Policy Priorities, September 13, 2013, https://www.cbpp.org/research/official-poverty-measure-masks-gains-made-over-last-50-years.

[10]Bruce Meyer and James Sullivan, "Winning the War: Poverty from the Great Society to the Great Recession," *Brookings Papers on Economic Activity*, Fall 2012.

[11]U.S. Treasury Department, "The Debt to the Penny and Who Holds It," Treasury Direct, accessed June 25, 2018, https://www.treasurydirect.gov/NP/debt/current. This does not include more than $80 trillion in unfunded liabilities for Social Security and Medicaid. Michael D. Tanner, "Medicare and Social Security Tabs Coming Due," Cato Commentary, February 6, 2015, https://www.cato.org/publications/commentary/medicare-social-security-tabs-coming-due. But for purposes of this discussion, those future costs should be considered separately.

[12]Author's calculations using Catalog of Federal Domestic Assistance; Congressional Budget Office, "The Budget and Economic Outlook: Fiscal Years 2011 to 2021," Appendix F, Table F-9: Outlays for Mandatory Spending; Bureau of Economic Analysis, "Current-Dollar and 'Real' Gross Domestic Product," Excel worksheet, June 28, 2018, bea.gov/national/xls/gdplev.xls.

[13]By some estimates, only around 15 percent of federal spending can be considered an investment, even using a broad definition of the term that includes "human investment," such as education. Congressional Budget Office, "Federal

Investment," December 18, 2013, http://www.cbo.gov/sites/default/files/cbofiles/attachments/44974-FederalInvestment.pdf.

[14]Tyler Cowen, "Does the Welfare State Help the Poor?," *Social Philosophy and Policy* 19, no. 1 (2002): 36–54, https://philpapers.org/rec/COWDTW.

[15]Martin Ravallion, "The Idea of Antipoverty Policy," National Bureau of Economic Research Working Paper no. 19210, NBER, Cambridge, MA, July 2013.

[16]In an ideal world, much assistance to the remaining poor would take place through the efforts of private charity and other voluntary programs. Numerous studies have documented a "displacement effect," whereby government programs crowd out private giving. See, for example, Russell Roberts, "A Positive Model for Private Charity and Public Transfers," *Journal of Political Economy* 92 (1984): 2136–48. In fact, there is evidence that the total amount of charity in a community remained relatively constant regardless of the mix of public and private sources. In 1899, Frederic Almy, secretary of the Buffalo Charity Organization Society, gathered data on public and private charitable activities in 40 cities. Almy ranked the cities in four groups from high to low in both categories of charity. He found that cities in the highest two categories of private charity had the lowest levels of public charity. Those with higher levels of public charity tended to have lower levels of private charity. Almy concluded that "a correspondence or balance between the amounts of public and private relief appears to be established." Frederic Almy, "The Relation between Public and Private Charities," *Charities Review* 9 (1899): 65–71. More recently, Charles Murray found a similar pattern. Charitable giving, which had risen steadily from the end of World War II until the mid 1960s, declined dramatically in the wake of the Great Society. In the 1980s, when the rise in welfare spending began to flatten (and not coincidentally the public was deluged with media stories warning of cutbacks to social welfare programs), the public responded with increased private giving. Charles Murray, *In Pursuit of Happiness and Good Government* (New York: Simon and Schuster, 1988), pp. 275–76. Moreover, although it appears that total charitable giving moves inversely to government welfare spending, so too does the portion of charitable giving that goes to human services rather than education or the arts. Following the Great Society, the portion of charitable giving devoted to direct human services fell from 15 percent to 6 percent. But during the Reagan years, social services giving rose again to 11.6 percent of total charity, only to decline once more to under 10 percent in the years that followed. American Association of Fund-Raising Counsel (AAFRC) Trust for Philanthropy, *New Times, Tight Money: How Corporate Leaders Respond: Giving USA Special Report: Trends in Corporate Philanthropy* (New York, AAFRC Trust for Philanthropy, 1995). However, whatever the ideal, I am not, for purposes of this book, calling for the end to all government welfare.

[17]See, for example, Hans Pitlik and Martin Rode, "Free to Choose? Economic Freedom, Relative Income, and Life Control Perceptions," *International Journal of Wellbeing* 6, no. 1 (2015): 81–100.

[18]Ben Gitis and Curtis Arndt, "Material Well-Being vs. Self-Sufficiency: How Adjusting Poverty Measurements Can Reveal a Diverging Trend in America," American Action Forum, Washington, March 9, 2017.

[19]Ron Haskins, Isabel V. Sawhill, and Julia B. Isaacs, *Getting Ahead or Losing Ground: Economic Mobility in America* (Washington: Brookings Institution, 2008), https://www.brookings.edu/research/getting-ahead-or-losing-ground-economic-mobility-in-america/.

[20]Barack Obama, "Remarks by the President on the Economy in Osawatomie, Kansas," Office of the Press Secretary, December 6, 2011, http://www.whitehouse.gov/the-press-office/2011/12/06/remarks-president-economy-osawatomie-kansas.

[21]Raj Chetty et al., "Is the United States Still a Land of Opportunity? Recent Trends in Intergenerational Mobility," National Bureau of Economic Research Working Paper no. 19844, NBER, Cambridge, MA, January 2014, http://www.nber.org/papers/w19844.

[22]Chul-In Lee and Gary Solon, "Trends in Intergenerational Income Mobility," National Bureau of Economic Research Working Paper no. 12007, NBER, Cambridge, MA, February 2006, http://www.nber.org/papers/w12007.pdf.

[23]U.S. Department of the Treasury, "Income Mobility in the U.S. from 1996 to 2005," November 13, 2007, https://www.treasury.gov/resource-center/tax-policy/Documents/Report-Income-Mobility-2008.pdf.

[24]I borrow this "prisoner's dilemma" formulation from Tyler Cowen, who actually disagrees with it. Cowen, "Does the Welfare State Help the Poor?"

[25]For a complete list of programs, see the appendix to Tanner, "The American Welfare State."

[26]Andrea Louise Campbell, *Trapped in America's Safety Net: One Family's Struggle* (Chicago: University of Chicago Press, 2014), p. 34.

[27]Author's calculations using Tanner, "The American Welfare State"; General Services Administration, *Catalog of Federal Domestic Assistance*, https://www.cfda.gov/?s=main&mode=list&tab=list; and Gene Falk, "Low-Income Assistance Programs: Trends in Federal Spending," Congressional Research Service report R41823, May 7, 2014, https://fas.org/sgp/crs/misc/R41823.pdf.

[28]U.S. Department of Agriculture, "WIC Food Package Regulatory Requirements," Food and Nutrition Service, https://www.fns.usda.gov/wic/wic-food-packages-regulatory-requirements-wic-eligible-foods.

[29]Office of Family Assistance, "Q&A: TANF Requirements Related to EBT Transactions: Question and Answer on TANF Requirements Related to Electronic Benefit Transfer Transactions," U.S. Department of Health and Human Services, March 25, 2013, https://www.acf.hhs.gov/ofa/resource/q-a-ebt-transactions.

[30]National Conference of State Legislatures, "Drug Testing for Welfare Recipients and Public Assistance," March 24, 2016, http://www.ncsl.org/research/human-services/drug-testing-and-public-assistance.aspx.

[31]Moreover, the fact that we don't drug test middle-class recipients of government benefits like Social Security suggests that these provisions are largely punitive and based on stereotypes (frequently racial stereotypes) of welfare recipients.

[32]Michael Tanner and Charles Hughes, "The Work versus Welfare Trade-Off: 2013," Cato Institute White Paper, August 19, 2013, p. 3, http://object.cato.org/sites/cato.org/files/pubs/pdf/the_work_versus_welfare_trade-off_2013_wp.pdf.

[33]Congressional Budget Office, "Illustrative Examples of Effective Marginal Tax Rates Faced by Married and Single Taxpayers: Supplemental Material for Effective Marginal Tax Rates for Low- and Moderate-Income Workers," November 2012, p. 13, https://www.cbo.gov/publication/43722.

[34]Elaine Maag et al., "How Marginal Tax Rates Affect Families at Various Levels of Poverty," *National Tax Journal* 65, no. 4 (December 2012): 759–82, http://www.urban.org/UploadedPDF/412722-How-marginal-Tax-Rates-Affect-Families.pdf.

[35]Erik Randolph, "Modeling Potential Income and Welfare-Assistance Benefits in Illinois: Single Parent with Two Children Households and Two Parents with Two Children Household Scenarios in Cook County, City of Chicago, Lake County and St. Clair County," Illinois Policy Institute, Special Report, December 2014, p. 45, https://d2dv7hze646xr.cloudfront.net/wp-content/uploads/2014/12/Welfare_Report_finalfinal.pdf.

[36]Elaine Maag and Adam Carasso, "Taxation and the Family: What Is the Earned Income Tax Credit?" in *The Tax Policy Briefing Book*, Tax Policy Center, http://www.taxpolicycenter.org/briefing-book/key-elements/family/eitc.cfm.

[37]Ron Haskins, "The Outcomes of 1996 Welfare Reform," testimony before the House Committee on Ways and Means, July 19, 2006, https://www.brookings.edu/wp-content/uploads/2016/06/20060719-1.pdf.

[38]Scott Winship, "Poverty after Welfare Reform," Manhattan Institute, August 2016, https://www.manhattan-institute.org/sites/default/files/R-SW-0816.pdf.

[39]Haskins, "The Outcomes of 1996 Welfare Reform."

[40]Robert Moffitt, "Welfare Reform: The U.S. Experience," Institute for Research on Poverty, Discussion Paper No. 1334-08, February 2008, http://www.irp.wisc.edu/publications/dps/pdfs/dp133408.pdf.

[41]Haskins, "The Outcomes of 1996 Welfare Reform."

[42]Ibid.

[43]Ibid.

[44]Robert F. Schoeni and Rebecca Blank, "What Has Welfare Reform Accomplished? Impacts on Welfare, Participation, Income, Poverty, and Family

Structure," Working Paper Series 00-02, Labor and Population Program, RAND, March 2000, https://www.rand.org/content/dam/rand/pubs/drafts/2008/DRU2268.pdf.

[45]Haskins, "The Outcomes of 1996 Welfare Reform." One thing welfare reform did not do was reduce welfare spending. Total welfare spending has increased significantly since 1996. It simply shifted from cash to in-kind benefits. This lack of reduction, as Scott Winship suggests, may have played a critical role in both moving welfare recipients into work and preventing them from falling into poverty after welfare reform. Yet it also means that welfare reform did not necessarily reduce the size of the welfare state or increase independence on the part of recipients. Winship, "Poverty after Welfare Reform."

[46]Department for Work and Pensions (UK), "Universal Credit Pathfinder Evaluation," Research Report no. 886, October 22, 2014, https://www.gov.uk/government/uploads/system/uploads/attachment_data/file/380537/rr886-universal-credit-pathfinder-evaluation.pdf.

[47]For a detailed discussion of the advantages of a universal basic income (UBI), as well as potential drawbacks, see Michael Tanner, "The Pros and Cons of a Guaranteed National Income," Cato Institute Policy Analysis no. 773, May 12, 2015. See also, Charles Murray, *In Our Hands: A Plan to Replace the Welfare State* (Washington: AEI Press, 2016); and Andrew Stern, *Raising the Floor: How a Universal Basic Income Can Renew Our Economy and Rebuild the American Dream* (New York: Public Affairs Books, 2016).

[48]Matt Jensen et al., "A Budget-Neutral Universal Basic Income," American Enterprise Institute Economics Working Paper no. 2017-10, 2017, https://www.aei.org/wp-content/uploads/2017/05/UBI-Jensen-et-al-working-paper.pdf.

[49]Paul Ryan, "Expanding Opportunity in America," discussion draft from the House Budget Committee, July 24, 2014, http://budget.house.gov/uploadedfiles/expanding_opportunity_in_america.pdf.

[50]Marco Rubio, *American Dreams: Restoring Economic Opportunity for Everyone* (New York: Penguin Books, 2015).

[51]Although more states have authorized lump-sum payments than any other type of diversion program, the U.S. Department of Health and Human Services reports that these programs are rarely used in practice. Utah, Virginia, and Montana appear to have the most extensive experience with the concept. Urban Institute, "Welfare Rules Database," Table I.A.1, "Formal Diversion Payments," http://anfdata.urban.org/databook_tabs/2013/I.A.1.XLSX.

[52]Ibid.

[53]Carmen Solomon-Fears, "Welfare Reform: Diversion as an Alternative to TANF Benefits," Congressional Research Service report no. RL30230, June 16, 2006, http://congressionalresearch.com/RL30230/document.php?study=Welfare+Reform+Diversion+as+an+Alternative+to+TANF+Benefits.

[54]Andrea Hetling, Kirk Tracy, and Catherine E. Born, "A Rose by Any Other Name? Lump-Sum Diversion or Traditional Welfare Grant?," *Journal of Policy Practice* 5, no. 2-3 (2006): 43–59.

[55]See, for example, Claudia Goldin and Lawrence Katz, *The Race between Education and Technology* (Cambridge, MA: Harvard University Press, 2008).

[56]Deirdre McCloskey, *Bourgeois Equality: How Ideas, Not Capital or Institutions, Enriched the World* (Chicago: University of Chicago Press, 2016).

[57]As a mathematical exercise, of course, a UBI could be designed to eliminate poverty. However, the cost of such a program would likely either be unsustainable or would require an intolerable amount of taxation, so I do not consider that a serious proposal.

Chapter Five

[1]Angela Davis, "Masked Racism: Reflections on the Prison Industrial Complex," Colorlines, April 18, 2015, https://www.colorlines.com/articles/masked-racism-reflections-prison-industrial-complex.

[2]Danielle Kaeble et al., "Correctional Populations in the United States, 2014," NCJ 249513, U.S. Department of Justice, Bureau of Justice Statistics, "Table 1 Estimated Number of Persons Supervised by U.S. Adult Correctional Systems, by Correctional Status, 2000, 2005–2010, and 2013–2014," January 2016, http://www.bjs.gov/content/pub/pdf/cpus14.pdf; Bureau of Justice Statistics, "Correctional Populations in the United States, 1992," U.S. Department of Justice, http://www.bjs.gov/content/pub/pdf/cpus92.pdf; Bureau of Justice Statistics, "Census of Jails: Population Changes, 1999–2013," NCJ 248627, U.S. Department of Justice, December 2015, http://www.bjs.gov/content/pub/pdf/cjpc9913.pdf.

[3]Kaeble et al. "Correctional Populations in the United States, 2014," "Table 3 Incarceration Rate of Inmates under the Jurisdiction of State or Federal Prisons or Held in Local Jails and Imprisonment Rate of Sentenced Prisoners under the Jurisdiction of State or Federal Prisons, 2004–2014; Roy Walmsley, "World Prison Population List," World Prison Brief, Institute for Criminal Policy Research, http://www.prisonstudies.org/sites/default/files/resources/downloads/world_prison_population_list_11th_edition.pdf.

[4]Walmsley, "World Prison Population List."

[5]Steven Levitt, "Understanding Why Crime Fell in the 1990s: Four Factors That Explain the Decline and Six That Do Not," *Journal of Economic Perspectives* 18, no. 1 (Winter 2004): 163–190, http://pubs.aeaweb.org/doi/pdfplus/10.1257/089533004773563485.

[6]Rucker Johnson and Steven Raphael, "How Much Crime Reduction Does the Marginal Prisoner Buy?," *Journal of Law and Economics* 55, no. 2 (2012): 275–310.

[7]Aaron Chaflin and Justin McCrary, "Criminal Deterrence: A Review of the Literature," *Journal of Economic Literature* 55, no. 1 (2017): 5–48.

[8]Council of Economic Advisers, "Economic Perspectives on Incarceration and the Criminal Justice System," April 2016, p. 43, https://obamawhitehouse.archives.gov/sites/default/files/page/files/20160423_cea_incarceration_criminal_justice.pdf. Note: This is the range for adults. The upper range for juveniles is as much as $350,000 per juvenile incarcerated.

[9]Ibid.

[10]Christian Henrichson and Ruth Delaney, "The Price of Prisons: What Incarceration Costs Taxpayers," Vera Institute of Justice, July 2012, https://www.vera.org/publications/price-of-prisons-what-incarceration-costs-taxpayers; Justice Policy Institute, "Sticker Shock: Calculating the Full Price Tag for Youth Incarceration," December 2014, http://www.justicepolicy.org/uploads/justicepolicy/documents/sticker_shock_final_v2.pdf.

[11]Council of Economic Advisers, "Economic Perspectives on Incarceration," p. 45.

[12]Robert DeFina and Lance Hannon, "The Impact of Mass Incarceration on Poverty," *Journal of Crime and Delinquency* 59, no. 4 (June 2013): 562–86, http://cad.sagepub.com/content/59/4/562.abstract.

[13]Robert DeFina et al., "The Impact of Mass Incarceration on Poverty," *Crime and Delinquency* (February 2009), https://www.researchgate.net/publication/228199876_The_Impact_of_Mass_Incarceration_on_Poverty.

[14]Robert Putnam, *Our Kids: The American Dream in Crisis* (New York: Simon and Schuster, 2015), p. 77.

[15]Sonja Siennick, Eric Stewart, and Jeremy Staff, "Explaining the Association between Incarceration and Divorce," *Criminology* 52, no. 3 (2014): 371–98.

[16]Ibid.

[17]Ernest Drucker, *A Plague of Prisons: The Epidemiology of Mass Incarceration in America* (New York: The New Press, 2013), p. 146.

[18]E. A. Miller et al., "Prevalence of Maltreatment among Youths in Public Sectors of Care," *Child Maltreatment* 16, no. 3 (2011): 196–204, http://www.ncbi.nlm.nih.gov/pubmed/21803778.

[19]Drucker, *A Plague of Prisons*, pp. 144–45.

[20]Nathan James, "Offender Reentry: Correctional Statistics, Reintegration into the Community, and Recidivism," Congressional Research Service report no. RL34287, January 12, 2015, https://fas.org/sgp/crs/misc/RL34287.pdf; Bruce Western, *Punishment and Inequality in America* (New York: Russell Sage Foundation, 2006); Joseph Murray, David P. Farrington, and Ivana Sekol, "Children's Antisocial Behavior, Mental Health, Drug Use, and Educational Performance after Parental Incarceration: A Systematic Review and Meta-Analysis,"

Psychological Bulletin 138, no. 2 (March 2012): 175–210, http://psycnet.apa.org/journals/bul/138/2/175/; Steven Raphael, "Early Incarceration Spells and the Transition to Adulthood," in *The Price of Independence: The Economics of Early Adulthood*, ed. Sheldon Danziger and Cecilia Elena Rouse (New York: Russell Sage Foundation, 2007), pp. 278–306.

[21]Matthew R. Durose et al., "Recidivism of Offenders Placed on Federal Community Supervision in 2005: Patterns from 2005 to 2010," Bureau of Justice Statistics, June 2016, http://www.bjs.gov/index.cfm?ty=pbdetail&iid=5642; Ilyana Kuziemko, "How Should Inmates Be Released from Prison? An Assessment of Parole versus Fixed Sentence Regimes," *Quarterly Journal of Economics* 128, no. 1 (February 2013): 371–424, http://qje.oxfordjournals.org/content/128/1/371.full. pdf+html.

[22]Rucker Johnson, "Ever-Increasing Levels of Parental Incarceration and the Consequences for Children," in *Do Prisons Make Us Safer*, ed. Steven Raphael and Michael Stolls (New York: Russell Sage Foundation, 2009), pp. 177–206.

[23]Pew Charitable Trusts, *Collateral Costs: Incarceration's Effect on Economic Mobility* (Washington: The Pew Charitable Trusts, 2010), http://www.pewtrusts.org/~/media/legacy/uploadedfiles/pcs_assets/2010/collateralcosts1pdf.pdf.

[24]Council of Economic Advisers, "Economic Perspectives on Incarceration," p. 43.

[25]Scott Decker et al., *Criminal Stigma, Race, Gender, and Employment: An Expanded Assessment of the Consequences of Imprisonment for Employment* (Washington: National Institute of Justice, 2014), https://www.ncjrs.gov/pdffiles1/nij/grants/244756.pdf.

[26]Drucker, *A Plague of Prisons*, pp. 143–44.

[27]Office of the Assistant Secretary for Planning and Evaluation, "Overview and Inventory of HHS Efforts to Assist Incarcerated and Reentering Individuals and Their Families. Projects in Support of the Prisoner Reentry Initiative (PRI)," U.S. Department of Health and Human Services, February 2011, https://aspe.hhs.gov/report/overview-and-inventory-hhs-efforts-assist-incarcerated-and-reentering-individuals-and-their-families/projects-support-prisoner-reentry-initiative-pri.

[28]Rebecca Vallas et al., "Removing Barriers to Opportunity for Parents with Criminal Records and Their Children: A Two-Generation Approach," Center for American Progress, December 2015, https://cdn.americanprogress.org/wp-content/uploads/2015/12/09060720/CriminalRecords-report2.pdf.

[29]Caroline Wolf Harlow, "Education and Correctional Populations," NCJ 195670, Bureau of Justice Statistics, Special Report, January 2003, https://www.bjs.gov/content/pub/pdf/ecp.pdf; Council of Economic Advisers, "Economic Perspectives on Incarceration," p. 43.

[30]Bernadette Rabuy and Daniel Kopf, "Prisons of Poverty: Uncovering the Pre-Incarceration Incomes of the Imprisoned," Prison Policy Initiative, July 9, 2015, http://www.prisonpolicy.org/reports/income.html.

[31]Drucker, *A Plague of Prisons*, p. 142.

[32]Charles Doyle, "Attempt: An Overview of Federal Criminal Law," Congressional Research Service report no. R42001, April 6, 2015, https://fas.org/sgp/crs/misc/R42001.pdf.

[33]Bernadette Rabuy and Daniel Kopf, "Detaining the Poor: How Money Bail Perpetuates an Endless Cycle of Poverty and Jail Time," Prison Policy Initiative, May 2016, https://www.prisonpolicy.org/reports/incomejails.html; Bureau of Justice Statistics, "Survey of State Prison Inmates, 1991," https://www.bjs.gov/content/pub/pdf/SOSPI91.PDF. Some might point out that the poor and minorities have higher arrest rates and more interactions with the police generally because they commit proportionately more crime. This argument does not appear to be the case for victimless crimes such as drug offenses, although it is true for many categories of violent crime. Still, this reasoning does not completely explain the disparities cited in this chapter. For example, studies suggest that 60 to 80 percent of the racial disparity in prison populations is due to higher levels of criminal involvement within African American communities. That still leaves an enormous disparity, as much as 20 to 40 percent, that is attributable, at least in part, to racial bias. Michael Tonry and Matthew Melewski, "The Marginal Effects of Drug and Crime Control Policies on Black Americans," *Crime and Justice* 37, no. 1 (2008): 1–44.

[34]Al Baker, J. David Goodman, and Benjamin Mueller, "Beyond the Chokehold: The Path to Eric Garner's Death," *New York Times*, June 13, 2015, http://www.nytimes.com/2015/06/14/nyregion/eric-garner-police-chokehold-staten-island.html.

[35]Eyder Peralta and Cheryl Corley, "The Driving Life and Death of Philando Castile," National Public Radio, July 15, 2016, http://www.npr.org/sections/thetwo-way/2016/07/15/485835272/the-driving-life-and-death-of-philando-castile.

[36]Michael Sances and Hye Young You, "Who Pays for Government? Descriptive Representation and Exploitive Revenue Sources, *Journal of Politics* 79, no. 3 (July 2017): 1090–94, http://www.journals.uchicago.edu/doi/abs/10.1086/691354.

[37]"Criminal Procedure, Policing and Profit: Developments in the Law," *Harvard Law Review* 128, no. 6 (April 10, 2015): 1706, http://harvardlawreview.org/2015/04/policing-and-profit/.

[38]United States Department of Justice, Civil Rights Division, "Investigation of the Ferguson Police Department," March 5, 2015, p. 13, https://www.justice.gov/sites/default/files/opa/press-releases/attachments/2015/03/04/ferguson_police_department_report_1.pdf.

[39]Ibid., pp. 11–12.

[40]Ibid., p. 14.

[41]*Harvard Law Review*, "Policing and Profit."

[42]Bureau of Justice Statistics, "Arrest Data Analysis Tool, Drug Abuse Violations—Total," https://www.bjs.gov/content/dcf/enforce.cfm.

[43]Katherine Beckett, Kris Nyrop, and Lori Pfingst, "Race, Drugs, and Policing: Understanding Disparities and Drug Delivery Arrests," *Criminology* 44, no. 1 (2006): 105–38.

[44]Substance Abuse and Mental Health Services Administration, "Results from the 2014 National Survey on Drug Use and Health: Detailed Tables," Table 1.19B—Illicit Drug Use in Lifetime, Past Year, and Past Month among Persons Aged 12 or Older, by Demographic Characteristics: Percentages, 2013 and 2014, http://www.samhsa.gov/data/sites/default/files/NSDUH-DetTabs2014/NSDUH-DetTabs2014.htm#tab1-1b.

[45]Ezekiel Edwards, Will Bunting, and Lynda Garcia, *The War on Marijuana in Black and White* (New York: American Civil Liberties Union, 2013), https://www.aclu.org/files/assets/aclu-thewaronmarijuana-rel2.pdf.

[46]Ibid.

[47]The high drug arrest rate for African Americans is probably not solely for racial reasons. For socioeconomic reasons, African Americans are more likely to sell or use drugs outdoors where they may be more likely to be seen by police. Many African Americans live in high-crime neighborhoods that are more aggressively patrolled by the police, leading to higher arrest rates. Regardless of motivation, the disproportionate arrest rate for drugs has a profound impact on the African American community, increasing black poverty.

[48]Department of Justice, Federal Bureau of Investigation, "Crime in the United States, 2013," Table 33, Ten-Year Arrest Trends, https://ucr.fbi.gov/crime-in-the-u.s/2013/crime-in-the-u.s.-2013/tables/table-33. The case of Melissa (full name withheld) provides an all too typical example of the drawbacks to the government's current stance toward sex work. At the age of 15, she met an older man who manipulated her into becoming a prostitute. By age 19, she had three convictions for prostitution. Today she is on welfare but trying desperately to find a job and to become self-supporting. Five days a week, she attends her local welfare-to-work program but is unable to find a job because of her criminal record. She was offered one job, a ticket taker for a tourist attraction, but the offer was withdrawn the day before she was to start after the employer ran a criminal background check. National Public Radio, "Check Yes or No: The Hurdles of Job Hunting with a Criminal Past," January 31, 2013, http://www.npr.org/2013/01/31/170766202/-check-yes-or-no-the-hurdles-of-employment-with-criminal-past. It's also worth noting that, like drug laws, laws against sex

work are frequently counterproductive. They make the work more dangerous than it should be, making it easier for clients to abuse the workers because clients know sex workers won't go to the police. There have been many cases in which the police themselves have been the abusers. Making matters even worse, the threat of abuse from clients and the police, as well as the threat of jail, forces many sex workers, especially so-called outdoor sex workers, to rely on pimps to protect them. Criminalization also drives sex workers into dangerous outdoor work by making it harder for indoor workers to vet potential clients. The government only hurts the service providers by shutting down sites with information on abusive clients, safe places to work, and other safety tips.

[49]Roland Fryer Jr. "An Empirical Analysis of Racial Differences in Police Use of Force," National Bureau of Economic Research Working Paper no. 22399, NBER, Cambridge, MA, July 2016 (revised January 2018), http://www.nber.org/papers/w22399.

[50]Council of Economic Advisers, "Fines, Fees, and Bail: Payments in the Criminal Justice System That Disproportionately Impact the Poor," issue brief, December 2015, https://obamawhitehouse.archives.gov/sites/default/files/page/files/1215_cea_fine_fee_bail_issue_brief.pdf.

[51]Darren Hutchinson, "There's Never Been a Better Time for Bail Reform," *Washington Post*, July 20, 2015, https://www.washingtonpost.com/posteverything/wp/2015/07/20/theres-never-been-a-better-time-for-bail-reform/.

[52]Council of Economic Advisers, "Fines, Fees, and Bail."

[53]Ibid.

[54]Ibid.

[55]Geoff Ziezulewicz, Bill Bird, and Lolly Bowean, "Family Wary after Naperville Woman's Death in Texas Jail; Grand Jury to Inquire," *Chicago Tribune*, July 16, 2015, http://www.chicagotribune.com/news/local/breaking/ct-sandra-bland-texas-jail-death-met-0717-20150717-story.html; Leon Neyfakh, "Why Was Sandra Bland Still in Jail? Our Bail System Puts People Who Can't Pay Behind Bars," *Slate*, July 23, 2015, http://www.slate.com/articles/news_and_politics/crime/2015/07/sandra_bland_is_the_bail_system_that_kept_her_in_prison_unconstitutional.html.

[56]Berkemer v. McCarty, 468 U.S. 420 (1984); Gideon v. Wainright, 372 U.S. 335 (1963).

[57]Lincoln Caplan, "The Right to Counsel: Badly Battered at 50," *New York Times*, March 9, 2013, http://www.nytimes.com/2013/03/10/opinion/sunday/the-right-to-counsel-badly-battered-at-50.html.

[58]Ibid.

[59]Andrew Cohen, "How Americans Lost the Right to Counsel: 50 Years after Gideon," *Atlantic*, March 13, 2013.

[60]Ibid.

[61]Caplan, "The Right to Counsel."

[62]Thomas H. Cohen, "Who Is Better at Defending Criminals? Does Type of Defense Attorney Matter in Terms of Producing Favorable Outcomes?," *Criminal Justice Policy Review* 25, no. 1 (January 2014): 29–58, http://cjp.sagepub.com/content/25/1/29.abstract.

[63]Michael A. Roach, "Indigent Defense Counsel, Attorney Quality, and Defendant Outcomes," *American Law and Economics Review* 16, no. 2 (December 2014): 577–619, http://aler.oxfordjournals.org/content/16/2/577.

[64]Michelle Alexander, *The New Jim Crow: Mass Incarceration in the Age of Color Blindness* (New York: New Press, 2015), p. 115.

[65]Caplan, "The Right to Counsel."

[66]Christopher Schmitt, "Plea Bargaining Favors Whites, as Blacks, Hispanics Pay Price," *San Jose Mercury News*, December 8, 1991.

[67]Darrell Steffensneier and Stephen DeMuth, "Ethnicity and Judges Sentencing Decisions: Hispanic-Black-White Comparisons," *Criminology* 31, no. 1 (March 2006): 145–78, http://onlinelibrary.wiley.com/doi/10.1111/j.1745-9125.2001.tb00919.x/abstract.

[68]Melissa Sickmund and Charles Puzzanchera, eds., *Juvenile Offenders and Victims: 2014 National Report* (Pittsburgh, PA: National Center for Juvenile Justice, December 2014), https://www.ojjdp.gov/ojstatbb/nr2014/downloads/NR2014.pdf.

[69]Steffensneier and DeMuth, "Ethnicity and Judges Sentencing Decisions."

[70]David Abrams, Marianne Bertrand, and Sendhil Mullainathan, "Do Judges Vary in Their Treatment of Race," *Journal of Legal Studies* 41, no. 2 (June 2012): 347–83, http://papers.ssrn.com/sol3/papers.cfm?abstract_id=1800840.

[71]United States Sentencing Commission, "Report on the Continuing Impact of *United States v. Booker* on Federal Sentencing," 2012, p. 108, https://www.ussc.gov/sites/default/files/pdf/news/congressional-testimony-and-reports/booker-reports/2012-booker/Part_A.pdf.

[72]Solem v. Helm, 463 U.S. 277 (1983).

[73]Families Against Mandatory Minimums, "Mandy Martinson," http://famm.org/mandy-martinson/. Take, for instance, the case of Mandy Martinson. An unemployed methamphetamine addict who had moved in with her dealer boyfriend after escaping from a previous abusive relationship, Martinson never personally sold drugs or carried a weapon, but she did accompany her boyfriend when he purchased marijuana and methamphetamines. She also reportedly helped him count the money he made from selling drugs. She was arrested along with her boyfriend on drug and weapons charges (there were guns in the apartment they shared). While awaiting trial, she got off drugs and found a job

as a dental hygienist. The judge at her trial noted that her involvement in the crimes was minimal and committed largely under pressure from her boyfriend. He praised her efforts to get her life back on track, saying, "The Court does not have any particular concern that Ms. Martinson will commit crimes in the future." Nevertheless, under federal mandatory minimum sentencing guidelines, she was sent to prison for 15 years. Her boyfriend, who cut a deal with prosecutors, went to jail for just 12 years.

[74]Charles Colson Task Force on Federal Corrections, "Transforming Prisons, Restoring Lives: Final Recommendations of the Charles Colson Task Force on Federal Corrections," Urban Institute, Washington, January 2016, p. 11, https://www.urban.org/sites/default/files/publication/77101/2000589-Transforming-Prisons-Restoring-Lives.pdf.

[75]Ibid.

[76]Equal Justice Initiative of Alabama (EJI), "Criminal Justice Reform in Alabama," EJI, Montgomery, AL, March 2005, https://eji.org/sites/default/files/criminal-justice-reform-alabama.pdf.

[77]American Civil Liberties Union, "Fair Sentencing Act," https://www.aclu.org/feature/fair-sentencing-act.

[78]Katherine Beckett and Alexes Harris, "On Cash and Conviction: Monetary Sanctions as Misguided Policy," *Criminology and Public Policy* 10, no. 3 (2011): 509–37.

[79]U.S. Department of Justice, "March 14, 2016, Dear Colleague Letter," Office for Access to Justice, https://www2.ed.gov/about/offices/list/ocr/letters/colleague-201702-title-ix.pdf.

[80]Jennifer Gonnerman, *Life on the Outside: The Prison Odyssey of Elaine Bartlett* (New York: Farrar, Straus, and Giroux, 2004), quoted in Drucker, *A Plague of Prisons*, p. 129.

[81]John Tyler and Jeffrey Kling, "Prison-Based Education and Reentry into the Mainstream Labor Market," in *Barriers to Reentry? The Labor Market for Released Prisoners in Post-Industrial America*, ed. Shawn Bushway, Michael Stoll, and David Weiman (New York: Russell Sage Foundation, 2007), http://users.nber.org/~kling/prison_ged.pdf.

[82]Jeremy Travis, Bruce Western, and Steve Redburn, eds., *The Growth of Incarceration in the United States: Exploring Causes and Consequences* (Washington: National Research Council, 2014), pp. 157–202.

[83]Work release opportunities have declined dramatically in recent years. In 1974, fully 62 percent of state prisons offered work release programs. That number has fallen to just 22 percent. And only 2 percent of federal prisons offer work release opportunities. Travis, Western, and Redburn, *The Growth of Incarceration in the United States*, pp. 157–202.

[84]Ibid.

[85]Christopher Bollinger and Aaron Yelowitz, "The Impact of Intensive Job-Search Assistance on Outcomes of Former Inmates," University of Kentucky, Lexington, 2016, http://yelowitz.com/Bollinger_Yelowitz_2016.pdf. Importantly, the difference was negligible for violent offenders.

[86]Society for Human Resource Management, "Background Checking—The Use of Criminal Background Checks in Hiring Decisions," July 19, 2012, https://www.shrm.org/hr-today/trends-and-forecasting/research-and-surveys/Pages/criminalbackgroundcheck.aspx.

[87]Alexander, *The New Jim Crow*, p. 149.

[88]Ibid.

[89]Tina Rosenberg, "Have You Ever Been Arrested? Check Here." *New York Times*, May 24, 2016, https://www.nytimes.com/2016/05/24/opinion/have-you-ever-been-arrested-check-here.html?_r=0.

[90]Brendan Lynch, "Never Convicted, but Held Back by a Criminal Record," *Talk Poverty*, December 9, 2014, https://talkpoverty.org/2014/12/09/held-back-by-a-criminal-record/.

[91]Shawn D. Bushway and Gary Sweeten, "Abolish Lifetime Bans for Ex-Felons," *Criminology and Public Policy* 6, no. 4 (2007): 697–706, http://www.albany.edu/bushway_research/publications/Bushway_Sweeten_2007.pdf.

[92]Rosenberg, "Have You Ever Been Arrested?"

[93]Merf Ehman and Anna Reosti, "Tenant Screening in an Era of Mass Incarceration: A Criminal Record Is No Crystal Ball," *NYU Journal of Legislation and Public Policy, Quorum*, March 2015, http://www.nyujlpp.org/wp-content/uploads/2013/03/Ehman-Reosti-2015-nyujlpp-quorum-1.pdf.

[94]U.S. Department of Housing and Urban Development, "Office of General Counsel Guidance on Application of Fair Housing Standards to the Use of Criminal Records by Providers of Housing and Real Estate-Related Transactions," April 4, 2016, https://portal.hud.gov/hudportal/documents/huddoc?id=HUD_OGCGuidAppFHAStandCR.pdf.

[95]Internal Revenue Service, "Publication 970 (2017), Tax Benefits for Education," chap. 2, American Opportunity Credit.

[96]Rebecca Vallas and Sharon Dietrich, "One Strike and You're Out: How We Can Eliminate Barriers to Economic Security and Mobility for People with Criminal Records," Center for American Progress, December 2014, https://www.americanprogress.org/issues/criminal-justice/report/2014/12/02/102308/one-strike-and-youre-out/.

[97]Ibid.

[98]U.S. Sentencing Commission, "Recidivism among Federal Offenders: A Comprehensive Overview," March 2016, p. 5, https://www.ussc.gov/sites/default/files/pdf/research-and-publications/research-publications/2016/recidivism_overview.pdf; Bureau of Justice Statistics, "Recidivism of Prisoners

Released in 30 States in 2005: Patterns from 2005 to 2010," Special Report NCJ 244205, U.S. Department of Justice, April 2014, http://www.bjs.gov/content/pub/pdf/rprts05p0510.pdf.

[99]Jeffrey Stinson, "States, Cities 'Ban the Box' in Hiring," *Stateline*, Pew Charitable Trusts, May 22, 2014, http://www.pewtrusts.org/en/research-and-analysis/blogs/stateline/2014/05/22/states-cities-ban-the-box-in-hiring.

[100]Amanda Y. Agan and Sonja B. Starr, "Ban the Box, Criminal Records, and Statistical Discrimination: A Field Experiment," University of Michigan Law and Economics Research Paper no. 16-012, June 2016, http://papers.ssrn.com/sol3/papers.cfm?abstract_id=2795795.

[101]Jennifer L. Doleac and Benjamin Hansen. "Does 'Ban the Box' Help or Hurt Low-Skilled Workers? Statistical Discrimination and Employment Outcomes When Criminal Histories Are Hidden," National Bureau for Economic Research Working Paper no. 22469, Cambridge, MA, July 2016.

[102]Bureau of Justice Statistics, "NCVS Victimization Analysis Tool," Household Victimization by Income Level, https://www.bjs.gov/index.cfm?ty=nvat.

[103]U.S. Sentencing Commission, "Report to the Congress: Impact of the Fair Sentencing Act of 2010," August 2015, http://www.ussc.gov/sites/default/files/pdf/news/congressional-testimony-and-reports/drug-topics/201507_RtC_Fair-Sentencing-Act.pdf.

[104]U.S. Sentencing Commission, "Sensible Sentencing Reform: The 2014 Reduction of Drug Sentences," 2014, http://www.ussc.gov/sites/default/files/pdf/research-and-publications/backgrounders/profile_2014_drug_amendment.pdf.

[105]U.S. Sentencing Commission, "Report to Congress: Impact of the Fair Sentencing Act of 2010," p. 26.

[106]Office of the Attorney General, Department Charging and Sentencing Policy, Memorandum for All Federal Prosecutors, May 10, 2017.

[107]Office of the Attorney General, Supporting Federal, State, Local and Tribal Law Enforcement, Memorandum for Heads of Department Components, and United States Attorneys, March 31, 2017.

Chapter Six

[1]Brown v. Board of Education, 347 U.S. 483 (1954).

[2]"Gary Becker's Concept of Human Capital," the *Economist*, August 3, 2017.

[3]James J. Heckman, "Is Job Training Oversold?," *Public Interest* 115 (Spring 1994): 91–115, https://www.nationalaffairs.com/storage/app/uploads/public/58e/1a4/e45/58e1a4e458813859492231.pdf .

[4]For instance, the Job Training Partnership Act (JTPA) was an improvement over the public work programs that it replaced. It created decentralized "workforce

investment councils," which were composed of local business representatives who would reflect local labor demands better than the government.

[5]Richard Dorsett and Andrew J. Oswald, "Human Well-Being and In-Work Benefits: A Randomized Controlled Trial," IZA (Institute of Labor Economics) Discussion Paper no. 7943, February 2014, http://ftp.iza.org/dp7943.pdf. While this study refers directly to a program in the United Kingdom, the program is similar enough to programs in the United States to provide a lesson for policymakers here.

[6]Erin Jacobs Valentine et al., "An Introduction to the World of Work: A Study of the Implementation and Impacts of New York City's Summer Youth Employment Program," Summer Youth Employment Program (SYEP), U.S. Department of Labor, Washington, April 2017, https://ssrn.com/abstract=2985651.

[7]Jonathan Davis and Sara Heller, "Rethinking the Benefits of Youth Employment Programs: The Heterogeneous Effects of Summer Jobs," National Bureau of Economic Research Working Paper no. 23443, NBER, Cambridge, MA, 2017.

[8]David Autor and Susan Houseman, "Do Temporary-Help Jobs Improve Labor Market Outcomes for Low-Skilled Workers? Evidence from 'Work First'," *American Economic Journal: Applied Economics* 2, no. 3 (2010): 96–128.

[9]James J. Heckman, Jora Stixrud, and Sergio Urzua, "The Effects of Cognitive and Noncognitive Abilities on Labor Market Outcomes and Social Behavior," *Journal of Labor Economics* 24, no. 3 (2006): 411–82, http://www.journals.uchicago.edu/doi/10.1086/504455.

[10]Interviews by the author with Harriet Karr-MacDonald from the Doe Fund, 2015, 2016.

[11]Roger Klein, Richard Spady, and Andrew Weiss, "Factors Affecting the Output and Quit Propensities of Production Workers," *Review of Economic Studies* 58, no. 5 (1991): 929–53, http://www.jstor.org/stable/2297945?seq=1#page_scan_tab_contents.

[12]Heckman, Stixrud, and Urzua, "The Effects of Cognitive and Noncognitive Abilities on Labor Market Outcomes and Social Behavior."

[13]James Riccio et al., "Conditional Cash Transfers in New York City: The Continuing Story of the Opportunity NYC-Family Rewards Demonstration," Manpower Demonstration Resources Corporation, September 2013.

[14]James J. Heckman, "Policies to Foster Human Capital," *Research in Economics* 54, no. 1 (2000): 3–56.

[15]For a detailed look at the question of preschool effectiveness, see David Armor, "The Evidence on Universal Preschool: Are Benefits Worth the Cost?" Cato Institute Policy Analysis no. 760, October 15, 2014, https://object.cato.org/sites/cato.org/files/pubs/pdf/pa760.pdf. This section draws heavily from Armor's analysis.

[16]Armor, "The Evidence on Universal Preschool"; Office of Planning, Research, and Evaluation, "Head Start Impact Study: Final Report," U.S. Department of Health and Human Services, January 15, 2010, http://www.acf.hhs.gov/opre/resource/head-start-impact-study-final-report.

[17]Mark Lipsey et al., "Evaluation of the Tennessee Voluntary Prekindergarten Program: Kindergarten and First Grade Follow-Up Results from the Randomized Control Design," Peabody Research Institute, Vanderbilt University, 2013.

[18]Armor, "The Evidence on Universal Preschool."

[19]Office of Planning, Research, and Evaluation, "Head Start Impact Study: Final Report."

[20]Lipsey et al., "Evaluation of the Tennessee Voluntary Prekindergarten Program."

[21]F. A. Campbell et al., "The Development of Cognitive and Academic Abilities and Growth Curves from an Early Childhood Educational Experiment," *Development Psychology* 37 (2000): 231–42.

[22]Lawrence Schweinhart, Helen Barnes, and David Weikart, *Significant Benefits: The HighScope Perry Preschool Study through Age 27* (Ypsilanti, MI: HighScope Press, 1993); James J. Heckman et al., "The Rate of Return to HighScope Perry Preschool Program," *Journal of Public Economics*. 94 (2010): 114–28.

[23]Grover Whitehurst, "Can We Be Hardheaded about Preschool: A Look at Universal and Targeted Pre-K," Brookings Institution, January 23, 2013, https://www.brookings.edu/research/can-we-be-hard-headed-about-preschool-a-look-at-universal-and-targeted-pre-k/.

[24]Heckman et al., "The Rate of Return to HighScope Perry Preschool Program." In fairness, Heckman argues that the return to society exceeds the cost of the program, although others disagree.

[25]Cheri Vogel et al., "Early Head Start Children in Grade 5: Long-Term Follow-Up of the Early Head Start Research and Evaluation Study Sample," OPRE Report no. 2011-8, U.S. Department of Health and Human Services, Washington, 2010.

[26]Reed Johnson, "A Closer Look at Income and Race Concentration in Public School," Urban Institute, May 13, 2015, http://www.urban.org/features/closer-look-income-and-race-concentration-public-schools.

[27]Ibid.

[28]Quoted in Robert Putnam, *Our Kids: The American Dream in Crisis* (New York: Simon and Schuster, 2015), p. 165.

[29]See, for example, Reyn van Ewijik and Peter Sleegers, "The Effect of Peer Socioeconomic Status on Student Achievement," *Educational Research Review* 5 (June 2010): 134–50.

[30]Diane Whitmore Schanzenbach et al., "Fourteen Economic Facts on Education and Economic Opportunity," Brookings Institution, The Hamilton Project, March 2016, http://www.hamiltonproject.org/assets/files/education_facts.pdf.

[31]Putnam, *Our Kids*, p. 163.

[32]Government Accountability Office, "K–12 Education: Better Use of Information Could Help Agencies Identify Disparities and Racial Discrimination," April 2016, http://www.gao.gov/products/GAO-16-345.

[33]Raj Chetty et al., "How Does Your Kindergarten Classroom Affect Your Earnings? Evidence from Project Star," *Quarterly Journal of Economics* 126, no. 4 (2011), http://qje.oxfordjournals.org/content/126/4/1593.full.pdf+html.

[34]*Budget of the U.S. Government, Fiscal Year 2017* (Washington: U.S. Government Publishing Office, 2016), Public Budget Database.

[35]National Center for Education Statistics, "Digest of Education Statistics," Table 236.10, Summary of Expenditures for Public Elementary and Secondary Education and Other Related Programs, by Purpose: Selected Years, 1919–20 through 2012–13, https://nces.ed.gov/programs/digest/d15/tables/dt15_236.10.asp.

[36]National Center for Education Statistics, "Digest of Education Statistics," Table 236.55: Total and Current Expenditures per Pupil in Public Elementary and Secondary Schools: Selected Years, 1919–20 through 2012–13, https://nces.ed.gov/programs/digest/d15/tables/dt15_236.55.asp.

[37]Organization for Economic Cooperation and Development, "Education at a Glance 2015: OECD Indicators," Chart B1.1, Annual Expenditure by Educational Institutions per Student, by Types of Service, from Primary to Tertiary Education (2012), http://download.ei-ie.org/Docs/WebDepot/EaG2015_EN.pdf.

[38]Eric Hanushek, "Assessing the Effects of School Resources on Student Performance: An Update," *Educational Evaluation and Policy Analysis* 19, no. 2 (Summer 1997): 141–64.

[39]Hanushek, "School Resources and Student Performance," in *Does Money Matter: The Link between School Resources, Student Achievement, and Adult Success*, ed. G. Burtless (Washington: The Brookings Institution, 1996), p. 69.

[40]Larry Hedges and Rob Greenwald, "Have Times Changed? The Relation between School Resources and Student Performance," in *Does Money Matter: The Link between School Resources, Student Achievement, and Adult Success*, ed. G. Burtless (Washington: The Brookings Institution, 1996), p. 90.

[41]Liz Bowie, "Passing High School Tests in Maryland Will Get Increasingly Difficult," *Baltimore Sun*, April 26, 2016, http://www.baltimoresun.com/news/maryland/education/blog/bs-md-parcc-score-requirement-20160426-story.html.

[42]Bethany Wicksall, "Detroit Public Schools Historical Budget Trends," House Fiscal Agency, February 24, 2016, http://www.house.mi.gov/hfa/PDF/SchoolAid/DPS_Historical_Budget_Trends(Feb16).pdf.

[43]Michigan Department of Education, "MI School Data," https://www.mischooldata.org/DistrictSchoolProfiles/StudentInformation/GraduationDropoutRate2.aspx.

[44]National Center for Education Statistics, "The Nation's Report Card, 2015 Mathematics Trial Urban District Snapshot Report, Detroit," https://nces.ed.gov/nationsreportcard/subject/publications/dst2015/pdf/2016049XR8.pdf; National Center for Education Statistics, "The Nation's Report Card, 2015 Reading Trial Urban District Snapshot Report, Detroit," https://nces.ed.gov/nationsreportcard/subject/publications/dst2015/pdf/2016048XR8.pdf.

[45]National Center for Education Statistics, "Digest of Education Statistics," Table 236.75. Total and Current Expenditures per Pupil in Fall Enrollment in Public Elementary and Secondary Education, by Function and State or Jurisdiction: 2012–13, https://nces.ed.gov/programs/digest/d15/tables/dt15_236.75.asp.

[46]National Center for Education Statistics, "The Nation's Report Card, 2015 Mathematics Trial Urban District Snapshot Report, District of Columbia," https://nces.ed.gov/nationsreportcard/subject/publications/dst2015/pdf/2016049XW8.pdf.

[47]No Child Left Behind (NCLB) is the common name for a George W. Bush–era amendment to the Elementary and Secondary Education Act conditioning federal education funding for disadvantaged students on the adoption of standards-based educational reforms. The Obama administration replaced NCLB with Race to the Top, which offered competitive grants to states on the basis of their reform efforts. Common Core was an attempt to set national standards for academic achievement. All three programs were highly controversial and represented a significant expansion of federal intervention into the traditionally local issue of education.

[48]For instance, math scores for African American nine-year-olds rose 10 points between 1986 and 1994, or 1.25 points per year, but only 5.00 points between 2004 and 2012, or 0.63 points per year. Similarly, reading scores for Hispanic students rose 9.0 points between 1994 and 1999, or 1.8 points per year, but only 8.0 points between 2004 and 2012, or 1.0 point per year. Neal McCluskey, "Has No Child Left Behind Worked?," testimony before the Committee on Education and the Workforce: Democrats, U.S. House of Representatives, February 9, 2015, http://www.cato.org/publications/testimony/has-no-child-left-behind-worked. However, high school seniors experienced no discernable improvement in either standardized test scores or graduation rates. At the very least, this fact suggests that any gains among younger students dissipate as they get older. NCLB failed to achieve its stated goal of full math and reading proficiency by 2014. Arne Duncan, "No Child Left Behind: Early Lessons from State Flexibility Waivers," testimony before the U.S. Senate Committee on Health, Education, Labor, and Pensions, February 7, 2013, http://www.ed.gov/news/speeches/no-child-left-behind-early-lessons-state-flexibility-waivers.

[49]National Center for Education Statistics, "The Condition of Education 2016," U.S. Department of Education, NCES 2016-144, https://nces.ed.gov/pubs2016/2016144.pdf.

[50]Thomas J. Kane et al., "Have We Identified Effective Teachers? Validating Measures of Effective Teaching Using Random Assignment," Bill & Melinda Gates Foundation, http://www.hec.ca/iea/seminaires/140401_staiger_douglas.pdf; Thomas J. Kane, "Validating Teacher Effect Estimates Using Changes in Teacher Assignments: A Replication of Chetty et al. in Los Angeles," http://studentsmatter.org/wp-content/uploads/2014/02/SM_Kane-Demonstratives_02.06.14.pdf.

[51]Daniel Aaronson, Lisa Barrow, and William Sander, "Teachers and Student Achievement in the Chicago Public High Schools," *Journal of Labor Economics* 25, no. 1 (January 2007): 95–135, http://www.jstor.org/stable/10.1086/508733?seq=1#page_scan_tab_contents.

[52]Raj Chetty, John N. Friedman, and Jonah E. Rockoff, "Measuring the Impacts of Teachers II: Teacher Value-Added and Student Outcomes in Adulthood," *American Economic Review* 104, no. 9 (September 2014): 2633–79, https://www.aeaweb.org/articles?id=10.1257/aer.104.9.2633.

[53]Vergara v. California—Tentative Decision (Superior Court of the State of California, County of Los Angeles, June 10, 2014), p. 11, http://studentsmatter.org/wp-content/uploads/2014/06/Tenative-Decision.pdf.

[54]Ibid.

[55]National Center for Education Statistics, "Schools and Staffing Survey," Table 8, Average Number of Teachers per Public School District in 2011–12, Average Number of Teachers per District in the Previous Year (2010–11) Who Were Dismissed or Did Not Have Their Contracts Renewed for Any Reason, and as a Result of Poor Performance, by Tenure Status of Teachers and State: 2011–12, https://nces.ed.gov/surveys/sass/tables/sass1112_2013311_d1s_008.asp.

[56]Jennifer Thomsen, "A Closer Look: Teacher Evaluations and Reduction-in-Force Policies," Education Commission of the States, May 2014, http://www.ecs.org/clearinghouse/01/12/43/11243.pdf.

[57]Lewis Solomon, "The Case for Merit Pay," in *Choice and Competition in American Education*, ed. Paul E. Peterson (Lanham, MD: Rowman and Littlefield, 2006), p. 106.

[58]Laura Goe, "The Link between Teacher Quality and Student Outcomes: A Research Synthesis," National Comprehensive Center for Teacher Quality, October 2007, http://www.niusileadscape.org/docs/FINAL_PRODUCTS/LearningCarousel/LinkBetweenTQandStudentOutcomes.pdf.

[59]Richard Vedder, "Should We Abolish Colleges of Education?," *Chronicle of Higher Education: Innovations* (blog), September 16, 2010, http://www.chronicle.com/blogs/innovations/should-we-abolish-colleges-of-education/26750. Teach for America is a charitable organization that recruits recent college graduates to teach for two years in schools with large numbers of underprivileged students. Volunteers do not need to be certified teachers, although teachers with certification may apply. Teach for America volunteers are full faculty members at

their schools, receiving the normal school district salary and benefits. They are not required to join the teachers' union; however, they are not prohibited from doing so.

[60]Quoted in "Reding, Wrighting & Erithmetic," *Wall Street Journal*, October 2, 1989.

[61]Sandra Black, "Do Better Schools Matter? Parental Valuation of Elementary Education," *Quarterly Journal of Economics* 114, no. 2 (May 1999): 577–99, http://www.ssc.wisc.edu/~scholz/Teaching_742/Black.pdf.

[62]National Center for Education Statistics, "State Education Reforms," Table 4.2. Numbers and Types of Open Enrollment Policies, by State: 2015, https://nces.ed.gov/programs/statereform/tab4_2.asp.

[63]U.S. Department of Education, "No Child Left Behind: Public School Choice, Non-Regulatory Guidance," January 14, 2009, https://www2.ed.gov/policy/elsec/guid/schoolchoiceguid.pdf.

[64]Black, "Do Better Schools Matter? Parental Valuation of Elementary Education."

[65]Jacob Gershman, "No Guarantee of Public School Choice in Constitution, Appeals Court Rules," *Wall Street Journal*, August 31, 2015, http://blogs.wsj.com/law/2015/08/31/no-guarantee-of-public-school-choice-in-constitution-appeals-court-rules/.

[66]Kyle Spencer, "For Some Parents, Search for Better Schools Could Lead to Jail," *Seattle Times*, May 16, 2015, http://www.seattletimes.com/nation-world/for-some-parents-search-for-better-schools-could-lead-to-jail/.

[67]Brittany Shammas, "Broward School District to Hire Private Investigators to Verify Home Addresses," *Sun-Sentinel*, June 3, 2016, http://www.sun-sentinel.com/local/broward/fl-private-investigators-students-20160604-story.html.

[68]Boston Public Schools, "BPS Residency Policy," https://www.bostonpublicschools.org/cms/lib07/MA01906464/Centricity/Domain/215/required_residency_documents_2013.pdf.

[69]Ibid.

[70]It could be argued that, because parents in wealthy school districts are paying for the quality of those schools through higher property taxes, the out-of-district students are, in effect, free riding on those taxes. Similar arguments are made in other situations by immigration restrictionists or advocates for zoning and land-use regulations (see following chapter). However, that seems a slender reed. There are many situations in which nontaxpayers place a burden on services provided by taxpayers, yet we insist on universal provision of those services. Consider traffic. Out-of-town drivers add wear and tear to a community's roads, but we generally don't allow cities to ban out-of-town cars. Or, under similar circumstances deny police, fire, or ambulance services to nonresidents of a community. There seems to be little reason that education should be treated differently. Regardless, the issue

could be solved by changing the tax base from education to something other than local property taxes.

[71]National Center for Education Statistics, "Digest of Education Statistics," Table 216.90. Public Elementary and Secondary Charter Schools and Enrollment, by State: Selected years, 1999–2000 through 2013–14, https://nces.ed.gov/programs/digest/d15/tables/dt15_216.90.asp.

[72]Ibid.

[73]Center for Research on Education Outcomes, "Urban Charter School Study Report on 41 Regions," 2015, https://urbancharters.stanford.edu/download/Urban%20Charter%20School%20Study%20Report%20on%2041%20Regions.pdf.

[74]Ibid.

[75]Susan Dynarski, "Urban Charter Schools Often Succeed; Suburban Ones Often Don't," *New York Times*, November 20, 2015.

[76]National Alliance for Public Charter Schools, "A Closer Look at the Charter School Movement," http://www.publiccharters.org/wp-content/uploads/2016/02/New-Closed-2016.pdf; Sara Mead, "Charter Schools Are Here to Stay," *U.S. News & World Report*, September 2015, http://www.usnews.com/opinion/knowledge-bank/2015/09/17/7-key-facts-about-charter-school-quality.

[77]Patrick Baude et al., "The Evolution of Charter School Quality," Cato Institute, Research Briefs in Economic Policy no. 16, December 16, 2014, http://www.cato.org/publications/research-briefs-economic-policy/evolution-charter-school-quality.

[78]National Center for Education Statistics, "Digest of Education Statistics," Table 205.50. Private Elementary and Secondary Enrollment, Number of Schools, and Average Tuition, by School Level, Orientation, and Tuition: Selected years, 1999–2000 through 2011-12," https://nces.ed.gov/programs/digest/d13/tables/dt13_205.50.asp.

[79]National Center for Education Statistics, "Trends in the Use of School Choice: 1993 to 2007," Table 1, Percentage of Private School Students Ages 5–17, Enrolled in Grades 1–12, By Poverty Status and Parents' Highest Level of Education: 2007, https://nces.ed.gov/pubs2010/2010004/tables/table_2a.asp.

[80]Becky Veeva, "What Is a School Voucher," *Great Kids*, March 7, 2016.

[81]David P. Smole, "School Choice: Current Legislation," Congressional Research Service issue brief, August 2003, p. 6, https://digital.library.unt.edu/ark:/67531/metacrs4411/m1/1/high_res_d/IB98035_2003Aug01.pdf.

[82]EdChoice, "School Choice in America," https://www.edchoice.org/school-choice/school-choice-in-america/.

[83]Greg Forster, "A Win–Win Solution: The Empirical Evidence on School Choice," Friedman Foundation for Educational Choice, May 2016, http://www.edchoice.org/wp-content/uploads/2016/05/A-Win-Win-Solution-The-Empirical-Evidence-on-School-Choice.pdf. Of the four studies that showed no

improvement, two involved the Louisiana program, which suffered from significant regulatory issues.

[84]Matthew M. Chingos and Paul E. Peterson, "The Effects of School Vouchers on College Enrollment: Experimental Evidence from New York City," The Brown Center on Educational Policy at the Brookings Institution and the Harvard Kennedy School Program on Education Policy and Governance, April 2012, https://www.hks.harvard.edu/pepg/PDF/Impacts_of_School_Vouchers_FINAL.pdf.

[85]William G. Howell and Paul E. Peterson, *The Education Gap: Vouchers and Urban Schools* (Washington: Brookings Institution, 2006).

[86]Zelman v. Simmons-Harris, 536 U.S. 639 (2002).

[87]Named after Congressman and House Speaker James G. Blaine, who unsuccessfully sought such an amendment to the U.S. Constitution in 1875, the Blaine amendments bar the use of public funds (or public lands) for the benefit of any religious group or sect. There is little doubt, historically, that Blaine amendments sprang from the anti-immigrant and anti-Roman Catholic bigotry that was widespread in the 19th century. Today, 38 states have some form of Blaine amendment as part of their constitution. Lindsey M. Burke and Jarrett Stepman, "Breaking Down Blaine Amendments' Indefensible Barrier to Education Choice," *Journal of School Choice: International Research and Reform* 8, no. 4 (2014): 642, Table 1.

[88]See, for example, the experience with the Douglas County Choice Scholarship Pilot Program. Jason Bedrick, "Colorado Supreme Court Strikes Down School Vouchers," Cato at Liberty, June 29,.2015, http://www.cato.org/blog/colorado-supreme-court-strikes-down-school-vouchers.

[89]National Conference of State Legislatures, "Accountability in Private School Choice Programs," February 18, 2015, http://www.ncsl.org/research/education/accountability-in-private-school-choice-programs.aspx.

[90]Atila Abdulkadiroglu, Parag Pathak, and Christopher Walters, "School Vouchers and Student Achievement: Evidence from the Louisiana Scholarship Program," National Bureau of Economic Research Working Paper no. 21839, NBER, Cambridge, MA, December 2015; Jonathan N. Mills and Patrick J. Wolf, "*The Effects of the Louisiana Scholarship Program on Student Achievement after Two Years*," Louisiana Scholarship Program Evaluation Report no. 1, School Choice Demonstration Project, February 2016.

[91]Jason Bedrick, "On Regulating School Choice: A Response to Critics," *Education Next*, January 14, 2016, http://educationnext.org/on-regulating-school-choice-a-response-to-critics/.

[92]Ibid.

[93]"Taxpayers choose to contribute to [scholarship organizations], they spend their own money, not money the State has collected." Arizona Christian School Tuition Organization v. Winn, 09-987, 563 U.S. 125 (2011).

[94]Jason Bedrick, Jonathan Bucher, and Clint Bolick, "Taking Credit for Education: How to Fund Education Savings Accounts through Tax Credits," Cato Institute, Policy Analysis no. 785, http://object.cato.org/sites/cato.org/files/pubs/pdf/pa785.pdf.

[95]*EdChoice*, "School Choice in America," https://www.edchoice.org/school-choice/school-choice-in-america/.

[96]Andrew J. Coulson, "Comparing Public, Private, and Market Schools: The International Evidence," *Journal of School Choice* 3 (2009): 31–54, https://object.cato.org/sites/cato.org/files/articles/10.1.1.175.6495.pdf.

[97]Michael Owyang and E. Katarina Vermann, "Measuring the Effect of School Choice on Economic Outcomes," *Regional Economist*, Federal Reserve Bank of St. Louis, October 2012, https://www.stlouisfed.org/publications/regional-economist/october-2012/measuring-the-effect-of-school-choice-on-economic-outcomes. Recently, however, some public education advocates claim the advantages of private schools are overstated because their student bodies are less diverse. Public schools must accept all comers, whereas private schools can skim off the best applicants, taking only the best performers or most motivated. Indeed, even the process of applying for a private school suggests some degree of parental involvement that many public school students lack. This line of thinking was perhaps best explored in *The Public School Advantage: Why Public Schools Outperform Private Schools*, by Sara and Chris Lubienski. The Lubienskis argue that if you control for the socioeconomic background of students, public schools actually outperform private ones by a small margin in standardized math and reading tests. Sara Lubienski and Chris Lubienski, *The Public School Advantage: Why Public Schools Outperform Private Schools* (Chicago: University of Chicago Press, 2014). Private school supporters respond that the Lubienskis' focus on the one metric—test scores—on which public school performance is comparable to that of private schools. Even if the Lubienskis' results are correct, they ignore many other areas where private schools are undeniably superior. Also, results from the math tests, in particular, were adjusted to make them align more closely with the public school math curricula. That is, public schools tend to emphasize math reasoning and problem-solving skills while private schools tend to focus on more traditional math content, such as computational skills. The tests tended to measure the former, rather than the latter, giving public school students an advantage. Patrick Wolf, "Comparing Public Schools to Private," *Education Next* 14, no. 3 (Summer 2014), http://educationnext.org/comparing-public-schools-private/. Regardless, the real issue is not comparing public versus private schools in the aggregate, but whether an available private school offers a better alternative to the public school that a child who is poor is attending now. Whether a different private school is better or worse than another public school is irrelevant to the child who is poor trapped in a bad school today.

[98]Stephen Cornman, Thomas Stewart, and Patrick Wolf, "The Evolution of School Choice Consumers: Parent and Student Voices in the Second Year of the D.C. Opportunity Scholarship Program," SCDP Report 0701, Georgetown University School Choice Demonstration Project, May 2007, https://eric.ed.gov/?id=ED508629.

[99]Michael Lovenheim and Patrick Walsh, "Does Choice Increase Information? Evidence from Online School Search Behavior," National Bureau of Economic Research Working Paper no. 23445, NBER, Cambridge, MA, May 2017.

[100]Jonathan Butcher and Lindsey M. Burke, "The Education Debit Card II: What Arizona Parents Purchase with Education Savings Accounts," Friedman Foundation, February 2016, http://www.edchoice.org/wp-content/uploads/2016/02/2016-2-The-Education-Debit-Card-II-WEB-1.pdf.

[101]"Together, Technology and Teachers Can Revamp Schools," *The Economist*, July 22, 2017.

Chapter Seven

[1]As quoted by Kevin Nance, "Matthew Desmond's 'Evicted' Details Cost of Evictions on Milwaukee's Poor," *Chicago Tribune*, March 10, 2016, http://www.chicagotribune.com/lifestyles/books/ct-prj-evicted-matthew-desmond-20160310-story.html.

[2]The Pew Charitable Trusts, "Household Expenditures and Income," issue brief, March 30, 2016, http://www.pewtrusts.org/en/research-and-analysis/issue-briefs/2016/03/household-expenditures-and-income.

[3]U.S. Census Bureau, "Consumer Expenditure Survey, 2015," Table 1101, Quintiles of Income before Taxes: Annual Expenditure Means, Shares, Standard Errors, and Coefficients of Variation, https://www.bls.gov/cex/2015/combined/quintile.pdf.

[4]For a discussion of the difficulties involved in incorporating home ownership in poverty measures, see David M. Betson, "Effect of Home Ownership on Poverty Measurement," Office of the Assistant Secretary for Planning and Evaluation, U.S. Department of Health and Human Services, November 5, 1997, https://aspe.hhs.gov/sites/default/files/pdf/106771/%21homeown.pdf. In a larger sense, the question of home ownership by the poor is illustrative of the difficulty in adequately describing American poverty. Simply put, Americans who are poor have a lot of material goods, especially when compared with poor in other countries. As the Heritage Foundation's Robert Rector and Rachel Sheffield point out, 99.7 percent of U.S. households that are poor have at least one television (two-thirds have more than one and 18 percent have a big-screen television), 81 percent have a microwave, 78 percent have air conditioning, 71 percent have a DVD player or DVR, 55 percent have a cell phone, 38 percent have a personal computer, and

one-quarter have a dishwasher. Robert Rector and Rachel Sheffield, "Air Conditioning, Cable TV, and an Xbox: What Is Poverty in the United States?," Heritage Foundation Backgrounder no. 2575, July 19, 2011. Likewise, if one uses the OECD Better Life Index, which measures such things as housing, health, safety, income, and life satisfaction, the poor in the United States have a quality of life very similar to that of the poor in such countries as Sweden and better than that of the poor in Great Britain, Germany, or France. In fact, the poor in the United States typically live better than the wealthiest 10 percent in Brazil, Israel, Italy, Russia, or Portugal. *The Economist*, "The Examined Life," Daily Chart, May 28, 2013, http://www.economist.com/blogs/graphicdetail/2013/05/daily-chart-17. All of this has led some conservatives to assert that there are no real poor in the United States. Yet the simple presence of material goods doesn't adequately define the lives of those whom I would consider poor.

[5]John Iceland, *Poverty in America: A Handbook* (Berkeley: University of California Press, 2015), p. 45.

[6]Gary Adamkiewicz et al., "Environmental Conditions in Low-Income Urban Housing: Clustering and Associations with Self-Reported Health," *American Journal of Public Health* 104, no. 9 (September 2014): 1650–56, http://www.ncbi.nlm.nih.gov/pmc/articles/PMC3954449/.

[7]Dorothy Brown, "Home Ownership Keeps Blacks Poorer than Whites," *Forbes*, December 10, 2012.

[8]David Rusk, "The 'Segregation Tax': The Cost of Racial Segregation to Black Homeowners," The Brookings Institution, October 2001, https://www.brookings.edu/wp-content/uploads/2016/06/rusk.pdf.

[9]Homeownership is not an unambiguous good. While it offers substantial advantages both as an investment and as a hedge against rent risk, homeownership also has potential drawbacks. As an investment, it is not diversified in some respects, and housing values have risen more slowly than some other investments. Owning a house can make it more difficult to relocate during labor market shocks. And so on. This suggests that we should not measure successful housing policies by whether they encourage the poor to own their homes at the same rate as the nonpoor. We have attempted that before, and the results were disastrous both for the poor and for the economy. See John Allison, *The Financial Crisis and the Free Market Cure* (New York: McGraw-Hill, 2012).

[10]Matthew Desmond, "Unaffordable America: Poverty, Housing, and Eviction," Fast Focus no. 22-2015, University of Wisconsin–Madison, Institute for Research on Poverty, March 2015, http://www.irp.wisc.edu/publications/fastfocus/pdfs/FF22-2015.pdf.

[11]U.S. Census Bureau, "American Housing Survey, 2013," Table S-08-RO, http://www2.census.gov/programs-surveys/ahs/2013/AHS_2013_National_Tables_v1.2.xls.

[12]Zumper, "Zumper National Rent Report: February 2015," https://www.zumper.com/blog/2015/03/zumper-us-rent-report-february-2015/.

[13]Raj Chetty, Nathaniel Hendren, and Lawrence Katz, "The Effects of Exposure to Better Neighborhoods on Children: New Evidence from the Moving to Opportunity Project," *American Economic Review* 106, no. 4 (2016): 855–902, https://www.aeaweb.org/issues/403.

[14]Peter Metayka, "Desire to Move and Residential Mobility: 2010–2011," U.S. Census Bureau, Household and Economic Studies, P70-140, March 2015, http://census.gov/content/dam/Census/library/publications/2015/demo/p70-140.pdf.

[15]Cited in Rebecca Cohen and Keith Wardrip, "Should I Stay or Should I Go? Exploring the Effects of Housing Mobility on Children," Center for Housing Policy, Washington, February 2011, http://mcstudy.norc.org/publications/files/CohenandWardrip_2009.pdf.

[16]Ibid.

[17]Desmond, "Unaffordable America: Poverty, Housing, and Eviction."

[18]Matthew Desmond and Carl Gershenson, "Housing and Employment Insecurity among the Working Poor," *Social Problems* 63, no. 1 (2016): 46–67, http://socpro.oxfordjournals.org/content/early/2016/01/09/socpro.spv025.

[19]Heather Sandstrom and Sandra Huerta, "The Negative Effects of Instability on Child Development," Low-Income Working Families Discussion Paper no. 3, Urban Institute, Washington, September 2013, http://www.urban.org/sites/default/files/alfresco/publication-pdfs/412908-The-Negative-Effects-of-Instability-on-Child-Development-Fact-Sheet.pdf.

[20]Cohen and Wardrip, "Should I Stay or Should I Go?"

[21]Matthew Desmond, "Poor Black Women Are Evicted at Alarming Rates, Setting Off a Chain of Hardship," How Housing Matters Policy Research Brief, MacArthur Foundation, Chicago, March 2014, https://www.macfound.org/media/files/HHM_Research_Brief_-_Poor_Black_Women_Are_Evicted_at_Alarming_Rates.pdf.

[22]There is also some evidence to suggest that evictions may be linked to the landlord's attitudes about race and gender. For instance, the Milwaukee study cited above found that African American women made up just 9.6 percent of the rental population but accounted for nearly 30 percent of evictions. Desmond, "Poor Black Women Are Evicted at Alarming Rates." Similarly, a Harvard study found that Latino tenants in majority white neighborhoods were twice as likely to be evicted as those in majority nonwhite neighborhoods, even after correcting for such factors as gender, age, marital status, children, criminal record, socioeconomic status, and violations of the rental agreement. Deena Greenberg, Carl Gershenson, and Mathew Desmond, "Discrimination in Evictions: Empirical Evidence and Legal Challenges," *Harvard Civil Rights-Civil Liberties Law Review* 51, no. 1 (2015):

115–58, http://scholar.harvard.edu/files/mdesmond/files/greenberg_et_al._.pdf?m=1462385261. Other evidence suggests that women who report spousal abuse are frequently targeted for eviction. Matthew Desmond and Nicol Valdez, "Unpolicing the Urban Poor: Consequences of Third-Party Policing on Inner-City Women," *American Sociological Review* 78, no. 1 (2013): 117–41, http://journals.sagepub.com/doi/full/10.1177/0003122412470829.

[23]Washington, D.C., had enacted height limitations in 1899, but that was a far more limited ordinance.

[24]Hadacheck v. Sebastian, 239 U.S. 394 (1915).

[25]Village of Euclid v. Ambler Realty Corporation, 272 U.S. 365 (1926).

[26]Christopher Silver, "The Racial Origins of Zoning in American Cities," in *Urban Planning and the African-American Community: In the Shadows*, ed. June Thomas Manning and Marsha Ritzdorf (Thousand Oaks, CA: Sage Publications, 1997). Zoning appears to have largely formalized practices of racial segregation that had been previously enforced through social norms and vigilantism. Werner Troesken and Randall Walsh, "Collective Action, White Flight, and the Origins of Formal Segregation Laws," National Bureau of Economic Research Working Paper no. 23691, NBER, Cambridge, MA, August 2017.

[27]Silver, "The Racial Origins of Zoning in American Cities."

[28]Quoted in A. Barton Hinkle, "Zoning's Racist Roots Still Bear Fruit," *Reason*, April 2, 2014, http://reason.com/archives/2014/04/02/zonings-racist-roots-still-bear-fruit.

[29]Silver, "The Racial Origins of Zoning in American Cities."

[30]Buchanan v. Warley, 245 US 60 (1917).

[31]Quoted in Silver, "The Racial Origins of Zoning in American Cities."

[32]See, for example, Laura Pulido, "Rethinking Environmental Racism: White Privilege and Urban Development in Southern California," *Annals of the Association of American Geographers* 90, no. 1 (March 2000): 12–40, http://onlinelibrary.wiley.com/doi/10.1111/0004-5608.00182/abstract.

[33]Matthew Resseger, "The Impact of Land Use Regulation on Racial Segregation: Evidence from Massachusetts Zoning Borders," Harvard University, November 26, 2013, http://scholar.harvard.edu/files/resseger/files/resseger_jmp_11_25.pdf.

[34]Jonathan Rothwell, "Racial Enclaves and Density Zoning: The Institutionalized Segregation of Racial Minorities in the United States," *American Law and Economics Review* 13, no. 1 (March 2011): 290–358, http://aler.oxfordjournals.org/content/early/2011/03/17/aler.ahq015.abstract.

[35]Edward L. Glaeser, Joseph Gyourko, and Raven Saks, "Why Is Manhattan So Expensive? Regulation and the Rise of Housing Prices," *Journal of Law and Economics* 48, no. 2 (2005): 331–69, http://citeseerx.ist.psu.edu/viewdoc/summary?doi=10.1.1.545.6618.

[36]Sanford Ikeda and Emily Hamilton, "How Land Use Regulation Undermines Affordable Housing," research paper, Mercatus Center at George Mason University, Arlington, VA, November 2015, http://mercatus.org/publication/how-land-use-regulation-undermines-affordable-housing.

[37]Ikeda and Hamilton, "How Land-Use Regulation Undermines Affordable Housing." One study at the time suggested that the rule was deliberately intended to prevent low-income families from moving into the township. Charles Haar, "Zoning for Minimum Standards: The Wayne Township Case," *Harvard Law Review* 66 (1953): 1051–63., cited in Ikeda and Hamilton.

[38]Donald Shoup, *The High Cost of Free Parking* (Chicago: American Planning Association, 2011).

[39]Although popular, these requirements appear to serve little purpose. Only 2.6 percent of the U.S. land area, barely 66 million acres, is currently classified as "developed lands." Roughly 75 percent of the U.S. population lives on this small portion of land. That would seem to leave plenty of undeveloped greenspace without limiting construction in areas where people want to live. U.S. Department of Agriculture Economic Research Service. "Major Uses of Land in the United States, 2012," https://www.ers.usda.gov/webdocs/publications/84880/eib-178.pdf?v=42972.

[40]Ikeda and Hamilton, "How Land Use Regulation Undermines Affordable Housing."

[41]Ibid.

[42]Vanessa Brown Calder, "Zoning, Land-Use Planning, and Housing Affordability," Cato Institute Policy Analysis no. 823, October 18, 2017, https://www.cato.org/publications/policy-analysis/zoning-land-use-planning-housing-affordability.

[43]States listed in descending order, from most regulation to least regulation added from 2000 to 2010 (scaled by state population).

[44]Glaeser, Gyourko, and Saks, "Why Is Manhattan So Expensive?"

[45]Salim Furth, "Costly Mistakes: How Bad Policies Raise the Cost of Living," Heritage Foundation Backgrounder no. 3081, November 23, 2015, http://www.heritage.org/research/reports/2015/11/costly-mistakes-how-bad-policies-raise-the-cost-of-living.

[46]John M. Quigley and Steven Raphael, "Regulation and the High Cost of Housing in California," *American Economic Review* (Papers and Proceedings of the One Hundred Seventeenth Annual Meeting of the American Economic Association, Philadelphia, PA, January 7–9) 95, no. 2 (2005): 323–28, http://www.jstor.org/stable/pdf/4132841.pdf.

[47]Haar, "Zoning for Minimum Standards: The Wayne Township Case."

[48]For instance, one of the most common models for urban economics is what is referred to as the "Tiebout model," which suggests that local governments

should be thought of as suppliers of public services. People can "vote with their feet" by moving to municipalities where the benefits of public services outweigh the costs for them. In the model, they can also leave places where the costs of public service provisions outweigh the benefits. Charles Tiebout, "A Pure Theory of Local Expenditures," *Journal of Political Economy* 64, no. 5 (1956): 416–24, https://www.unc.edu/~fbaum/teaching/PLSC541_Fall08/tiebout_1956.pdf. However, one of the critiques of the Tiebout model is that it does not account for free riders, including people who live in multifamily housing and benefit from the municipality's services at higher rates than they pay for them through property taxes. Zoning provides barriers to entry for free riders. As William Fischel, father of zoning economics, argues, "Property taxation without zoning does not work very well." William Fischel, "Fiscal Zoning and Economists' View of Property Taxes," Dartmouth College, June 20, 2013, https://papers.ssrn.com/sol3/papers.cfm?abstract_id=2281955. It is possible there are other ways to remedy this, for example, by reforming public services like schools and roads. It is also possible that zoning does not act as a benefit tax at all, in which case zoning reform may avoid many of the stipulated inefficiencies. George Zodrow, "Reflections on the New View and the Benefit View of the Property Tax," in *Property Taxation and Local Government Finance*, ed. Wallace Oates (Cambridge, MA: Lincoln Institute of Land Policy, 2001). Moreover, to the degree that zoning hinders mobility, it actually prevents people from "voting with their feet," undermining the relatively efficient outcomes suggested by the Tiebout model.

[49]Diana Thomas, "Regressive Effects of Regulation," Mercatus Center Working Paper no. 12-35, Mercatus Center at George Mason University, Arlington, VA, November 2012, http://mercatus.org/sites/default/files/RegressiveEffects_Thomas_v1-0.pdf.

[50]Roderick Hills and David Schleicher, "Balancing the 'Zoning Budget'," *Regulation* 34, no. 3, (2011): 24–32, https://object.cato.org/sites/cato.org/files/serials/files/regulation/2011/9/regv34n3-6.pdf.

[51]Jared Walczak, "How High Are Property Taxes in Your State?" Tax Foundation, July 1, 2016, http://taxfoundation.org/blog/how-high-are-property-taxes-your-state-2016.

[52]Ibid.

[53]Jack Goodman, "Houses, Apartments, and Property Tax Incidences," paper presented at the annual meeting of the American Real Estate and Urban Economics Association, Philadelphia, PA, January 2005, http://www.jchs.harvard.edu/sites/jchs.harvard.edu/files/w05-2.pdf.

[54]Robert Fisher, *State and Local Finances* (Chicago: Irwin, 1996). There are essentially two critiques of the argument that property taxes are regressive. First, the relationship between income and property taxes is less robust when alternative income measures are used. And, second, some economists have begun to view property taxes less as an excise tax and more as a form of capital tax. Because the

capital, in this case housing, is disproportionately owned by the wealthy, the tax can be seen as progressive in this view. See, for instance, Henry Aaron, *Who Pays the Property Tax? A New View* (Washington: The Brookings Institution, 1975). Still, this seems a largely semantic argument. The fact remains that property taxes are a significant burden on low-income families, especially when you consider the degree to which the tax is passed through in the form of high rents.

[55]Goodman, "Houses, Apartments, and Property Tax Incidences."

[56]Leah J. Tsoodle and Tracy M. Turner, "Property Taxes and Residential Rents," *Real Estate Economics* 36, no. 1 (Spring 2008): 63–80, http://onlinelibrary.wiley.com/doi/10.1111/j.1540-6229.2008.00207.x/full.

[57]Goodman, "Houses, Apartments, and Property Tax Incidences"; James Edward Kee and Terrance Moan, "The Property Tax and Tenant Equity," *Harvard Law Review* 89, no. 3, (1976): 531–51.

[58]Goodman, "Houses, Apartments, and Property Tax Incidences."

[59]"T11-0264—Tax Expenditure Benefits; Mortgage Interest Deduction; Baseline: Current Law; Distribution by Cash Income Level, 2011," Tax Policy Center, August 9, 2011, http://www.taxpolicycenter.org/model-estimates/major-individual-income-tax-expenditures-2011/tax-expenditure-benefits-mortgage-1.

[60]In fact, the mortgage interest deduction doesn't even appear to increase homeownership, because any increase in homeownership from reduced user costs is neutralized by the negative effect on homeownership rates from increasing the cost of homes. Jonathan Gruber, Amalie Jensen, and Henrik Kleven, "Do People Respond to Mortgage Interest Deduction? Quasi-Experimental Evidence from Denmark," National Bureau of Economic Research Working Paper no. 23600, NBER, Cambridge, MA, July 2017, http://www.nber.org/papers/w23600. Other studies suggest that the primary effect of the mortgage interest deduction is to encourage people who would have purchased homes even in the absence of the deduction to buy larger or more expensive homes. Andrew Hanson, "Size of Home, Homeownership, and the Mortgage Interest Deduction," *Journal of Housing Economics* 21, no. 3 (September 2012): 195–210.

[61]Teresa Wiltz, "As Rent Skyrockets, More Cities Look to Cap It," *Stateline*, Pew Charitable Trusts, July 27, 2015, http://www.pewtrusts.org/en/research-and-analysis/blogs/stateline/2015/07/27/as-rent-skyrockets-more-cities-look-to-cap-it.

[62]Adam Davidson, "The Perverse Effects of Rent Regulation," *New York Times Magazine*, July 23, 2013, http://www.nytimes.com/2013/07/28/magazine/the-perverse-effects-of-rent-regulation.html?_r=0.

[63]Elizabeth Roistacher and Charles Brecher, *Reforming Residential Rent Regulations* (New York: Citizens Budget Commission, 1991).

[64]Tore Ellingsen and Peter Englund, "Rent Regulation: An Introduction," *Swedish Economic Policy Review* 10 (2003): 3–9.

[65]David Sims, "Out of Control: What We Can Learn from the End of Massachusetts Rent Control," *Journal of Urban Economics* 61, no. 1, (2007): 121–51, http://www.sciencedirect.com/science/article/pii/S0094119006000635.

[66]Peter Navarro, "Rent Control in Cambridge, Massachusetts," *Public Interest* 78, no. 4 (1985): 83–100.

[67]Scott James, "How the Rich Get Richer, Rental Edition," *New York Times*, February 17, 2012.

[68]NYU Furman Center, "Profile of Rent-Stabilized Units and Tenants in New York City," June 2014, http://furmancenter.org/files/FurmanCenter_FactBrief_RentStabilization_June2014.pdf. Among the celebrities who live in rent-controlled apartments are Mia Farrow, Cindi Lauper, Carly Simon, Bianca Jagger, and Steve Kroft. See Jim Epstein, "New York City's Affordable Housing Bonanza for the Rich: Housing Subsidies Go to Families Making up to $193k," *Reason*, July 3, 2014, http://reason.com/archives/2014/07/03/new-york-citys-affordable-housing-bonanza.

[69]This program was created under Section 8 of the Housing and Community Development Act of 1974. While public housing has largely been phased out, Section 8 vouchers have become the primary mechanism for subsidized housing.

[70]Congressional Budget Office, "Federal Housing Assistance for Low-Income Households," September 2015, https://www.cbo.gov/sites/default/files/114th-congress-2015-2016/reports/50782-LowIncomeHousing-OneColumn.pdf.

[71]Howard Husock, *America's Trillion-Dollar Housing Mistake: The Failure of American Housing Policy* (Chicago: Ivan R. Dee Publishing, 2003). This, however, may change under recently announced HUD policies. See Vanessa Brown Calder, "HUD's Latest Proposal Is Big on Good Intentions and Unintended Consequences," Cato at Liberty, July 21, 2016, https://www.cato.org/blog/hud-proposal-intentions-consequences.

[72]Howard Husock, "Public Housing and Rental Subsidies," *Downsizing Government*, February 23, 2017, http://www.downsizinggovernment.org/hud/public-housing-rental-subsidies.

[73]Ibid.

[74]Calder, "Zoning, Land-Use Planning, and Housing Affordability."

Chapter Eight

[1]Michael Sherraden, "Assets and the Poor: Implications for Individual Accounts and Social Security," Testimony to the President's Commission on Social Security, October 18, 2001, Washington University, St. Louis, https://csd.wustl.edu/Publications/Documents/P01-17_78.AssetsAndThePoorImplications.pdf.

[2]Cynthia Rocha, "Factors That Contribute to Economic Well-Being in Female Headed Households," *Journal of Social Service Research* 23, no. 1 (1997): 1–17; Signe-Mary McKernan and Michael Sherraden, "Poor Finances: Assets

and Low-Income Households," Office of the Assistant Secretary for Planning and Evaluation, U.S. Department of Health and Human Services, September 2007, https://aspe.hhs.gov/basic-report/poor-finances-assets-and-low-income-households-introduction-series#Why.

[3]Robert Lerman and Signe-Mary McKernan, "Effects of Holding Assets on Social and Economic Outcomes of Families; A Review of Theory and Evidence," prepared by the Urban Institute for the Office of the Assistant Secretary for Planning and Evaluation, U.S. Department of Health and Human Services, November 2008, https://aspe.hhs.gov/sites/default/files/pdf/75706/report.pdf.

[4]Caroline Ratcliffe, "Asset Poverty and the Importance of Emergency Savings," Urban Institute, Presentation for the Congressional Savings and Ownership Caucus, September 24, 2013, http://www.urban.org/sites/default/files/alfresco/publication-pdfs/412911-Asset-Poverty-and-the-Importance-of-Emergency-Savings.pdf.

[5]Ibid.

[6]Board of Governors of the Federal Reserve System, *Report on the Economic Well-Being of U.S. Households in 2015* (Washington: Board of Governors of the Federal Reserve System, May 2016), https://www.federalreserve.gov/2015-report-economic-well-being-us-households-201605.pdf.

[7]Ratcliffe, "Asset Poverty and the Importance of Emergency Savings."

[8]Lerman and McKernan, "Effects of Holding Assets on Social and Economic Outcomes of Families."

[9]Ratcliffe, "Asset Poverty and the Importance of Emergency Savings."

[10]Michael Barr, "Banking the Poor," *Yale Journal on Regulation* 21 (Winter 2004): 121–237, http://ssrn.com/abstract=556374.

[11]Federal Deposit Insurance Corporation (FDIC), "2013 FDIC National Survey of Unbanked and Underbanked Households," FDIC, October 2014, https://www.fdic.gov/householdsurvey/2013report.pdf.

[12]Joe Valenti, "Millions of Americans are Outside the Financial System," *Economy*, Center for American Progress, October 30, 2014.

[13]Michael Barr and Rebecca Blank, "Savings, Assets, Credit, and Banking among Low Income Households: Introduction and Overview," in *Insufficient Funds: Savings, Assets, Credit, and Banking among Low-Income Households* (New York: Russel Sage Foundation, 2009).

[14]FDIC, "2013 FDIC National Survey of Unbanked and Underbanked Households."

[15]Ibid.

[16]While such alternative banking operations are frequently vilified, that criticism is often unjustified. Such operations are extremely competitive, assume a lot of risk, and provide a market that is extremely valuable for the poor. Their

outcomes certainly could be worse without such institutions. Victor Stango, "Some New Evidence on Competition in Payday Lending Markets," *Contemporary Economic Policy* 3, no. 2 (2012): 149–61.

[17]FDIC, "2013 FDIC National Survey of Unbanked and Underbanked Households."

[18]Ibid.

[19]Frank Bass and Dakin Campbell, "Predator Targets Hit as Banks Shut Branches amid Profits," Bloomberg, May 2, 2013, http://www.bloomberg.com/news/articles/2013-05-02/post-crash-branch-closings-hit-hardest-in-poor-u-s-areas.

[20]Michael Sivy, "Why So Many Americans Don't Have Bank Accounts," *Time*, November 20, 2012.

[21]Dean Karlan, Aishwarya Lakshmi Ratan, and Jonathan Zinman, "Savings by and for the Poor: A Research Review and Agenda," *Review of Income and Wealth* 60, no. 1, (March 2014): 36–78.

[22]Hester Peirce, Ian Robinson, and Thomas Stratmann, "How Are Small Banks Faring under Dodd-Frank?," Cato Institute Research Briefs in Economic Policy no. 20, February 2015, https://www.cato.org/publications/research-briefs-economic-policy/how-are-small-banks-faring-under-dodd-frank.

[23]Karlan, Ratan, and Zinman, "Savings by and for the Poor."

[24]Patricia Zengerle, "Young, Hispanics, Poor Hit Most by U.S. Voter ID Laws: Study," Reuters, September 26, 2012, https://www.reuters.com/article/us-usa-campaign-voterid/young-hispanics-poor-hit-most-by-us-voter-id-laws-study-idUSBRE88P1CW20120926.

[25]Federal Deposit Insurance Corporation (FDIC), "The 2011 FDIC National Survey of Banks' Efforts to Serve the Unbanked and Underbanked," FDIC, https://www.fdic.gov/unbankedsurveys/.

[26]Aimee Chin, Léonie Karkoviata, and Nathaniel Wilcox, "Impact of Bank Accounts on Migrant Savings and Remittances: Evidence from a Field Experiment," University of Houston working paper, June 2011, http://www.uh.edu/~achin/research/ckw_banking_june2011.pdf.

[27]Federal Deposit Insurance Corporation (FDIC), "Alternative Financial Services: A Primer," *FDIC Quarterly* 3, no. 1, (2009): 39–47, https://www.fdic.gov/bank/analytical/quarterly/2009-vol3-1/fdic140-quarterlyvol3no1-afs-final.pdf.

[28]Winnie Hu, "As Check Cashers Expand Services in Poorer Areas, Criticism Grows," *New York Times*, August 5, 2012, http://www.nytimes.com/2012/08/06/nyregion/as-check-cashers-expand-services-in-poorer-areas-criticism-grows.html.

[29]Deborah Figart and Thomas Barr, "Inside the World of Check-Cashing Outlets," *Dollars and Sense*, January/February 2015, http://www.dollarsandsense.org/archives/2015/0115barr-figart.html.

[30]Zoë Neuberger, Robert Greenstein, and Peter Orszag, "Barriers to Saving: The Dilemma for Low-Income Families," *Communities and Banking* 19, no. 3 (Summer 2006): 25–27, https://www.bostonfed.org/-/media/Documents/cb/PDF/barrierstosaving.pdf.

[31]Ibid.

[32]Urban Institute, "Welfare Rules Database," Table 1.C.1 Asset Limits for Applicants, http://wrd.urban.org/wrd/data/databook_tabs/2015/I.C.1.xlsx.

[33]United States Department of Agriculture, "Broad-Based Categorical Eligibility," https://www.fns.usda.gov/sites/default/files/snap/BBCE.pdf.

[34]Ibid.

[35]LIHEAP Clearinghouse, "LIHEAP Heating Assistance Eligibility: Assets," U.S. Department of Health and Human Services, Administration for Children and Families, https://liheapch.acf.hhs.gov/tables/FY2015/assets.htm.

[36]Social Security Administration, "Supplemental Security Income (SSI) Resources," Understanding Supplemental Security Income SSI Resources—2018 Edition, https://www.ssa.gov/ssi/text-resources-ussi.htm.

[37]Jonathan Gruber and Aaron Yelowitz, "Public Health Insurance and Private Savings," *Journal of Political Economy*, 107, no. 6 (December 1999): 1249–74, http://www.jstor.org/stable/10.1086/250096.

[38]Robert Hubbard, Jonathan Skinner and Stephen Zeldes, "Precautionary Saving and Social Insurance," *Journal of Political Economy* 103, no. 2 (1995): 360–99, https://www.jstor.org/stable/2138644?seq=1#page_scan_tab_contents. Both this study and the one cited in endnote 37 of this chapter found that social welfare programs discouraged savings in two ways. First, the programs themselves discouraged precautionary savings because they provided their own form of protection against future events. And second, that asset tests imposed an effective 100 percent tax on wealth accumulation.

[39]Aleta Sprague and Rachel Black, "State Asset Limit Reforms and Implications for Federal Policy," New America Foundation Asset Building Program, Washington, October 31, 2012, https://www.newamerica.org/asset-building/policy-papers/state-asset-limit-reforms-and-implications-for-federal-policy/; and Asset Building Program, Washington, May 2005, https://community-wealth.org/content/save-or-not-save-reforming-asset-limits-public-assistance-programs-encourage-low-income.

[40]Ray Boshara, "The Rationale for Assets, Asset-Building Policies, and IDAs for the Poor," in *Building Assets: A Report on the Asset Development and IDA Field*, ed. Ray Boshara (Washington: Corporation for Enterprise Development, 2001).

[41]Gene Falk, "Individual Development Accounts (IDAs): Background on Federal Grant Programs to Help Low-Income Families Save," Congressional Research Service report no. RS22185, July 10, 2013, https://www.fas.org/sgp/crs/misc/RS22185.pdf.

[42]Administration for Children and Families, "Report to Congress: Assets for Independence Program: Status at the Conclusion of the Fifteenth Year," U.S. Department of Health and Human Services, 2014, https://www.acf.hhs.gov/sites/default/files/ocs/fy2014_15th_afi_report_to_congress_final_8_5_16b.pdf.

[43]Annamaria Lusardi, "Financial Education and the Saving Behavior of African-American and Hispanic Households," Dartmouth College, September 2005, http://www.dartmouth.edu/~alusardi/Papers/Education_African%26Hispanic.pdf.

[44]Marianne Hilgert, Jeanne Hogarth, and Sondra Beverly, "Household Financial Management: The Connection between Knowledge and Behavior," *Federal Reserve Bulletin*, July 2003, pp. 310–22, https://www.federalreserve.gov/pubs/bulletin/2003/0703lead.pdf.

[45]Ryan Bourne and Chris Edwards, "Tax Reform and Savings: Lessons from Canada and the United Kingdom," Cato Institute Tax and Budget Bulletin no. 77, May 1, 2017, https://www.cato.org/publications/tax-budget-bulletin/tax-reform-savings-lessons-canada-united-kingdom.

[46]Legislation to establish this type of savings vehicle has been introduced in the U.S. House of Representatives by Rep. David Brat (R-VA) and in the Senate by Sen. Jeff Flake (R-AZ), respectively titled officially as The Universal Savings Account Act Senate (H.R. 937) and the Universal Savings Account Act (S. 323).

[47]Quoted in Bourne and Edwards, "Tax Reform and Savings."

[48]Ibid., citing HM Revenue and Customs, *Individual Savings Accounts (ISA) Statistics*, Data for 2013–14, p. 25, and Canada Revenue Agency, Tables 1C and 3C.

[49]For a detailed discussion of this issue, see Michael Tanner, "Privatizing Social Security: A Big Boost for the Poor," Cato Social Security Choice Paper no. 4, July 26, 1996, https://www.cato.org/publications/social-security-choice-paper/privatizing-social-security-big-boost-poor.

[50]The wealthy may well dis-save, or stop some of their current savings, if given the chance to save a portion of their Social Security taxes. If they continue to save, they may shift some of their current savings into lower risk, lower return investments. As a result, they may see little overall gain from personal accounts. However, the poor have little or nothing to dis-save. Personal accounts would likely increase their overall investments. They are also more likely to receive the full benefit of the higher returns from capital investment.

[51]Technically, the tax is split equally between the employer and employee, but most economists believe that the employee bears most of the cost of the tax through forgone wages and benefits. Ángel Melguizo and José Manuel González-Páramo, "Who Bears Labour Taxes and Social Contributions? A Meta-Analysis Approach," *Journal of the Spanish Economic Association* 4, no. 3 (2013): 247–71, https://doi.org/10.1007/s13209-012-0091-x.

[52]Martin Feldstein, "Social Security and the Distribution of Wealth," *Journal of the American Statistical Association* 71, no. 365 (December 1976): 800–807, https://www.researchgate.net/publication/254284867_Social_Security_and_the_Distribution_of_Wealth.

[53]Jeffrey Brown, "Redistribution and Income: Mandatory Annuitization With Mortality Heterogeneity," Boston College Center for Retirement Research Working Paper no. 2001-02, April 2001, p. 26.

[54]Thomas Piketty, *Capital in the Twenty-First Century* (Cambridge, MA: Belknap Press, 2013).

[55]We should be careful, of course, not to oversell the benefits or the feasibility of personal accounts. President George W. Bush's bungled campaign for Social Security reform has largely taken personal accounts off the table for the moment. Moreover, Social Security's finances have continued to deteriorate in the years since Bush released his proposals. That will make the short-term cost of any transition greater and may complicate any personal account plan.

Chapter Nine

[1]Barack Obama, "Remarks by the President in Conversation on Poverty at Georgetown University," The White House, Office of the Press Secretary, Washington, https://obamawhitehouse.archives.gov/the-press-office/2015/05/12/remarks-president-conversation-poverty-georgetown-university.

[2]Deirdre McCloskey, *Bourgeois Equality: How Ideas, Not Capital or Institutions, Enriched the World* (Chicago: University of Chicago Press, 2016).

[3]Daniel Bennett and Richard Cebula, "Misperceptions about Capitalism, Government, and Inequality," in *Economic Behavior, Economic Freedom, and Entrepreneurship*, ed. Richard Cebula et al. (Northampton, MA: Edward Elgar Publishing Inc., 2015), pp. 1–21.

[4]Eugene Smolensky and Robert Plotnick, "Inequality and Poverty in the United States: 1900 to 1990," University of Wisconsin-Madison Institute for Research on Poverty Discussion Paper no. 998-93, March 1993, https://www.irp.wisc.edu/publications/dps/pdfs/dp99893.pdf.

[5]James Tobin, "Macroeconomic Trends, Cycles, and Policies," in *Confronting Poverty: Prescriptions for Change*, ed. Sheldon Danziger, Gary Sandafeur, and Daniel Weinberg (Cambridge, MA: Harvard University Press, 1994), p. 150; Gerald James and Robin Williams Jr., eds., *A Common Destiny: Blacks and American Society* (Washington: National Academy Press, 1989), p. 278.

[6]U.S. Census Bureau, "Poverty Status of Families, by Type of Family, Presence of Related Children, Race, and Hispanic Origin: 1959 to 2016," Historical Poverty Tables: People and Families—1959 to 2016, table 4, https://www.census.gov/data/tables/time-series/demo/income-poverty/historical-poverty-people.html.

[7]Tyler Cowen, "Does the Welfare State Help the Poor?" *Social Philosophy and Policy* 19, no. 1 (2002): 36–54, https://philpapers.org/rec/COWDTW.

[8]McCloskey, *Bourgeois Equality*.

[9]Brink Lindsey, ed., "Editor's Introduction," in *Reviving Economic Growth: Policy Proposals from 51 Leading Experts* (Washington: Cato Institute Press), p. 3, note 11. By "economic growth," I am referring to growth in gross domestic product (GDP). While GDP is perhaps the best measure that we have for national wealth, it is arguably a flawed one. For instance, GDP includes government activity, not just the private sector. It also includes activity that does nothing to increase national wealth, such as exploding bombs. Furthermore, numerous critiques have been leveled against the way its components are measured. Still, GDP remains the dominant measure of a country's material well-being.

[10]Lena Groeger, "The Immigration Effect: There's a Way for President Trump to Boost the Economy by Four Percent, but He Probably Won't Like It," *ProPublica*, July 19, 2017, https://projects.propublica.org/graphics/gdp.

[11]Mitra Toossi, "A Century of Change: The U.S. Labor Force, 1950–2050," *Monthly Labor Review* (May 2002): 15–28.

[12]Nicholas Eberstadt, *Men without Work: America's Invisible Crisis* (West Conshohocken, PA: Templeton Press, 2016), p. 3.

[13]Author's calculations using data from: U.S. Department of Labor, "American Time Use Survey—2016 Results," USDL-17-0880, Table 4: Employed Persons Working and Time Spent Working on Days Worked by Full- and Part-Time Status and Sex, Jobholding Status, Educational Attainment, and Day of Week, 2016 Annual Wages, June 27, 2017, https://www.bls.gov/news.release/pdf/atus.pdf; U.S. Census Bureau, *Historical Statistics of the United States, Colonial Times to 1970*, Part 1, Series D 655, p. 94, https://www.census.gov/library/publications/1975/compendia/hist_stats_colonial-1970.html.

[14]Groeger, "The Immigration Effect."

[15]U.S. Department of Commerce, U.S. Census Bureau, Current Population Reports, Series P-25; and U.S. Census Bureau, *Historical Statistics of the United States, Colonial Times to 1970*; Current Population Reports, Series P-25; U.S. Department of Education, National Center for Education Statistics, Digest of Education Statistics, various issues.

[16]Ryan Avent, "Diminishing Returns to Schools," *The Economist*, April 14, 2011.

[17]James Heckman and Dimitriy Masterov, "The Productivity Argument for Investing in Young Children," *Review of Agricultural Economics* 29, no. 3 (2007): 452, http://jenni.uchicago.edu/papers/Heckman_Masterov_RAE_2007_v29_n3.pdf.

[18]The cost of a 1908 Model T took about four times as many work-hours to purchase at the average hourly wage as does the 2017 Ford Focus today (3,900 hours in 1908 versus about 950 hours today). Author's calculations using data from the following: Carol Boyd Leon, "The Life of American Workers in 1915," *Monthly*

Labor Review, Bureau of Labor Statistics, February 2016, https://www.bls.gov/opub/mlr/2016/article/the-life-of-american-workers-in-1915.htm; Toossi, "A Century of Change"; Philip Van Doren Stern, *A Pictorial History of the Automobile as Seen in Motor Magazine: 1903–1953* (New York: Viking Press, 1953), p. 44, https://babel.hathitrust.org/cgi/imgsrv/download/pdf?id=mdp.39015024198692;orient=0;size=100;seq=50;num=44;attachment=0; U.S. Census Bureau, "May 2016 National Occupational Employment and Wage Estimates," May 2016, https://www.bls.gov/oes/current/oes_nat.htm#00-0000.

[19]Adam Thierer and Andrea O'Sullivan, "Preparing for the Future of Artificial Intelligence," Mercatus Center Public Interest Comment, Mercatus Center at George Mason University, Arlington, VA, July 22, 2016, https://www.mercatus.org/publication/preparing-future-artificial-intelligence.

[20]Ian Hathaway and Robert Litan, "Declining Business Dynamism in the United States: A Look at States and Metros," Brookings Institution, May 5, 2014, https://www.brookings.edu/research/declining-business-dynamism-in-the-united-states-a-look-at-states-and-metros/.

[21]Adam Thierer, "Embracing a Culture of Permissionless Innovation," Cato Institute Online Forum, November 17, 2014, https://www.cato.org/publications/cato-online-forum/embracing-culture-permissionless-innovation.

[22]Cowen, "Does the Welfare State Help the Poor?"

[23]James Gwartney, Robert Lawson, and Joshua Hall, *Economic Freedom of the World: 2017 Annual Report* (Vancouver: Fraser Institute, 2017), https://www.fraserinstitute.org/studies/economic-freedom-of-the-world-2017-annual-report.

[24]Ibid.

[25]The World Bank Group, "Starting a Business," June 2016, http://www.doingbusiness.org/data/exploretopics/starting-a-business.

[26]"Corruption Perceptions Index 2016," Transparency International, January 25, 2017, https://www.transparency.org/news/feature/corruption_perceptions_index_2016.

[27]For instance, in 2011 taxpayers spent more than 6 billion hours complying with the tax code, which would be equivalent to an annual workforce of 3.4 million people. Jason Fichtner and Jacob Feldman, "The High Costs of a Terrible Tax Code," *U.S. News & World Report*, May 28, 2013, https://www.usnews.com/opinion/blogs/economic-intelligence/2013/05/28/the-complex-tax-code-hurts-the-economy.

[28]David Kamin et al., "The Games They Will Play: An Update on the Conference Committee Tax Bill," *SSRN* (December 18, 2017), https://ssrn.com/abstract=3089423.

[29]For more on how the tax exclusion of employer-provided health insurance and pension benefits and the home mortgage-interest deduction distort economic activity, see Jason Fichtner and Jacob Feldman, "When Are Tax

Expenditures Really Spending? A Look at Tax Expenditures and Lessons from the Tax Reform Act of 1986," Working Paper no. 11-45, Mercatus Center at George Mason University, Arlington, VA, November 2011, https://www.mercatus.org/system/files/Tax_expenditures_FichtnerFeldman_WP1145.pdf. For more details on why the charitable tax deduction may not be worth keeping, see Ed Dolan, "Is the Charitable Deduction Worth Keeping?," Niskanen Center, April 17, 2017, https://niskanencenter.org/blog/charitable-deduction/. Finally, regarding how the deductibility of state and local tax deductions distorts communities' budgetary decisions, see Douglas Holtz-Eakin and Harvey S. Rosen, "Tax Deductibility and Municipal Budget Structure," National Bureau of Economic Research Working Paper no. 2224, NBER, Cambridge, MA, 1987, http://www.nber.org/papers/w2224.pdf.

[30]U.S. Treasury Department, "The Debt to the Penny and Who Holds It," Treasury Direct, accessed June 25, 2018, https://www.treasurydirect.gov/NP/debt/current.

[31]Congressional Budget Office, "The 2017 Long-Term Budget Outlook," March 2017, https://www.cbo.gov/system/files/115th-congress-2017-2018/reports/52480-ltbo.pdf.

[32]Maeve P. Carey, "Counting Regulations: An Overview of Rulemaking, Types of Federal Regulations, and Pages in the *Federal Register*," Congressional Research Service report no. R43056, October 4, 2016, https://fas.org/sgp/crs/misc/R43056.pdf.

[33]Clyde Wayne Crews Jr., "Ten Thousand Commandments: An Annual Snapshot of the Federal Regulatory State, 2016 Edition," Competitive Enterprise Institute, May 2016, https://cei.org/sites/default/files/Wayne%20Crews%20-%20Ten%20Thousand%20Commandments%202016%20-%20May%204%202016.pdf.

[34]David Kocieniewski, "G.E.'s Strategies Let It Avoid Taxes Altogether," *New York Times*, March 24, 2011, http://www.nytimes.com/2011/03/25/business/economy/25tax.html?_r=4&ref=business.

[35]Elizabeth Powers, "Growth and Poverty Revisited," *Economic Commentary*, Federal Reserve Bank of Cleveland, April 15, 1995, https://www.clevelandfed.org/newsroom-and-events/publications/economic-commentary/economic-commentary-archives/1995-economic-commentaries/ec-19950415-growth-and-poverty-revisited.aspx.

[36]Rebecca Blank, "Why Were Poverty Rates So High in the 1980s?," in *Poverty and Prosperity in the USA in the Late Twentieth Century*, ed. D. B. Papadimitriou and E. Wolff (New York: St. Martin's Press, 1993), chapter 2.

[37]Powers, "Growth and Poverty Revisited."

[38]Isabel Sawhill, "Poverty in the U.S.: Why Is It So Persistent?," *Journal of Economic Literature* 26, no. 3 (1988): 1076–119, http://www.jstor.org/stable/pdfplus/2726525.pdf.

[39]Ibid.

[40]U.S. Department of Labor, "Minimum Wages for Tipped Employees," Wage and Hour Division, January 1, 2018, https://www.dol.gov/whd/state/tipped.htm. There also is a separate federal minimum wage of $2.13 for tipped employees, with an expectation that tips will fill any gap between the minimum and $7.25 per hour. Employers are responsible for making good on any shortfall. However, eight states mandate that employers pay the full minimum to tipped employees.

[41]James Sherk, "Who Earns the Minimum Wage? Suburban Teenagers, Not Single Parents," Heritage Foundation, Issue Brief no. 3866, February 28, 2013, http://www.heritage.org/research/reports/2013/02/who-earns-the-minimum-wage-suburban-teenagers-not-single-parents.

[42]Joseph Sabia and Thanh Tam Nguyen, "The Effects of Minimum Wage Increases on Means-Tested Government Assistance," Employment Policies Institute, Washington, December 2015, https://www.epionline.org/wp-content/uploads/2015/12/EPI_MW_GovtAssist_Study_V2.pdf.

[43]Jeffrey Clemens, "Redistribution through Minimum Wage Regulation: An Analysis of Program Linkages and Budgetary Spillovers," in *Tax Policy and the Economy, Volume 30*, ed. Jeffrey R. Brown (Chicago: University of Chicago Press, forthcoming), http://papers.nber.org/books/brow-14. I use the draft version NBER provides.

[44]David Neumark, "Reducing Poverty via Minimum Wages, Alternatives," Federal Reserve Bank of San Francisco, Economic Letter no. 38, December 28, 2015, http://www.frbsf.org/economic-research/publications/economic-letter/2015/december/reducing-poverty-via-minimum-wages-tax-credit/.

[45]Greg Mankiw, "How Are Wages and Productivity Related?," *Greg Mankiw's Blog*, August 29, 2006, http://gregmankiw.blogspot.com/2006/08/how-are-wages-and-productivity-related.html.

[46]The best known of these studies is David Card and Alan Kruger's, "Minimum Wages and Employment: A Case Study of the Fast Food Industry in New Jersey and Pennsylvania," *American Economic Review* 90, no. 5 (2000): 1397–420. Following Card and Kruger's line of analysis, others suggested that previously observed job losses following a minimum wage hike might be due to broader employment trends rather than the wage hike itself. For example, a study by economists at University of California–Berkeley found that after correcting for differences in employment trends and long-term growth differences between states increasing minimum wages and those that did not, there was no reduction in employment. Sylvia Allegretto, Arindrajit Dube, and Michael Reich, "Do Minimum Wages Really Reduce Teen Employment? Accounting for Heterogeneity and Selectivity in State Panel Data," *Industrial Relations* 50, no. 2 (April 2011): 205–40, http://www.irle.berkeley.edu/cwed/allegretto/pubs/166-08.pdf.

[47]David Neumark, J. M. Ian Salas, and William Wascher, "Revisiting the Minimum Wage-Employment Debate: Throwing Out the Baby with the Bathwater?,"

ILR Review 67, no. 3 (suppl., May 1, 2014): 608–48, http://ilr.sagepub.com/content/67/3_suppl/608.abstract.

[48]See, for example, Daniel Aaronson, Eric French, and Isaac Sorkin, "The Long-Run Employment Effects of the Minimum Wage: A Putty-Clay Perspective," VoxEU, Center for Policy and Economic Research, Washington, March 19, 2016, http://voxeu.org/article/long-run-employment-effects-minimum-wage; Jonathan Meer and Jeremy West, "Effects of the Minimum Wage on Employment Dynamics," *Journal of Human Resources*, 51, no. 2, (2016): 500–22, https://ideas.repec.org/a/uwp/jhriss/v51y2016i2p500-522.html; and Peter Brummund and Michael R. Strain, "Real and Permanent Minimum Wages," American Enterprise Institute Working Paper no. 6, February 2016, https://www.aei.org/wp-content/uploads/2016/02/brummund-strain-minwage.pdf.

[49]Meer and West, "Effects of the Minimum Wage on Employment Dynamics."

[50]Harry J. Holzer, "A $15-Hour Minimum Wage Could Harm America's Poorest Workers," *Fortune*, July 30, 2015, http://fortune.com/2015/07/30/1223726-15-hour-minimum-wage-workers-fast-food/?iid=leftrail.

[51]Alan B. Krueger, "The Minimum Wage: How Much Is Too Much?" *New York Times*, October 9, 2015, http://www.nytimes.com/2015/10/11/opinion/sunday/the-minimum-wage-how-much-is-too-much.html?_r=0.

[52]Council of Economic Advisers, "Technology and Innovation" in *Economic Report of the President Together with the Annual Report of the Council of Economic Advisers*, February 2016, https://www.gpo.gov/fdsys/pkg/ERP-2016/pdf/ERP-2016-chapter5.pdf.

[53]Jeffrey Clemens and Michael Wither, "The Minimum Wage and the Great Recession: Evidence of Effects on the Employment and Income Trajectories of Low-Skilled Workers," Cato Institute Research Briefs in Economic Policy no. 22, March 2015, https://object.cato.org/sites/cato.org/files/pubs/pdf/research-brief-22.pdf.

[54]Ibid. Even if one sees it as the proper role of government to ensure wages of a certain level, the minimum wage is an inefficient mechanism to do so, especially when compared with other available tools, such as the earned income tax credit (EITC) or other wage supplements.

[55]Council of Economic Advisers, "Occupational Licensing: A Framework for Policymakers," July 2015, https://obamawhitehouse.archives.gov/sites/default/files/docs/licensing_report_final_nonembargo.pdf.

[56]Council of Economic Advisers, "Occupational Licensing"; Morris Kleiner, "Reforming Occupational Licensing Policies," Brookings Institution, Hamilton Project, Discussion Paper no. 2015-01, March 2015, https://www.brookings.edu/wp-content/uploads/2016/06/THP_KleinerDiscPaper_final.pdf.

[57]Dick Carpenter et al., "License to Work: A National Study of Burdens from Occupational Licensing," Institute for Justice, 2012, https://www.ij.org/images/pdf_folder/economic_liberty/occupational_licensing/licensetowork.pdf.

[58]Timothy Sandefur, "Testimony to the U.S. House Committee on Small Business," Pacific Legal Foundation, March 26, 2014, https://smallbusiness.house.gov/uploadedfiles/3-26-2014_sandefur_testimony.pdf.

[59]Morris Kleiner and Alan Krueger, "The Prevalence and Effects of Occupational Licensing," *British Journal of Industrial Relations* 48, no. 4, (2010): 676–87, http://onlinelibrary.wiley.com/doi/10.1111/j.1467-8543.2010.00807.x/abstract.

[60]Carpenter et al., "License to Work: A National Study of Burdens from Occupational Licensing."

[61]Kelly Edmiston, "Entrepreneurship in Low and Moderate Income Communities," in *Entrepreneurship in Emerging Domestic Markets: Barriers and Innovation*, ed. James R. Barth and Glenn Yago (Springer: New York, 2008), http://harbert.auburn.edu/~barthjr/publications/Stumbling%20Blocks%20to%20Entrepreneurship%20in%20Low-%20and%20Moderate-Income.pdf.

[62]Stephen Slivinski, "Bootstraps Tangles in Red Tape: How State Occupational Licensing Hinders Low-Income Entrepreneurship," Goldwater Institute Policy Report no. 272, February 23, 2015, https://slideblast.com/bootstraps-tangled-in-red-tape_59ab8acd1723dd8d1c30ac04.html.

[63]Ibid.

[64]Council of Economic Advisers, "Occupational Licensing."

[65]For an excellent discussion of the history of occupational licensing and minorities, see Clint Bolick, *Unfinished Business: A Civil Rights Strategy for America's Third Century* (San Francisco: Pacific Research Institute, 1990).

[66]Quoted in Walter E. Williams, *The State against Blacks* (New York: McGraw-Hill, 1982), pp. 91–92.

[67]Cited in Michael Goldberg and Peter Horwood, *Zoning: Its Costs and Relevance for the 1980s* (Vancouver: Fraser Institute, 1980), p. 11.

[68]One recent study reaches a different conclusion, however, suggesting that African Americans and others may benefit from occupational licensure because in its absence potential employers may resort to other, more discriminatory criteria to judge an applicant's competence. Peter Blair and Bobby Chung, "Occupational Licensing Reduces Racial and Gender Wage Gaps: Evidence from the Survey of Income and Program Participation," Working Paper no. 2017-050, Human Capital and Economic Opportunity Global Working Group, Chicago, May 15, 2017, https://econresearch.uchicago.edu/sites/econresearch.uchicago.edu/files/Blair_Chung_2017_licensing_gender_racial_wage_gaps.pdf. This seems similar to instances when employers have responded to "ban the box" restrictions on asking about criminal records by using race as a proxy, thereby increasing discrimination against minorities. Although we should be aware of this study, it remains an outlier, and the overwhelming preponderance of the evidence suggests that occupational licensure does more harm than good.

[69]Sandefur, "Testimony to the U.S. House Committee on Small Business."

[70]Ibid.

[71]Thomas Snyder, "The Effects of Arkansas' Occupational Licensure Regulations on the Poor," University of Central Arkansas, 2014. http://uca.edu/acre/files/2015/04/Occupational-Licensure-Regulations1.pdf.

[72]U.S. Census Bureau, "2012 Survey of Business Owners," Statistics for All U.S. Firms That Were Home-Based by Industry, Gender, Ethnicity, Race, and Veteran Status for the U.S.: 2012, http://factfinder.census.gov/faces/tableservices/jsf/pages/productview.xhtml?pid=SBO_2012_00CSCB19&prodType=table.

[73]Garrett Atherton, "Half of U.S. Businesses Are Home-Based: Why Do Some Cities Want to Kill Them?," Institute for Justice, May 5, 2015, http://ij.org/action-post/half-of-us-businesses-are-home-based-so-why-do-some-cities-want-to-kill-them/.

[74]Ibid.

[75]Jared Meyer, "Uber-Positive: The Ride-Share Firm Expands Transportation Options in Low-Income New York," Manhattan Institute Issue Brief no. 38, September 2015, https://www.manhattan-institute.org/sites/default/files/ib_38.pdf.

[76]"Mobility Challenges for Households in Poverty: 2009 National Household Travel Survey," FHWA NHTS Brief, U.S. Department of Transportation, Federal Highway Administration, 2014, http://nhts.ornl.gov/briefs/PovertyBrief.pdf.

[77]Biz Carson, "Why There's a Good Chance Your Uber Driver Is New," *Business Insider*, October 24, 2015, http://www.businessinsider.com/uber-doubles-its-drivers-in-2015-2015-10.

[78]Diana W. Thomas and Devon Gorry, "Regulation and the Cost of Child Care," Mercatus Working Paper, Mercatus Center at George Mason University, Arlington, VA, August 2015, https://www.mercatus.org/system/files/Thomas-Regulation-Child-Care.pdf.

[79]Ibid.

[80]Ajay Chaudry et al., "Child Care Choices of Low-Income Working Families," Urban Institute report, Washington, January 2011, https://www.urban.org/sites/default/files/publication/27331/412343-Child-Care-Choices-of-Low-Income-Working-Families.PDF.

Chapter ten

[1]Senator Robert F. Kennedy paraphrased George Bernard Shaw, "You see things; and you say 'Why?' But I dream things that never were; and I say 'Why not?'" *Back to Methuselah*, act I, in George Bernard Shaw, *Selected Plays with Prefaces*, vol. 2 (New York: Dodd, Mead, and Company, 1949), p. 7. Kennedy used the paraphrase as a theme for his 1968 presidential campaign.

[2]American Enterprise Institute and *Los Angeles Times*, "2016 Poverty Survey: Attitudes toward the Poor, Poverty, and Welfare in the United States," survey conducted by Princeton Survey Research Associates International, August 18, 2016, http://www.aei.org/wp-content/uploads/2016/08/2016-Poverty-Survey_AEI_Los-Angeles-Times_Topline.pdf.

[3]James Truslow Adams, *The Epic of America*, 2nd ed., (Westport: Greenwood Press, 1931), p. 404.

INDEX

Note: Information in figures and tables is indicated by f and t; n designates a numbered note.

ABOUT THE AUTHOR

Michael Tanner is a senior fellow with the Cato Institute, where he heads research into a variety of domestic policies, with a particular emphasis on poverty and social welfare policy, health care reform, and Social Security. Recently Tanner has undertaken a major project to develop innovative solutions to poverty and inequality.

Tanner is the author of numerous books on public policy, including *Going for Broke: Deficits, Debt, and the Entitlement Crisis*; *Leviathan on the Right: How Big-Government Conservatism Brought Down the Republican Revolution*; *Healthy Competition: What's Holding Back Health Care and How to Free It*; *The Poverty of Welfare: Helping Others in Civil Society*; and *A New Deal for Social Security*. *Congressional Quarterly* named him one of the nation's five most influential experts on Social Security.

Tanner's writings have appeared in nearly every major American newspaper, including the *New York Times*, the *Washington Post*, the *Los Angeles Times*, the *Wall Street Journal*, and *USA Today*. He also writes a weekly column for *National Review Online*. A prolific writer and frequent guest lecturer, Tanner appears regularly on network and cable news programs. The *New York Times* refers to him as "a lucid writer and skilled polemicist."

You can follow Tanner at www.TannerOnPolicy.com or @mtannercato on Twitter.

ABOUT THE CATO INSTITUTE

Founded in 1977, the Cato Institute is a public policy research foundation dedicated to broadening the parameters of policy debate to allow consideration of more options that are consistent with the principles of limited government, individual liberty, and peace. To that end, the Institute strives to achieve greater involvement of the intelligent, concerned lay public in questions of policy and the proper role of government.

The Institute is named for *Cato's Letters*, libertarian pamphlets that were widely read in the American Colonies in the early 18th century and played a major role in laying the philosophical foundation for the American Revolution.

Despite the achievement of the nation's Founders, today virtually no aspect of life is free from government encroachment. A pervasive intolerance for individual rights is shown by government's arbitrary intrusions into private economic transactions and its disregard for civil liberties. And while freedom around the globe has notably increased in the past several decades, many countries have moved in the opposite direction, and most governments still do not respect or safeguard the wide range of civil and economic liberties.

To address those issues, the Cato Institute undertakes an extensive publications program on the complete spectrum of policy issues. Books, monographs, and shorter studies are commissioned to examine the federal budget, Social Security, regulation, military spending, international trade, and myriad other issues. Major policy conferences are held throughout the year, from which papers are published thrice yearly in the *Cato Journal*. The Institute also publishes the quarterly magazine *Regulation*.

In order to maintain its independence, the Cato Institute accepts no government funding. Contributions are received from foundations, corporations, and individuals, and other revenue is generated from the sale of publications. The Institute is a nonprofit, tax-exempt, educational foundation under Section 501(c)3 of the Internal Revenue Code.

CATO INSTITUTE
1000 Massachusetts Ave., N.W.
Washington, D.C. 20001
www.cato.org